THE CAUTIOUS REVOLUTION

THE

CAUTIOUS

REVOLUTION

Britain Today and Tomorrow

BY ERNEST WATKINS

FARRAR, STRAUS AND COMPANY

For my wife
Jenny
With my deepest gratitude

FOREWORD

The intention of this book is clear enough, to give a dispassionate account—dispassionate, that is, to the extent that one man can be dispassionate—of events in Britain between July, 1945, and February, 1950, and beyond, with a sufficient factual background to support the story. The reality in what follows may be quite different. Certainly, I am uneasily conscious of subjects left out—education, for instance—that should have been included. Equally, I am aware that the reader may not stop short at complaining of the sins of omission. But there it is. I can say that it is an honest attempt. And I must say that the mistakes—in fact the whole book —is no one's responsibility but mine.

That is not true of the work in it. I am deeply grateful for the help I have received from so many people, from Mrs. Margaret Atkinson and Miss Molly Drury, who acted as secretaries at various times; from individual members of the staffs of the *Economist* and the B.B.C.'s News Information Service, who aided me with research; from the editor of the *Economist,* who permitted me to incorporate some material I had written for him; and above all, I am grateful both for the help and for the forebearance of my wife, who had to put up with a very great deal while this book was in preparation.

Ernest Watkins

London, S.W.1.

Contents

ix

x   *Contents*

INTRODUCTION

Here is an extract from a letter I received last year:

New York City, N.Y.
18 June 1948.

My dear Ernest,

. . . Yesterday, I had a very vivid reminder of the day I last saw
you, in that shabby old house just off Grosvenor Square. An aircraft
cut off its engine just as it came over our house and I sprang to the
window, as I did then, more than half expecting to see another buzz
bomb in the sky, and as I did so I suddenly remembered your voice
saying, "I still like to keep away from windows that have their glass
left in them." That was June 1944 and this is October 1950. I guess
there's some difference—. But how much?

Maybe in June 1948 one can't help thinking of wars but, aside
from that, that reminder set me thinking pretty hard again—my
excuse for dawdling in the morning—and at the end of it all I
found myself asking how far have we come since VE day—and by
"we" I mean your side of it. Here at home I can keep abreast of
things, but what has been happening in Britain? I know I've had
occasional letters from you, there's the radio and the news commentaries and God knows how many million words have been
written about it all. But the focus is too close. It's all yesterday and
tomorrow stuff. It doesn't give me the chance to stand back and see
it whole. And I guess there are plenty like me.

Has it been all one long crisis or not? What is this "socialism"
that you English seem to like and we don't? Why did no owner of a
gas works barricade himself in and go down with his guns firing?
Are candies still rationed—its just plain incredible to us that they
should be? Why don't your trade unions like high wages and high

production? And what's it feel like to lose an Empire almost over-night?

Maybe someone has explained all that. Maybe about twenty-thousand foreign correspondents have explained it over and over again. Maybe I'm just dumb. But again I think there are plenty like me.

I'd like someone to write a book about Britain—I mean the people of Britain—over the last five years. Just a plain, ordinary book, with no ideas to sell, no axe to grind, no mirages to conjure up. Let's get the successes and the mistakes—or the mistakes and the successes—whichever way you like to put the emphasis. In fact, you ought to write precisely such a book.

You spent some of the war telling your guys what the war was about and how it was going. So did I. You called it an A.B.C.A. publication. We called it "Army Talks." And I did get to Isigny before you, when they were still shelling the road, and all you could write about afterwards was the smell of the over-ripe Camembert cheese coming from the town. So you owe me that one. But I'm not going to get nostalgic. All I'm doing is reminding you of your bounden duty, since we both write the same language.

Maybe you're still too lazy . . ."

I think it was the stab in that last sentence that did it.

PART I

THE CIRCUMSTANCES, THE TASKS AND THE MEN

CHAPTER I

The Background

If this were a play, you would now be reading the stage directions; your eyes, hesitating a little over the italics, might make out these words:

The curtain rises on a partially wrecked factory. The floor is littered with unfinished shell cases. From the skylights in the roof the blackout material has been roughly torn away . . .

And as you read, you would begin to see in your mind the lights coming up slowly to silhouette the broken girders and the tattered black paper hanging down in untidy strips. And perhaps, while the empty stage brought back memories, or fears, an insecurely poised shell case would slip and clatter downstage, starting a small avalanche of others, and you would suddenly laugh a little, perhaps from relief. But so much would have been explained in an instant.

I can only start with facts and figures. I am even uncertain about the date to be written in the first paragraph. The date I will choose is July 1, 1945. It has the merit of being practical. It was a date used by the British Government in casting up its account of the war then on the point of ending. It is a date halfway through that confused period between the end of the war in Europe and the end of the war in the Pacific. It is the date, to within a day or so, when the people of Britain were choosing their government for the next five years. Arbitrary or not—and all dates are arbitrary—it is a date that marks the end of one phase, and the beginning of another.

No nation consists solely of its material possessions. No nation is anything more than the sum of the individuals who belong to it. Yet facts and figures, the accountant's shorthand for the story of an enterprise, are at least symbols of a reality, a record of what is over and done with, co-ordinates of what must follow. The first marks on any undrawn map are the faint black parallel lines, arbitrary rulings on the virgin sheet, and yet the only safe guide to use when filling in the outlines of the map itself.

Britain finished the war economically crippled, owing debts far beyond her immediate capacity to pay, having put into her effort to survive a greater percentage of her total capacity than any other country on the Allied side. The total effort of the United States may have been greater. The total destruction within Soviet Russia may have been greater. Nevertheless, Britain's problem remained the more complex. The United States could switch her production from war to peace in her own time, by her own methods. Soviet Russia could find—indeed, was determined to find—all the material and labor she needed from resources under her own command. Whether Britain liked it or not, she could not reconvert her industries to peacetime production nor repair her damage solely by her own decision, nor solely from her own resources.

For well over a century, Britain had lived on international trade, on her exports. To fight the war she had given up a large percentage of her export trade, and international trade remained a question of bargaining. In July, 1945, after a six-year break, these bargains had to be negotiated again, and any single one of the former customers could say "no."

The figures speak for themselves:

COMMERCIAL EXPORTS

	£ millions	Index of volume
1938	471	100
1939	440	94
1940	411	73
1941	365	56
1942	270	36
1943	233	29
1944	258	30

This cut in export trade was a deliberate decision. Britain could not produce for export and provide the shipping needed for export and at the same time produce for war and provide the shipping needed for the essential materials of war. In cutting that trade,

Britain acted as instinctively as does a man in danger of drowning when he strips himself of clothes and boots, the better to be able to swim. But when he has saved his life he is still without his clothes. From 1941 onward, Lend-Lease provided Britain with the food and the raw materials these exports would normally have purchased, but on July 1, 1945, Britain had hardly begun to switch her industrial machine back to its peacetime uses, and the end of Lend-Lease was only two months away.

Loss of an export trade was not the only consequence. The figures for all the wartime losses are available. In connection with the Anglo-American Loan Agreement negotiations in the fall of 1945, the British Government prepared certain sets of statistics showing the effect on Britain of the war, and of the decisions made by Britain during the war in the course of deployment of her resources. These figures were subsequently published in the form of a "White Paper," or official government statement. The principal items of loss, as shown by this white paper, are covered in the appendix to this chapter, as are some figures and information taken from an economic survey of Europe published by the United Nations in 1948. I have also added some statistics showing the degree of British war recovery during the years 1945 to 1950.

I have put forward these facts as a framework for the rest of the book. They have, inevitably, political implications and explanations. They do not by any means tell a plain and unequivocal story by themselves. But they are essential to the understanding of this book, to the understanding of the motivations of the Labour Government and, indeed, to the understanding of Britain.

It is the people who write history, every kind of history. They have leaders who, on occasion, stride forward in the blind certainty that they will be followed. More frequently, these leaders, while appearing to lead, are walking uneasily in front, looking backwards in an attempt to interpret what the people behind them really want—and, incidentally, there is a great deal to be said for that kind of leadership. But what did the people of Britain want when the war was over?

In general, of course, they are very like people everywhere else. They are fond of sport and gossip and regard work as a necessary means of earning money and preferable to complete idleness. But the people of Britain have certain characteristics which stand out when set against those of other nations. They have a respect for law and order, not because it is imposed—on the contrary, they have an immense capacity for ignoring laws, such as the betting laws, which they consider to be unrealistic—but because for so long they have had a government which they can feel to be part of themselves, a government whose merits and demerits they have been able to argue without let or hindrance.

Politically, too, they have the advantage of a certain national consistency. There are local characteristics but they are no more than freckles on the skin. There is a difference between townsman and countryman, but one townsman thinks very like another, from whatever town he may come. A British political leader choosing a cabinet, for instance, never need select a Yorkshireman to balance a Devonian. That simplifies politics.

Again in Britain, the social classes are well established. The visitor to Britain may leave with the impression that its inhabitants are excessively class conscious. So they are, but it is important not to draw the wrong conclusions from that. The British people draw a sharp distinction between the rights and duties attached respectively to social classes and to economic classes.

Social classes in Britain are both complex and rigid, but they allow, paradoxically, considerable freedom of movement to any individual who has any capacity for change. Change from one social class to another is not only a matter of money; profession, even one's accent come into it, as well. But the man or woman who is prepared to play his part in any class, as carefully as he would play a stage role, has no difficulty in climbing to the top—and, after all, the same actress may play Portia, Juliet and, perhaps, Lady Macbeth, but she does not play them all in the same way. All that is asked is that each individual shall stick to whatever social part he is playing at the moment, and this, basically, is no more than a social request that the individual shall be natural, natural against the social background he claims as his own.

But this acceptance of social classes is now accompanied by a remarkably well-developed demand for economic egalitarianism. Increasingly, the majority of people in Britain no longer accept the proposition that increase in personal wealth should automatically carry with it increase in economic power. They are very conscious of what economic power is, of how it affects a whole community if it is used for personal ends, without regard for social consequences. So an individual may accept and even delight in social inequality, and yet vote for a party that demands economic equality, just as he may stand for hours to see a royal wedding and yet murmur with full approval when Mr. Aneurin Bevan speaks of all Conservatives as vermin.

Superficial judgments on Britain are to be avoided. The visiting Communist may jump to the conclusion that the socialism of the British Labour party is a complete sham, while the visiting capitalist may imagine that he is seeing what the foreigner in Paris saw in 1788, the shadow of the tumbril round the next corner of time. I don't think either of them really gets the story straight.

That is all I want to say about social classes and their oddities. To go on would be to describe what a person is wearing, and to remain silent over his thoughts. The results of general election of 1945 were determined by political and economic, not social causes.

The fifteen years between 1930 and 1945 fall into two periods, from 1930 to 1939, and from the outbreak of war to the election in June, 1945. And that first decade, from 1930 to 1939, was not a happy period, either in Britain or in Europe. It was a decade of insecurity, materially and mentally, at home and abroad. It saw the slump of 1929–31, the growth of the Nazi Party in Germany from 1932 onward and the Spanish Civil War of 1936–39. The United States, in the same period—and faced with parallel problems—experienced President Roosevelt and the New Deal. Europe could see only Adolf Hitler and Joseph Stalin. Most Europeans would consider the United States to have been the more fortunate.

On June 30, 1929, the number of unemployed in Britain was 1,164,000, 9% of an insured (unemployment insurance) population of 12,094,000. By the same date in 1931, the number had risen to 2,707,000 (22%). By 1936, when rearmament was beginning, the number had fallen to 1,708,000 (14%), but even this measure of recovery was not uniform over the country. And in June, 1939, two months before the war started, there were still 1,270,000 people out of work. That was the material insecurity which has haunted everyone born before about 1915.

The mental uneasiness came from the spectacle of external affairs, close at hand in Europe. It was possible, for at least part of the twenties, to believe that the League of Nations was a new-found solution to the threat of another international war. But insecurity seeped back as Mussolini dragged open the door of the police state in a country which Western Europe had thought to be, with France, its most civilized. The smell of Fascism and Nazism, of Hitler and Goebbels and Goering, of anti-semitism, rose before the peoples of Europe like a dank mist rising from an evil swamp. Long before the road reached the edge of the morass many men and women had some intimation of what might lie ahead. Savagery could still boast and kill. France floundered at the nadir of parliamentary democracy, and Britain seemed to have produced no more than men like Mr. Baldwin and Mr. Chamberlain.

What was wrong? It was easy to ask, hard to find an answer, any answer. The average working man in Britain never really understood why the Labour Government of 1929 collapsed in 1931; and to account for it he invented the theory of a "bankers' ramp." But that did not explain away the socialist, Mr. Ramsay MacDonald, or the trade-union leader, Mr. J. H. Thomas, when they went over to the enemy, as the average man called it, and joined the National Government. What he did understand was the figures in the unemployment returns and the queues of men outside the labour exchanges —a name satirically in contrast to their actual function of paying out unemployment benefit—"the dole"—to men who would have been glad to exchange almost anything for a steady job.

The actions of this government in European affairs provided no greater comfort. When Germany reoccupied the Rhineland with troops, it was the British Government that hung back. When Italy invaded Abyssinia, it was a British minister who signed the Hoare-Laval pact designed to dismember the victim. When Hitler and Mussolini openly supported General Franco's rebellion in Spain, it was a British government that invented the policy of "non-intervention." The government of the prewar years may have had excellent reasons on each of the occasions on which it refrained from action, but successful government, like successful courtship, requires something more than an ability to go on saying "Not now."

The men and women who were over thirty in 1939 had spent the formative years of their lives in an atmosphere of insecurity and under a government that seemed more clearly right wing every time it proclaimed itself to be "National." A great many of them did not like either.

The war changed all that, and dramatically. Here was something bloody but positive. Here was something to resist and defy, here a chance to share with David his emotions when he fitted the stone to his sling. And, from out of the past—but not from out of the National Government's past—came a man capable of telling the nation why it resisted and defied and why it would be successful in the end. There was not only work to be done and wages to be earned, but there was a purpose behind it as well.

The younger men and women (and by 1945 they had a vote) felt a little differently. Chronic unemployment had left its scars on their youth, but it had not made them doubt their own individual capacity to earn a living when they did go to work. They could still look forward to times that would be very much better than those they had seen while they were growing up. The war saved them from industrial disillusionment, and it went on long enough for that hope to become a habit of mind. For Britain, those six years of war were a series of campaigns, and in the intervals a great many men and women in the forces and in the war factories had time to think. For various reasons, the authorities helped them to think.

On Christmas Eve, 1944, I remember coming across a friend of mine, in command of an engineers' unit, sitting in a bitterly cold attic in the shattered town of Nijmegen in Holland studying, by the light of a small paraffin burner, an officially issued army textbook on the law of town planning. During those six years, vast numbers like him read about law and medicine, sociology and bee-keeping, economics and mining engineering, and if you had asked them why, their answers would have been some variation of "I just thought I would try and catch up on things."

In time of war, the British people naturally begin to think of what should happen when this particular war is over. They are optimistic by temperament. They have never doubted that they would emerge from any war as the masters of their own fate and responsible for all that comes next.

It is not difficult, after the event, to find smooth answers to the question of why the Labour party won in 1945 and why Mr. Churchill lost. There is no single easy answer. With a poll of some eleven million votes to the Conservatives' eight million, it would be plausible to say that it was the men and women in the forces who turned the scale. Indeed, there were then five million of them, all with votes.

One basic fact is that the Labour party had become a recognized, constitutional and orthodox political party, and the alternative to the Conservatives. From 1918 to 1929, it had fought with and defeated the Liberal party on the issue of which was the second party in the country. In 1931, it shed its top growth of men from a past period of time, and between 1931 and 1939 it had learned, in opposition, some of the lessons and rules of government. During the war, it had shared the risks and the glories (lesser) of triumph. Above all, at the start of 1945, it had seized its chance. It had said what so many were thinking, that Britain would not survive the peace with the kind of government it had possessed before the war.

July, 1945, was a moment when most men and women still believed that unity among the Allied powers was a fact, and that the main task ahead of Britain was no worse than putting to order her own house and her own affairs. Few of them guessed what damage the structure of that house had sustained, or what was still to threaten it. The moment was one of climax to a past, not sober acceptance of the challenge of the future.

Mr. Churchill chose his election allies badly. Perhaps, not having been a member of the National Government before the war, he was too charitable about its failings. But his principal handicap was that he remained a man who thought in terms of military and political events. The world, to him, is a vast arena in which men fight and talk and argue and die, gloriously or ignominiously. But it is also a world without weekly pay envelopes, salary checks, or, indeed, any kind of practical economics. The British are a fighting people but not a military one. When the battle is over, they like to go home to a job. And jobs were the things in which the Labour party seemed to be interested.

The Labour party cannot be accused of winning the election on false pretenses. Nevertheless, it won the election because at the time, all party programs were pretenses and theirs was nearest to the popular dream. These five years, from 1945 onward, are a history of the relation between pretense and reality, and of the difficulty of knowing which is which.

CHAPTER II

Who Governs Britain?

The most important and the most difficult question you can ask about any country is: Who governs it?

There are various easy and superficial answers. Parliament, Congress, the civil service, the administration, the cabinet, the banks, the trade unions; anybody can add to that list. The real answer is infinitely more complex, particularly in Britain, if only because the seat of governmental power isn't static.

A democracy is governed by people acting through institutions, and commonly each institution multiplies by many times the power possessed by the individual actively in control of it. At the same time, each individual in control acts upon every other individual in charge of another section of the machine, and is affected in his turn by what those others do and think. Nor do the institutions themselves yield fixed results. One man will derive more power out of the section he is handling than can another. The whole sum of central government is a vast complex of personalities, powers and customs, and what is called "The government" is the result of all their mingling forces.

In a parliamentary democracy, of the kind that has flourished in the English-speaking world, it is necessary that the number and importance of the matters on which the major political parties agree should be greater than the number and importance of matters over which they disagree. If the "opposition party" is in fact in complete opposition to the basic assumptions on which the other party acts, then the country itself is an arena for continuous conflict, a revolutionary conflict in which the majority party may tend to become a tyranny and the opposition an underground insurrectionary movement, and where a successful revolution may do no more than reverse the roles of the individual parties.

Equally, the majority party may have a strong tradition of parliamentary democracy and may hold fast to its intention to maintain that tradition. The situation in France over the last few years has been thus. There the major conflict between the Communist and non-Communist parties extends throughout the structure of the state. Parliamentary democracy in France only exists when the Communist party is defeated or at least rendered impotent. And a healthy parliamentary democracy is not permanently twisted into a tyranny by such a struggle. It can and does maintain its essential qualities.

It is important to make it clear at the outset that Britain is and has been during these five years a parliamentary democracy by this strict definition. The Communist party in Britain has not had strength enough to produce even minute distortions of the traditional pattern; definitely less, for example, than the distortions produced in Northern Ireland by the pressure of the revolutionary Irish Republican movement. The Labour party, as a whole, is not a revolutionary party, although it may contain a few members who regret that fact. On fundamentals, it has as a party more points of agreement with the Opposition than the reverse. This may mean that some useful things are not done and that some injustices are not remedied, but the resulting stability of the country has its compensating advantages, including the fact that no one is shot or sent to a concentration camp.

This rather slight glance at the foundations of government is intended as no more than a preliminary to the main question: who are the men who have governed Britain between 1945 and 1950? Politicians are not the engineers of railroad trains, destined to follow a set of tracks, and guided from start to destination by automatic signals. Far more do they resemble the drivers of long distance busses whose individual mistakes may result in wrong turnings or complete disasters. These men have the forces of a vast mechanism under their control. Who are they? How did they fight their way to this authority?

At the apex of the pyramid of power in Britain, there have been three men during this period: Mr. Clement Attlee, Prime Minister; Sir Stafford Cripps, Chancellor of the Exchequer; and Mr. Ernest Bevin, Foreign Secretary. Below them is another pair: Mr. Herbert

Morrison, whose titular office is Lord President of the Council and whose duties in fact are to lead the House of Commons and be responsible for the day-to-day management of the Labour party; and Mr. Aneurin Bevan, Minister of Health (which includes Housing) and the real leader of the left wing of the Labour party.

Below that, the field widens suddenly and very extensively. The main difference between the men I have named and those in the layers below them is that these five men can and do make their influence felt in every section of government. Each of the others exerts considerable influence in one field, a good deal less outside that field. Many of these others are not cabinet ministers, and some are not even politicians. Each has his own corner. The word and the influence of each counts heavily but not to anything like the same degree as the influence possessed by the five leaders.

For example, Field Marshall Sir William Slim, in 1949, was Chief of the Imperial General Staff. When the cabinet was concerned about military strategy over Hong Kong and over the general problem of compulsory military service, Sir William Slim was called in to advise, and what he said must have had considerable influence. Lord Catto was Governor of the Bank of England at the time of the devaluation of the pound sterling; Mr. Arthur Deakin is secretary of one of the largest trade unions, the Transport and General Workers Union; Mr. Harold Wilson is President of the Board of Trade. Each of them was bound to be consulted about matters in his own sphere and therefore played his part on the decisions of government.

It is at this level, too, that the senior civil servants are involved. They have considerable control over the formation of departmental policy and complete control over its execution. The political influence of some cabinet ministers, does not exceed the total of the work done for them by their departmental civil servants. Equally important is the influence of leading industrialists. They are grouped together in various organizations, formally as in the Federation of British Industries, informally as in the Board of the Bank of England. But these civil servants and industrialists have one thing in common: in matters of major policy, they influence others rather than make direct decisions themselves. They govern by remote control, which gives the greater power to the man who actually handles the controls.

This process can almost be described as government by friendly conversation. All these men are in constant contact with each other in London. All of them have other contacts throughout the rest of the country. They meet at dinners, or in their clubs for lunch. They talk. They telephone each other. Each has some channel of approach to the men who are responsible for decisions. So they become a part of government, and there they serve as two-way radios, transmitting opinions and receiving them.

Of only slightly less importance today are the leaders of the larger trade unions. They are consulted by the government as a matter both of principle and expediency; principle because the Labour Government thinks of itself as the instrument of organized labor, expediency because the trade-union leaders control the voting on policy at the annual conferences of the Labour party. But it is impossible to attach quite the same importance to the trade-union leaders as to the industrialists. The industrialist has behind him far more self-confidence. He expects to be consulted and listened to. The trade-union leader, however, hopes to be consulted and is determined to talk when he is.

A list of those who possess some influence would contain hundreds of names. Most of the effective members of the House of Lords, the retired parliamentarians like Lord Samuel, the Law Lords and the Bishops, ought to be included. In addition, the list would name the heads of a hundred or so voluntary bodies, from the Royal Society through the Royal College of Physicians to the secretary of the Commons and Footpaths Society. And there is the press, which will be dealt with separately. But there is one further name to be added, that of His Majesty King George VI.

The influence of the King is very difficult to define exactly. King George does not govern. He influences those who do, but with the difference that his influence is indirect and is not intended to serve any particular personal or factional end. It exists because, by custom, he is informed of everything that goes on in Parliament and in the cabinet. Few men have better knowledge of public affairs than he. Furthermore, he is continually meeting, formally and informally, people who themselves possess both knowledge and influence and who are leaders in their own circles. Prestige gives a king of England the power to exert influence based on this knowledge and information, but what influence is in fact exerted, how and with what result, depends very largely upon the personality of the particular King.

But let us go back to these five leaders of the Labour Government.

There was a time when Britain's politicians were drawn exclusively from one social class, a class small in numbers. There has never been a period during the last two hundred years when that class was limited to those born into certain families. True, to be born in one of the ruling families gave the child (if politically minded) an enormous advantage. But money could always buy land, and the ownership of land carried social prestige and the right of entry into political circles. Now even this is no longer necessary. While the tradition of social exclusiveness dies hard, the recollection of that tradition lasts even longer. But those times are gone, and today it is almost as much a liability as an asset to be a nobleman or an aristocrat in politics.

Two of these five men are Sir Stafford Cripps and Mr. Ernest Bevin, and their careers could not be in greater contrast to each other.

Cripps was born in 1889, Bevin in 1881. Cripps is the son of a family with money, influence and position. His father was Lord Parmoor, a man of Conservative mind who, oddly enough, edged gradually leftwards with advancing years. Richard Stafford Cripps, his son, was inevitably destined for Winchester, one of the first six public schools, and the university, and from there quite as naturally took to the law.

Bevin had no such advantages at all. He was born into a working-class family, and from the age of thirteen has been literally dependant upon himself, even for food. He has learned all he knows by and at work, and in the creation of a trade union.

Cripps served with the Red Cross in France in 1914, and was called back a year later to manage a munitions factory. By 1910, Bevin was already organizing the Dockers Union. Between 1919 and 1930 Cripps was building up a career at the English bar, with little thought of politics, and moved to the higher rank in his profession by becoming a King's Counsel in 1927. He did not enter politics and Parliament until 1929, and was Solicitor-General between 1930 and 1931. It was only after the fall of the Labour Government in 1931 that his political life became really a part of himself. He organized a left-wing socialist group known as the Socialist League and, between then and 1938, was generally at odds with the orthodox leaders of his party.

Bevin reached the position of secretary to his union, which became the Transport and General Workers Union in 1921, and from then until 1940 he lived and breathed trade unionism and the intricate balance of strike and negotiation which trade unionism means. He did not enter Parliament until 1940, when he had already been chosen by Mr. Churchill as his Minister of Labour. Trade unionism, on Bevin's level, is certainly politics but not parliamentary politics.

All his life, Cripps has fought a campaign against a gastric weakness which has compelled him to treat every particle of food as a separate problem. Bevin has lived in complete defiance of his doctors, ignoring every symptom of overwork. Cripps is intellectually brilliant and capable of exposition which is as clear as his grasp of the subject. Bevin has the terrier's instinct for knowing which is the neck of the situation and of holding on until that neck is broken and a corpse lies at his feet.

Clement Attlee, again, is a quite dissimilar individual. He is a man built around a sense of duty. He comes from a middle-class family, and he too became a lawyer. Born in 1883, he was called to the bar in 1905. Duty drew him to work in the East End of London from then until 1914, and the first reward that duty provided was merely the mayoralty of the London Borough of Stepney for the year 1919–1920. Duty had taken him with the infantry in 1914, and kept him as a front line soldier for five years when he finished with the rank of Major.

But from then on duty produced rather more from its hat. It provided him with a safe seat in Parliament, the Limehouse Division of London, which he represented without a break from 1922 to 1950 when the constituency was merged with another. Limehouse could never conceivably have elected a Conservative. On his election, he became personal private secretary to Mr. Ramsay Macdonald, in Opposition, and was rewarded with a minor post in the 1924 Labour Government. He has moved gradually and sedately upwards, always along the right political channels, until, in 1935, he became leader of the Labour Party. From there he was naturally carried into office, both in the wartime Coalition Government and in the postwar Labour Government.

Attlee is often described as a good chairman who holds his commanding position as a result of the existence of opposing forces, each of which is stronger than he. In part that is true. The Labour party was reluctant to choose between Herbert Morrison and Ernest Bevin, and the choice fell upon Attlee because those strong antagonists would serve under him more easily than either would have served under the other. But it is not the whole truth.

Many aspects of personality usually found to be highly colorful in politicians are a plain gray in the case of Attlee. He has a poor voice, an inability to project himself into the public mind sufficiently to see that popular government must not only be for the people but also with them. But there is a hard core of sincerity and of ruthlessness to his character—inevitably so, for no man holds the reins of office for so long without some ability to cut down rivals when they appear. Attlee is loyal to his friends. But he does not forgive his enemies, nor forget who they are; and that includes those few in his own party who have proved themselves enemies.

Duty, sincerity and loyalty are fine attributes. Their effect can be seen in Britain's actions in India and Burma, and in the persistence with which the Labour Government has pursued its election aims. But even these virtues have within them their own shortcomings. The man who sincerely believes he is right may become the man who cannot understand why others still go on being wrong. Attlee is neither revolutionary nor dictatorial. But he is becoming obstinate.

The remaining two names on the short list of five also provide a fine pair of contrasts, not so much in their backgrounds as in their natures. Herbert Morrison is the son of a London policeman, Aneurin Bevan of a South Wales miner. Morrison was born in 1888, Bevan in 1897. Both had a public education. From his London elementary school Morrison went on to become errand boy, shop assistant and deputy circulation manager of a newspaper. Bevan left school at thirteen to go into the pit and it was his fellow miners who paid his tuition at a labor college. Morrison entered politics to organize the business side of the London Labour party, Bevan to organize disputes among the miners in the South Wales coalfield. That distinction has followed them throughout their political lives.

Morrison is the party organizer, whose test of a party platform is how it will go down with the voters. Bevan is the agitator whose greatest fear is that the voters will accept things too easily. Morrison struggles to maintain the middle of the road. Bevan walks willfully in the left-hand gutter, daring the respectable householders on either side to come out and fight him.

Morrison owes his place and his power to his judgment and to his manipulative skill as a politician, learned over twenty years of building up a powerful political machine on the London County Council. Bevan has something more valuable, and more dangerous, than this. Of all these five men, he alone is haunted by an emotional vision, a genuine fire in the belly that both prophets and agitators share, to mankind's immediate discomfort, and perhaps to his future gain.

Cripps and Attlee think; Morrison arranges. Bevin knows that security is about 90% of what most people want. Bevan feels.

But party leaders are one thing. Men who are at the top seem to solidify, to assume set shapes and achieve set reputations which are distinct from the parties which gave birth and form to their political careers. They no longer seem to mirror so accurately the thoughts and ideas which pervade the common mass of their supporters. I believe that if you want to see a political party clearly, you must choose as your illuminant a man a few rungs below the top of the ladder, one who can, and who probably will some day be a leader in his own right but who is at present more affected by, and so more typical of, the pressure of public opinion.

Here are the profiles of three such individuals in the 1945–50 parliament.

The first is a socialist, Lieutenant Colonel D. R. Rees-Williams,* appointed in 1948 to be parliamentary Under-Secretary of State for the Colonies in the Labour Government. He is a lawyer and looks the part. He is forty-six but seems older. He is well-built and about aver-

* Lieutenant Colonel D. R. Rees-Williams was created Lord Ogmore in the summer of 1950.

age height. His hair is light, his face ruddy like that of a countryman, which is as it should be, since he was born in Glamorgan, Wales. He has the shrewd eye of his profession. But he differs from the norm of that profession in two respects. One was imposed upon him by events held in common with the majority of others born between 1900 and 1920. That is six years of military service. The other is individual to himself.

When World War II broke out in 1939, Rees-Williams had been in practice as a solicitor in Cardiff for four years. He was also a major in a Territorial Army artillery unit based in that city. He went away with his unit on August 12, 1939, for a month's training in camp. He returned six years later. He was by then a lieutenant-colonel, and his last appointment had been as presiding officer in the first British Army military court in Berlin. He was also a member of Britain's Parliament. In this, he had fulfilled his major ambition.

His father was a veterinary surgeon in Glamorgan, his mother a woman deeply interested in public affairs and a local councilor. He went to Mill Hill school, completed his legal studies at the University of Wales and was admitted as a solicitor in 1929. However, a young lawyer in Britain without family connections must either take the chance of opening his own office or accept a clerkship with an established firm. Rees-Williams decided upon the latter, but the firm was in Penang, in the Straits Settlements, as they were then known. His wife felt that the East would be a fascinating place in which to begin married life. He believed that it would be useful experience for a future political career. (It was this, too, that influenced his return four years later.) By 1934, he had built up a considerable reputation as a lawyer in the Settlements and was compelled to decide whether or not to join permanently the firm which employed him. But if you intend to be an M. P. in Britain, you must live in Britain. The Rees-Williamses returned to Cardiff and he began his career again. Four years later World War II ended that practice.

Of his twenty-one years of professional life, four have been spent in a colony, six on military duties, five as an M. P. Rees-Williams has ceased to be a typical solicitor, yet the influence of legal training remains.

Rees-Williams himself gives this example of the effect of his experience. As a British lawyer in Malaya he saw quite a different side
of the country and its people than could any other European. Alone
among foreigners, the lawyer is the servant of the man who retains
him, be he Malay, Chinese, Arab or European. And very often he is
fighting for that individual against a more powerful machine, be it
State or private trading corporation. The lawyer learns what an individual is like even before he learns anything about the politics or
economics of the territory.

Rees-Williams became part of (and in part responsible for) the
machinery of the British Colonial Service. He dealt with innumerable problems from all over the world, each superficially different.
But because of the ways in which he acquired his knowledge of men
and events, he believes that all these problems have a common base,
the individual in each colony, his family and his tribe. What Britain can do for them, he believes, is to extend their way of life to take
in wider political and economic responsibilities, to build up these
responsibilities from tribe to district and from district to province,
to help the natives extend their own activities in their own way. To
do that, every people needs political stability, and all that Europe
can find in the way of experience, science and equipment. But, as is
the case of the lawyer, whatever skill is brought in from outside, it
must be brought for the benefit of the client first and foremost. He
believes that all this can be done and that a Labour Government in
Britain should do it.

Rees-Williams is the administrator type. Commonly, administrators have a belief in their powers of organization and a delight in
exercising them. Sometimes they are content with that. Sometimes
they have in addition a positive feeling as to the kind of pattern that
they are trying to create. Rees-Williams has; it concerns economic
equality, a feeling that the mass of people must be looked after and
protected—and, of course, that he is the man to do it. Such men are
rarely torn by ideals or passions. They inspire very little. They create
by the process used in the formation of a coral reef. They very
rarely become revolutionaries, because revolutions destroy order and
tear up the card indexes. None the less, I think Rees-Williams is
more typical of the British Labour party today than, say, Mr. Aneu-

rin Bevan. His mind works parallel with the minds of the trade
unionists. He is of the fabric of the Party rather than of its spirit, and
today the fabric is the more influential.

The Conservative M. P. I would choose is Mr. David Eccles.

David Eccles is the son of a doctor and he married the daughter of
a doctor, Lord Dawson of Penn. He was born in 1904. He went to
Oxford University and when he left college he entered business,
starting as a ledger clerk at thirty shillings a week. By 1939, at the age
of thirty-five, he was managing director of a group of South African
mining companies and earning well over £5,000 a year. Up to that
point he had displayed no interest whatsoever in politics of any complexion. If he voted at all, he voted Conservative, but politics was
for chaps who talked in debates and at street corners, for men who
would not be successful in business anyway.

Appropriately, Eccles looks like a doctor, a fashionable and successful consultant. His face is fresh, his color boyish, his hair is gray
and has a faint curl around the side of his head. He is tall and slim.
He dresses with care, in the kind of clothes which successful specialists wear after they have taken off formal morning attire. His is the
perfect bedside manner; it can reassure those despondent Conservatives who think their party is on its deathbed.

The war pried Eccles loose from private business and harnessed
him to the war machine, first as economic adviser to the embassies in
Lisbon and Madrid. (It was a feature of the early stages of the war
immediately to equip British embassies and legations with "economic
advisers," economics being a department of human activity on which
the prewar Foreign Office was not well-informed.) In 1942 he came
back to the Ministry of Production, and there he saw government at
work. He came to the conclusion that the politicians who were ultimately responsible for its operation were sadly ill-equipped by nature for running such an undertaking in the kind of world which he
saw would exist after the war. But where many guessed this and were
content to leave it at that, Eccles was not. He felt he ought to do
something about it.

He talked it over with his wife. As he saw it, politics must inevitably be a full-time job. If he went in for a political career, it would
be impossible to return to the old job. (He was not alone in think-

ing that; the directors of his former companies bluntly told him so.)
But why should a man be reluctant to leave commerce, particularly
when postwar taxation was going to take away most of the income he
earned in the high-level brackets? Unless you liked living in a world
of shiny cars and of elegant evasions to obtain foreign currency for
long vacations abroad, unless the people in that world had a real
fascination for you, what was the incentive left in business? Power
and responsibility? Power could be found in politics, if you put your
mind to it. But that was secondary to responsibility. If you had
come to believe—if you really knew—that you could do the job well,
responsibility would not let you leave the effort to someone else.

At about that time the Conservative M. P. for Chippenham, an
agricultural community in Wilshire seventy miles from London, was
killed. Eccles already lived close to the area, and suggested to Conservative party headquarters that he would like to become the member for Chippenham. They agreed. He was returned unopposed in
1943. And he held the seat by a majority of 4,023 in the general
election in 1945. Since then, he has become one of the rising young
Conservatives, as the saying is.

As a politician, he has several major advantages. He knows the
business world, the world in which the effects of politics are as a
whole best seen. The war forced him to realize the part which government action was bound to play in British politics during the era
that lay ahead. He made his decision at an age when his mind was
young and resilience great enough for him gladly to make a new
jump. He has the time and experience to work out for himself a clear
conception of what he thinks are the essential political objectives; but
he has never had time to acquire the commonplace habits of political thought.

Eccles is a Conservative because he sees himself as the present up-
holder of a tradition that stretches far back into the past and which
should, if possible, be extended into the future. It is a tradition
which is as much West European as British. It is far older than the
British Empire, and, at its best, the British Empire was only the extension of this tradition over the world; the tradition is the responsibility of the few for the many.

There are always a few who are fitted by nature to govern, to accept the responsibility of government. Eccles does not believe that

heredity is a determining factor there; he comes from the British middle classes who do not attach very great importance to hereditary privilege. But education and environment do come into it, for they make it easier for these few to understand each other. His belief is that if you accept the privileges which education, environment and, of course, your own inherent qualities secure for you, you must accept the responsibilities as well.

You must look ahead. Leave to others the task of thinking out changes; there are always too many who think of change. Your task is to discover what is most worth while preserving, and to work out means of preserving it. That is the really difficult thing in politics, to make the right choices. And that is the major reason which brought and keeps Eccles in politics today.

Frank Byers is a Liberal, and his approach to politics is at bottom emotional. He grew up in the thirties, at the time when Fascism in Europe was spreading and maturing. He is a Liberal because he believes in freedom.

Freedom is an abused word. I use it to denote a state of mind. I call a man free when he is able to weigh all the factors involved in any course of action and to decide, entirely within his own mind, what to do and what to refrain from doing. No man is or can be free from the emotions that compel action, fear, love, hatred, desire; but he should be free to balance them, to make his own estimate of how they affect him and how they should affect him.

The events of the decade in which he grew up gave Byers a natural tendency to join the Liberal party. When he went to Oxford University he looked for the Liberal club. After a three weeks' search he found a man who confessed to being the secretary. He said he wanted to join the club. The secretary said, "That's easy. At the moment the club consists of myself, secretary, and my brother, chairman. You had better be treasurer." In a year, the three had increased the membership to 350. The two brothers were in their final years and soon left the university, leaving Byers in control of the club, and, as such, the representative Liberal undergraduate whom Liberal politicians wanted to meet. He was invited to become a Liberal candidate, and did so in 1939 at the age of twenty-two and for the constituency he represented until February, 1950.

He joined the Army Artillery in September, 1939. He was commissioned the following year, and was sent to the Middle East, the Western Desert. In 1942, he was given a staff job on the planning of the invasion of Sicily. He went through the Sicilian and early Italian campaigns, came back to Britain to prepare for Normandy, and in 1944 and 1945 fought through France, Belgium and Germany. He was released in June, 1945, with the rank of Lieutenant Colonel, to return to Britain to fight the general election, and he won his Dorset seat with a majority of 1,965. (He lost it by an even smaller majority in the February, 1950, election.)

Byers owes his early success to differing aspects of his personality; his prowess as an athlete and his ability as a poultry farmer. The poultry farming provided the cash with which to work his way through college. His athletics persuaded school masters to overlook the amount of time he was devoting to his business enterprise, for he started poultry farming at the age of sixteen.

Poultry farming is an occupation to which time and motion study of the most intensive kind can be most usefully applied. Byers had to attend school five days a week. In the remainder of his spare time he built up, virtually singlehanded, a flock of some 1,000 birds, organized the feeding, collection and sale of their eggs. As a result, his academic study suffered. Fortunately, he was an athlete. He captained the Westminster School football team and broke his school record for the quarter mile. At college, he broke the British record for the quarter mile hurdles. He ran in the International Athletic meeting at Brussels in 1937. He was, in addition, a member of the Oxford and Cambridge team that visited the United States and beat Harvard, Princeton and Cornell universities on their own grounds. But it was the poultry farming that paid for it. It also paid for a six-month tour of the United States and Canada and for a period at Milton Academy, in Massachusetts, where he graduated. It likewise financed a period of study at Geneva with Sir Norman Angel.

Byers is more than ten years younger than the other two, but he is part of the same generation.

These are three politicians, one from each of the main political parties. Each of them is a man with the capacity and the stamina to lead his party, despite the fact that two of them, the Labour and the Liberal, suffered a temporary set back in that they were defeated in the February, 1950, election. It will only be a matter of luck which holds cabinet rank first. All of them have some characteristics in common; ambition, capacity for hard work, willingness to accept and flourish under responsibility. All of them have good minds and varied backgrounds, and all of them have benefitted from their war experiences. None of them is parochial or blinkered, intolerant or narrow. Each of them would subject personal inclinations to his sense of public duty. All these things they have in common.

None of them could belong to any party but their own, yet all of them have an even deeper thing in common, a love of liberty—and I use the word "liberty" in distinction to the word "freedom"; freedom being the personal thing, liberty the social characteristic.

It can be argued that these three men are not representative, that they are above average. That is true, but the argument is irrelevant. All political parties contain the stupid, the smart and the self-seeking. When you get down to the lower orders, party allegiance and party platforms cease to matter. For the stupid and the selfish, membership in any one party as opposed to another is a matter of chance or of opportunism. Britain contains its share of politicians interested in skullduggery and little else, but you can only illustrate what parties aim to be by choosing as examples those men most capable of demonstrating these aims in their personal actions and beliefs.

These three men started their political thinking from the one fact; in Britain, over the last fifty years, political power has shifted from the middle class to the working class, from the man who lives on the profits of his own trading to the man who lives on a weekly wage or monthly salary.

Eccles, and the intelligent Tories, consider it their political function to be the representatives of the people who once had exclusive political power but who now have lost it; that amalgamation of the wealthy middle classes and the aristocracy whose day as rulers of Britain really ended in 1914. They are in the position of Charles II in 1660, or William III in 1698, or the Duke of Wellington in 1832. They have certain cards in their hands. They have prestige, knowledge and experience. But they must come to terms with the new orders. They must make a bargain, a new Grand Settlement, to give

Britain political stability for a fresh term of years. Because they are the defeated, it is they who must make the proposals. And in doing so they must be careful to decide correctly where they will give way and where they will stand.

Eccles will stand for some freedoms, and he and the Conservative party are choosing these freedoms carefully. Freedom for the individual to make profit at anyone's expense will have to go. Freedom to be an individual, to vote, to object, to criticise, to defy regimentation, are the more important freedoms. Those the Conservatives stand for and will continue to, not only in Britain, but in all Western Europe as well.

Rees-Williams is in the other camp. He is a representative of the victors, and the freedoms for which he is concerned are the freedoms the Labourites do not feel they have completely won. Freedom from want, from insecurity, from humiliation and contempt, all freedom to be an individual and not a "hired hand" or "factory personnel" or a number in a card index or a statistic in an unemployment return.

Byers is between the two and yet a little apart from them, because the other two are concerned not only with freedoms, but also with privileges; the Conservatives with the privileges they are losing, the Labourites with the privileges they are winning. Liberals are not concerned so much with privilege as with responsibility, which is one explanation of why the Liberal party is so small.

The contest of power and privilege and freedom is going on in every country, sometimes actively and violently, sometimes, as in Britain, calmly and within set limits. Sometimes there is a pause, when one side holds all the weapons and seems to be permanently entrenched. But, while the contest continues, it is real and intense, whatever it may seem on the surface. For it has to do with the realities of everyday life.

CHAPTER III

The Labour Party Wins

The Labour party's program for the 1945 election was published in April of that year. It consisted of a pamphlet of some 5,000 words, prepared by the National Executive of the party for approval or rejection by the annual conference of the party due that Whitsuntide. The policy was approved.

Party programs are commonly not held in as much respect in the United States as in Britain, for Britain is devoid of sectional interests based on geography, and admittedly the greater part of the pamphlet was written in that vague but uplifting style commonly associated with political publications. Yet the program contained some concrete proposals, and these proved to be important.

First, they gave the party a positive social and economic policy, and made it public knowledge. The program said that certain specific consequences would follow if the majority of the electorate voted for the Labour party, and there is no doubt that a considerable body in the electorate wanted those things to happen and therefore voted for the Labour party in the expectation that they would happen. The proposals later provided substance to the Labour Government's argument that it was not for the House of Lords to stand in the way of specific reforms which the party in office had, before the election, said it intended to make, and which a majority of the electorate had specifically endorsed. (The pamphlet also said, "We give clear notice that we will not tolerate obstruction of the people's will by the House of Lords.")

Finally, the proposals made up the political program on which Mr. Attlee himself accepted office as Prime Minister and which he therefore regarded as his guiding testament throughout the five years that followed. To Mr. Attlee, election proposals and promises offered by a party and accepted by the electorate become a bond, and duty demands that bonds be honored.

Of course, the pamphlet talks airily of freedom. It was a wartime publication and freedom is always a wartime aim. It spoke more definitely of one freedom in particular, release of the trade unions from the old chains imposed on them by the Trades Disputes Act of 1927, and this release was the subject of one of the first acts passed by the new Parliament. And it did announce certain definite measures of nationalization: the Bank of England "must be brought under public ownership"; the fuel and power industries, inland transport, iron and steel. Of the latter it said: "Private monopoly has maintained high prices and kept inefficient high-cost plants in existence"—a comment which, perhaps, is true but concerning a state of affairs which the Labour Government itself, judging by its performance, would have found extremely difficult to alter.

Then followed proposals for agriculture; a housing and building program with no dangerously definite commitments over figures and targets; proposals for the land, education and recreation, health and social insurance; and inevitably it included plans for the supervision of monopolies and cartels; for a firm and clear-cut program for the export trade; the shaping of suitable economic and price controls; and the better organization of government departments.

(Two sentences on the pamphlet when put in juxtaposition have, in the light of after events a sad, nostalgic note: "There is no good reason why Britain should not afford such programmes, but she will need full employment and the highest possible industrial efficiency in order to do so. . . . The economic purpose of Government must be to spur industry forward and not to choke it with red tape.")

But it is dangerously easy, in the light of afterevents, to poke fun at a party program. There is this to be said for the program. It was a fighting document, and in that respect it mirrored more accurately the mood of the rank and file of the party than that of their leaders. The leaders themselves were then part of a coalition government. They had been concerned for five years with securing one common end, and many of them still believed, prior to the annual party conference at Whitsuntide 1945, that it might be a good idea to continue this association until after the Japanese war was over and the peace treaties were signed. Not so the rank and file. They had never accepted the argument that a wartime political coalition in government implied that there must also be a truce in party activity. The delegates at the conference wanted to fight for socialism. It was they who told their leaders to do that, or else—and the delegates had the shrewder immediate political judgment. The election was fought on that program and the party won.

It was also a backward-looking program. It summed up all that the party had felt and thought in the thirties. It was a compound of theory and emotion. It assumed that if unemployment could be conquered, the last dragon would be slain. It assumed that the cost of the war was no more than a paper cost or, at least, that the maturity date of the bills to be paid could be deferred as long as the debtor found it convenient to have them deferred. It assumed that nationalization would have an effect on the workers in an industry, similar to a religious conversion. And it presupposed that once Germany and Japan were defeated, all the major outstanding questions in foreign relations were settled. In those assumptions it certainly did represent the beliefs of the majority of the electorate. It had something of the quality of the resolutions a young man makes when he leaves home for the first time.

The election came in July, 1945. The Labour party polled 11,982,874 votes against the Conservative party's 8,660,560. It won 392 seats in the Commons to the Conservative's 189. It had written out its check when it approved its party program three months before, not quite believing that the check would ever be presented for payment. Now it had been presented. There were five years in which to redeem promises, and for the first time in history a member of the Labour party with a clear-cut majority had to sit down as Prime Minister, choose his cabinet and draft his legislative proposals. This time he would do it with the knowledge that the electors might well hold himself, his colleagues and his party responsible for any failure to carry the program successfully to a conclusion.

The election results were announced at the end of July, in the middle of the Potsdam Conference. Mr. Attlee started in the conference as an observer and finished it as Prime Minister of Great Britain and Britain's principal delegate. When the new Parliament met for the first time in August, 1945, the Labour party members flooded the government benches in the House of Commons and began the proceedings by singing the "Red Flag." The day to which all the members of the cabinet had looked forward so intensely all their working lives had actually arrived.

The first blow came about a month later, with the sudden ending of Lend-Lease. The decision by President Truman to end Lend-Lease was the real turning point of international relations at the end of the war, and its effects will be felt for a very long time. No other political act could be as decisive, because all subsequent decisions were conditioned by the fact that Lend-Lease had ended as and when it did. The United States Government had a perfect right to end it at any time and in any way. Yet it is impossible not to feel that the manner of its ending did not display the same instinctive understanding of world politics that went into its inception.

This is not said in any spirit of recrimination. Lend-Lease was a weapon of the United States in the war, and for the purposes of the war. It provided her with men, munitions and supplies which, had she had to provide them herself, would have doubled the burden upon her, and perhaps more than doubled her losses. Lend-Lease or some equivalent provision had to be made. It was followed by the Anglo-American loan and the Anglo-American loan agreement, which were transactions of a quite different nature.

One essential point about Lend-Lease was that it was not a gift of money, nor a gift connected with trade, nor a gift to a particular nation. It was a gift of goods for a particular purpose. It recognized that all the Allies were in the war together and that a shot fired by one was as effective as a shot fired by any other. Its termination was based on two assumptions: that the problems of war ended when the last shot was fired, and that the problems of peace after a war were of the same nature as the problems of the peace that preceded the war. Neither was true. Lend-Lease was in effect continued by Marshall Aid and by a supply of arms under the North Atlantic Treaty. But the Anglo-American loan intervened, and nothing can expunge that, and its effects, from the record.

It has already been made clear that war dislocated Britain's trade and forced upon her a dependence on the United States for a number of essential commodities to a greater extent than had ever existed previously. The total British imports from the United States in 1938 valued £118,000,000; in 1944 £532,000,000. Imports of meat had risen from £3,400,000 to £40,100,000; dairy produce from £200,-000 to £44,300,000; iron and steel from £2,500,000 to £27,300,000; non-ferrous metals from £2,600,000 to £14,700,000. Imports of machinery had quadrupled, and those of gasoline, oils and resins had multiplied no less than seventeen times. Without aid in some form Britain was, in 1945, unable to pay for continuance of these imports on anything like the quantity still needed. As Mr. Oliver Lyttelton, Conservative ex-Cabinet Minister, said in that year, "the standard of life of every citizen of Britain . . . depends on our receiving . . . a large measure of financial aid from the United States."

In August, 1945, it was up to the United States to continue or discontinue aid to Britain. It would have been perfectly fair had the United States administration said, in effect, "We intend to help wipe out the worst of the war damage, and do that by a gift of relief in kind administered through the UNRRA. If you qualify for aid under that heading, well, that's fine. If you don't, we don't propose—we have no right—to give you preferential treatment." That would, in Britain, have hurt, but it would have made sense.

Instead, the United States said to Britain, in effect, "Let's get back to normal trade—and let's make it snappy."

Well before the election, the wartime Coalition Government and its experts had opened talks with the United States on the trade and financial agreements that subsequently became the Washington loan agreement and the Bretton Woods trade agreement. The American thesis—which does not need elaboration here—sounded simple enough. The objective, when the war was over, was to return as rapidly as possible to world multilateral trade, to a state of affairs in which the American export surplus of raw materials and manufactured goods could be sold outside America without the handicap of artificial discriminations against them (which meant such things as imperial preferences) and in which America could buy freely, and without interference from state organizations, such raw materials as she needed and such manufactured goods as she chose to buy, while retaining her own existing tariffs. Such a system suited America; the rest of the world would soon find it suited them too. It would be necessary to allow certain exceptions to the general rules, to meet special cases of war-damaged countries, but expanding world trade would quickly cure the strains and hurts of the war.

The official British point of view was different, not so much over the ultimate ends to be attained but in its ideas on how to attain them and how long it would take. As Britain saw it, there were certain inescapable present-day facts.

First, trade between different currency-areas must balance; if it did not, the difference must be paid either in gold or in a currency. Second, Britain did not possess sufficient gold or dollars to pay any continuing adverse balance of trade with the United States. She could earn dollars only by increasing her exports to countries paying in dollars, and even in 1945 it could be seen that the increase needed was over 175% of the 1938 volume. With manufactured articles, Britain would need to export twice as much as she did before the war, in order to balance her external trade.

Britain's natural markets were with Europe and the Empire; even here, the war had shattered the former foundations of trade. Europe was still so damaged that her ability to pay for exports from Britain was doubtful. And as for the Empire, Britain finished the war owing some of the countries of the Empire, particularly India and Egypt, such large debts for war supplies that if the debts were taken at face value, Britain would be sending goods to these countries in payment of debts for decades, and receiving nothing in exchange. Yet, at this stage and in these circumstances, the United States was thinking, talking and acting in terms of multilateral trade and, moreover, as though she had reason to fear Britain's "discrimination" against her. In fact, the American argument over discrimination went as far as to say that if Britain reduced the level of her purchases of any commodity from the United States she must also reduce the level of her purchases of that commodity from every other source by the same amount.

A most vexing question to Americans was imperial, or empire, preference. In origin, it is as old as the British Empire itself. In the seventeenth century, it was a system of bounties, preferences and prohibitions. Of the methods employed, the prohibitions, being the least successful, were the first to be discarded; they seemed to lead to disintegration of the Empire rather than any mutual increase in trade. But preferences did succeed in promoting, even in creating trade. The Canadian lumber industry was materially assisted in its growth by a preference granted in 1807. It was only with the adoption of a general system of free trade by Britain a century ago that preferences disappeared.

They began to return with the granting by the dominions, never full free-trade communities, of import duty preferences to those countries (of which Britain was the major one) which admitted their products freely. Canada led the way, in 1898. On the British side, preferences within the empire were restored when Britain abandoned a general policy of free trade and reimposed import duties in 1919. The new preference policy was continued by various statutes enacted between 1920 and 1932, and culminated in the Import Duties Act, 1932, and the Ottawa Conference of 1933, which provided for a duty-free entry of certain goods into Britain, and a promise by Britain not to cut its 10% ad valorem duties on certain foreign imports lately imposed without the consent of the dominion concerned. The agreements covered, in the main, foodstuffs and raw materials, and the majority of the British duties imposed, in consequence, on non-empire goods fell within scope of the existing 10% ad valorem duty.

Nor is imperial preference simply a matter of trade with Britain. Interdominion agreements were also arranged, between Australia and New Zealand in 1922, Canada and Australia in 1925, South Africa and Southern Rhodesia in 1925, and Canada and New Zealand in 1932. In 1935, Australia and South Africa signed a most-favored-nation trade agreement and in 1937, Australia and Newfoundland made a treaty dealing with the exchange of specified categories of goods.

Opinion in Britain—still less in the Dominions—did not defend imperial preferences solely on the basis that they were a natural expression of common sovereignty. They were defended on the grounds that they were an expression of an existing pattern of international trade, and that before you abandoned one pattern you were entitled to some assurance that the succeeding pattern was likely to be better.

So, in the fall of 1945, the Americans seemed to be thinking that the first requirement was to put multilateral trade onto its feet again as soon as possible. To do that, the world outside the United States would need more dollars than it then had. America must put up a substantial amount of dollars as working capital. As Britain, and the sterling area, were a natural center of world trade, those dollars would be loaned to Britain. But Britain ought to do two things in return: cut out discrimination, which hindered a return to multilateral trading, and scale down her war debts, otherwise they would drain off most of the working capital of dollars before they had become effective internationally.

The situation that faced the British government in response was that the United States was prepared to give Britain financial aid, but only as loan, and only as part of a general trade agreement (the Bretton Woods agreement) containing terms which would inevitably cut down Britain's capacity to recover by means of external trading (which simply meant cutting down Britain's capacity to recover). If Britain accepted the aid on these terms, she would be signing an agreement which, if enforced, would injure her still further or, if not enforced, would destroy her reputation as an honorable nation. If she refused to accept the terms, she condemned her citizens to an absence of imported essential raw materials, to expensive and scanty food and an indefinite continuation of rationing. There would be a limitation of government expenditure on defense outside Britain (which included Greece and the Middle East, as well as Germany) and a distortion of her policy on dominion and colonial development. No wonder Lord Keynes, in the British delegation in Washington, fought so hard to obtain the dollars as a gift and without conditions—in fact, he asked for the kind of plan that Marshall Aid came to be.

The Economist, by no means a periodical hostile to the United States, put the British viewpoint clearly in an editorial on the agreement in December, 1945.

We cannot accept the American doctrine of "non-discrimination" and hope to get our exports up to the required level. We cannot survive without methods that are called "reciprocal" by those that practise them and "bilateral" by those who object. Unless we are free to use our great import market as a bargaining lever we cannot hope to find the necessary markets for our exports. . . . The Americans discriminate quite openly and forcefully in their loan policy, in their shipping policies and most ostentatiously in their immigration restrictions. We have at least as much right as they to employ the methods of discrimination that we find useful.

In the end, the two governmental delegations in Washington reached an agreement for a loan which provided Britain with a line of credit totalling $3,750,000,000 net, and with a positive obligation not to discriminate. In the end, the British Parliament ratified the loan agreement, by 345 votes to 98 in the Commons, by 90 to 8 in the Lords. Twenty-three Labour members voted against it. Of the Conservatives, 8 voted for it, 71 against, and 88 abstained from voting either way.

Was the British Government right in accepting the loan on those terms? It believed that it ought not to impose on the people the even greater austerity of life, which refusal of the loan would have meant. Perhaps it guessed that America's good sense would, over the years, convince her people not to attempt to enforce those provisions in the agreement which could not usefully be enforced. Such has been the case. Probably the government sensed that to break with America at that time, on a question of money and trade, would weaken Europe to an extent which would leave it an easy prey to communist disruption. Refusal of the loan would have been, politically, a slap in the face to the United States. But it was no easy decision, and I for one still am not convinced that a refusal would not have brought about some improved alternative.

Has world stability been increased or diminished by the acceptance of the loan and its terms? Certainly world trade generally benefitted from the dollars placed in Britain's possession. If the dollars had not gone to Britain, there is no certainty that they would have gone to any other nation on the same scale. There is no doubt that the existence of the loan indirectly facilitated the grant of independence to India and so increased stability in Asia as well as in Europe. Even more important, it prevented the immediate split of the world into two ideological groups as would, in 1945 and 1946, inevitably have followed an American refusal to make the loan to Europe, and which would have found all Europe on the wrong side of the iron curtain.

The United States bought, with this loan, immediate freedom

from Soviet aggression based on wartime confidence. That freedom has been not secured in the sense that aggression did not re-emerge. But when it did re-emerge, Western Europe itself faced it with greater resources and, more important, with greater self-confidence.

None the less, the tragic event was the way in which Lend-Lease ended. Tragedy it is, because the need to make some decision was forced upon President Truman too soon in his political life and growth, at a time when he felt himself to be no more than a man nominated for office by one solitary elector, Death.

These arguments can never be conclusive. History never gives anyone the chance to know for certain what would have happened if one had taken the other road.

PART II

THE PROGRAM AND ITS CONSEQUENCES

CHAPTER IV

Five Years in Parliament

When a political party takes office in Britain, it has two missions. As His Majesty's Government in the United Kingdom, it is solely responsible for the state of the nation. It is not divorced from the legislature, since its members are a part of Parliament. It is not subject to a Supreme Court as is the case in the United States; there is nothing in the British Constitution that may not be changed by Act of Parliament. Therefore, its two missions are these. It may have a political philosophy to further—the Labour Government certainly had that—which will require a legislative and administrative program. But it must wrestle with, and defeat if it can, all the events that confront a national administration from day to day as, for example, the mining of the two Royal Navy destroyers in the Corfu Channel in 1946, or the implicit threat to Hong Kong that developed after the collapse of the Nationalist Government in China in 1949. The latter chapters of this section deal with the specifically socialistic experiments of the government. This chapter is intended to give something of the background of the events that demanded plain government, to estimate how the party and its members stood up to these daily responsibilities and shaped their policy accordingly.

In 1945, the main figures in the Labour Cabinet were Mr. Attlee, Prime Minister, Mr. Bevin at the Foreign Office, and Mr. Herbert Morrison, Leader of the House. Close behind, all men of potentially great influence in government, were Mr. Hugh Dalton at the Treasury, Six Stafford Cripps at the Board of Trade, and Mr. Aneurin Bevan at the Ministry of Health. Again how did all these men fare in the five-year context?

In 1945 the parliamentary Labour party did not contain 392 identical members. It consisted of two wings with a debatable ground between them, and at first those two wings were inclined to test their relative strengths (hence their respective importance) within the party. The larger group consisted of the trade-union members, the majority of them solid, unimaginative men prepared to accept party authority with loyalty. It was sufficient for them that their chosen leaders were in office. The smaller group was made up of socialists, and on occasion they felt the pull of two loyalties: loyalty to the party as such, loyalty to the aims of the party as declared when it had been in opposition, for there were times when they believed that they saw the leaders drifting away from the party ideal.

Their two most serious interventions occurred early: In 1946, when they challenged Mr. Bevin's foreign policy in general, with particular reference to Germany and Indonesia, and in 1947, when they disagreed with the policy of the Minister of Defence, Mr. A. V. Alexander, over military service. This left-wing group, of course, was not consistently of the same mind, nor did it always consist of the same people. Its unity, when it existed, was occasioned by the fact that individual members of a party must combine if they are to achieve any result at all. And, to summarize its story before it starts, the group won no outstanding success, if success is to be judged by an overthrow or reversal of the declared policy of its leaders. But it pushed hard in the direction in which it wanted action taken, and if it had not pushed so hard against opposing influences, things would have been shaped differently in the end.

The Labour Government itself can be said to have passed through five periods of crisis. The first came with the revolt of the left-wing group over foreign affairs; the occasion was the debate on the King's Speech at the opening of the session in November, 1946. Then came the fuel crisis of February, 1947, and the sterling crisis of July and August, 1947. These two were the most severe. Finally, there were the devaluation of the pound sterling in September, 1949, and the collapse of the East African groundnut project (as originally planned) toward the end of that year.

Nineteen forty-six was an encouraging year for the Government. It had been able to surmount, without too much difficulty, the first problem that invariably presents itself after a war, the method and rate of demobilization of men and women from the armed forces. It had found, with the Coal Nationalisation Bill, that it would not have to engage at once in deadly combat with the House of Lords. Reconversion of industry was proceeding smoothly, and the indices of production were showing healthy rises. The American loan had covered a very vulnerable flank for what seemed likely to be the period of worst weakness. And the war was still so close that it was possible to blame all failures on its after-effects.

The revolt on foreign policy of some of the left-wing members, in November, 1947, never seriously threatened the Government, and it had the effect of making two things perfectly clear thereafter to the party as a whole. The first was that for the purposes of that government, Mr. Attlee and Mr. Bevin could be considered as twin stars, bound together by forces too strong for any minority movement of revolt to defeat or weaken. It also made it clear that the foreign policy of the government would be the foreign policy of Mr. Bevin, pure and simple, and that any resemblance between that and a "socialistic" foreign policy would be purely coincidental. Its remaining effects were on personalities, and relative personal positions within the party itself.

It hardened the feeling of the trade unionist elements in the party against the intellectuals to their left. They had always known that they were the hard core of the party, when it came to money, to votes at the party conferences, and to seats in the safer Labour constituencies. Now they could feel satisfied that in foreign affairs Mr. Bevin was their man, and that his policy must be their policy. Mr. Bevin established an ascendancy that was never shaken, not even after events in Palestine.

The other important result was a definite decline in the influence of Mr. Herbert Morrison, and an increase in that possessed by Mr. Hugh Dalton. The left-wing group had not only challenged Mr. Bevin, they had also challenged party discipline, for which Mr. Morrison was responsible. For that, the trade union members would have liked a few "examples" to be made. As leader of the House and as party tactician, Mr. Morrison had to ride roughshod over the non-union section of the party. His position was difficult; a tactical mistake at that stage and there would be martyrs around, showing their dreadful wounds, and if any martyrs were to be burned at the stake, Mr. Morrison could see his own future going up with the first whiff of smoke. He emerged well from the test. There were no martyrs.

But the experience had not been made any happier for him by the skill with which Mr. Dalton had managed to keep himself free from identification with one side or the other. Like a Chinese Buddha, he had sat through the debates and nodded and smiled and kept silent, and no one knew for certain what it meant. Mr. Dalton might hint that he had been too busy with international money to concern himself about international politics; no one called his bluff by pointing out that there was a connection between the two.

A little shaken by this attack, but not seriously disturbed, the cabinet spent the last two months of 1946 thinking out its economic plans for 1947. If the revolt had shown that some members of the party were prepared to vote against their leaders, it had also shown that by far the larger number of them were not prepared to do anything of the kind.

The long-term economic difficulties of the cabinet remained as they had been; the gap between British exports and imports, how that gap could be bridged and finally closed. All the problems of dollar shortages, the terms of convertibility, trade, even internal wages and prices, were pangs of the larger headache. But the immediate problem at home was something much more vividly in the minds of the public. That winter was cold, and coal and electricity consumption jumped rapidly upward. But supplies of coal were short. What would happen if Britain actually ran out of coal? That could bring on a crisis within 24 hours, which is precisely what happened.

So far as the general public was concerned, the coal situation, as 1946 passed into 1947, intruded itself on its notice in two ways—by the increasing number of newspaper reports that individual factories all over the country were stopping production because coal supplies were at an end, and by the almost daily announcement on the radio, before the 8 A.M. news, that the Central Electricity Board would cut electricity supplies somewhere in the country within the next few minutes. This was usually followed very promptly by the actual cut.

The second was not a direct consequence of the coal shortage at all. It was primarily due to demand for electricity overtaking productive capacity, as the following figures show:

Year	Total installed capacity (in thousand kilowatts)	Total consumption (in millions of units)
1938	9,365	25,708
1940	10,159	29,976
1942	11,585	36,903
1944	12,248	39,649
1945	12,297	38,611
1946	12,498	42,742

In short, consumption between 1938 and 1946 had increased by approximately 68% while capacity had only increased by 37%. Nor was there any speedy remedy. A modern generating station costs as much, and takes almost as long to build, as a modern battleship, and no stations of that size had been started during the war.

The coal situation in Britain was equally simple, if equally inconvenient. Before the war, Britain produced roughly 230,000,000 tons of coal a year, consumed 180,000,000, and exported 50,000,000. In 1946, production was down by 40,000,000 tons, and consumption at home up by 4,000,000, leaving a margin of only 6,000,000. Moreover, the home consumption figure was kept down only by a reduction by one-third of residential consumption. Even then, the margin of 6,000,000 was more apparent than real. All coal produced is not of the same quality, and the last 6,000,000 tons (of which 5,000,000 were exported in 1946) was low grade coal, of which continental importers were bitterly aware.

The fall in coal stocks tells its own story:

COAL STOCKS
(in thousands of tons)

Year		Distributed	At Opencast mines	Colliery stocks at pithead
1939	monthly	14,550		5,186
1941	average	18,850		3,353
1943		17,376	1,602	3,064
1945	Jan.	13,205	2,367	2,732
1945	July	12,644	1,640	2,401
1946	Jan.	9,763	587	2,167
1946	July	9,438	137	1,674
1946	Dec.	8,466	326	1,439

By the end of January, 1947, the position was really serious. Some 300 factories in the Northwest of England were faced with a complete stoppage. The scene had a disquieting similarity to that predicted during the war for the final stage of oil shortage in Germany. "When the stage is reached," the experts used to say, "that local shortages arise and can only be met by rushing supplies in from another area on an emergency basis, then the whole system is near collapse." There was certainly a good deal of rushing in of supplies on an emergency basis.

If the problem was simple, the solution was not. The output of the mineworkers themselves per manshift in 1946 compared reasonably well with that of the rest of Europe. It was 90% of the monthly average for 1935–38, and the highest comparable percentage in the rest of Europe was in the French-run Saar mines, which showed a figure of 83% of the 1935–38 average. The percentage in France, Belgium and Czechoslovakia was no better than 73%. Further, there was trade union support for increased output. The Mineworkers' Union that year had spent £20,000 from union funds in a campaign to increase production, an event unique in trade union history. As with electricity, all the solutions required time to make their influence effective; in this instance in the amount of usable coal actually leaving the pits.

Another weak link in the chain of supply was transportation. Due to shortage of rolling stock, the railroads were strained to the utmost. In December, 1946, Mr. Shinwell, as Minister of Fuel and Power, had reported this to the cabinet and had asked that coal freight be given priority over passenger traffic, particularly in the allocation of locomotives. This request was refused, and one of the more permanent personal repercussions was that Mr. Dalton expressed in such terms his skepticism of the need for the request that the breach between Mr. Shinwell and himself lasted for the remainder of the life of that Parliament.

It was against this background that the economic program for 1947 was discussed. It was placed under the direct responsibility of Mr. Morrison, and it was intended to give industry, workers and employers their goals for the year, and to explain why they were necessary and how they were to be achieved. The facts of the situation were clear enough. The civil servants had written innumerable memoranda on them. The battle within the cabinet was over how much should be said in public and how it should be phrased.

The first phase of the battle was fought over the white paper containing the government's *Economic Survey for 1947*, which appeared at the end of January. That was intended to be the diagnosis of Britain's position. Broadly speaking, the quarrel was whether the full magnitude of the economic difficulties should be made public, thereby arousing the public to action, but also providing ammunition for the opposition. Mr. Attlee, Mr. Bevin and Mr. Isaacs, Minister of Labour, were in favor of plain speaking.

Their main opponents, at this stage, were some of the trade union members of the cabinet, who foresaw that a confession of such an emergency would inevitably result in pressure being put upon the unions to do things they do not want to do. On this occasion the Prime Minister's faction won, though only after some very straight speaking, and a most stubborn stand by Mr. Attlee himself, who threatened resignation if his view were not accepted.

The second and much more crucial stage of the fight arose from the promised economic budget—that is, the document intended to contain the plan for recovery. Many, if not all, of the obvious remedies—longer hours of work, no more increases in pay, payment by results rather than by time, and so on—were then still anathema to the trade unions. A second serious struggle took place, with Attlee, Bevin and Isaacs again taking one line, and Shinwell, Bevan and Strachey taking the opposite. Not that the issues were at all clear cut. For instance, Mr. Aneurin Bevan, though in favor of speeding up the socialist program, wanted to insist on piecework and longer hours in the building industry while the trade unions, though a little wary of more nationalization experiments, were still adamant against any retreat on conditions of work.

That left three important members of the cabinet, Mr. Morrison, Mr. Dalton and Sir Stafford Cripps, uncommitted to either side. Mr. Morrison was nominally responsible for economic affairs, and he had always foreseen such a conflict. He preferred to keep himself free to rush to the assistance of whichever side appeared likely to be victorious, although his own inclinations drew him, other things being equal, to the Attlee-Bevin-Isaacs view. Mr. Dalton was equally prepared to take either side (for a consideration paid in the hard cash of prestige and power within the government), but his personal inclination, unlike Mr. Morrison's, was towards the socialist side of the dispute. Sir Stafford Cripps remained quiet, thinking.

That situation could not remain static for long. First, Mr. Morrison fell victim to a serious attack of thrombosis, which kept him out of politics for the following six months. The second blow was completely impersonal. The February weather struck Britain and converted a conflict confined to the minds of the few into a physical struggle which dominated the thoughts of everyone in the country.

The events of that first week in February had a dramatic swiftness. As a rule, Friday in the Commons is not a day for major issues. The House sits early and leaves early, and the business for the day is arranged to dispose of minor measures, known to be noncontroversial. The afternoon is usually left free for members who wish to raise a discussion which does not merit debate on a more important day.

Friday's debate was on the newly imposed coal allocations, but only so far as they affected one particular area. Mr. Blackburn, the member opening the debate, represented the constituency in which Austin, the motor manufacturer, has its factory. Austin had been talking of closing down because of insufficient coal allocation, and Mr. Blackburn wanted to know why they had not been given a better priority. On the face of it, it looked as though there would be a mildly acrimonious debate, mainly centered around the motor industry and the export trade in automobiles.

Behind the scenes, however, things were far from happy. The previous week of bad weather had meant that coal could not be moved either by land or by sea, and a week's interruption in deliveries had resulted in exhaustion of coal stocks in certain areas. On Thursday, the Fuel Ministry began to panic. It hastily imposed a ban on bunkering foreign ships—and as hastily canceled it. On Friday morning, there was an emergency cabinet meeting. Mr. Shinwell was given authority to impose an absolute ban on the use of electricity in certain areas between certain hours, and he came to the House to announce that decision—as late in the debate as possible, to take advantage of the approaching weekend of closed factories (and of a closed Stock Exchange). But Mr. Shinwell was rattled, and showed it. The most damning comment of all, that day, came from someone on his own side: "Lack of foresight." That weekend, the Labour Government was nearer to collapse and failure than it had ever been before, or was to be during its whole period of office.

It survived, and it survived because the physical crisis caused by the weather deepened, and compelled everyone to stop thinking about politics and to think instead about the concrete problems of food and fuel supplies. It survived because the seriousness of the situation forced cabinet agreement on immediate emergency action to be taken, and this restored its members' nerve. Life in Britain, even on a governmental level, became a matter of improvisation and emergency. And it survived because Sir Stafford Cripps stepped, carefully and tentatively, into the gaps left by the illness of Mr. Morrison, and the fallen idols, Mr. Dalton and Mr. Shinwell. As the *New Statesman* said afterwards, in its comment on the debates in the Commons: " . . . in a period when hard decisions are required, Stafford Cripps' austere integrity rings true, while Hugh Dalton's jollying tone is in danger of acquiring a hollow ring." The writer continued, in a prophetic note, "As for the dead wood, both old and new, which litters the Treasury Bench, there is an uneasy awareness that it will take several more crises to excise it." (In fact, there were never enough crises to excise it completely.)

The coal crisis was basically a physical one, induced by exceptional weather and thus a phenomenon not likely to recur. Yet it had important consequences. Mr. Attlee realized that his cabinet organization was too loose for effective control of the machinery of government, working on the scale and at the pressure demanded by the government's program. Previously, the cabinet had itself been the coördinating committee of government, and it had worked very unevenly. Henceforward, the cabinet was divided into layers of responsibility. Three groups were established, one under the Foreign Secretary, another under the Chancellor of the Exchequer (trade and finance), the third (for general matters) under the Lord President of the Council, Mr. Morrison. The holders of the more important cabinet offices became members of one or more of these groups. The remainder were departmental heads, called in for consultation only on matters directly affecting their departments. The groups, or committees, were further strengthened by the inclusion of high officials. All were directly responsible to the Prime Minister.

This alteration materially increased the power available to Sir Stafford Cripps when he became head of the trade and finance group.

There were also repercussions among personalities. Mr. Morrison had not done too well as economic leader of the country up to the time of his illness, and when he returned from convalescence he never quite regained the position, still more the prospects, that he had once had. It was felt that he had driven past too many red lights. On the other hand, he remained the tactician of the party. In that field, his absence was noticed and regretted.

Mr. Dalton gave no overt sign of any reduction in his confidence in himself, but there were signs that the confidence of the cabinet in Mr. Dalton had been shaken. The real change was the position of Sir Stafford Cripps. He had always been deeply ambitious, but from sense of purpose and responsibility far more than from a desire for greater personal power. In all that had happened, he saw that there would be more work for him to do, more responsibilities for him to accept. He continued his quiet preparations for that stage.

For the rest of the party, and for the public, the aftermath was a sense of uneasiness. Things had gone wrong. The theoretical calculations had been made and applied, yet disaster had appeared just the same. What next?

"Convertibility" of sterling had hung like a shadow in the background to Britain's economic position ever since the middle of 1946. Under the Anglo-American loan agreement made in December, 1945, Britain had accepted, at American insistence, an obligation that "not later than one year after the effective date of this agreement..." she would "impose no restriction on payments and transfers from current transactions," and this clause in the agreement was followed by one that imposed a complementary condition that releases from accumulated sterling balances should be freely available for current transactions in any currency area, without discrimination. The effective date of the loan agreement was that of its final ratification by the United States government, which was July 15, 1946. That made "Convertibility Day" July 15, 1947.

"Convertibility," then, applied in two fields. It meant that, once it was applied, currently earned sterling could be converted into any currency—dollars was the currency that really mattered, and convertibility came to mean just the right to use pounds sterling to buy dollars from Britain. It also meant that accumulated sterling debts could be exchanged for dollars up to whatever amount the creditor could persuade the British authorities to release.

The first problem, in the early part of 1947, looked much the less dangerous. Britain had trading relations with all parts of the world. With some countries, her trade almost balanced. With others, Britain might be buying more than she sold, or the reverse. If Britain were selling more than she bought, or if her purchases and sales broke even, the authorities believed that they had nothing to fear. They judged that their liability to convert currently earned sterling extended only to the net balance struck at the end of any twelve–month accounting period, a net balance reached after all individual transactions, private and state, had been totaled. In the events that happened, it is by no means certain that some individual foreign creditors of Britain did not jump the gun, and convert their own sterling claims into dollars, to the detriment of their compatriots. But that was a possibility which did not figure very largely in the public mind before July. It was assumed that the exchange machinery would take care of that.

This left those countries from which Britain bought more than she sold. These would have net balances of currently earned sterling. What risk was there of an immediate run of conversions by them of sterling into dollars?

There, the authorities were relying mainly on the goodwill of those countries, and with some justice. By and large, the creditor nations on current accounts were the food–producing countries, and most of them were in the Commonwealth. Canada was all right— there were special arrangements with Canada. Australia and New Zealand were two others, and Britain had never had any serious currency disputes with either. South Africa was another; there the ties of sentiment were not so strong, but they seemed strong enough to insure at least a square deal. There remained Argentina, and Argentina did make the best of her position. It cost Britain the ownership of the Argentinian railways to make an acceptable bargain.

The accumulated sterling balances were quite a different problem; for one thing, their totals were astronomical. Quite apart from the United States and Canada, Britain had been forced to run up external debts to the tune of at least £3,600,000,000 by the middle of 1946, and the two biggest individual creditors were India and Egypt. Clearly, from a point of view of liquid reserves, Britain was insolvent. If every creditor asked for payment at once, Britain had neither the money nor the goods with which to pay. That was obvious, so obvious, indeed, that the very fact itself was a help, not a hindrance, in the inevitable negotiations. What Britain had to negotiate with each country was an agreement that regulated the portion of that total debt which each creditor country could convert each year. By making such an agreement, Britain contracted to make so much sterling available for conversion into dollars, and to send that country goods in the value of the amount so released, without requiring it to pay for them out of its internal resources. Those are called "unrequited" goods.

Hence, 1946 and the first half of 1947 was a period of intense Treasury activity. Each creditor country had to be seen, and with each the long process of negotiation undertaken. Fortunately, both India and Egypt were countries with which Britain had a favorable balance on current trade, so the problem of currently earned sterling did not arise with them so acutely. But, fantastically large as the problem looked, in reality the technical arrangements necessary to meet it were not quite so immense. The United States was out of those discussions, and with them the countries in the American currency area. Bilateral agreements existed with France, Switzerland and the Scandinavian countries, and these could be adjusted to meet convertibility. A system governing transferable accounts had already been arranged with Canada, Newfoundland, Argentina and the Belgian, Dutch and Portuguese currency areas. A special agreement existed with Italy. In short, judged by financial standards, the situation early in 1947 did not look as though it would get out of hand.

It was possible for *The Economist* to say, as late as April, 1947, "if the promise of convertibility costs Britain as much as £50 million in hard currencies this year, we shall have to deem ourselves very unfortunate."

Opinion in Britain, before July, had two main themes. It accepted the coming of convertibility as an inevitable step; to quote *The Economist*, it was "an essential prerequisite to the continued readiness" of countries to go on supplying Britain with the goods she needed. On the other hand, many people felt that the fixing of a definite date for convertibility so long ahead had weakened Britain's bargaining power with her creditor countries. It meant that each creditor country was only too aware that time was on its side, that if it did not agree to limit the amount of sterling it could convert, after July 15, 1947, it would, in theory, be able to convert into dollars every pound sterling it possessed. It could afford to sit back and let the British set the pace in the negotiations.

These were difficulties in the way of making an agreement, but it was natural to feel that once the agreement was made, the troubles were over. There was general confidence that the Treasury and the Bank of England were capable of making every agreement watertight.

This feeling of confidence continued to the beginning of July— in some quarters it lasted longer. At the end of June, Mr. Dalton announced that imports of newsprint would be cut and other cuts in imports were to follow. There was a general feeling that it was a pity that he had decided to start with newsprint, but that was accompanied by some confidence that other cuts would inevitably follow. Then, on July 3, Mr. Dalton said in the Commons that there would be no significant change in the volume of imports. It was that *volte face* that started the uneasiness that was to grow so rapidly in July.

At first, the uneasiness did not spread to the government. It affected the nonofficial world and was reflected on the London Stock Exchange. (It is said that the Exchange is an excellent barometer of short-term and long-term influences, less reliable over medium-term considerations, and in July, 1947, it justified that view.) By the middle of July, there was a sharp and sudden drop in security prices, the sudden, cold wind that precedes the storm.

Still, the official world was undisturbed. There are arguments as to whether or not the United States administration made suggestions that the convertibility date should be postponed. Even if these were made, they were rejected. The Treasury was content to abide by the figures of actual dollar conversions and, for the first week or so after July 15, that indicator gave no cause for alarm. About three-quarters of each weekly drawing of dollars was for British expenditure, and the total of drawings by other countries remained reasonably constant. The government went on with its plans for the August recess. Parliament would rise early in August. Cabinet member and civil servant would take their holiday break in August and everyone would return, refreshed, to cope with the situation in October. In October, the next danger signal, the end of the line of dollar credit under the loan agreement, might be so much the nearer, but then everyone would be in a better position to estimate if and when any dollars would be forthcoming under the Marshall Plan.

But that timetable was wrecked. Between July 15 and the end of that month, dollar drawings for British expenditure remained at the rate of $60,000,000 each week, but in August the demand for sterling conversion from other countries began to mount. In the second week of August they rose to $115,000,000. In the last six days before convertibility was suspended, they were no less than $237,000,000. This was a crisis in credit, a run on a fund, accelerating, as such runs do, with enormous velocity towards the end.

So the storm at last descended on the official world. There is no doubt that the financial authorities were very badly surprised at the run on dollars that followed. All through the preceding months, the Treasury had been so very confident that everything had been arranged, that there could be no flight from sterling. They repeated that confidence in private as well as in public. They were wrong and for a few days officials were as badly scared by the fact that they had miscalculated as by the actual results of the miscalculation.

The currency crisis had immediate political repercussions. Early in July, the government had committed itself to a two-day debate on the economic situation before Parliament adjourned for the summer. It was suddenly put upon notice, both by the general state of public opinion and specifically by a warning from the Trades Union Congress, that it would be expected to produce a policy for the crisis. Nothing had been further from the ministers' minds than that they should be prodded into producing, and taking responsibility for, a coherent and necessarily unpleasant policy before they had their holidays. But they suddenly realized that they could not escape.

There began a process of hurried improvisation. Perhaps it is not quite fair to call it improvisation. The departments had prepared, months previously, a program of economies designed to save dollars and stimulate exports, all—as is the civil servants' duty—within the framework of the government's general policy. The document could be, and was, taken out again and dusted off; there was no improvisation there. But ministers had never accepted this painful document. They were all ready to agree that some such program would be necessary when the "twelfth hour" struck in the fall, and when (or if) that time came, they would screw up their courage to take the plunge. But in the meantime, there were unanswerable objections to every item in the list.

Mr. Attlee was attacked from both sides. One of his troubles was Mr. Ernest Bevin. Mr. Bevin's attitude was that of a weary Titan, returned from unexampled labors overseas and entitled, like Ulysses, to find all well at home. But what does he find? He finds that his colleagues, who are cast in lesser molds, have made a mess of things again. In particular, with the deliberate and personal object of weakening his foreign policy, they had failed to produce any coal for export. He had been saying this, loudly and emphatically, for some time. He had some support from Mr. Dalton, much of whose bouncing self-confidence had gone, and who would even then have been glad to get out of the Treasury before he had to start making himself unpopular.

On the other side, the Prime Minister had to meet the attack of the left-wing section of his party, represented in his cabinet by Mr. Aneurin Bevan, Mr. Strachey and Mr. Shinwell. Logically, their conception of a proper policy ought to have involved even more restrictions at home. But two of them were personally committed to supplying the people with houses and food. Only two gigantic professions of faith could make that possible. One was that the immediate application of socialist principles would achieve a great increase in the productive efficiency of the British economy. The other was that the advent of Marshall Aid should be treated as a certainty.

While this conflict was developing within the cabinet, the departments had been at work to see what they could contribute to the drastic program that the Prime Minister had promised and the Trades Union Congress would expect. Naturally, this gave rise to inspired leaks in the press. Day by day, some horrible new restriction was freely and "authoritatively" predicted. The public was led to expect that the meat ration would be halved, the fats ration reduced, the basic petrol allowance for pleasure driving withdrawn, foreign holidays banned, a capital levy imposed, and so forth. The government departments have plenty of means of preventing this sort of talk from spreading. They did not use them. The chorus became louder and more unanimous; the public believed it and, by and large, the public resigned itself to what was coming.

With immense solemnity, the government produced its anti-climax. There were to be fresh restrictions, but once again the cabinet had illustrated its lowest common denominator of agreement, and pretty low it was. The restrictions were not nearly so harsh as had been predicted. The cracks were to be plastered over, not repaired. Everyone breathed a sigh of the wrong kind of relief, relief that he had been spared, not relief that the job had been well tackled.

That was the August crisis. On the technical side it was met by the suspension of convertibility on August 20, and Treasury officials set out on a second long and weary round of foreign capitals to negotiate fresh agreements for the gradual release of blocked sterling. On the political side, the horse that had refused to jump had somehow scrambled through the fence. But it was the major crisis of the whole five years because it determined the shape of things to come. It underlay the devaluation crisis of September, 1949, and the reasons for that decision. It was the background to the dogged insistence of Sir Stafford Cripps on the importance of the sterling area, with all the consequences that had on the prospects of European Union.

The cause of it all? Confidence. There was an almost visible loss of confidence by the country in the government. There was an almost equally visible loss of confidence by ministers in themselves. Their divisions had become public property; they could no longer conceal the fact that these prevented them from reaching the decisions necessary to formulate a policy. The verdict can be put in a single paragraph from an article on the crisis by the financial editor of the *Manchester Guardian* in September, 1947: "If we [Britain] had taken a grip on our production troubles sooner and if the Loan Agreement had left us as much freedom as the Bretton Woods Agreement, the crisis would have been delayed until next year, and it might never have taken the form of a sterling crisis. A few months might have made all the difference in the world, because renewed American aid might then have come in time."

The consequences?

Domestic politics were affected. Because the government's own confidence had been shaken, the left wing of the party scored two political successes almost immediately. It obtained a promise that a bill to nationalize the iron and steel industry would be introduced in the 1949 Session, coupled with the necessary rider that an attempt would be made in 1948 to alter the Parliament Act of 1911, in such a way that an iron and steel nationalization bill, introduced and passed in 1949, would become law in 1950 before a general election. It also secured a promise that the rate of new house construction and of the importation of the essential raw materials should be maintained.

The iron and steel industry cannot help being an industry in which the level of production dominates everything else in an industrial state. Just as the corresponding industry in the Ruhr Valley is the key to so many problems, in Germany; so in Britain. The middle-road members of the government, exemplified by Mr. Morrison, whose illusions about the virtue of this nationalization proposal had long since faded, might heartily wish that the word "steel" had not been so casually slipped into the party program for an election they were never persuaded that they would win. The left–wing members of the cabinet felt otherwise. They insisted that the real test of the government's ability to pull the country out of the crisis would be the determination with which it pressed on with the nationalization of iron and steel. To the Conservatives, by the same token, the industry became the last ditch in which they must do or die—at least, they must do and the House of Lords must, if necessary, die.

The left–wing members rarely stopped long enough to explain exactly what it was they would do—if they had ownership of the industry—that they could not do with existing powers. Conservatives might admit in private that the British steel industry could hardly be called a shining example of efficient private enterprise, certainly not of the virtues of competition, in that it was already controlled from the center about as tightly as any industry could be. That did not matter. Steel became a test case, a symbol which had for both sides far more importance than its inherent significance, great as that was.

But, as a counterpoise there was another result of the crisis. It made it certain that Sir Stafford Cripps would, before long, become the leader of the government in economic and financial matters. Sir Stafford was a socialist. He could and did support the nationalization of the iron and steel industry. But he had one attribute that the left–wing group lacked in public affairs. He had patience.

The collapse of the plan to make the pound sterling freely convertible with the dollar was a joint Anglo-American failure. An essential part of the original 1945 agreement, the American negotiators had insisted, was that convertibility should take place at a time fixed in advance, and fixed not very far in advance. That had been tried, and it had not worked.

Not very much is to be gained by attempting to apportion blame for that failure. Clearly, there had been an original misjudgment on the American side of the difficulties in the way of success. It is equally clear that the trade and financial policy of the United Kingdom during that eighteen months had not won the confidence necessary to carry the whole thing through. Possibly no British government could have satisfied all the countries and the individuals concerned in international trade that a pound sterling was the equivalent of four dollars for all purposes. But even a different approach, on the part of the Labor government itself might, as the writer in the *Manchester Guardian* suggested, have carried the pound sterling over the awkward gap between the convertibility date and the effective start of Marshall Aid without such a complete loss of international confidence. Recriminations apart, there had been failure, and it meant that the next attempt to make the pound freely convertible with the dollar was bound to be postponed for a long time. No responsible person could risk a second fiasco.

Faced with these circumstances, there were three possible policies open to a United Kingdom government. These policies were not mutually exclusive. They had common features. Their differences were more matters of emphasis. They were, so to speak, different roads up the same valley, but they were certainly not intended to reach the same ultimate point.

The first policy, commonly held by Conservatives, was that Britain ought to bring her whole economy more closely into line with that of the United States and Canada. How, and to what extent this could be done, depended upon reactions in North America. Its keynote would be an abandonment of what was pure socialism in the economy of the country, to allow greater opportunities for competition for both capital and labor; and above all, an end to what the Americans were calling "discrimination" and "state buying" in international trade (not that the Conservatives were at all willing to give up Imperial Preferences). The general effect of such a policy can best be described by saying that if it were to be successfully followed, the pound sterling would not be asked to achieve convertibility with the dollar on its merits, but to become an American dollar of a different size and shape. Such a policy would, no doubt, in American eyes produce a Britain all of a piece with Belgium, Germany, France and Italy, but with greater internal stability than any of the others.

The left wing of the Labour party would have had the party follow another line. The crisis had made the extremists very conscious of the difficulties in the way of what they called a full socialistic policy, and very conscious of their need to prepare their own long-term policy.

They did not pretend that they knew of any means by which Britain could escape dependence on American dollars in the immediate future. They were worried about the position that would arise when the aid was no longer there, how Britain could escape the need to rely on something of the kind indefinitely. They agreed that, granted the present organization of international trade, the level of Britain's exports was inevitably tied to the level of United States production. The reasons for that were complex but valid; the proposition could be demonstrated by a comparison of the relevant figures. The real drive behind their policy came from their belief that the national economy of the United States was inherently unstable and that, in consequence, any country tied to the American economy would be bound to suffer industrial disturbances and unemployment, despite all it could do for itself.

The left wingers urged that Britain should consciously plan, with the rest of Europe, to make Europe into an economic unit comparable with that existing in the United States, and that this combination should be based upon Europe's productive capacity, and Africa's supplies of raw materials. It would not be sufficient, they said, to increase Britain's exports of manufactured consumer goods to the world in general—in that, she could never alone compete with the

United States for long. Salvation could only come from a closer integration of all Europe, a Europe organized to make the best of its traditional skills and various facilities. Britain and Europe must adjust their export programs, and hence their production programs, to meet such a changed situation. But—and this was a point they did not stress—to achieve all this Europe must also be prepared to plan as one, under single direction from above; in short, under the equivalent of British socialism. And the advocates of this point of view never provided a convincing answer to any question of how this miraculous change could be wrought in a Europe that so obviously was thinking along the reverse lines.

Had Mr. Dalton remained Chancellor, his inclinations would undoubtedly have been to follow such a policy as far as he could. Such a happy combination of finance and foreign policy would have appealed to him strongly. Equally, he would have welcomed the opportunity to lecture the rest of Europe on what it must do to be saved. But he was to lack the opportunity. He made an attempt to recapture this golden moment at Strasbourg in 1949, but much water had flowed under the bridge by then.

No writer of fiction would dare to make use of chance to the extent that fate did in deposing Mr. Dalton from the Treasury. Mr. Dalton had been among the leaders of the Labour party since long before the war. He was an economist, a professor at the London School of Economics, a man who had played a leading part in teaching and encouraging the young men of the party. He had all the paper qualifications for his post. And he had, at the start, all the confidence needed to carry the task off with a flourish. He was excellent in debate, his grasp of figures was lucid and tenacious, and although unkind critics had sometimes said he was more the headmaster of the House of Commons than master, he never hesitated to treat the financial world, and the financiers, as roughly as he thought they deserved.

By June, 1947, he had begun to lose ground. From his room in the Treasury he had pushed many buttons, and many of the right answers had come up. Yet, by then, there was a mounting number of buttons which, when pushed, had produced some rather disconcerting results. Even among his supporters there were those who wondered if the grand design really resembled the blueprints of the national economy, so confidently described by Mr. Dalton before taking office.

Nevertheless, Mr. Dalton remained Chancellor of the Exchequer. He talked as though the country had been through a natural calamity as inevitable and as unpredictable as the cold spell of the previous February. However many might fail to share his view of himself as a man dealing with the bludgeonings of a blind fate, there was nothing they could do about it. Mr. Attlee had already made it clear that he did not intend to change his major office holders lightly —not that the full extent of his ability to forgive was already apparent.

The events of the first six months of the financial year required that the Chancellor should produce an autumn budget. The tradition that the contents of a budget must remain absolutely secret until the Chancellor reveals them in his speech to the Commons is absolute in Britain. On the afternoon of November 12, 1947, on the way into the chamber in which the Commons was sitting—what is called the Lobby—Mr. Dalton was stopped by a journalist, a personal friend. The journalist asked him half jokingly (for he could never have expected a straight answer) what he had in store for the country. Mr. Dalton told him, in outline, but he said enough to enable an experienced Parliamentary journalist to complete a full story. The journalist, hardly realizing the implications of all that had happened, phoned his news room; he represented a London evening paper, *The Star*. By chance, his story reached the news desk just in time to make a new edition of the paper. By chance that edition of the paper reached the streets before the Chancellor had finished his speech, and it contained not a journalist's forecast of what the Chancellor might say, but the Chancellor's summary of what he intended to say. The rule had been broken. The following day, Mr. Dalton sent his resignation to the Prime Minister, the Prime Minister accepted it; he handed over his seals of office on November 14, 1947.

The whole story is one of chance. The story traveled from the phone booth in Westminster to the printing machines in Bouverie Street, off Fleet Street, so fast that no one had time to think about it on the way. No one thought to check up the times; had any one man stopped to think, he could have saved Mr. Dalton from the consequences of an incredible indiscretion. But no one did, and within a week Sir Stafford Cripps was sitting at the desk of the Chancellor of the Exchequer in Treasury Chambers, Whitehall, planning what he would do. His power to carry through whatever he planned became all the more clear when it was announced that he would also become technically Minister for Economic Affairs, and that both the Treasury and the Board of Trade were to be under his control.

The policy that Sir Stafford decided to follow differed appreciably from the two outlined earlier. Its essence was development of the sterling area. Every action, every decision, came to be judged by the one test, its effect on the fortunes and progress of the sterling area. In December, 1949, Sir Stafford gave an interview to Mr. Charles Kline, the London correspondent of the *U.S. News and World Report.* He was asked to state his attitude toward "the so-called integration of Europe." In the course of his reply he said:

> It very much depends, of course, what you mean by the term integration, which has never been defined exactly and means a great many different things to a great many different people . . . if it means some sort of linking up of the economies through organisation like customs unions which might jeopardise the position of the Sterling Area as a whole, then I think we should not want to go in for such close linkages . . . before joining some smaller area as yet untried, we need to see a good prospect that it will be a success, and in any event that it will not jeopardise the success of the Sterling Area.

That is the policy Sir Stafford Cripps—and the Labour Government—have pursued since the fall of 1947. There is, despite its utterly different context, a touch of Churchillian determination and patience in the persistence with which Sir Stafford shepherded the whole labor movement along this road. It is one they can never have expected to follow; there was no reference to it in their election program. It ignores the claims of any crusade to socialize the rest of Europe. Indeed, if the sterling area were called the British Commonwealth—which would not be an inaccurate approximation—many Labour members might feel a hot blush of shame at all the earlier protests they had so quickly abandoned. All that made no difference. Sir Stafford piped and they followed; at least, they did not turn and walk the other way.

The origins of what came to be called the sterling area date back to 1931. When Britain left the gold standard and the pound sterling became a managed currency—that is, a currency not remaining inertly passive to changes in world currency rates—the Bank of England was given formal authority to set up an Exchange Equalisation Fund, and to use that fund as an implement with which to protect the exchange rate commanded by the pound sterling in world markets. Thereafter, all currencies which were directly linked with sterling in international trade became automatically a part of this "Sterling Area." They were bound to share the results, good or ill, of the Bank of England's use of its equalization fund, and this provided an additional reason why they should attempt to co-ordinate their trade policies with those of Britain. At the outset, the areas directly involved included the dominions and the colonies, but the pound sterling came to have an appreciable influence on the currencies of the western fringe of Europe, from Scandinavia to Portugal, and a large part of the Middle East.

From 1939 onward, this concept of a series of linked currencies managed from a central point became immensely more important because it became both an active weapon of war against Germany and an active implement in procuring for Britain the supplies and services needed to build up her own war strength. The sterling area had two years of independent existence before the United States entered the war, two years in which it had had to fight an all-out struggle. The sterling area could not help being an instrument designed first and foremost to protect the interests of Britain; it was molded to do exactly that. Once America was in the war, the rope that secured the dollar area to the sterling area was Lend–Lease. The two areas were made fast; they had a common policy, but they were never united. In 1945, the United States cast off the rope, and once again the sterling and dollar areas were free, independent and unequal.

The real strength of the sterling area, after 1945, lay in its vast trade within itself (it was and remained the greatest area of multilateral trade in the world) and the vast debts that Britain owed to most of the countries within it. In its more complex way, it had the strength of the bond between the trader with the over-draft and his banker. While the trader continues to trade, while the turnover of the account with the banker is high, the banker is reluctant to close down the account and call in the overdraft. If he does, he fears that he may not be paid, while if he continues, the vitality of the account becomes the best token he can have that some day all will be well.

Sir Stafford Cripps drew some major lessons from the convertibility failure of August, 1947. First, what had enabled Britain to survive that fiasco had been the strength of the sterling area. Up to that point, the relationship between pound and dollar, based on the 1945 loan agreement, had done the pound as much harm as good. Contrariwise, the sterling area had survived this powerful shock without falling apart. Britain's repudiation, on August 20, 1947, of the convertibility clause in the loan agreement was not only a breach of an agreement with the United States, it also tore up scores of agreements made with other countries under which Britain had promised them that a portion of the sterling they owned would be freely convertible into dollars. Without the support of the countries in the sterling area, Britain would have suffered all the complications of international bankruptcy.

Moreover, the sterling area had important political implications. Relations between Britain and India were the most delicate in the year 1947. India was a member of the sterling area, and if the area were to be abandoned, or even compromised, India would sever every link with Britain. And if this occurred, who could be certain that chaos and conflict might not overwhelm her? A conflict of race and religion, an extension of the Punjab massacres, might produce calamities a hundred times worse than those which had already befallen Burma.

Sir Stafford's second lesson was that he should put no trust in salvation as the result of economic co-operation with Europe, and that was his biggest break with the left-wing theorists of his party. As he saw it, the peoples of Europe were one thing; their desires for a closer unity were real and urgent. But their financial workings were another kettle of fish. These, he thought (and he was basing his judgment on the events of the three months before August) were an anarchistic horde, with the fierce and short-sighted individualism of the shark. Europe's statesmen might proclaim, and honestly believe, that Europe without Britain was unworkable, unthinkable, but a thousand little men in Paris, Rome, Brussels and Amsterdam had used all their ingenuity—which was considerable—to turn Britain's difficulties into profits for their individual accounts. It was not a question of morals or politics or political theory. That was how these men were made. They were living in a system that allowed them to behave that way, and to omit that fact from the calculations would be madness.

The third lesson was that Britain must win some independence from the United States. The over-all government of the United States suffered from one dreadful handicap, in the eyes of those dealing with it. It had no mechanism by which it could create and follow a policy in world economics which was consistent on a day-to-day basis. Certainly, the United States pursued a general line in world affairs, for its people were sufficiently of one mind to give their country an ultimate direction. You could tell for what port the United States was making, but it was quite impossible to forecast the precise course she would follow. The United States government is without an organ singly responsible for shaping policy and for putting it into effect. There is nothing to stop the State Department from formulating a policy, the Treasury another, with congressional foreign affairs committees damning both. And who could tell which group would win? There was another factor affecting the strength of American foreign policy, the two cycles of public disinterest, one a four-year cycle based on the presidential election, the other, slightly milder, based on the mid-term elections. For the rest of the time, there would be scores of contradictory voices, and no two Americans would agree on the importance to be attached to each. The safest assumption did not go beyond the belief that the United States was on the side of the angels, and that she would give aid where aid was needed in her own time and in her own way. But to forecast what would be happening in any one particular week. . . .

With these lessons in mind, Sir Stafford Cripps could see two main lines of advance. To hold the sterling area together, the countries in it needed two things, a secure and fairly priced market for their produce, and a supply of manufactured goods, equipment and technical help. Britain and Europe could provide a reasonably secure and expanding market for a great deal of their raw materials. Equally, Europe—particularly Britain—could supply a great many of these countries' demands. It was therefore essential for Britain to maintain full employment, and to increase her productivity to meet this mounting call on output. It was also essential that the sterling area should possess dollars, as many dollars as possible, earned dollars if possible, and that none of these dollars should be wasted in buying non–essentials. For that reason, it was vital that control of the sterling area's funds should be left centralized in the hands of Britain. Granted all that, he felt he could guarantee that these dollars would produce the minerals, raw materials and specialized goods of all kinds that were needed for the well-being of the whole area.

The other objective was to reduce, as far as possible, any absolute dependence by the sterling area on the dollar area for anything that was really a necessity—and that is something quite different from a desire to eliminate trade with the dollar area. An expanding trade with the dollar area was all to the good, provided it balanced. What was dangerous was being in a position in which a vital supply might be cut, and nothing could be done about it.

Seen in the light of these considerations, the policy pursued by Sir Stafford Cripps was positive and consistent. It satisfied no one completely (it would have been damned if it had), but it persuaded those involved that no alternative in sight offered more. As a result, the devaluation of the pound sterling in September, 1949, did not jolt world trade, or Britain's position in it, nearly so much as had the suspension of convertibility two years previously. Devaluation was not an involuntary decision, of the kind forced on the Chancellor in August, 1947, to his surprise and dismay. Nor was it a voluntary decision, in the sense that Britain could have avoided taking it if she had wanted to. But it was a foreseeable decision; above all, it was foreseen and prepared for.

The causes lay in the setback to domestic trade in the United States in the early part of 1949. That reduced American imports, and some of the main cuts were in raw materials produced by the colonies of the British Commonwealth. Those cuts in their turn reduced the dollar earnings of the sterling area, without reducing the desire and the need of the constituent countries to continue their dollar purchases. Devaluation was the only means left by which the volume of imports into the United States could be maintained. But that sequence of events could be plotted in advance as soon as the figures for domestic trade in the United States began to show a decline. Sir Stafford fought to defer the moment of devaluation, but his course had been one in which devaluation would be a logical and expected step at the time when it was made. Nevertheless, this policy contains one weakness, for which the government failed to find a solution. This is the problem of "unrequited" exports, and it can be illustrated simply enough.

It is estimated that in mid-1948 the sterling balance owed by the United Kingdom to the Dominion of India was £760,000,000, after allowing for the cost of pension payments, etc., for which the United Kingdom had assumed direct responsibility. This balance was "blocked" in the sense that India had agreed not to attempt to spend it all at once. Britain had on her part agreed that India, during the financial year 1948–49, should have the right to spend £15,000,000 in hard currencies from this blocked balance, and additional £50,000,000 (approximately) in sterling. This agreement would give the government of India the opportunity to grant licenses to various Indian merchants to import British goods to the value of £50,000,000. In fact, in that year, the actual releases of sterling and hard currencies to the Dominion of India were £36,000,000 in hard currencies and £130,000,000 in sterling.

Merchants in India, relying on the availability of this money overseas, were at liberty to place orders in Britain for goods totaling that amount, and British manufacturers would be making goods to that value to meet those orders. The British manufacturer would be paid in the long run by the Bank of England. But the Bank of England would not be reimbursed for that amount by the Indian Government. Instead, it would debit the account of the British Government, and the Indian Government would reduce the amount of the British debt to India by a similar amount as it collected the money payable from the various Indian merchants. At the end of 1949, the estimated indebtedness of Britain to India was down to £630,000,000 but the British Government had been unable to spend the £130,000,000 its manufacturers had earned in India. The export of the goods they had made was "unrequited" in that those exports would bring back no equivalent volume of goods from India to Britain.

Such a process carried with it many advantages for Britain. Apart from the fact that it resulted in a partial re-payment of the debt, it facilitated the sale of British goods to India and elsewhere within the sterling area. It kept up employment in Britain. But equally, the process was bound to work against attempts to expand the trade between Britain and the dollar area. While a British manufacturer found it comparatively easy to sell his goods to India, he would have all the less incentive to attempt to sell those goods to the United States or Canada. The effects went further than that. While industries, manufacturing the kind of goods required in India (which might be very different from the goods likely to sell in America) were busy and prosperous, they would generally offer to workers the prospect of a steady job at a good wage, and a man earning a good wage is far from inclined to abandon that job to look for another in an industry making goods for America. Likewise, the manufacturer who had no existing market in the United States would not attempt to break into an admittedly more difficult market so long as India provided one more easy.

It can be said that the whole process amounts to a discrimination against the American export trade, yet the British debts to India are facts, and India has made it plain that she intends to continue to regard them as facts, as debts to be paid. That these debts are a handicap to multilateral international trade is no reason for ignoring their existence. Until they are paid off, or written off, they will continue to influence the patterns of trade as the magnet influences the pattern of the iron filings. It is useless to blame either the magnet or the filings.

It is too much to expect any democratic government to be wholly logical, consistent and clear-headed. Certainly, it would be too much, if it were omniscient, for the ordinary man and woman whose destinies it has to control and whose conveniences it has to study. The paradox of the Labour Government, even more of the Labour party in Parliament, was not that it was able to live in two worlds at once but that it was able to do so with so few outward signs of mental distress. After the skirmishings and upsets of 1946 and 1947, the party in Parliament, to all outward appearances, was stable—almost static.

Its two worlds were that of the thirties and that of the forties, prewar and postwar. Most of the party program belonged to the first; the policies of Sir Stafford Cripps belonged to the second. Some clash was unavoidable. The whole conflict between Sir Stafford's policy of freezing wages and profits (a deceptive phrase; the process was far more akin to that of bottling new wine in old bottles) and the natural inclinations of both trade unionists and employers, was a conflict between the postwar world and the world of before the war. Yet while this argument continued, there was a stream of Fabian acts of Parliament, nationalizing the utility and coal mining industries in the manner of the daring pamphlets of the twenties. It was a remarkable period, a time in which, as so often before in British history, the country carried through a series of changes which must still be called revolutionary, although the revolutionary fire had long since gone, just as champagne left for weeks in an uncorked bottle is still champagne, although not a bubble stirs in its depths.

So Mr. Attlee was able to sit serenely at the head of a party that still liked to think it had a coherent policy for the times in which it lived and worked. He built his reputation as the steady worker accumulates his pension rights, by staying a long time in the same job with the same people. His performance was a great triumph of personal confidence. After all, it is an achievement to have won five years of peaceful recovery after a violent war by pretending that the past was the present, and that the present hardly existed at all.

Similarly, Mr. Bevin remained Foreign Secretary, but that required the full exercise of a powerful personality, a personality which did, incidentally, prove to be nonsense the 1945 claim that Labour would find it easier to get along with Soviet Russia than had the Conservatives. Mr. Bevin, as a trade-union leader, had always seen Communists as disrupters of his idea of a well-run trade union; as Foreign Secretary, he had greater opportunities for treating all Communists as minority movements inside a trade union, to be hit violently on the head as soon as they spluttered a protest.

Mr. Bevin's performance as Foreign Secretary was in keeping with his background and training. His greatest success was his instantaneous reaction to the offer implied in Mr. Marshall's speech at Harvard in July 1947. There he was the skilled negotiator, seeing in an almost casual utterance (at that time Mr. Marshall could not have foreseen all that would spring from that speech) a hint of a fresh line of approach, capable of producing an agreement, so desired and so needed.

His greatest failure was over Palestine. The irrational and extreme speeches and behavior of the American Zionists raised all his rebellious pride and resentment. His inability to estimate the strength of emotion driving towards non-economic ends made it only too easy for him to accept the advice of those who told him that the Arab world was strong enough, and united enough, to prevent a Jewish state from coming into effective existence. That was the advice he wanted.

Within his own field, he remained a matchless negotiator, but he relied upon the game's being played according to the rules. Two of the most important of these rules are that the man with whom he negotiates must be assumed to be working for ends comparable with his—greater security and comfort for his own people—and that, if and when an agreement is reached, the other party to the negotiations will honor it sufficiently at least to try to make it work. In that, in many ways, Mr. Bevin was a prisoner of his own early environment, precisely as was Mr. Neville Chamberlain. He could grasp the Russians no more successfully than Mr. Chamberlain understood Hitler.

The greatest relative changes in fortunes among leaders of the party were in the rise of Sir Stafford Cripps, and the decline of Mr. Hugh Dalton, and I think the differences between the two men explain a good deal more than the changes in their political positions. The plain fact is that the roots of Sir Stafford's whole personality go much deeper than those of Mr. Dalton. Sir Stafford is religious, analytical and logical. (The last two characteristics explain his inability, in Britain, to win as great a liking as respect.) He has a sense of mission, a combination of Christian belief and indomitable will, strengthened by his battle with the nerves of his stomach, as President Roosevelt was strengthened by his battle with paralysis. His socialism is a reflection of his Christianity, a parallel to his Christian belief that material power and possessions are the enemies of man's soul. It is that which makes it possible for him to work without rancor in a partially capitalistic society. He believes that money—industrial capital, cash, personal possessions—are a natural phenomenon of this world, and therefore to be accepted as part of its structure, giving men opportunities to fulfill their duties; that and no more. In his scheme of things, neither capitalism nor socialism is more than a means through which men can achieve some far greater destiny.

Mr. Dalton was brought up in an Anglican household, and that gave him a sense of sin. In manhood, he rejected that society, that elegant and rigid world which gave everything a fixed and permanent place in a heaven-sent social order. He entered another material world, an inversion of the former one, a world whose co-ordinates were figures, and whose logic was that of Euclid. But he brought too little with him, or found too little when he arrived. His new world had only two shades, black and white. For him, accumulations of capital under individual, irresponsible control (as he would term it) were natural enough, like sin, but creations incapable of appreciating public duties, and therefore possessing few public rights. Neither Sir Stafford Cripps nor Mr. Dalton has many of the common failings of common people, but there is this vital difference between them. Sir Stafford seems to have the greater humility. He is the one who recognizes that, at the core of it all, there is something which even he does not fully understand.

So the Parliament of 1945 passed into its fourth and last year, and the fourth year in the life of any British Parliament is bound to be dull and uninspired. Inevitably, the government will have carried through, or abandoned, most of the plans with which it began, and it will be too late in the day to introduce any fresh or startling novelties. If the party leaders conjure up a new plan which they believe is likely to appeal to the electorate, they will prefer to save it for inclusion in their election program. If the party leaders are faced with a problem that is politically dubious, they will tend to keep it out of sight until the oncoming election is over. In the last session of Parliament, the two Houses passed over a hundred different statutes. Only two of them, the Iron and Steel Bill and the Parliament Bill, aroused any considerable political dispute.

Even the revelations from East Africa on the groundnut plan made remarkably little stir in Parliament (they are discussed more fully later in this book). The opposition in the Commons did not handle its case well, and the Conservative speakers never seemed to come to grips with the real points on which they could have driven home their criticisms. The truth was that by then the average M.P.

was a very tired man. He believed that his leaders had at last found some sort of policy, and he was content to leave it at that. He had come to realize that everything could not be changed by act of Parliament.

As 1949 drew to its close, the preoccupation of each member became increasingly the size of his majority on polling day. Everything said or done had to have the greatest possible appeal to the greatest possible number. His constituents were at work, and by far the greater number of them were drawing a living wage. Was this the moment to look for alternative policies or alternative idols? Still less was it the moment to shake them with new and unpleasant ideas. When he knew whether he was to return to the House, when he knew the result of the election and the size of the working majority of the new government, then it would be time to think again.

CHAPTER V

First Steps in Nationalization

The bill for the nationalization of the Bank of England, the first item on the Labour Government's list, was introduced in the first session of the new Parliament in October, 1945. The proposal was expected, and the first reaction, even of those opposed to nationalization of anything at all, was not very strong. Why interfere, they asked nevertheless, with an institution which was already working harmoniously as part of the financial and economic structure of the country?

So far as its stockholders were concerned, it was a public institution. Its dividend had remained unchanged at 12% since 1923; its semiofficial historian, Sir John Clapham, could write that "The Bank has ceased to think of raising the dividend on its stock." The stockholders, as such, had no control over its activities; they did not even elect its Court of Directors. The court itself was a self-perpetuating oligarchy, its replacements selected by the existing court from those leading figures in finance and industry who, they felt, would fit in with and continue the tradition of the institution. Although the Governor of the Bank under its charter was bound to come up for re-election every two years, the last Governor, Lord Norman, better known as Mr. Montagu Norman, had been Governor for twenty-four years in succession. What the Bank possessed above all things was continuity of experience.

In the words of *The Economist:* "When other and younger central banks ask for its rules or statutes, they are told that there is no book of the rules, that its charter would be of very little use to them and that its relations with the Exchequer have never been codified."

The defenders of the old regarded this as an almost perfect arrangement. Here was the substance of a sound working institution, with no nonsense about trying to put it into writing. They said, in effect, "You may imagine you can paint a better picture than an old master—you may be able to do so, in fact—but there is one thing you can't do, and that is to improve an existing masterpiece by altering its details."

But most of the rank and file of the Labour party had in their minds an equally simple, if very different picture of the Bank. "Here," they said, "is the central point of the whole financial power of Great Britain, the power that in some way (rarely described in detail) wrecked a Labour Government in 1931. It is essential that this body should be made answerable to us, the people."

Public opinion accepted, placidly enough, quite a number of the provisions in the bill when it appeared. The compensation paid to the stockholders was felt to be fair. They were given £400 of a newly created 3% government stock in exchange for each £100 of Bank stock they held, a sum sufficient to yield them in perpetuity an income equivalent to that which they had drawn since 1923. The terms of the appointment of directors were changed, most people agreed, for the better. The Governor and Deputy Governor were to hold office for five years, the others for four. The number of the Court of Directors was to be fixed at sixteen, a small reduction, and four were to retire every year. An entire new Court was to be appointed by the Goverment immediately after the bill was passed, but thereafter a goverment could only appoint four fresh directors each year, which meant that no government would possess the legal means of packing the Court. (In fact, the new Court, appointed after the Act came into effect, was very much the old Court, with one or two veteran trade-union leaders added.) The Government agreed that the Bank should publish an annual report, that there would be no interference with the day-to-day working of the Bank, and that the Bank's employees should remain independently recruited and not be absorbed into the Civil Service. In short, these provisions added up to no more than a formal change in ownership, and the opposition was entitled to feel that, in this case, the government was simply soothing its supporters, even if it were perhaps wasting parliamentary time in doing so.

But there was one controversial clause in the bill when it appeared: Clause 4. Clause 4 proposed to give the Treasury the power to issue general directions "in the public interest" to the Court of

Governors of the Bank, and to give the Bank itself power to direct other banks and to require those banks to give the Bank of England information regarding their own activities. Colorless those words might sound, but in the debates on the bill Mr. Dalton said that it was essential "to establish priorities in the disposal of short-term funds," and those words, to bankers, were ominous. Everybody recognized that the Treasury had inherent power, of its own volition, to manipulate medium and long-term funds, and that its own resources enabled it to do so. Indeed, in 1946 and 1947 it did precisely that, for a great deal of Mr. Dalton's cheap money campaign was waged with Treasury funds and by means of the control and influence upon the market that those funds provided. But the short-term funds in the possession of the trading banks were another matter.

Short-term funds came into being in two ways. One portion of them consisted of Treasury bills and Treasury deposit receipts; in other words, the floating debt, a government creation and an important implement in government financial policy. This was not, nor had it ever been, under Bank of England control although, no doubt, the Bank was regularly consulted over what was being done with it. The other portion of short-term credit consisted of the loans and advances made by the joint-stock banks to their individual customers, and this was by far the more important to industry. These are the credits on which industry and trade rely for every transaction that needs borrowed money. Were these to be controlled too, or even supervised, by a socialist Treasury? If so, then the Socialists really would have their foot on the neck of private enterprise.

The act of Parliament that resulted from the debates was something of a compromise. The government accepted amendments to the bill that made it clear that the Bank of England could not use its powers under Clause 4 to victimize or even seek information about any individual customer of any individual bank, and that the initiative in taking action under this clause must lie with the Bank of England and not the Treasury. Further, it was specified that no order could be given to any banker without prior discussion of the order, and the banker had the right to appeal to the Chancellor of the Exchequer himself, if he was still not satisfied. By implication, he was given the right to complain publicly, if he saw fit, and the implication was pretty clear, in fact, because the only weapon left to the Treasury to silence an "awkward" banker was the Official Secrets Act.

Yet Clause 4 of the act still starts with the sentence that the Treasury may give the Bank directions "in the public interest" with respect to the employment of money, and "public interest" is a phrase that no one has been able to define satisfactorily in an act of Parliament.

And this clause has had some meaning. In the fall of 1949, after the government had announced its plans to meet the dollar shortage crisis, Sir Stafford, as Chancellor of the Exchequer, published the text of letters he had exchanged with the Governor of the Bank of England. The purpose of the Chancellor's letters was to ask the joint-stock banks to co-operate in putting into effect the government's policy of limiting capital expenditure as a means of reducing the risk of inflation. The letters were courteous in tone and vague in their terms. At their face value, the letters from Sir Stafford were no more than a friendly jolt to the Governor's memory that the government had a policy, coupled with a faint hint that in view of the friendly relationship existing between government and Bank, it would be rather nice if the Governor could help promote this policy. The government, at the same time, released the information that there had been letters between the same parties on earlier occasions, but neither the text of those letters, nor the occasion, was made public.

On reading this correspondence, my mind went back eighteen months. In the first half of 1948, the retail radio trade in Britain began to suffer a considerable setback in sales. It had been one of the first to recover its peacetime rate of production, and there is not much doubt that the volume of sets produced had by early 1948 almost exhausted the cash available for the purchase of that kind of luxury. "However," the trade must have thought to itself, "there is always the installment market, the people who cannot pay cash but who can be lured into a small down payment."

In Britain, almost all retail credit is financed by a number of financial companies which specialize in that business. Either they themselves make the credit-selling agreement with the customer, or (where prestige is involved) the retail house signs the agreement and at once discounts it for cash with the finance company. Almost all these finance companies trade with money borrowed from banks. They usually supplement their own cash resources with bank loans of amounts perhaps two or three times as great. The finance company carries the risk and charges the customer interest on the credit-sale at rates above those charged them by the bank. If well managed, it is a profitable business.

But in 1948, the finance houses found that the banks were not prepared to lend money for the financing sales of radio sets to customers on credit. There was no law—in fact, nothing at all about it appeared in print. Only in 1949 did the Chancellor think it desirable to make public what he was doing. It was just one of those conversations, a little talk by a senior bank official with a senior official of the finance company, and the word went round the whole trade. Credit-buying of radio sets was out; bicycles, agricultural machinery, all sorts of things, "yes"; radio sets, "no". Possibly, some bankers added something vague about inflation, about the desirability of encouraging people, in general, to save money. Possibly some said nothing at all. In the close-knit financial circles of Britain, there are many occasions when it would be a little gauche to offer an explanation, or to ask for one.

I think it extremely probable that somewhere in the files of the Bank of England there is another letter from the Chancellor of the Exchequer to the Bank's Governor referring, possibly by implication, to Clause 4, and going on to talk about the need to limit the uses of short-term credit in credit-buying. But of course I don't know. Perhaps the nationalization of the Bank of England was only a matter of form. But I doubt it.

It would, of course, be lamentable if the policy of the Treasury and the policy of the Bank of England should fall out of step. It would be equally lamentable if the joint-stock banks of the country ignored a government's efforts to limit inflation and granted loan facilities to all and sundry, to spend as they liked. It may equally be arguable that in 1948 it was not necessary for large numbers of people to buy radios on credit. But the most unfortunate thing of all would be to imagine that Clause 4 of the Bank of England Nationalization Act did not make it perfectly plain that, in the last resort, the whip is firmly in the hands of the government of the day.

The second item in the Government's nationalization list was the coal mining industry, but that demands a chapter to itself. The third was inland transport, the railways, the canals, the docks and harbors, and the road transportation services for passengers and goods where, in magnitude and importance, the railways were easily supreme. The remaining industries nationalized can be grouped together, not because of similarity in their activities but because of the similarity of their political circumstances.

Electricity in Britain was nationalized by the Electricity Act, 1947, under which the industry was taken over on April 1, 1948, and the gas industry by the Gas Act, 1948, effective from May 1, 1949. Both had certain features in common. All existing undertakings in each industry were taken over by especially created public corporations— the British Electric Authority and the National Gas Council—and the former private owners of securities were given government securities based on the Stock Exchange values of their holdings, where quoted, or on a valuation, where unquoted. Holders of gas stocks in areas where the earning power of the undertakings had been adversely affected by war conditions were given an especially increased compensation on that account.

The electricity industry in Britain can be divided into three parts: The producing section, the wholesale distributing section and the retail distributing section. The producing section, the major power stations, were in part owned by public trading companies and in part by public authorities, such as municipalities. There are 142 principal generating stations and about the same number of secondary stations. All fed their supplies into a common "grid," or high voltage transmission system, covering the whole of Britain except North Scotland. (North Scotland has its own hydro-electric system.) The price at which each station sold its product was limited by statute, and so the profits of each had a ceiling. Bulk distribution over the grid was undertaken by the Central Electricity Board, a nonprofit body, which charged a price for the electricity it sold based on cost, plus the interest and amortization of its capital outlay. The retail distribution undertakings were variously owned.

They totalled 541 individual concerns, and about 60% were publicly owned, very many by local authorities. The remainder were owned by private companies, in business for a profit. All were regulated by statutory order, made under acts of Parliament stretching back fifty years or more, which limited the territory in which they could operate and controlled their maximum prices; but within that range they could and did make good profits. All of them were subject to the risk that under existing acts of Parliament their business might end in some 40 or 50 years.

Similarly in the gas industry, while most producing concerns were also distributors, the end price of the product was controlled. Further, a gas company could only increase its dividend provided it simultaneously cut its price to the consumer, a condition not easy to fulfill. For the most part, gas companies paid a fixed and steady dividend.

Incidentally, one admirable arrangement disappeared with the end of private ownership in the gas industry; one of the most comprehensive profit-sharing plans in operation in Britain. In 1937, a typical prewar year, one half of the capital employed in the industry was affected by some such plan. Fifty-nine undertakings, with a capital of £113,000,000, paid out just under £400,000 in bonuses to 52,779 employees, and the average bonus equaled 5.83% of the average year's wage. The plan in one company now submerged, the South Metropolitan Gas Company, provided that after paying a 5% dividend on the capital of the company, 75% of the remaining profits were to be applied toward the reduction of prices to the consumer, 12½% went to the shareholders' addition to their dividend, and the remaining 12½% was to be divided among the employees of the company, 8,802 in number. The bonus was not all paid in cash. One half was converted into an issue of stock. Administratively, perhaps, it would have been difficult for the new authority to have carried on the plan; when the gas industry was nationalized, administrative convenience won the day.

Two other nationalization projects carried through by the Labour Government must be mentioned: the completion of government control over all forms of external communications, summed up in the final absorption of the main operating company, Cables and

Wireless, Ltd.; and over the regular civil airlines (the independent charter companies were not included), now organized in British Overseas Airways and British European Airways. These created very little stir. Both steps could be said to have been a continuation of a prewar policy and little more than a formalization of a state of affairs that for obvious reasons had existed during the war.

No one could honestly employ the word "competitive" about the activities of this group of undertakings. All of them performed a "service" but the companies in each industry did not compete with one another; it would have been blatantly uneconomic to do so, just as a single house does not need two competing water suppliers. Talk of killing competition in these industries only fogs the issue; competition had long since died, even if it had once existed.

The real problem of these industries is that of their organization. Are they to become a series of bureaucratic institutions, with every possible trace of initiative wrung out of them? Or are they to become enterprising public servants, searching out ways in which to improve and cheapen the services they offer?

These questions remain unanswered. It would also be encouraging but false to say that in these five years the Labour Government has seriously asked it, at least in public.

Nationalization of inland transport is a live issue still, in part because it is not complete and in part because there is no pretense that nationalization has, in itself, solved the problem. The supply of electricity or gas is a technical problem of efficiency. The product sold is uniform, and no one can say that nationalized electricity is inferior in quality to that produced by privately owned generators. Transportation is a different problem. If the customer orders a five-ton truck for his deliveries he will not be satisfied if you send him a bicycle or a canal barge to do the job.

In 1939, there were five major railway companies in Britain. One, the London Passenger Transport Board, was a special statutory body set up in 1933 to own and operate all forms of passenger transport in the London area. The other four were the London Midland Scottish Railway, the Southern Railway, the London North Eastern Railway and the Great Western Railway. Each of the four was an amalgamation of a greater number of smaller railway undertakings (brought about in 1922) and each had a different financial structure and a different financial result. Here are the major figures:

Railway	Debenture Capital	Share Capital 1945	Amount required for Deb. interest	Available for Dividend on Share Capital	
				1937	1945
L.M.S.....	£109,141,619	£304,637,238	£4,439,170	£9,917,106	£11,779,571
L.N.E.R...	119,105,839	257,427,804	4,178,460	6,832,884	5,885,168
S.R......	55,187,605	114,102,398	2,218,263	4,608,957	4,746,134
G.W.R. ...	39,997,897	109,728,016	1,648,199	5,236,673	5,293,730

These show how uneven were the earnings available for dividend among the four companies. For example, the G.W.R. could earn 5% on its share capital, while the L.N.E.R. can earn only about 2%. Nor was that the only trouble. A great deal of the capital of the companies was in prior charges with fixed rates of interest so that, in the case of the L.N.E.R., while the total capital earned income at the rate of 2%, when all prior claims to fixed dividends had been met, nothing was left to pay a dividend on the ordinary capital— £78,000,000 out of the total of £257,000,000.

During the war, the companies operated under a special agreement with the government, whereby they were guaranteed a minimum yearly sum for their net operating receipts and surrendered the surplus above a certain amount. The last normal year was 1938, when their net operating receipts were:

L.M.S............	£10,803,000	L.N.E.R...........	£6,026,000
G.W.R..........	£4,630,000	S.R..............	£5,041,000

The position vis-à-vis railway and road transport was complicated by the fact that in 1929 the railways were given power to invest money in existing road passenger transport undertakings and, as a result, they acquired (jointly with three large outside financial groups) ownership and control of all the major passenger transport undertakings in Britain. The railways also bought all the stock of three large road transport concerns carrying freight only: Carter Paterson & Co., Pickfords, and Hays Wharf Cartage Co. In 1942, they had also, as a group, bought the ownership of Thomas Cook & Son, the travel agency.

Canals and internal waterways were a comparatively simple problem. There were eighteen separate undertakings, of which the major one was the Grand Union Canal, connecting London and the Midlands. All operated under statute, and only one had any special function besides that of maintaining its canal system in good condition.

So much for the railways and waterway concerns. Because of their size and number, nationalization was not, from a legal standpoint, a complicated matter. It was otherwise with road transport.

In Britain, the division between passenger and goods transport by road was virtually complete. A few passenger transport undertakings had small parcel-delivery services. A few commercial vehicles were used for transporting passengers. (Contractors were allowed to use their own transport to take their own employees to and from their place of work.) Otherwise, even on the financial side, there was little connection between the two. In the twenties, which was a period of rapid growth in road transport of all kinds, some of the early undertakings combined the transportation of both passengers and goods, but the division between the two branches was formalized by the two acts of Parliament, the Road Traffic Act of 1930, and the Road and Rail Traffic Act of 1933.

The Road Traffic Act of 1930 established a system of control over all passenger road services. Until then, anyone with sufficient capital to buy a vehicle could start a passenger service. After the passage of that act, any person who wanted to enter the business was compelled to obtain a license from a traffic commissioner before he could put a vehicle on the road. Britain was divided into a number of traffic zones and no vehicle could carry more than seven paid passengers without a license from the traffic commissioners in the zones in which it was to run. The traffic commissioners were charged with the duty of eliminating redundant or unnecessary services, the establishing of routes to be covered, the fares to be charged and the timetables of each route. A license was good for three years, but before any license was granted, either on first application or renewal, the applicant must have shown that the services he wished authorized were necessary to the public interest and that other services already licensed—including railway facilities—were not adequate for the existing public need.

The Act of 1933 extended this licensing system to truck transport. The same system of traffic zones, commissioners and licenses were utilized and (with one exception) the same standards of justification by public need applied, but there were some major variations.

There were three types of licenses. The first was the "A" license, permitting an operator to carry for compensation only the goods of others, but imposing no condition on the kind of freight to be carried or the distance it was to be hauled. The second was the "B" license, entitling the holder to carry either his own goods or the goods of others, but, in the case of the latter, imposing strict limitations on the kind of freight to be carried or the distance traveled, or both. The third was the "C" license, allowing the holder to carry only his own goods but without restriction on their nature or the distance of the haul. "C" licenses were free from proof of public need. No machinery was set up to fix rates or routes of trucks. The act and later amendments to it established the hours a driver might be continuously employed, the wages paid the drivers and standards of maintenance for the vehicles operated.

This system remained in force until the beginning of the war, at which time the government took over some 400 main road operators and paid them a fixed rental, based on profits of earlier years, very much as they took over the operation of the railways. Smaller concerns continued to operate, under supervision, but were given defence permits instead of licenses, which eliminated, to a large extent, the distinction between B and C licenses and restricted the operators to work within 60 miles or less of their base. That form of wartime control ended in August, 1946. On the passenger side, there was no such over-all control. Passenger carriers remained under the supervision of the existing traffic commissioners, who exercised their restrictions mainly by limitations on fuel.

The Acts of 1930 and 1933 were necessitated by the increasing disorganization resulting from cut-throat competition between road and rail transport. There was a bias towards the preservation of the economic life of the railways. In effect the acts created a closed association between road and rail haulage. It was very difficult for a newcomer to enter the road business and, while competition between existing road operators and railways was not eliminated, it was no longer necessary for each to cut rates to attract business. Charges to the public were in effect stabilized and decent working conditions for the employees made more likely.

On the financial side, the structures of the two groups were very different. In the passenger lines there was virtually a monopoly combine. In the freight business, there were a number of separate undertakings, operating in well-defined areas and routes, but capable of fierce competition if any concern should show signs of losing its grip.

To take the passenger services first. Britain was covered by a network of passenger bus and coach routes. In London, the London Passenger Transport Board had a complete monopoly. In each zone outside London there was almost invariably one concern which carried 80% to 90% of all the traffic. That was the concern which provided the framework of regular highway passenger service for the whole area, and it might own as many as 500 vehicles. In addition, there were a few small operators, with generally not more than five vehicles each, operating shorter and more special services. In the larger towns, particularly in the north, the major concern was the municipalities themselves. Their vehicles had replaced the former trolley lines, now generally abandoned, and had considerably extended the mileage covered. Elsewhere, with two exceptions, the major interest was a member of one of three combines. Each of these combines consisted of one or more of the railways together with the British Electric Traction Company, Ltd. or Thomas Tilling, Ltd. or one of their subsidiaries or the Scottish Motor Traction Company. In consequence, these companies had become very prosperous.

In the freight business the position was more complex. Here are the figures for January, 1946:

	No. of license holders	No. of licensed vehicles
A licenses........................	19,950	86,750
B licenses........................	27,800	54,000
C licenses........................	149,200	306,400
	196,950	447,150

By December, 1947, just before the Transport Act took effect, the total of licensed vehicles was some 650,000. The majority of long-distance highway freight traffic (hauls over 40 miles) was in the hands of the larger concerns which might own between 50 and 100 vehicles each. The small man, with two or three trucks, would not undertake long runs as he lacked the organization necessary to obtain return loads and so make the journey a profitable one.

One of the complexities was the great variation in capital employed by each operator. A small man with one vehicle might keep it under a tarpaulin in the yard of his house, use his home as an office, and his wife as a bookkeeper and secretary. His tangible capital would be his vehicle, worth anything from £500 to £1,500, and nothing else. But some basis for a more commercial valuation could be found in the balance sheet of Transport Services, Ltd., a public company formed to amalgamate some two dozen operators in different parts of the country. Land and buildings accounted for £128,019, motor vehicles for £192,066, plant and equipment for £19,811 and goodwill, £265,974. Translating that into the terms of the one-vehicle business, and evaluating the vehicle at £1,000, the value of its necessary garage and office accommodation would be £600, the value of essential plant and tools £100, but its owner might hope to claim up to £1,400 for goodwill.

That was the technical situation facing any attempt at the nationalization of transport. The actual plan materialized in the Transport Act of 1947. Its brief outline is this: Railways, road passenger transport, long-distance road-haulage services (those with scheduled runs of over 40 miles), hotels, docks and canals were to be transferred to a British Transport Commission. Transport undertakings which operated on routes of under 25-mile radius were to be left to private ownership, but under the public control of the traffic commissioners, as before. Private concerns, using vehicles under C licenses, were still entitled to own and use their trucks for carrying their own goods where they pleased, without any restriction at all. Certain specialized forms of road transport, mainly transport requiring special vehicles or special skill (for example, the transportation of livestock or the removal of furniture) were also exempted from acquisition.

The British Transport Commission operates through various

executives, one each for the railways, the docks and inland water-ways, road transport, London transport (virtually the old London Passenger Transport Board) and for hotels (the railway companies had maintained some 64 hotels scattered all over Britain).

The process of taking over was staggered. The railways and all their assets (including hotels) passed directly under public ownership on the day the act came into operation, January 1, 1948. So did the canal companies. The majority of the stocks in the nationalized undertakings were quoted on the Stock Exchange and valued by reference to that quotation. The total capital of transport stock issued to the former holders of shares in railway and canal companies was £1,065,000,000. The railway executive also took over all railway cars.

The Road Transport Executive also came into existence on January 1, 1948, but it has been proceeding in a more cautious manner. Under the act, no date was set for automatically assuming control of property. It was left for the commission to take the first step in the acquisition of any freight transport undertaking. This it did by giving formal notice that it claimed the undertaking to be one to which the act applied. If the owners disputed that claim, the argument was to be settled by a specially constituted independent tribunal. The act also empowered the commission to acquire concerns by agreement, and during 1948 the commission had taken over 248 separate freight transport concerns by agreement, and none by use of the procedure laid down by the act. As a result, at the end of 1948 it owned 8,208 motor vehicles, 1717 trailers and 1567 horse–drawn vehicles.

The transfer of bus and coach lines appeared to be an even longer drawn-out process. The act did not give the executive concerned the power to acquire individual concerns by compulsion. It provided first that the executive must prepare a separate plan for simultaneously taking over all concerns operating in one zone. No such plan could come into actual operation without a specific order from the Minister of Transport. In the interim, however, there was nothing to prevent the commission from taking over any individual business by a negotiated agreement. For example, by the end of 1948 they succeeded in reaching such an agreement with Thomas Tilling, Ltd., whose transport interests changed hands at the price of £22,000,000.

The docks figure in the last part of the act. In Britain, each port has developed differently, and each has its own dock and harbor authority. Usually, these are separate bodies set up by individual acts of Parliament, but the plans under which most function have certain common features. Generally, the controlling body is nominated partly by local authorities and partly elected by users of the harbor. It has power to borrow money for harbor works and improvements, and equally the power to levy charges or tolls on those using the facilities provided. As a rule, the governing body of the authority is made up of local men. The charges levied are usually fixed so that the annual income will meet the annual expenditure on operating and maintaining the harbor, and pay the interest and amortization on the capital outstanding. Some systems of docks, notably those at Southampton and Cardiff, were owned by railway companies. Those were automatically transferred to the Transport Commission.

For the rest, the act goes no further than to authorize the Minister of Transport, at some time in the future and at his own discretion, to work out schemes for co-ordinating dock authorities or for setting up local authorities where none exist. No plans under this part of the act have yet been made, but two dock systems formerly owned and operated by railway companies, those at Cardiff and King's Lynn, have been transferred to the Docks Executive.

While the Transport Bill was being debated, the principal outcry was over the measure of compensation payable to the holders of railway and canal stocks. In the case of the Bank of England and the coal mines, the government had accepted the principle that the compensation should be related to the "net maintainable revenue." In the case of railways and canals, it fixed the compensation by reference to the Stock Exchange quotations for the various securities taken over from their individual holders. Protest from the highway freight industry was equally vociferous, but there the protest was at the loss of so many privately owned businesses. The compensation terms aroused less debate. The Transport Commission was taking over physical assets and, with respect to price at least, the dispossessed were treated on a basis that made sense; in some cases it was fairly generous.

On the general principle of nationalization, few could reasonably claim that in transferring the railways to a Transport Commission, a great edifice of private enterprise had been brought low. The railways were not in competition with one another, and for years they had been desperately anxious to avoid the competition of the road services. These were good technical arguments for unification of management, techniques, equipment and experience and no Labour Government could have been expected to unify the railways into one monopoly without bringing that monopoly under public control. Further, the government was bound to use the chance so presented to attempt to solve once and for all the old problem of road and rail co-ordination.

One of the three companies with the largest interest in road transport was Thomas Tilling, Ltd. At its annual general meeting early in 1947, its chairman, the late Sir Frederick Heaton, said, ". . . in order to get the utmost use out of the railways of this country during the war and to work them with the greatest efficiency, they had to be operated as nearly as may as a unified system. The advantages derived from this measure of unification were manifest and it was my view that we could not afford to sacrifice them in the difficult days that would follow the end of the war." He then went on to refer to an abortive plan put forward, before the threat of nationalization grew so close, for the co-ordination of all long-distance traffic, including canal and road transportation. "Co-ordination . . . would have resulted in the elimination of the various restrictions which, against the public interest, now exist, including the uneconomic protection given to many operators. . . ." This plan was submitted to the various bodies representing both the industry and its users. "There was," he went on, "a very definite desire to be left alone on the part of most of those who were to be directly affected; they either would not, or could not, see the inevitable trend of events. For my part, I was satisfied that unless some such scheme were to be adopted, the alternative would prove to be complete nationalization. . . . The strength of the Labour party's position is in this need for unification."

It is certainly likely that the individual owner of railway stocks will in the future be better off than he would have been if the four main-line companes had been left to face the unrestricted road competition likely by 1948 or 1949. In 1937, the amount available for dividend among the stockholders of the four companies was some £26,500,000. The Transport Commission's accounts for the year 1948 showed that the net traffic receipts of the railways were no more than £26,000,000, from which was deducted some £5,750,000 of general charges. The comparison is not a true one, but it illustrates the trend: falling railway receipts.

The Transport Act of 1947 did not destroy all competition between public and private enterprise. It left in private ownership the vehicles with B licenses, although, as of February 1, 1950, it restricted them to no more than twenty-five miles from their operating bases. It also left in private control the vehicles with C licenses, those used by their owners to carry their own goods. And the number of vehicles on C licenses—on the issue of which there is no restriction—has mounted fast. The Report for 1948 of the Traffic Commission gave these totals:

June 1938	365,025
Jan. 1946	306,443
Dec. 1946	383,738
Dec. 1947	487,151
Dec. 1948	590,561

Viewed dispassionately, it may be foolish for a manufacturer to insist on buying and operating—perhaps only part-time—his own transportation when there are public service carriers available to meet all his reasonable needs. It may be, nationally speaking, uneconomic to allow so many people to tie up so much capital in road equipment which is not fully used. Some Labour party experts in transport have said this freedom must also be "curtailed," that is, brought to an end. The Transport Commission itself in its 1948 Report said more cautiously, "it is plain that the increased use made of "C" licensed vehicles is a circumstance which vitally affects the policy of the Commission in planning, in fixing charges and in the eventual integration of their services." But the individual owner has clearly said in reply that he is not going to surrender the last card in his hand.

The major battle over the future organization of freight transportation in Britain is centered in the C license.

CHAPTER VI

The Coal Mining Industry

Why were the coal mines in Britain nationalized?

The simple answer is that the coal mining industry had reached a state of development in which reorganization and unification were essential if it was to survive, and that it was politically impossible for this to be done while the industry itself remained in private ownership. A minority of the population, the Labour party voters, may have desired nationalization on ideological grounds, but technical reasons made the essential difference. They induced many of those opposed to nationalization to accept the fact of unification because they considered that to be a necessity in the national interest. I doubt very much if the majority in the country would now like to see the industry revert to private ownership, granted that very many, including some who have always been supporters of nationalization, would like to see the existing administrative machine remodeled.

What are the technical reasons that rendered private ownership of each pit an impossible barrier to efficiency? In one mining area it is water. The following was written in 1934, concerning the South Wales coalfield: "In the past . . . water has not created sufficient widespread difficulties to make it a question of general concern to the majority of colliery companies in the area. . . . The position is now assuming a different aspect . . .

"It only requires that the collieries on the rise side of the coalfield shall stop their pumping operations for those who are now in the happy position that the water does not trouble them to find the burden transferred to their shoulders. . . . The Tredegar Company are in 1934 pumping large quantities of water . . . coming from an area in which another colliery company worked the coal."

By 1943, the annual quantity of water which had to be pumped out of the mines in South Wales was 34,208,000,000 imperial gallons, and the cost of doing so added 8d. to the price of each ton of coal. Water was one very good reason why the mining engineer, for instance, hoped to see the mines of the area worked as one. There were hosts of others.

The history of the industry between wars, in barest outline, is as follows: 1914-18; government control, reduced man power and greater demand, rising wages and rising prices. In 1919-20; export boom, due to the aftermath of the war and the French occupation of the Ruhr. Export price of coal rises to 7 a ton, leaving the continental importer of British coal keenly anxious to find an alternative supply as soon as possible. In 1921; relapse and first general coalminers' strike. In 1921-28; general period of confusion, particularly in export markets. Demand falls by 10% and prices by 23%. Increasing unemployment in all mining areas accompanied by increasing cuts in wages. General strike of 1926, which about finishes any hold Britain had on export markets, and encourages the continental countries to overhaul their whole mining system. In Britain, it made a final break between the coal owners and the miners. Neither trusted the other again.

Between 1924 and 1928, the average price of coal fell from 19s. 9d. per ton at the mine to 13s. 3d., which converted a profit of 1s. 2d. per ton into a loss of 11d. per ton. The remaining 4s. 5d. in the reduced price received was borne by wage cuts and a reduction in the amount available for development, even for replacements and renewals.

From 1928 to 1934, prices remained steady, although sales contracted by an additional 20%. From 1934 on, there was a small but steady increase in prices and profits, the latter rising from 6d. per ton in 1934 to 1s. 7d. per ton in 1939.

The decisive years were between 1926 and 1929. During those years the industries on the Continent reorganized their entire operation, and found the finances with which to do it. In Britain, it was during those years that the mining industry became least able to reorganize itself from within, and least attractive to any introduction of capital assistance from without. The European industry, in general, was helped by government-imposed price regulation plans which subsidized and extended the export of their coal. The British industry was hindered by taxation allowances which gave insufficent inducement to operating concerns to invest in new installations.

In 1945, there was published what came to be known as the Reid Committee's Report on Coal Mining. The committee consisted of the chairman, Sir Charles Reid, a mining engineer and formerly general manager of a Scottish colliery company, and six other mining experts, all managing directors or general managers of substantial colliery companies. They had been appointed in 1944 to "examine the present technique of coal production," and to advise what technical changes were necessary to bring the industry to a state of full technical efficiency. It is worth noting that these terms of reference use the word "technical" on three occasions. The government did not want a political solution from a committee inquiring into coal.

That report became the bible of the technical men in the industry and of the National Coal Board as well. Its conclusions were unanimous; they spared no feelings and they shied at no hedges. As a whole, the report was severely technical, but, inevitably, it did not avoid points which had been or were likely to become occasions for political argument. Summarized, the committee's conclusions on why the British industry was technically so inefficient are these:

1. The natural conditions in which coal in Britain is found are comparable to those of the Ruhr Valley in Germany and coal beds in Holland. However, output per man-shift obtaining in Britain is lower than in European countries due to financial advantages of those countries over Britain: adequate resources of capital were available and taxation on mining undertakings was more favorable. Further, the long-standing uncertainty surrounding future ownership of the industry in Britain was not conducive to any considerable capital expenditure.

2. In Britain, coal as a mineral was the possession of the owner of the land in which it existed. In the rest of Europe, the mineral was owned by the state. British mine owners usually leased small areas of land around a single pit, and often the result was an unduly small or awkwardly shaped lease. Elsewhere, both the concession and the mine were established on a much larger scale. Under the British system, there was often pressure on the mine operator, as leaseholder, to develop seams producing imme-

diate results, a short-term policy that piled up difficulties for the future.

3. Grouping of mines under the same ownership facilitates the closing down or merging of uneconomic mines, and a more concentrated use of common hoisting and surface operations. In Britain, ownership was widely dispersed and, although the Coal Production Act of 1930 had increased the machinery for carrying through amalgamations, recourse to it was optional and few made use of it.

4. In European mines the basic skeleton layout was straight passageways through solid strata, from which coal seams could be reached directly and efficiently. In Britain, the underground layout, in the main, followed the inclinations of the coal seams. The passageways were undulating and circuitous, and the task of reconstruction was thereby infinitely more difficult and costly. The report suggested that, as the seams in European fields were steeper than those available to the first mining engineers in Britain, haulage considerations, from the outset, demanded a level passageway. In Britain, at the start, the easier beds could be worked along the seam. The British failed to change their technique to meet the changing circumstances of their own mines.

The final point in the report deserves quotation:

The employers, as a body, have been prepared neither to accept the principal of survival of the fittest nor fully to abandon their traditional individualism. In relation to their own undertakings the short view has too often prevailed.

In the end, it is the employer who must lead his men. If he inspires neither appreciation of his technical efficiency nor respect for his capacity to manage his business, he leaves himself defenseless to attacks on his basic right to remain in charge of his industry.

The demand for nationalization, as part of the Labour party's electoral program in 1945, and as part of its policy as a Government from 1945 onward—and the reactions of the Opposition to that demand—must be judged in the light of the Reid Committee's report.

The situation facing Britain at the end of the war precluded any conventional solution of the coal mining industry's troubles.

So far as the mine owner is concerned, capitalist economics are a relatively straightforward affair. As owner, you spend money on buying mining leases and equipment, and on hiring labor, at a time when you think that the price you will get from the coal will more than cover your outlay. If you are wrong, if conditions begin to prove you are wrong, your first action is to try to cut costs. If that does not succeed in the end, after a long or short period of running at a loss (depending on your capital resources and other business interests) you write the venture off and close down the mine. The mine worker is part of the cost of running the job. So is new equipment of any kind. What you pay for them has to be balanced, in the long run, by the profit that can be made out of them.

That attitude had its obverse. The miner may argue about nationalization—but employment is a business of to-day. He will also argue, with quite a different end in view, about present wages and conditions of work, about every one of the details that go to determine what is left in the wage packet at the end of each week. He will argue about every action, or lack of action on the part of the management about such things as safety precautions, pithead baths, canteens and fatigue-eliminating machinery. He too has an ultimate resort. He can stop work, or he can leave mining altogether for another job. (The latter is usually the more difficult, for the mining village is commonly small and isolated, and other jobs which don't involve a violent plunge into the depths of the unknown world, are few.)

The trade-union leader began as no more than the paid mouthpiece and organizer of a small body of men. However—because no one can rest content with a purely passive role—he grew to provide these men with a bigger organization and an extended policy. He came to be the one who decided which concessions to demand and which to reject. In doing so, he could not ignore what took place on the employer's side of the fence. Yet fundamentally, he remained on the employees' side. It was essential for him to know how much money came into the industry by way of earnings, and in the end his main task was to divert as much of that as possible into the wage packets, and to lose no sleep over how much went into dividends.

The six years of war made very many serious changes in these relationships. It cut off export markets for coal. It was difficult to get new or even replacement equipment. It provided many of the younger men in the industry with new jobs and new ideas. At the end of it all, it produced one answer to the miner's hope—a Labour

Government pledged to nationalize the mines. It also produced an economic situation in which the country as a whole was dominated by how much coal, both for export and home consumption, was raised to the surface. In capitalist phraseology, it was a seller's market. In political language, a ton of exportable coal was a bargaining counter as different from the raw material of which it consisted as a cruiser was from the tons of steel from which it was made.

These men were compelled to face this changed situation, and to adjust themselves to it if they could. The history of the five post-war years is a record of that adjustment.

All coalfields have their individual characteristics. There is no such thing as a typical coalfield. So let us talk about South Wales, remembering that some of their problems are unique, some are common to all coalfields and some have been escaped by South Wales.

The main South Wales coalfield is a basin 90 miles long, with an average width of fifteen miles. It is saucer-shaped. To the north, the coal veins rise gradually toward the northern outcrop. To the south, the veins turn sharply upward, becoming in places almost vertical. The whole area is crossed by numerous flaws, varying in size from a few yards to almost half a mile. The surface strata are of sandstone; beneath are the Lower Coal Series. In the Rhondda Valley there are sixteen main seams of coal actually being worked, and they extend to a depth of 2,000 feet.

To the east, the coal is bituminous. Traveling to the northwest, the distance increases between the strata in which the coal is found. The coal becomes harder, with a high carbon and a low oxygen content. To the east lies the gas coal, in the center the steam coal, to the northwest the anthracite. And the anthracite is the most difficult to work. Its seams are folded and broken and the dust is bad. In 1903, there were nine collieries at work there, in 1945 only two.

The output of coal, and persons employed in the South Wales coalfield, is shown in this table:

Year	Output of Saleable Coal (tons) Gt. Britain	South Wales	Output of S. Wales as percentage of Gt. Britain	No. of persons employed in S. Wales	Output of coal per person per annum in S. Wales (tons)
1901	219,046,945	39,209,260	17.90	150,394	260.7
1907	267,830,962	49,978,211	18.66	190,603	262.2
1913	287,430,473	56,830,317	19.77	244,800	243.1
1916	256,375,366	52,080,765	20.31	214,100	243.2
1919	229,779,517	47,522,306	20.68	257,163	184.8
1922	249,606,864	50,325,094	20.16	243,015	207.1
1925	243,176,231	44,629,522	18.35	218,053	204.7
1928	237,471,931	43,311,966	18.24	168,465	257.1
1931	219,458,951	37,084,852	16.90	158,271	234.3
1934	220,726,298	35,173,317	15.94	139,935	251.39
1937	240,409,436	37,773,013	15.71	136,088	277.6
1940	224,308,699	32,351,990	14.42	130,394	248.1
1943	194,500,359*	25,115,673	12.91	116,167	216.2
1944	184,114,525*	22,395,200	12.16	112,337	199.34

* Excluding output from government open-cast workings.

Set those figures against these:

INCREASES IN OUTPUT PER MANSHIFT

Country	Basic yr.	O.M.S. in Basic Year (cwt)	O.M.S. in 1936	Percentage increase (%)
Holland..............	1925	16.48	35.94	118
The Ruhr............	1925	18.62	33.66	81
Poland..............	1927	23.44	36.20	54
Britain..............	1927	20.62	23.54	14

The South Wales coalfield suffers from the fact that serious large-scale development started there a century ago. Other coalfields all over the world have benefitted from the mistakes that were made in developing it. But it is always more costly to remedy a mistake than to avoid it.

The Reid Report contains this description of the men who developed the industry—in all of Britain. "The employers and the mining engineers . . . were hard-working, adventurous and self-reliant men. They set out to get cheap coal and the country reaped the fruit of their efforts. If they were hard taskmasters, they worked hard themselves, and they depended on the work of men's hands rather than on machinery. They believed in competition and were prepared to meet it. Their capital resources were often limited and, as soon as a mine was sunk, the cry was for output. Whatever planning was done was, for the most part, done on a short-term basis. In their work they met many difficulties, and they were not always successful in their ventures . . . Though they left the mining engineers with a legacy of mines not easy to reconstruct to fit the requirements of today, these men were the product of the days in which they lived, and the circumstances of the time dictated their actions."

But they left a legacy of more than mines that are difficult to reconstruct. They left men like Trefor Williams.

Trefor has lived in the same mining village in the Rhondda Valley all his life. His father was killed underground by the fall of a roof when Trefor was 12. His mother blamed the mine owners for it, because there was some argument about the timbering. So did Trefor, in consequence, but he still went into the same pit.

He is now 37. He is able, determined and ruthless. He has one loyalty, to the men in the pit. He has one antagonist, the pit management. He is now secretary of the Mineworkers Union Lodge for that pit, and is not interested in union promotion beyond that level. But he is interested in everything that affects the men in that pit, from the price of food in the canteen, to the number of beds in the maternity ward at the local hospital which his union has supported from its funds. He knows intimately every section of every agreement affecting every classification of job in and around the pit, whether the agreement is written or based on the customs of the area.

He also sings in the village choir, and is studying architecture so as to be able to help his elder son, who thinks he would like to become an architect.

Trefor Williams cannot change himself over night, any more than can a mine be changed. If he wins an argument which results in an increase in the money any man takes home on Friday, he is doing no more than his duty. If he allows any new machine into the pit, without being sure that no man loses pay in consequence, again he is doing no more than his duty as he sees it. To him, a man from the Polish Resettlement Corps is not primarily a refugee from Germany or

Russia. He is a potential blackleg, a stranger. He comes from the outside world and so may be without the fundamental loyalty to his mates possessed by the rest of the men in the village.

Trefor Williams has a respect for learning and music. He reads about the American elections, the plan for growing groundnuts in East Africa. He likes to hear people talk about them, just as he likes to hear the Bach Choir on his radio. But all these things belong to another world. So do Mr. Attlee and Sir Stafford Cripps, and government white papers on personal incomes. What they say and do are not directly connected with tomorrow's argument over the the rates of pay for the man on the new conveyor on Number 5 face.

The disposal of coal, the quantity of coal to be disposed of, its price and destination, its effect on the steel industry, or on European recovery—all these are management problems. His job is to see about the pay of the men who are finished with that coal when the freight cars move out of the colliery yard.

"National Coal Board," he says, and spits. "The old faces at the top of a new suit of clothes. I am not taken in so easily as that, man."

In 1930, the second Labour Government passed a Coal Production Act, a rather pathetic compromise between what a Labour Government wanted to do and what the Liberals (on whom their majority in the House of Commons depended) and the House of Lords would allow them to do. The principal consequences of that act were to demonstrate beyond doubt the failure of the two methods it proposed for improving the industry. Part I of the act laid down certain minimum home prices for coal; yet the selling price of coal still fell. Part II dealt with technical improvement of the mines themselves, by improving the conditions for the voluntary amalgamation of colliery companies with adjoining interests in the same coalfield; yet almost all the colliery companies with adjoining interests refused to amalgamate voluntarily.

In 1938, the mineral coal itself was nationalized, by the Coal Act of that year. That is to say, the ownership of the unworked portion of each seam, known or unknown, both in a mine already open or elsewhere, became vested in a public body known as the Coal Commission. The Coal Commission took this property, subject to all existing leases and agreements, and issued to the former owners of the mineral its own stock in amounts based on a valuation of their individual rights. On December 31, 1946, the total amount of such stock in issue was £78,457,089, allotted to the former owners of coal. It carried interest at 2.5% and the terms of its issue required in addition that an annual payment of £2,766,245 should be set aside to provide for its final redemption by 1996. The Coal Commission continued to draw the royalties payable by the colliery companies under their leases and agreements with the former owners. The Commission was in a position to begin to plan each coalfield as a unit, but only as the existing mining leases and agreements expired. Obviously, progress on that basis was going to be pretty slow. The mining industry remained unchanged. The royalties it paid were a first claim on its earnings.

In 1942, the Coalition Government was compelled by wartime needs to devise some plan capable of removing financial difficulties likely to hold up coal production, which did not allow prices of coal to get out of control. Production costs were rising and, even by this time, the rise in costs was sufficient to put some pits out of production, unless their selling prices were increased. In outline, the plan finally adopted, and known as the Coal Charges Account, was this: Each colliery company paid into a central account a flat amount for each ton of coal it produced. From the funds so created, augmented by a government subsidy, each colliery could draw varying sums to offset additional wage and production costs. The Coal Charges Account was used to make certain that no colliery closed down simply because it was no longer profitable for it to continue operation. The money necessary to do this was found, in part, by the more prosperous concerns in the low-cost districts, in part by government subsidy. The account was maintained until the end of 1946, and over the whole period of its operation the government subsidy had totaled £27,500,000. The plan and the subsidy came to an end on December 31, 1946.

That was the immediate background to the general election of 1945. The Labour party wanted nationalization of the industry, and the Reid Committee's report was a strong electioneering argument in their favor. Here was the first essential industry of the country, run down and bankrupt, needing unification and a new approach, if the dreary history of 1919–1926 was not to be repeated.

Coal mining needed a salvage operation on a national scale. Let the nation take it on.

The Coal Nationalisation Bill was introduced into the House of Commons in December, 1945. It proposed to set up a National Code Board of nine members, charged with the duty of finding and mining coal, of securing the efficient development of the coal mining industry, and of "making supplies of coal available in such quantities and at such prices as may seem to them best calculated to further the public interest." The board was to balance its books on the average of the good and the bad years. It was to be watched by two advisory councils, one representing consumers and the other distributors, which were to have considerable powers of investigation, but not the power to interfere with the management.

Generally, the board was to be free from government control and interference as well. The bill provided that the Minister of Fuel and Power could give the board general directions on the operation of the industry. Otherwise, responsibility for management rested with the board. The bill did not propose to nationalize existing coal mining undertakings as such. It proposed to transfer, by compulsion to the new board, all coal, the surface land of each colliery, its essential plant and machinery, the service installations—like coal preparation plants and electric power plants—the colliery coke ovens and the stocks of coal and other products. It would leave the former operating companies with ownership of their investments outside the coal industry, their cash and their other liquid assets.

Between the assets completely to be taken over and the assets left undisturbed there was a border country. Part of it would consist of property owned by the companies which had some association with the industry, such as water works, wharves, workmens' homes, surplus land, farm property in the neighborhood of the pit. These assets could be transferred to the board either at the option of the board or the option of the owner, whether or not the other party acquiesced.

The remainder were undertakings not organically connected with the business of coal mining but which might be owned and worked by a particular company for its own convenience, such as a brickmaking plant. These assets could be taken over by the board if both parties agreed. If one party wished them to be taken over, and the other disagreed, an independent arbitrator was to decide the issue.

Compensation for the assets to be taken over had already been the subject of conversations between the government and the mine owners' representatives, before the bill appeared. No sum had actually been agreed upon, but the government had accepted the argument that the compensation should be based on the net maintainable revenue from the assets acquired. A straight average of the net yearly revenue between 1923 and 1938, based on figures accepted by owners, trade union and government, was £6,900,000.

In addition to its power to issue stock in satisfaction of the compensation payable, the board could borrow up to £150,000,000 in the first five years of its life, for the purpose of modernizing and improving the properties it was acquiring.

On the whole, the bill was well received, by the socialists with acclamation, by the opposition with rather the air of "we object to the whole thing, but if you must do it, this is not an unfair way of doing so." The bill passed through Parliament in the 1946 Session and the Minister fixed January 1, 1947, as the day on which it would come into full operation with all the assets vested in the Board.

There were over 800 separate companies having assets affected by the Nationalisation Act in one way or another; in fact, by the end of 1946 the board had accumulated a remarkable range of miscellaneous properties. They included 30 plants for the manufacture of prepared fuel and briquettes, 55 coke ovens, tar distillery plants, and plants for the recovery of benzol, sulphuric acid, and pyrites, and 85 brick works and pipe works. In addition to the land actually in use at the pithead, the board owned about 250,000 acres of farm land, and other land undeveloped, and 141,000 houses, which included 2,000 farm houses and agricultural cottages. In addition, it owned shops, hotels, swimming baths, a cinema, a holiday camp, a bicycle track and a slaughter house.

The board had an enormously complicated accountancy job. First, there was the compensation for the main assets transferred. After an independent inquiry, that was fixed at a total of £164,660,000 for the whole country. This figure was accepted by the industry as reasonable. It was generally believed that their highest hopes of compensation, under this heading, had not exceeded £180,000,000.

But that calculation was merely phase one. It represented only the total value of all the assets of individual undertakings automatically acquired by the board. This total had again to be divided among the various districts and a portion allocated to each district. That amount had again to be subdivided among each company or individual who had owned any of the assets acquired in that district. On top of that, the value of each asset taken over by the board under the statutory options, or by agreement, had also to be evaluated. This task was not nearly completed, even by the end of 1948. Whatever else the act might have done, it brought enormous fees to the accountancy and appraisal professions.

There also remained the 480 mines in Britain—out of a total of 1,400—which did not employ more than 50 underground workers. A mine of this size was not automatically tranferred to the board under the act. The Coal Board was authorized to allow the owner to continue to work it under license. As a result, the owner faces an entirely different situation. He has ceased to be an owner of property. He has become a licensee from the Coal Board, entitled to mine coal under the terms of his license, but with no right to renewal of his license at the end of its period of currency. He must always face the fact that the location of his present operation may someday conflict with a large scale development, and that his license may not be renewed. In 1946, these small mines produced nearly 2,000,000 tons of coal—1% of the country's total output. His best security today is the fact that neither the Coal Board nor the country can allow any mine producing coal, however small the quantity, to fall into disuse while anyone is prepared to work it.

The National Coal Board faced its future with some considerable advantages. It was free from the physical shackles imposed by the division of ownership among the mineral, the mines and the equipment. It could begin by treating each coalfield or potential coalfield as a unit. It was free from the financial burden of having to produce an immediate profit, and from the financial difficulties of raising fresh money. It had a government-guaranteed credit for capital expenditure of £150,000,000. And it possessed the continued support, or at least the interest of the technicians of the industry. Few of them were "owners" in the old sense of the word. They might be expected to welcome the board if it merely improved the opportunities for work and advancement within the industry. Finally, it could count on support from the government, which above all desired the experiment to succeed, and from the Mineworkers' Union because the board represented the culmination of two decades of political battle.

Yet it had two enormously difficult problems to solve, the one technical, the other one basically of human relations. Ideally, the best technical solution to the problem of increasing the output and efficiency of the whole mining industry would have been to close a number of pits at once for complete overhaul and reconstruction. It would have been better to employ a greater proportion of available skill on preparatory work on improved underground layouts, equipment and methods, and to have accepted a 25% cut in total output for the three years that this would have involved. The industry needed at least a three-year breathing space for overhaul and re-equipment. In that time, it could have made up leeway and emerged in 1951 as an industry technically as good as any in the world.

Of course, that was impossible. World conditions demanded an immediate increase in Britain's output of coal. The board could no more pause to absorb the lessons of the past than can an army in the middle of a war. It had to re-equip in order to increase output, and suffered many technical hitches in doing so.

Its other task was to change the spirit of the industry and find some new way of giving the men in that industry an incentive to work harder. It could no longer use the stick of dismissal and employment with any freedom. It could not demand, from a Labour Government, privileges for the miner in the shape of wages, food allocations or clothing priorities (such as were offered in Germany) which would make the miner a privileged class of worker. It had to confront many industrial miners, whole communities of miners with complete uprooting from their old surroundings—and each mining community, in its way of life is inherently conservative. It had also to redesign a system of administration, based on geography and not ownership, and yet, if it could, avoid the evils of bureaucracy and overcentralization.

Some idea of its successes and failures can be glimpsed from its report for the first full year of operation, the report of 1947, published in July, 1948.

Obviously, the first point on which its critics would seize would be its profit and loss statement. That, after all, is some test of efficiency. Even in a socialized industry, and even to most socialists, a loss has to be supported by a pretty good defense, if those who have made it are to escape immediate condemnation.

Publication of the report had been preceded by a rumor campaign in the press that it would reveal losses of approximately £25,000,000. Who started the campaign it is difficult to say. Whoever it was gave the Coal Board considerable help, for that campaign had one result. When the report was published, and the loss was found to be below that figure, the criticism it received was rather less severe than many had expected. Even a detailed study did not seem to provide much ammunition. It was still easy enough to damn the board in a negative way. It was not so easy to offer any positive or constructive suggestions.

The board had made a loss, a net loss of £6,187,300. The collieries had lost £9,203,905, and the loss on housing was £202,653. But a profit had been made on the ancillary undertakings, the largest profits being from the operation of its railway cars (£1,203,407) and its coke ovens (£925,555). And the report also showed that the board had made a profit on some of its mining operations. The complete figures for the areas are:

Division	Costs per ton	Profit (+) or loss(−) per ton	Total profit (+) or loss (−)	Average weekly earnings (including allowances in kind)
	s. d.	s. d.	£	s. d.
Scottish..........	38. 9.4	+1.50	+1,574,097	137.10
Northern..........	45. 3.4	−4.10.8	−8,795,131	142. 3
Northeast.........	38. 7.6	+ 3.9	+623,022	137. 3
Northwest.........	46.10.0	−2. 4.5	−1,570,675	132. 8
East Midlands......	33. 0.4	+4. 4.0	+7,510,621	155. 6
West Midlands.....	37. 9.4	+3. 2.7	+2,686,092	133. 0
Southwest.........	52.11.7	−9. 7.0	−10,741,405	128. 5
Southeast.........	52.11.9	−7. 1.6	−490,526	139. 5
Total..........	41. 3.0	−1. 0.0	−9,203,905	138. 9

One of the areas producing primarily export coal, the Southwest —South Wales—had operated at a loss. The other, the Northeast, had managed to make a small profit. Yet the average wage in the Southwest area was the lowest of any coalfield. One line of criticism collapsed. It could not be said that the board did know how to make a profit nor that it had increased its losses by paying all its employees too well.

The next question on which criticism might seize was that of working hours. If high-cost, inefficient pits had to be kept open simply because their coal was needed, surely the miners could work longer hours. The question of working hours had been neatly avoided for the government in 1946 by Mr. Shinwell, Minister of Fuel and Power, before the board took over. The men were then working a five-and-a-half-day week. He said at that time that the government had no objection to the five-day week if it were properly organized and the country's need for more coal were recognized. The union view was clear. If public relations had not prevented plain speaking, any mine union leader would have said, "We are opposed to a six-day week, unless, of course, the men are paid overtime for the sixth day."

The board, at least, had no illusions. They knew that a decision either way would be attacked. As the 1947 report said, "Could the country afford the early introduction of the five-day week? Alternatively, could the country afford to defer it? The stakes were high and the Board had to play." There was substance in the second alternative. With recruitment of new miners still falling, the board could not afford to dismiss any possible disincentive to recruiting with a slight shrug.

The five-day week was introduced in May, 1947. Arguments, and unofficial strikes over its application, alone cost the country some 800,000 tons of coal. To quote again from the report, "the response to the appeal by Board and Union for greater tasks was disappointing." Could the board be blamed for that? Yet the tide of recruitment had turned. The net inflow of workers in 1947 was 26,000, as compared with a net decrease of 4,200 in 1946.

And in the fall of 1947, the miners went back to longer hours at higher wages. Introduction of the five-day week added 4s. a ton to the price of domestic coal in September, 1947. The longer hours put another 2/6d. on the price on January 1, 1948.

Then there was the general question of personnel relations in each pit. Before taking over, the Coal Board and the mine workers had worked out a pretty comprehensive plan for conciliation in the industry, based on a plan worked out between colliery owners and the union in 1943, and introduced by an agreement made in December, 1946. At the top level, the agreement set up a Joint National Negotiating Committee, made up of nine men from the Coal Board and not more than 14 from the union, plus a National Reference Tribunal—an arbitrator—of three. Each district had bodies with similar but local functions, and at the pit level there was a new system for rapid conciliation by consultation on the spot. In an attempt to side-track the unpleasant consequences of delay, a rigid timetable was laid down. If pit officials and pit union officials could not reach agreement in three days, the dispute automatically passed upwards to the manager for settlement, and with similar timetables upwards if the manager failed as well. Again the board was honest. Its report said, "it is hard to say how successful the Pit Scheme was during the year." Certainly, it had not reduced the number of unofficial strikes, 1,635 in 1947 as compared with 1,329 in 1946. But "without the conciliations schemes . . . there could certainly have been many more strikes. . . ." Despite the formal perfection of the scheme on paper, it did not work perfectly in practice. There were complaints of delays.

There was still, for the critics, the question of output per man. That was still not satisfactory. Again the board disarmed criticism by admitting as much in its report. Nor had it any firm answer why. Nor did it say what could be done about it. But neither did the critics. If miners in high-cost pits could not be fired, because of the need for the coal they produced, if the industry as a whole needed more man-power, what methods were there of inducing, or compelling, the men in the industry to work harder and to produce more? On that the critics were in just as much of a quandary as the Coal Board.

So, indeed, was the Mineworkers Union. Its annual conference was held in July, 1948, just before the publication of the 1947 report. It was a conference remarkable for the steady and sensible thinking of both the leaders and the majority of delegates. The mood of the conference was realistic, no longer obsessed by political visions or nightmares. As union members, they had achieved, on paper, most of the objectives for which they had been striving for fifty years. They too felt a little tongue-tied when asked, "What next?" They had no unanimous answer to the question, "How can more coal be produced, here and now?" (Nor had they found that unanimous answer by their 1949 conference).

None the less, there had been some increase in the output of saleable coal in 1947, compared with 1946, of some 10,000,000 tons. Of that, the report estimated that increases due to purely technical changes accounted for 3,500,000 tons. The remainder, 6,500,000 tons, "must be attributed to better efforts and attendance on the part of the men, and to the increase in the total labour force." But, it added, "The operation of cutter-loaders has sometimes been hampered, and even prevented, by difficulties over wages."

So the 1947 report continued. I have discussed it in detail, not only because it was the Coal Board's first report, but also because it was the board's first detailed survey of the task that it had ahead, of the difficulties it could see on the horizon.

The 1948 report appeared in the fall of 1949. So far as trends were concerned, its contents were not so very different. True, higher prices of coal had converted a loss of £6,000,000 in 1947 into a trading profit of £17,500,000 in 1948, but costs had risen even higher, by 4s.4d. a ton, and the average number of shifts worked by a worker each week had fallen from 4.85 at the end of 1947 to 4.74 at the end of 1948. Production was still rising slowly, but was that due to greater mechanization or harder work. In fact, was not the rise in production so small as to be ominous when placed against the degree of mechanization achieved at the coal face itself? Everything pointed to the obvious facts that nationalization was solving some problems, that it was not solving others, and that the tempo of improvement was very slow.

The publication of the 1948 report had one noticeable result. It led to a debate on the report in the House of Commons, in November, 1949, the first debate ever to be held specifically on the annual report of a nationalized industry. The indictment of the coal mining industry under nationalization, as prepared by the Opposition, is summarized in the following comparison of figures (published in this form, perhaps a little maliciously, by the *Financial Times* on the morning of the Commons debate):

	1937	1948
Output Salable Coal (tons million).......	240.4	197.6
Output per Worker per annum (tons)......	309	272
Total number of Workers................	777,800	724,030
Shifts worked per Worker (over-all) per annum	270	245
— do — (Coal face) per week.....		4.42
Output per Manshift worked (Coal face)...	60 cwts.	58.4 cwts.
— do — (Over-all)....	23.96 cwts.	22.2 cwts.
Total Cost per ton of Output............	13s.11d.	45s.6d.
Wages — do —	9s.6d.	29s.9d.
Earnings per Manshift Over-all...........	11s.8d.	33s.1½d.
Earnings per Worker per week............	£3.0.8d.	£8.3.10d.
Coal Shipped Abroad (tons millions)......	56.3	15.93.

And these figures can themselves be compressed into one sentence: coal mining, in 1949, with all the new equipment poured into it by the Coal Board, was not producing as good results as it did in 1937 under private ownership.

Nationalization had solved one technical difficulty, that of providing the industry with the new capital it so desperately needed in its attempt to climb back to its highest levels of production. But neither nationalization, by itself, nor the activities of the board had for certain converted men like Trefor Williams, and the thousands who feel as he does, into devoted enthusiasts for their newly nationalized management. It had not been able to give Britain the production of coal it would like to have. It had not yet devised an administrative machine which gave proper freedom to management and yet won the confidence of the majority of workers. If it had shown one thing, it was that nationalization produced no automatic paradise for anyone.

The truth was, and is, that the mining industry has been operating these three years under the terms of an uneasy compromise between the ideas of both public and private ownership, with many of the worst features of each. Under private ownership, those mines which were permanently operating at a loss would have been closed down long since, and the men dismissed. That would have kept down the cost of coal but would have resulted in a reduction of output, both directly and indirectly. On the other hand, too many miners have thought of the Coal Board in the same terms as they once thought of a prosperous private owner and, as a result, they have demanded concessions and benefits of one kind and another by methods which are based on the national need for more coal, not on the industry's inherent ability to grant them.

This is no place in which to attempt to dig deeper into each separate problem of the industry. Instead, I would like to concentrate on two particular points, because I believe them to have an application in Britain far beyond this one industry.

One is absenteeism. In Britain, one has a feeling that the rest of the world regards this as a peculiarly British disease. It is a disease of full employment. So far as coal mining is concerned, practically every other national coal mining industry in Europe suffers from it, and to the same degree. Absenteeism has increased since 1938. In that year, 6.4% of all possible shifts were not worked. In 1946, the percentage was 16, in 1948, 11.6%, and in 1949 it was 12.5%. And despite this fact, output per manshift in Britain has made the greatest recovery in Europe. Taking the 1937 figures as 100; in September, 1949, Britain's index was 101, France 87, Belgium and Holland 81, the Saar 80 and Poland 72. But even these figures can deceive, for in 1937 Britain's output per manshift was below those of other European countries.

Absenteeism is made up of two elements, involuntary absenteeism —due to sickness or accident—and voluntary absenteeism. Increase in involuntary absenteeism may be a good thing. It may mean that a man is not driven by fear to return to work before he is well. In 1949, it was estimated that the figure for voluntary absenteeism was about 5.5% of all shifts, as compared with 6% in 1948 —that change is not one for the worse. But even that figure means that each man misses an average of 11 to 12 shifts a year, and that, in its turn, means that a small percentage of men in the industry are missing vastly more shifts than that. Why?

Various reasons are put forward: the tradition in some districts that the coal industry is still one for casual labor; the absence of monetary incentives (that is not true of the mine face worker—the basis of his pay is designed to encourage a full week's continuous work); high taxation; poor housing conditions; the suggestion that by now the mine worker values greater leisure more than higher weekly earnings. All these add up to one answer; the industry has lost three forms of discipline, fear of dismissal, wage cuts and unemployment. It has not found a substitute which is equally effective as a spur to all the men in the industry. Absenteeism is a problem of a minority, a very small minority, but it runs like a thread through every industry in which employment is as stable as it is in coal mining.

The other point is the organization of the industry under the Coal Board. There I would quote from the speech of Col. Lancaster, a Conservative M. P. who was a former director of a nationalized coal undertaking, in a Commons debate on the 1948 report of the Coal Board:

The indictment will be, not that they [the Coal Board and the government] made their initial mistakes—those are incidental—but that they rushed into this problem without sufficient thought . . . Having made this mistake, they have not been prepared to make the changes and alterations which were required.

I believe they started their task with two false premises. First, the view was taken that everything was wrong with the coal industry. Whereas in fact there were . . . a number of concerns which were as efficient, both technically, as anything either in Europe or in the United States. I think it would have been far better too in the first instance for them to have modelled their organisation on these good concerns. . . .

The second mistake . . . was to ignore the fact that there were and there are two parties to management . . . There are and almost always must be the administrator and the technician . . .

I think it is possible to reduce all this to a series of propositions:

(A) In 1945, nationalization of the industry was a political necessity, and unification of the industry was a technical necessity. It is unfortunate that these two needs arose in compelling force at the same time.

(B) Nationalization found some solution for those problems still outstanding from the years 1922 to 1939. It contributed very little, and that indirectly, to answering the political questions that confront the industry in 1950.

(C) The effects of nationalization, because they have been colored by politics, have been, since 1946, more of a hindrance than a help to the technical improvement of the industry.

(D) The outlook for the industry is better than it was before 1945 for these reasons:

(1) The crippling effects of shortage of capital are disappearing.

(2) The union leaders have shown themselves capable of facing the real problems of their position and their real responsibilities— although they have not yet solved them.

(3) The tension that culminated in the demand for the political solution of nationalization is on the wane, since it was the product of insecurity, low wages and bad conditions never likely to return in so acute a form.

All this is going to take a considerable time in its working out. The pressing need for coal will remain. So will the necessity to attract more new workers into the industry. The inevitable technical changes over the next ten years will impose their own fresh problems of personnel relationships, and the need to avoid precipitate action. It will become necessary to close down more pits and to put an end to certain processes or routines which now provide employment. And it would be foolish for anyone to antagonize the men in the industry by clumsy methods at the very start of that process.

At its conference in July, 1948, the Mineworkers Union pledged its support to all essential plans for reorganizing the industry, even though that might result in loss of work for many men. But the men who are displaced, and their mates who are not, have yet to be subjected to the discipline of the actual test itself on any large scale. The day will come when Colliery X is closed down, its effective workers transferred to the books of Colliery Y, and the unneeded workers paid off. What will happen then? What will the excess men do? And what of the men who see in the move an end to all hopes of further employment, because they are too old, or too disabled to be employed elsewhere, or to learn a fresh trade?

That will be the real testing time of the board, of the union, of the industry itself. There is no alternative but to let the Coal Board and the miners alone, to allow them to learn by themselves and gradually.

In the meantime, here are two tailpieces:

The Central West area of the Scottish Division of the Coal Board comprises the counties of Stirling, Dumbartonshire and part of Lanarkshire. It contains 51 collieries, producing nearly 5,000,000 tons of coal a year, and in 1947 the area lost 3/5d. per ton raised, the output per manshift being only 18.4 tons.

These coalfields were once the most prosperous in Scotland. The coal was of fine quality; it lay at fairly shallow depths, and as a result it was worked fast and hard. Now some mines are nearly worked out, and the seams remaining to be worked are only from 17 inches to 24 inches wide. The economic answer is to close the area down. Its houses are old and not worth repairing. Its pits are often damp. Above all, it does not pay. If 19 of the 51 collieries were closed, only 5,000 tons of coal a day would be lost, but 6,000 miners would be put out of work.

If all the mines close, the shops and services of the area will be left derelict. A mining area is a community. A miner will not readily move unless he is moving to a reasonably equivalent locality. Is the shopkeeper, the local publichouse owner, the manager of the local gas-works to be left stranded, surveying a dead and empty town? How are his equivalents in the new area to be found and established in business?

And where are the men to go to? To the pits of another area of the Scottish coalfield, if possible. It is planned that the coalfields now being developed in Fife and Ayrshire will produce some 5,000,000 more tons of coal per year than the recently-closed Lanarkshire mines have done. The local authorities have already planned a new town, to be called Glenrothes, for 30,000 people. But where can it be located? Centrally? In that case it sterilizes every ton of coal under it. Away from the coalfield? In that case what about transportation to and from the shafts?

Again, shall the industries that use the coal of the Central West area of Scotland move, and follow the coal, or must they pay more for it because of extra haulage costs? Shall the old ports that shipped the coal elsewhere be abandoned in favor of new? Who will build and pay for the new railways facilities necessary to handle the new tonnage? Who will pay for the housing, schools—the list continues.

The Coal Board began this operation of closing down the one coalfield and developing the newer fields in November, 1948, and it will extend possibly over 25 years. By June, 1949, seven pits had been closed, 824 men had moved voluntarily, and 311 more had agreed to settle in one of the new coalfields when their pit was closed. Four out of every five men who have moved have been provided with houses in their new locality.

The details of the closing of two pits in the Shotts area in April, 1949, provide some illustration of the complexities. The two pits produced no more than 360 tons of coal daily and they were losing money at the rate of £83,000 a year. They employed 448 men, of whom forty-four could be retained at the collieries on salvage work.

Before the pits were closed, 98 men migrated voluntarily. Another 144 followed them when the pits were closed. Another 114 found work in neighboring pits to replace men from those pits who had themselves moved voluntarily. Others found other work locally, but in the end there were thirty-six men left for whom no suitable alternative work could be found. Some of these would inevitably be men suffering from early injuries and capable only of light work. For others, local ties—possibly the occupations of the rest of the family—would be too strong to allow them to migrate. They are the core of the problem. They will be the core of the problem every time a pit is closed.

In all, it is estimated that the closing down of these pits of the Central West area will, in one way or another over the next ten years displace some 100,000 people. That is the nature and magnitude of the problem which faces the coal industry, management and unions, in Scotland.

Nantgarw Colliery, seven miles north of Cardiff, lies on the edge of the southern end of the South Wales coalfield. The coal veins run much more vertical than horizontal, but workable coal in the area—some of the world's finest coking coal—exists in quantities expected to last 200 years at the estimated future rate of mining. Attempts to work this area began in 1911. The main seam is the "Black Vein," about 7 ft. in thickness, but angled from 14 to 26 inches per yard. Five seams were partially worked, but they had failed because coal could not be mined economically by the old method of laying the underground roads. The mine was abandoned in 1927.

It was later bought by the Powell-Duffryn Company which planned to open the colliery again, basing the underground workings on level roadways. They began planning in 1938, resumed again in 1944 and began work in 1946. When the National Coal Board took over, they adopted and extended that plan. As revised, from 1950 onward, a maximum of 780,000 tons of salable coal will be mined each year.

During the first twenty-five years, only the coal lying between a depth of 280 yards and 350 yards in the Nantgarw shafts will be worked; nine seams in all, all dipping steeply northwards. They contain about 19,000,000 tons of reserves and to work the area out, some 17 miles of hard headings must be driven.

When the mine has been fully developed, 1,750 underground workers, 355 surface workers and 150 coke oven workers will be employed at the colliery. They will live in a newly built model village, and the responsibility for that will rest with the local authority, the Caerphilly Urban District Council. The colliery itself will be equipped with a modern canteen, pit-head baths and first-aid accommodations. Men working below ground will change in the baths and be under cover all the way from there, through the lamp-room to the pithead itself.

Both shafts will be equipped for hoisting men, but all the coal will be raised at the south pit, and the north pit will be kept for taking in stone and materials. The coal will be tipped near the shaft and conveyed either into a bunker or direct to the coal preparation plant. The washery will be a Chance two-process type, the grades of eight to one and one-sixteenth inches in one box and the fine grades treated by froth flotation. A flocculation plan will clarify the water, to avoid pollution of the river, and to allow the water to be recirculated. A crushing plant will treat the stone from the mine and the washery refuse, so that it may be used subsequently for the pneumatic filling of the coal faces underground, after the mining of the coal has been completed. Stone and washery refuse will be loaded into mine cars and returned underground down the north pit.

When the colliery has been fully developed, it will, so the Coal Board proudly announces, "give a satisfactory return on the capital invested and compare favorably with any other colliery producing coking coal in the country."

I saw the area on a day in May. Like all South Wales, the valley was one of contrast, the dirty shale and stone from the old slag heaps then being spread on the floor of the valley to support the rail marshalling yards, a somber comment on the green of the trees and the hedgerows and grass on the hills around. Climb a hundred feet and industry was all below you. Beyond, upwards, there was only grass and heather, stone walls and bare mountain pasture.

The engine house for the new pit was finished, white concrete and red brick. The coke ovens were rising in the valley, a vast concrete tower 150 feet high, surrounded by steel scaffolding, like a secular cathedral. Curling around the colliery entrance was the old canal, unused, weed-grown, the first artery ever to carry coal from the valley to the sea, a century ago. All South Wales was in that valley, as it is in every South Wales valley.

The men there were more intent on working out the future than in tidying up the past, but they could have looked for blackbirds' eggs in the hedgerows on the way home from work.

CHAPTER VII

The Battle Over Iron and Steel

Various factors decreed that the issue of iron and steel nationalization should be deferred until the final period of the Labour Government's administration. These were entirely political. The circumstances of the industry itself did not change in such a way as to strengthen the arguments in favor of public ownership. On the contrary, the industry defiantly insisted on blooming and flowering while its nationalized sisters seemed to wilt. The arguments remained as effective or as ineffective as they had been in 1945. What did change, and change more than once, was the resolution of the Cabinet when faced with the immense political battle an iron and steel nationalization bill would provide, and with the equally immense practical difficulties in the way of changing ownership and control of such a vast industry.

This political issue arises from and is part of the history of the industry in Britain, a history of rise and relative decline. Modern steelmaking originated in Britain in the third quarter of the last century, but Britain did not retain that lead for long. By 1890, the United States had taken first place, followed by Germany. Britain fell behind, not only in size of plant and total output, but in method, in output per worker, in fuel economy and in the over-all cost per ton. The Labour party, as representing the worker dependent on the industry, has not within living memory had occasion to look upon the leaders of the industry as complete masters of the craft of producing cheap steel.

Many of the advantages won by foreign competitors were gained by political weapons, by rigid exclusion of imported steel, by differential selling prices to compel the home producers to subsidize exports; but those political weapons were supported by technical advance and flexibility. The British steel industry was late in winning any political weapons with which to fight; it was slower still in backing them up on the technical side of quantity production—despite its skill in the field of special steels.

In 1932, the British industry was given political aid, in the shape of tariffs on imports, operating through two agencies. The first was a government organization, the Import Duties Advisory Committee, which supervised the tariffs then imposed on imports of steel. The second was an internal body, the Iron and Steel Federation, created by the leading men in the industry. In return for a promise to reorganize and re-equip the industry, the Federation was given practical means of fixing steel prices within Britain, of reserving such proportion of the home market for home products as it chose, of subsidizing high-cost home producers and exports, and of preventing newcomers from entering the industry save on such terms as the Federation might fix. In addition, it won the right to compel co-operative buying of raw materials. The steel industry then ceased to be one which could be described as fully competitive internally, as the word "competitive" is generally understood. The Federation, by accepting these powers, and the practical support of the Imports Advisory Committee, also accepted responsibility of management for the public benefit, and so by implication a liability to be criticized from that standpoint.

Its record since 1932 is not wholly favorable. Like the coal industry, it spent too little on modernization, replacement and research. There was one new major installation set up, at Corby in Lincolnshire, to take geographical advantage of local deposits of iron ore. For the rest, the industry continued to operate the high-cost plants, to refuse to consider any general relocation of its installations, to oppose new companies in the industry (as at Jarrow, an area then suffering acutely from unemployment by reason of the closing down of local shipyards). It hesitated over the introduction of modern techniques to supplant older, more traditional processes. And it preserved in its price structures and buying controls—now universal over the country—many of the old deterrents to efficiency and competition. Prices rose, and no one could really feel convinced that the increases were not intended to enable the least efficient plant to make some profit.

Above all, from the labor point of view, it failed even to think in terms of full employment. Because the labor cost in its installations was high per ton of steel produced, the industry habitually layed men off at the first sign of a fall in demand, and always contrived to retain a pool of unemployed workers. In 1929 and 1937, good years in steel output, unemployment in the industry was 10% of the total labor force; between 1931 and 1935 as much as 35%. And it failed, again like the coal mining industry, to attract the young worker in it. At some periods and in some areas, over 50% of the boys apprenticed to the industry left it after their apprenticeship was complete and they were fully skilled men.

There were, then, adequate arguments, and the right psychological atmosphere, for a Labour party while in opposition to accept the idea of nationalizing the industry. A majority of the rank and file of the Labour party wanted and expected the industry to be nationalized, by which they meant that the actual production of iron and steel should be undertaken by a public board responsible to Parliament. Their view was that if socialism meant anything at all it meant that the essential basic industries of the state should be directly owned and operated by the state. It meant that socialism should not stop merely at services such as the post office or transport, nor at the nationalization of decaying industries like coal mining, where, at the end of a period of government control, nationalization might well become acceptable to both sides if only because management and labor mistrusted each other too much ever again to resume normal industrial relations.

The inclusion among the party's electoral promises of a proposal to nationalize iron and steel during the lifetime of the 1945 Parliament, was largely due to Mr. Hugh Dalton. It was not generally liked by the Executive in 1945, when it was working out its election program, but it was accepted largely in the spirit of, "Oh, well, it is very unlikely we shall have a working majority anyway!"

Mr. Herbert Morrison was the leading figure in the faction within the Executive that did not want to touch iron and steel at all in the lifetime of the first Labour Parliament. Mr. Morrison was only indirectly interested in political theory. He was more concerned with what would lose votes and what would gain them. An abortive attempt to take over iron and steel in a bad year would almost certainly lose votes. A promise to take over iron and steel after a successful general election in 1950 might attract them.

A curious feature of the situation before the election, and since, has been the negative part played by the trade union principally concerned, the Iron and Steel Confederation. Judging from the public utterances of its officials, the union could almost be described as neutral. Its relations with management were good. It was an amalgamation of a number of old craft unions which had never been much concerned with political theory—in fact, this union is a good illustration of the argument that a trade union is not inevitably a socialistic body—and while it seemed prepared to follow the labor movement as a whole, it did not bring pressure to bear on the cabinet to do something quickly. The union of the allied engineering trade, the Amalgamated Engineering Union, was quite different, being a leftist and pugnaciously led organization.

The obvious first step for any such government after the election was an examination of the industry as it stood, and of what proposals the Iron and Steel Federation, as the controlling body, had for reorganization and expansion.

In May, 1945, the Coalition Government had asked the Federation to submit its postwar plans for a "substantial volume of modernization and new construction" for the industry. That plan was completed by the end of the year and was published by the government as a white paper in May, 1946, when the Commons had its first important debate on the future of the industry.

The plan first attempted some estimate of future demand for British steel. Home and export demands had fluctuated between wars. From 1910 to 1915 yearly domestic production ran at about the 5,000,000 ton level. It rose to 7,300,000 in 1918, fell again to 5,000,000 between 1923 and 1926, but by 1931 had reached 7,650,000 tons. Nineteen hundred and thirty-four brought another ebb to 6,500,-000 tons: by 1939 output was up to 10,500,000 tons. Exports had varied in roughly the same way over these periods, but their fluctuations had kept them near the level of 3,000,000 tons a year. The Federation concluded that on the basis of full employment there should, by 1950, be a demand for 13,000,000 tons of steel for home use and 3,000,000 tons for export; total ingot requirements 16,000,000 a year.

To provide raw material for that demand, scrap would make up about 55% of the total, which would mean the industry would have to increase basic and hematite pig-iron production to 8,500,000 tons per annum. This would consume 20,000,000 tons of ore, of which it was estimated 7,500,000 tons would be imported and 12,500,000 tons home produced, 11,000,000 tons of which would come from the Midland areas of Britain.

One of the initial considerations discussed in the report was the location of the various plants. Cautiously, it listed the factors affecting location: costs of the raw material; the required quality of the finished product; the cost and quality of coal at the site; the full utilization of gas; distance from markets; "availability of personnel, houses and social amenities" (a dry way of referring to people); and it concluded with the even more cautious phrase, "generalisation is difficult."

The report then considered in detail what would be needed to create such a production capacity in both branches of the industry, and to improve the manufacturing installations and equipment. It estimated that the total cost of executing the detailed plans for modernization and development suggested would be £168,000,000, an expenditure to be spread over seven and one-half years. The effect of that expenditure would be to replace 40% of the capacity of the industry. The major projects suggested were:

1. A new strip mill and ancillary plant in South Wales which would annually produce 1,000,000 tons of strip for sheet and tinplate.
2. A new broad–flange beam mill and steel-works on the North East Coast —to be the first in Britain.
3. Five new continuous–billet mills, backed by modern blast furnaces and steel plants, in Northamptonshire.
4. New blast furnaces and steel plants in both Lincolnshire and Scotland.

The final section of the report dealt with how the money could be raised. The report estimated that the annual expenditure on the plan would be £22,500,000. It calculated that the industry could contribute £3,000,000 a year based on its prewar rate of depreciation, and another £3–4,000,000 from what it had saved during the war through suspension of new construction. Up to £3,000,000 might come from the government's promised contribution to war damage and the companies' own provision for deferred repairs. In all, the Federation thought that about half the annual cost could be found within the industry. The rest would require the investment of new money and there was a strong hint that a great deal of that ought to be provided by the government.

In the light of subsequent criticisms, two further points about the report should be noted. It assumed that the Federation would continue to have considerable powers of control over the industry. For example, in its discussions of a possible concentration of heavy steel rail production, it listed eleven individual firms which, in 1937, had produced a total 463,453 tons of steel rails. It proposed to concentrate production among four firms: Colvilles; United Steel Company at Workington, Cumberland; Dorman Long and Guest Keen Baldwins. Together, these firms would produce 650,000 tons, two producing about 200,000 tons each, the other two about 125,000 tons each. The remaining seven would apparently fade out of the picture, since they were unnoticed in the report and unsung.

The report was also silent on the question of the compensation (if any) payable to those concerns whose high-cost plants were to be closed down on general reorganization, scrapped and replaced by more modern plants built elsewhere, possibly an installation by some other ownership. It is unlikely that the Federation had overlooked this question of compensation altogether, but whatever views its members had, none of them appeared in the report.

This was the background of the iron and steel industry at the end of 1945. No one expected that any attempt to nationalize it would take precedence over the corresponding bill to deal with the coal industry. But many people can at least be excused for thinking that the Government would have a plan.

Those who thought that way were too pessimistic. The Government had a plan—more than one, in fact, a whole series of considerable variety. Four years passed before the Government introduced a bill to nationalize the major individual companies engaged in the industry, a bill very closely related to the draft bill which they had first considered in 1946. But a remarkable number of other bills had flowed into wastepaper baskets during those three years.

Soon after the election, Mr. Wilmot, Mr. Attlee's first choice as Minister of Supply, was presented by his experts with a plan to nationalize the industry simply by securing—through mandate—financial control of the major iron and steel companies. That process completed, the Government, as the major shareholder of each company, would carry through modernization of the industry largely on the lines of the Federation's own report. That plan had many advantages. It was straightforward. It avoided the complicated task of defining where steel-making ended and heavy engineering began. It left the position of principal executives in the industry unchanged, and at that stage, the government could hope to secure their support. It also avoided the technical form of nationalization, the dislocation of contracts resulting from the liquidation of individual companies, and the transfer of those contracts to a new body. All these points were important in an industry depending on the import of raw materials and the export of the finished product.

This plan would have an historic interest in any event, for it was adopted four years later, without very considerable alteration, as the foundation on which the nationalization bill of 1948 was based. But in 1946 its manifest advantages did not outweigh its one apparent disadvantage. It was not socialistic enough, so Mr. Wilmot and Mr. Dalton thought. It did not propose that the whole industry should be transferred to a new board and run as one vast centralized concern. That was the acid test, apparently, of socialism in 1946, even though no one, expert or politician, was agreed on how to define in words where the steel industry began and ended. So Mr. Wilmot sent his experts away, and told them to study the draft of the Coal Nationalization Bill and follow humbly in those steps.

The second stage came when Mr. Wilmot found that all the merits of that abandoned plan were real, and very important, and that the objections to any alternative were also very real, beyond his capacity to surmount. He changed his mind. But by that time, the steel executives, headed by Sir Andrew Duncan, had retreated inside the Federation, taking their records and files with them. Mr. Wilmot had lost not only the possibility of their acquiescence in the original plan, but also the information necessary to enable him to work out another. That was the stage of the desperate and abortive call for aid to Mr. van der Bijl, head of the South African government-controlled steel industry, in the late summer of 1946. He came, he looked around and he advised against nationalizaton. The cabinet faced the situation with courage; it deferred action again.

The next move was the creation by Mr. Wilmot of an Iron and Steel Board, with the aid of Sir Archibald Forbes, ostensibly to gain some control over iron and steel production and allocation, but actually to set up some machinery which would provide his ministry with the data necessary to know what was going on in the industry. This step meant that an attempt at nationalization would be impossible during the 1947 Session, but it was the only action he could take which even looked like a step forward.

Incidentally, whatever motives may have possessed Mr. Wilmot when he called this Iron and Steel Board into being, the next two years showed that his child had some of the qualities of a Frankenstein. Here was a new chessman on the political board, and it was the Federation which seized the initiative in using it. In 1949, they were claiming, in effect, that in this board the country had the real instrument of control and supervision that it needed. To quote from the Federation's own bulletin:

The public interest has been safeguarded by the existence of a public board drawn from both sides of the industry, the consumer and the State, which guides the development of the industry. The success of the organisation which has been evolved is clearly seen in the outstanding contribution which the industry has made to post-war recovery.

That may have been making a virtue of necessity, but virtues are are not so numerous that any should be condemned solely on the grounds of its origin.

Stage four came while Mr. Herbert Morrison was away ill, during the first six months of 1947. The ordinary members of the Parliamentary Labour party were becoming increasingly restless at the delay and uncertainty over the whole project, and in the course of time that uneasiness penetrated within the ambit of the Prime Minister. The first task he gave Mr. Morrison on his return to work was that of getting steel nationalization into shape. Mr. Morrison naturally settled down to attempt to work out a compromise, and the result was an even more cautious proposal. The government was to ask for statutory power to take over any inefficient steel firms, but to leave the remainder alone. No trouble about definitions. An answer to the Tory critics. Above all, co-operation from the industry itself; in fact, this plan might well be described as a proposal to nationalize Sir Andrew Duncan, coupled with a hope that Duncan would bring the iron and steel industry along with him under the new umbrella.

Again, bad luck dogged the Cabinet. Mr. Morrison, owing to his illness in 1947, had not been able to complete his plan for submission to the Cabinet before July, 1947, and July brought with it the dollar crisis, the clash within the Cabinet and the early stages of the Marshall Aid negotiations. Rumors drifted around (originating usually from British rather than American sources) that the Labour Government would be required, as a condition of the Marshall Plan, to slow down its nationalization program, and this had the effect of stiffening the backs of the left-wing members of the cabinet. Mr. Aneurin Bevan demanded nationalization, something more full-blooded and immediate than the Morrison plan. "That," he said in effect, "is not socialism as I understand it, and I won't have it." He went on to threaten resignation and most people in his party had a shrewd feeling that he was about the only member of the cabinet who would make such a threat, and mean it. Mr. Attlee tacked again; August, 1947, was not quite the moment for a cabinet resignation. The Morrison plan was dropped. There was a cabinet reshuffle; Mr. Wilmot disappeared from office, and the Ministry of Supply went to Mr. George R. Strauss, a much more definite character.

The concluding stage of these preliminaries can be foreseen. August, 1947, saw the emergence of Sir Stafford Cripps as the man with the greatest say in economic affairs, and both Mr. Harold Wilson at the Board of Trade, and Mr. Strauss at the Ministry of Supply, can be considered almost as protégés of Sir Stafford. Sir Stafford had little difficulty in deciding that the original plan suggested to Mr. Wilmot was the only practical plan from which a bill, strong enough to survive the battles in Parliament, could be constructed. By the summer of 1948, the draft bill was taking shape. What would be nationalized in the industry would be individual firms, not industrial processes.

But Mr. Aneurin Bevan and his group had scored one success during the 1947 fall crisis. They pointed out that if the bill to nationalize the industry were not introduced before the 1948 Session, there would be no time left, between its final stage in Commons and the dissolution of Parliament in 1950, for the bill to be carried into effect over the heads of the Lords under the provisions of the Parliament Act of 1911, and it was already clear enough that the Lords would never pass this bill, in a form acceptable to the government, as they had passed the earlier nationalization bills.

That act is a product of the intense battle between Commons and Lords over the land taxation proposals in the Liberal Government's budget of 1909–1910. Until then, the three elements in the United Kingdom Parliament, King, Lords and Commons, had to agree on a parliamentary bill before it became law. The consent of the King had, since the middle of the eighteenth century, been a constitutional formality. Not so the consent of the Lords. The Lords of 1910 did not agree to the Commons' taxation proposals, and they threw out the budget when it came before them. The Parliament Act of 1911 was a hard-won compromise. Under it, a "money" bill (a bill containing only provisions for taxation) does not require the consent of the House of Lords. Any other bill may receive the Royal Assent despite the failure of the House of Lords to accept it, provided it is passed by the Commons, in identical form, in three separate sessions of Parliament spread over a period of two years.

In November, 1947, a bill to amend the Parliament Act of 1911 appeared in the House of Commons. Its proposals were simple. They cut down the period of delay imposed on a bill by the 1911 act from two years to one, and the number of sessions from three to two. But it also contained this important rider. It provided that these alterations to the 1911 act should be retroactive; in other words, any bill passed in two separate sessions of the 1945–50 Parliament, on occasions not less than twelve months apart, could become law without the Lords' consent.

It was, of course, indignantly denied that there was any specific connection between the Parliament Bill of 1947 and the fact that there was to be no steel nationalization Bill before 1948. And, of course, a great many people disbelieved these denials.

The Parliament Bill of 1947 went through its required stages. Introduced for the first time in November, it went through its third stage in the House of Commons, in its third separate session, on November 14, 1949, and became law under the Parliament Act of 1911, on December 16, 1949. Thus it provided a means of carrying a steel nationalization bill onto the statute book in 1950. But that became unnecessary. Government and Opposition made one compromise over the bill.

To complete the parliamentary history of the steelization bill (its formal title as introduced was "The Iron and Steel Bill"), the bill passed the Commons during 1949. Inevitably, it was considerably amended by the Lords. In October, when Parliament resumed after the summer recess, the Commons was due to consider the Lords' amendments, some sixty in all. Unless it accepted them, the bill would lapse as unagreed at the end of the 1948–49 session, that is, at the end of that year. From this point of view, the major amendment made by the Lords was to postpone the date on which the bill could come into operation The date fixed in the original bill had been May, 1950, a date which might have preceded the 1950 general election. The Conservative members of the House of Lords insisted that this date should be altered to a later one, one late enough to make it certain that a general election would have first taken place. The reason is obvious. They wanted to make certain that, if a Conservative government came into power after the 1950 election, it would be free to scrap the whole plan. To that, at first, the Government objected.

It changed its mind soon enough. If the Cabinet had wished to use the machinery of the amended Parliament Act to pass its bill, it would have been necessary to call a further session of Parliament in 1950, and the formalities connected with the passing of the bill through all its stages again would have occupied at least the first three months of 1950. Therefore, it would have been impossible to hold the 1950 election before April, 1950, and impracticable to hold it much before late May or June, because there must be a Parliament sitting in April and May every year to pass the year's budget. In September, 1949, Mr. Attlee was prepared to defer his general election until June, 1950. By November, he was not.

The final result was that the Government amended its own bill to provide that the vesting of the various companies in the newly created Iron and Steel Corporation could not take place before January, 1951, and that the new Corporation itself could not come into existence before October, 1950. That amendment was accepted by the Conservatives in both the Commons and the Lords and the bill became law on November 24, 1949. And, on the occasion of its final appearance in the Commons on November 16, 1949, Mr. Churchill said: " . . . should we be returned to power one of our first steps will be to expunge this wanton, wasteful partisan measure which many of those associated with it do not in their hearts believe in; this measure which strikes this country a bitter blow at a bad time."

What was the plan for nationalization contained in the Iron and Steel Bill introduced into Parliament at the end of October, 1948? It was a plan to nationalize certain companies in the industry, very like the first plan put up to Mr. Wilmot in 1946.

The principal companies to be taken over totaled 96 (of over 2,000 supervised by the Iron and Steel Board) and were listed by name in the bill. The named companies were the leading concerns in the industry. All their issued stocks and securities were to be transferred to a new public corporation, the Iron and Steel Corporation of Great Britain, which would then become a holding company owning about 90% of the productive capacity of the industry. The date for the change-over was to be May, 1950, or within eighteen months thereafter, as decided by the Minister of Supply. (This, of course, was a date subsequently amended by the time the bill became law.)

Existing executives would not be disturbed or turned into employees of the new corporation. They would remain directors and managers of their former companies, but responsible to a new shareholder. In the meantime, until the transfer, the old companies were to be continued in operation, but without taking on fresh commitments or dispersing existing assets unless the Minister gave his consent.

Some companies not specifically named in the bill would be caught in the nationalization net. Concerns with a total yearly production of less than 5,000 tons of either pig iron or steel escaped all control. Those annually producing more than 5,000 tons but less than 50,000 tons of pig iron, or 20,000 tons of steel, could only operate—if and when the bill became law—under license from the main corporation. All subsidiaries of the companies named in the bill were also included in the change-over except those whose main activity was the production of motor vehicles; these were specifically excluded (a gesture, it was generally felt, to the Ford Motor Co., Ltd.).

So far as general policy was concerned, the bill provided that the new corporation would have the duty of procuring, in the public interest, adequate supplies of iron and steel at the right price, in the right quantities and of proper quality. For that purpose, it would have power to give general directions to the individual operating companies which were, in effect, its subsidiaries. It was not intended that the corporation would interfere with the day-to-day management of each subsidiary's business. It was required to be certain that the combined revenues of the whole undertaking were sufficient to meet the combined expenditures properly chargeable to revenue, when averaged out over the years.

In short, not only would the new Iron and Steel Corporation of Great Britain—if and when it came into existence—combine the functions of both the Iron and Steel Federation and the Iron and Steel Board as far as general supervision of the industry was concerned, it would also own the whole industry, with all that this implies. The profit element would be eliminated. But the taxpayer could make a loss. There still might not be enough steel. And the price of the steel produced could still go up.

Clearly, no government could allow the uncertainty of this situation to hold up work on the industry's own plans for development. Nor could the industry itself afford it. The government made use of the recently created Iron and Steel Board to fix prices of steel on the basis of the information it was now collecting from the whole industry. Each pig iron and primary producer submitted to the board a regular statement of its costs and selling prices for all main products. Similar information was collected, but at longer intervals, in respect to lighter and more highly finished products. In addition, the board obtained, direct from each firm, an annual statement of its total profits. As a result, the board had information covering current costs and the relation between costs and total profits. With that information, it was able to fix a standard price for a product, not a standard rate of profit for a particular undertaking. The price rulings were made effective within the industry by statutory order. The industry claimed that this prevented any monopolistic increase in prices but left room for price competition within the industry and for competition in service.

Details of the profit margin (before allowing for depreciation) of individual undertakings producing plates, sections, rails and ordinary quality billets were published by the Federation during the course of 1948. Of the concerns, 12% included in one survey carried on production at a loss. The return, for the second quarter of 1948, showed that profit margins ranged from £2.17s. a ton on ingots (the average was nearer to £1. a ton) to a loss of £1.10s. a ton. But the Federation gave no quantitative figures of how much profit or loss was made.

The industry also continued to operate some forms of subsidy payments. These were of two kinds, one originating within the industry, the other provided by the government. In neither case, the Federation claimed, was there any arrangement for pooling profits, nor for subsidizing the less efficient at the expense of the more efficient firms.

The internal arrangements involved an adjustment to compensate for the relatively high cost of pig iron, when compared with the low (artificially low) price of scrap metal. Firms using only scrap paid into a financial pool 17s.6d. per ton of ingot steel produced by the firm and the pool made a payment of a corresponding amount to a firm using only pig iron. The government grant took the shape of a subsidy towards the freight cost of imported ore. Each firm paid no more than its prewar freight cost, plus 100 per cent. While freight charges remained higher than this, the government paid the difference between that arbitrary figure and the actual cost. The amount contributed by the government in 1948 represented about 10s.6d. per ton of steel prices, or 3 per cent. The government also bore the excess of the cost of imported steel over the internal selling price of home-produced steel.

A comparison of British and foreign steel prices, made by the Federation in 1948, showed that on the whole British prices compared favorably with those of similar products in most other countries. Australia was the major exception. The exceptionally low cost of local ore and coal in Australia makes the internal price of Australian steel about the lowest in the world—between 15% and 20% lower than prices in Britain. But the Federation did not point out that the wage rates within the industry were only about one-half of those prevailing in the United States.

The industry was also producing expanding results, in the shape of steel for the home market and for export. Output rose as follows:

PRODUCTION OF CRUDE STEEL
(ingots and metal for castings)

Year	Tons
1937	12,984,000
1938	10,397,900
1947	12,724,500
1948	14,876,600
1949	15,552,900

Net deliveries of finished steel showed a corresponding expansion and the figures for the total steel available are:

(Figures in millions of tons)

	Imports	Total supply	Exports	Home deliveries
1937	1.48	14.54	2.92	11.62
1938	0.97	11.22	1.98	9.24
1947	0.47	14.33	1.95	12.38
1948	0.53	15.79	2.10	13.69
1949	1.14	16.93	2.49	14.44

In the first half of 1949, direct exports of iron and steel, and of steel manufactures, rose in value as compared with the same period of 1947. Not only that. The British industry was showing a rate of increase in output comparable with any achieved in any other European country involved in the war.

PRODUCTION OF FINISHED STEEL
(millions of tons)

Country	1938	1948	1949
Belgium and Luxembourg	2.8	4.7	4.4
Sweden	0.6	0.7	0.9
Britain	6.6	10.3	11.3
France	4.1	5.1	6.2
Italy	1.7	1.5	1.6
Czechoslovakia	1.3	1.8	1.8

It is easy to understand the political reasons why steel management was concerned with improving output. But it also persuaded the workers in the industry to extend their hours of work, and to adopt a continuous–process operation, which deprived them of a regular free weekend. The industry was also co-operating reasonably well in the distribution of its products.

A new steel allocation system was introduced at the end of March, 1948. As far as its immediate object was concerned, it had a reasonable success. It speeded up actual deliveries and removed the backlog of paper, or formal allocations estimated at 2,000,000 tons at the end of 1947, which had acted as a drag on the steel-consuming industries. But, in the main, this success was due to the increased quantities of steel coming from the producers. In 1948, an actual production rate of 15,000,000 tons per annum meant that government departments did not, in fact, have to cancel on a large-scale allocation made in 1947. Further, the Materials Sub-Committee of the Cabinet, the body responsible for the over-all distribution of steel, had deliberately under-allocated when deciding amounts for the second quarter, April to June, of 1948.

But the main advantage of the new plan was that the bulk of the supplies was allocated for six months ahead, not for three months, as previously. Doling out allotments of steel, quarter by quarter, had obvious disadvantages. Even greater flexibility was shown where concerns were compelled by the nature of their business to rely on future plotting of production. As much as 100% of their supplies could be authorized for nine months ahead, and for even longer where the product manufactured required an extended period of production; in heavy electrical equipment, for example. A company with a foreign civil engineering contract, for instance, could receive an authorization covering its needs for two years ahead. Flexibility in the management of the program was increased by decentralization to regional officers of the various ministries.

The system was not perfect; it is doubtful if any such scheme could ever be perfect, in the sense of making the volume of paper authorizations exactly equal the volume of supplies. Neither the exact amount of demand nor the exact supply of steel are predictable for six months in advance. Fortunately, departments were sensible enough to decide that it was better to over-allocate rather than to under-allocate, to take the risk of delay in some deliveries rather than to leave industry unnecessarily short of supplies because of a paper decision.

By the middle of 1948, supplies of most types of steel in Britain were reasonably good. An inventory of stocks held by steel-using firms showed that, on the average, their reserves were equivalent to a little less than three months' normal supply. Acute steel shortages in Britain were confined to special types of steel, wire and strip and small billets, mainly due to the fact that before the war Britain had relied wholly on imports of these. With this improvement, could it not have been possible to abolish steel rationing altogether? That argument can best be answered by a quotation from an article in *The Financial Times,* a paper not commonly a supporter of any form of government control.

Would the large steel-consuming industries—the railways, the mines, the vehicle and shipbuilding industries—find supplies sufficient to meet the whole of their demand, if controls over distribution were removed? It is unlikely that they would. . . . Although some firms are undoubtedly getting more than their immediate requirements, the removal of these anomalies would not provide ample supplies to the main metal industries. Both the shipbuilding and the motor car industries are at the moment working well below capacity, because of the shortage.

Steel for railway coach building is also extremely short, and in the collieries the better supplies of timber now coming forward have not resulted in any reduction of the demand for steel supports and other metal products.

The answer is no. The general shortage remained. Even 15,000,000 tons of steel a year in 1948 was not enough to satisfy everyone. And that, of course, is a serious criticism of the Federation's own 1945 plan which had forecast a demand rising to only 16,000,000 tons by 1950. Even by 1948, British industry, home and export markets together, could have absorbed such a production. Sir Stafford Cripps put the level of real demand at 20,000,000 tons a year.

In the meantime, work on the reorganization of the industry along the lines of the Federation report went ahead. In April, 1947, the government gave its approval to a large redevelopment plan affecting the sections of the industry located in South Wales which were later grouped into what became the Steel Company of Wales. The plan involved the building of a three-stand, wide strip cold reduction plant and a hot-strip mill at Margam, near Port Talbot, and two additional cold mills at Swansea and Llanelly. A third cold mill was also proposed, but for the moment no decision was made. The ultimate total cost of the program was to be in the neighborhood of £50,000,000, almost one-third of the total of £168,000,000 which the steel industry had announced it would, if left to itself, spend on redevelopment in the seven years after the war.

In July, 1947, the Steel Company of Wales Limited was incorporated, with a capital of £50,000,000, £35,000,000 of which was furnished by the government-sponsored Finance Corporation for Industry, and £15,000,000 by public subscription of an issue of 3% debenture stock in multiples of £100 at par. (It was this stock that later, under the Steel Bill, the government proposed to take over at £98.18.7d. per £100.)

Plans for the future development of the industry did not cause friction, in matters of principle, between the industry and the Government. The industry, through the Federation, accepted the fact that its plans could not be its sole concern. As the Federation itself said:

It has seemed quite appropriate to the industry that any plan drawn up should be submitted to a public body for criticism, not only in regard to the programme as a whole, but in order that any individual firm who may feel aggrieved by some aspect of it should have access to a broadly based public body. This was one of the functions of the Iron and Steel Board . . .

But the Federation did not remain on the Iron and Steel Board throughout the whole period. The original members were appointed for two years from October 1, 1946. In October, 1948, the chairman and four other members of the Board declined the Minister of Supply's invitation to take office for a further period. They said:

. . . in the changed conditions likely . . . to arise from the Government's proposals for bringing sections of the iron and steel industry under public ownership, they are not willing to continue on the Board . . .

They were unwilling to linger in the vicinity of something which they regarded as a poisonfest. But it is clear enough that if the bogey of public ownership were laid, the industry would accept the kind of public control which it had experienced from the Iron and Steel Board.

The following are some of the arguments in support of nationalization:

1. The iron and steel industry is inefficient. Its plant location is seriously at fault; its equipment is uneconomic, out of balance, outdated and badly run-down. Its research work has been inadequate. It has failed to supply the right quality at the right price. It has failed to solve its labor problems.

2. The leaders of the industry have failed to learn their lessons; they cannot be trusted for the future. The recent record of steel output is only a bluff, designed to convince the man in the street that the industry is doing very well as it stands.

3. The steel workers only worked as hard as they did because they expected the industry to be nationalized not later than 1950.

4. The industry is already a monopoly in which so-called "enterprise" of the individual has long since ceased to exist. And the industry is too important to leave in private hands. Every other industry, whether nationalized like coal or transport, or privately operated like construction engineering, shipbuilding—in fact, most other trades—is too dependent on supplies of cheap steel to allow this industry to be in the hands of the few almost anonymous men who control the policy of the Federation.

5. The industry cannot raise more than half the sum needed to modernize it without government assistance. "Is it," as one socialist M.P. wrote, "the function of Government to build a brand new industry for capitalists who have failed to build one for themselves?"

Obviously some of these criticisms, true or not, have little bearing on the issue of nationalization.

Nationalization will not change plant location. Full-scale modernization needs a government subsidy, whoever runs the industry. Poor research work is not, in Britain, a fault peculiar to only one industry. This industry has been without a serious strike for longer than any other major industry. Must the fact that the workers in an industry desire its nationalization have precedence over all other considerations?

Some of the arguments on the Labour side are propaganda arguments, designed to prevent thought, not to promote it. But something remains. This is Britain's key industry, and it has a poor record for planning ahead, and for technical efficiency. Despite the fact that the number of individual shareholders may be many, it is so organized that a few men control all of it, and wield the immense influence that this control gives them.

Since 1932, the industry has been subject to some form of centralized control, control extending to all major aspects of policy. It would be impossible to abandon that amount of control, and attempt to force the constituent concerns in the industry to resume competitive trading among themselves. They do not want to do it; there is no power strong enough to compel them to do it, and it is very doubtful—if they were to return to competition—that the advantages would outweigh the disadvantages. It is technically impossible, in a country the size of Britain, to attempt to break up this monopoly and restore effective competition among every kind of equivalent works within the industry. The monopolies, tinplate in South Wales, flanged beams on the northeast coast, must remain sole producers because it would be silly to duplicate the colossal plants on which they are based. But the query still remains: Is nationalization of the industry the sole means of controlling such a monopoly? Has the government shown that it will be likely to give an alternative controlling body more intelligent direction, more virile leadership?

Again, it would be difficult to argue that a government should have no say at all in the central direction of the industry—nor does the Federation itself advance that argument. It is an industry vital to every form of industrial enterprise, and the size and cost of each modern steel plant make that plant a dominating influence in the economic lives of hundreds of thousands of people living around it. All sorts of considerations, economic, social and strategic, make government decisions over the industry inevitable today.

For example, were location of industry no more than a technical problem, certain sections of the steel industry should be taken out of South Wales altogether. The Corby area in Northamptonshire, with its new plant, its reserves of iron ore and better access both to coalfields and convenient harbors (European ore is landed on that side of Britain), is the area in which future growth should be encouraged. Yet, as the Steel Corporation of Wales shows, the government was drawn to South Wales because, rightly or wrongly, it felt this to be an area needing aid in its redevelopment for social reasons. And, had the industry been miraculously nationalized, would the decision of the Government have been any different?

It is true that it is socially less disturbing to redevelop the site that exists than to remove a modern steel plant in its entirety to a new location, even to one in which it will be more efficient. The efficiency of that plant is not the only consideration. Skilled workers must be persuaded to move, and new towns must be built for them. New industries must be sought out and their managing bodies persuaded to move into the abandoned area, if only to keep the whole social and economic life of that area from collapsing completely. The technical arguments in favor of a move may be very strong. If they do prevail, again it is impossible to leave private enterprise to solve all the problems left behind, as the people of South Wales remember bitterly to this day, when they think of that very move to Corby before the war.

Yet all these arguments skirt the main problem posed by the 1949 act. They do not answer it. Is the method of control embodied in this act likely to work well, at least as well as the Iron and Steel Board, for example, had operated?

There are two objections as yet unanswered. So far, the Government has given little evidence of capacity to formulate any clear policy for the industry. Its vacillations over the form nationalization was to take have been described, and they are no credit to any government. Regarding development, it has been content to swallow the Federation's 1945 plan almost intact. It has convinced no one within the industry that it has the capacity to handle the problems of the future. The effect of the bill itself, which from 1948 onward put every problem requiring a major policy decision into cold storage until 1950, reflects another aspect of this unwillingness or inability to think and decide. The Government's record over these four years is one of *ad hoc* decisions, of improvisations, ingenious but never impressive.

The other objection also shows lack of top-level thought. The spring that drives the man in private enterprise is the prospect of profit, some form of pecuniary gain. The spring that drives a man in public service is a sense of service coupled with a sense of power. The whole design for the operating companies, as they would function under the new Iron and Steel Corporation, eliminates both of these motives. The executive from the old era who stays on will no longer feel free to work for some personal profit, yet the organization of each company, the very fact that it is preserved in its former shape, will prevent men with the public–service type of mind from entering the industry and climbing to the top. If ever there was a case of new wine being poured into old bottles it is the steel nationalization bill.

When the terms of the bill were made public, Sir Ellis Hunter, President of the Federation, said:

> The whole structure of the Bill is such as to create controversy and conflict between the State and private enterprise over a wide area of industry without the slightest indication being given of the terms or principles on which public money and public powers would be used in this conflict.
>
> The industry has always been prepared for further constructive development of public co-operation but the Government have abandoned their own experiment of control through the Iron and Steel Board, in favour of a policy grievously prejudicial not only to iron and steel output and development, but also to the industries which iron and steel serve.

It is fair enough comment.

PART III

THE IMPACT OF SOCIALISM

CHAPTER VIII

The Ordinary People During These Five Years

In November, 1949, at a time when the fall crisis in Britain was off the boil but still simmering, a Conservative M.P., suffering perhaps from a desperate feeling of frustration, worked some of it off by writing to *The Times* as follows:

Sir—Yesterday the Archbishop of York and today the Lord Mayor of London are reported as demanding that the nation be told the bitter truth about our awful economic position. Both believe this would produce a greater willingness to work. But why should it? Why should the industrial worker believe that there is a crisis at all? He is told constantly how much better off he is than under Conservatism before the war. He knows that his average wage packet has doubled. He now gets canteen meals, holidays with pay, and works a shorter week. Unemployment which before the war was about 1,500,000 is today under 300,000. He is boss and fears nobody. In 1935 he smoked under 14 m. pounds of tobacco monthly. Today he consumes 17,500,000 lb. He drank 1,900,000 barrels of beer monthly—last August he drank 2,790,000 barrels. He has more, bigger, and brighter cinemas, theatres, dance halls, and dog tracks, and he spends ten times as much on football pools. Finally, his food rations are guaranteed.

If these are crisis conditions, he never wants to go back to pre-war prosperity. That his wife is faced with increased difficulties and has to stand in queues is immaterial. That is her look-out. If told that the value of sterling abroad has fallen, he does not comprehend. Government stocks may have dropped sharply, but he has none. The value of savings may have gone down, but he is unmoved. Nor is it the working man alone who thinks we are living in a Socialist paradise. Far too many business men have found profit earning too easy to be dissatisfied. Many whose incompetence and idleness should have put them into bankruptcy are still making fat profits and reiterate the workers' thought: "May it go on for ever."

No, Sir, telling the truth is not enough. The responsible trade union leaders—who have perhaps the most difficult task today—would confirm this. What is wanted is discipline, stern, swift, and inevitable.

And, of course, the figures in this letter are true. The rest of it? But I did not quote the letter to raise that argument at this point. I raised it as a preliminary to a deeper question: Do people live a better or worse life than before? I know such a question begs many others. Which people? What was the life that most people lived before? What is "better" or "worse"? Such questions may turn up later, occasionally bringing their answers with them.

The pattern of life for a great many people in Britain between 1945 and 1950 has been different from that which they led ten years previously. More people have a larger income and fewer people have very large incomes.

These are the figures on net income, after deduction of all state income taxes, as published by the Board of Inland Revenue.

Range of net income (In pounds per annum)	No. of individuals drawing income		
	1938–39	*1945–46*	*1947–48*
£120 to £149......................	(*not available*)		2,030,000.
£150 to £249......................	4,500,000	7,950,000	8,470,000.
£250 to £499......................	1,820,000	5,225,000	8,740,000.
£500 to £999......................	450,000	652,000	1,378,000.
£1,000 to £1,999..................	155,000	137,500	320,000.
£2,000 to £3,999..................	56,000	34,615	58,500.
£4,000 to £5,999..................	12,000	840	3,430.
Over £6,000......................	7,000	45	70.

Despite the rise in the cost of living (or the depreciation in the value of money), that is a considerable change.

In 1938, a man with an income of £10,000 a year had 43.4% of his income after paying all income taxes. In 1949, he had no more than 23.6% of his income. For a man with £1000 a year, the drop is only from 91% to 80%.

From another angle, one of the invaluable charts compiled by *The Economist* (issue of October 8, 1949) shows most clearly, in summary form, the general situation of the average man earning the average wage.

	WAGES, COST OF LIVING AND HOURS OF WORK						
	Average Weekly Earnings			*Weekly Wage Rates (All Workers)*			
Date	*Men*	*All Workers*		*Index Oct. 1938 = 100.*		*Weekly Hours Worked (All Workers)*	*Cost of Living Index, 1938 = 100.*
	s. d.	*s. d.*	*Index Oct. 1938 = 100*	*Industries corresponding to earnings.*	*All Principal Industries.*		
Oct., 1938	69.–.	53.3.	100	100	100	46.5	100
July, 1943	121.3.	93.7.	176	130	137	50.0	143*
July, 1944	124.4.	96.8.	182	136	144	48.6	146*
July, 1945	121.4.	96.1.	180	143	151	47.4	148*
Oct., 1946	120.9.	101.–.	190	158	164	46.2	—
April, 1947	123.5.	103.6.	194	161	166	45.0	—
Oct., 1947	128.1.	108.2.	203	162	171	45.2	162
April, 1948	134.– .	114.–.	214	168	175	45.3	174
Oct., 1948	137.11.	117.4.	220	172	179	45.3	175
April, 1949	139.11.	119.4.	224	173	180	45.3	176
Aug., 1949	—	—	—	—	182	—	179

*Annual Averages.

NOTE: Weekly earnings and hours worked are from special reports by the Ministry of Labour and cover a large number of manual wage earners in industry. Certain industries are excluded—notably agriculture, coal mining and dock labour. The increase in wage rates for the industries included in the enquiries is shown separately from the more comprehensive scope of the general index. The cost of living index is the index of retail prices published by the London and Cambridge Economic Service which links back to prewar the official "interim" index of retail prices.

For those who wish to pursue this matter further, three actual family budgets from this period have been placed in the appendix to this chapter at the end of the book.

It is true that people with the lowest income obtained relatively more value for the money they spent. The smaller the family income, the greater proportion of it that must be spent for the two major essentials, food and shelter. The cost of these two items has been kept down by deliberate policy. Retail food prices have been reduced by means of subsidies toward the cost of all the staples in the average diet; bread, meat, milk and vegetables. These subsidies amounted to £336,000,000 in 1946; £395,000,000 in 1947; £485,000,000 in 1948 and £484,000,000 in 1949. (In each case about 8% of the subsidy was specifically earmarked to provide "welfare" foods for mothers, children and the sick.) For the year ending March 31, 1950, the estimate of the total was £440,000,000. Their effect is estimated to be equivalent to a reduction of 12s. 6d. in the weekly expenditure on food of an average family of four. Likewise, rents of new houses are subsidized, and the rents of all houses in existence before September, 1939, are controlled at their 1939 level (in some cases at earlier levels).

That is not all. There is more certainty of work. The unemployment figure of 297,000 for 1947 is only a fifth of what it was before the war. At the same time, the whole array of social benefits under the national insurance plan has removed many of the fears formerly associated with prospects of unemployment, sickness or old age.

People are healthier, particularly children. The infant mortality rate in 1947 was 39 per 1,000, the lowest ever recorded, 2 per 1,000 below the rate in 1946, the previous low.

Equally important, the effective reproduction rate was 1,206, which means that in 1947 the births taking place were 21% above the figure required to maintain the population at its present level, higher than in any other year since 1920.

Those are some of the advantages. I know they do not provide the whole answer. There is the inevitable comment, "But what of the spirit of the people? Of what value is material security to them if, by gaining it in this way, they lose their grip on the spiritual things that determine whether a nation has the capacity to meet its fate and master it?" But let us clear our minds of humbug. It is part of the duty of the state to increase the material comfort and well-being of its inhabitants, to improve their standard of living. It is a confession of failure on the part of the state if it leaves its people degraded by unemployment, weakened by insufficient food, brutalized by bad standards of housing.

I cannot feel moved to shed many bitter tears over the fiscal fate of the very rich. They are heavily taxed. Over three-quarters of their earned income is taken away from them. The inland revenue officials pry into their private affairs and block up their avenues of escape—at least, some of them. At times, life is grim and hard—(relatively, of course)—and they miss the past.

Such a citizen's most solid complaint is over the amount spent on the various subsidies; food and housing and social insurance. These are things that he feels—not altogether correctly—are bought exclusively with his money; but even these have brought him indirect advantages in the shape of industrial peace and a reduction in the pressure for increases in wage rates.

The disadvantages for the very rich are obvious enough; too obvious, at times. It is possible to be hypnotized by the loss through taxation of 76.4% of an income of £10,000, and to ignore the fact that the remaining 23.6% amounts to over £2,000 in the year, still a figure handsomely above the average. But the very rich usually manage to find their own ways out.

If they so desire, they have their capital to spend in supplementation of their income, and a great many do. The habit and tradition of individual saving is dying. For those wealthy people who are not in business, it is impossible, on the income their possessions now produce, to maintain the standard of living to which they were accustomed before the war. So they spend capital and as a result this group of the rich is dying out—which usually means that their children more frequently have to go to work.

But most people with money are interested in some business, either one they have built up themselves or one which they have inherited from an ancestor. They have two escapes from real austerity, the expense account and the fact that capital gain is not taxed.

I doubt that even the inland revenue authorities, the tax-collectors, have really exact statistics on the amounts claimed by individuals as expenses, incurred in their businesses and thus allowable as deductions from the profits or salaries they earn. By now, under various enactments by various governments, the avenues of direct escape from tax have become almost non-existent. It is no longer possible to distribute capital among relatives, or to tie it up in private family trusts to escape tax by reducing the legal income of the principal money earner. It is no longer possible for amiable boards of directors to vote themselves large allowances for expenses out of the company's money, and to escape any inquiry from the tax authorities as to how the money is spent. But I should imagine that most men in big executive position add from £500 to £750 to their effective incomes by charging as business expenses items which the less fortunate man has to pay out of net income. The family car is owned and maintained by the business, not the household. Entertainment is business entertainment, rarely charged to the private purse. The list is long, and the ingenuity of the business man and his accountant is in constant battle with the inspector of taxes over its contents.

Then there is capital gain. After all, the distinguishing mark of the successful entrepreneur is his ability to see what investment is capable of increasing in value if properly handled. This individual is still successfully at work. He buys cheaply, he applies his talents to the project, he develops it and he expands it. He makes it capable of producing a larger annual profit and then very frequently he sells the whole undertaking to the public through an investment broker or, as it is called in Britain, an issuing house, at a price far above what he paid for it. He pays no tax on this profit. He is subject only to those controls, probably in Britain less stringent then those in the United States, which any capitalist country imposes on that kind of activity to insure a reasonable standard of honesty.

I came across a curious instance of the convolutions of this system. A man with a large income bought a country house from the executors of the former owner for £15,000, a price well below its costs of construction even before the war. It was not an easy house to market again, but after some months he was able to interest the trustees of an orphanage in buying it. He offered it to them at £20,000. He persuaded them to pay this price for it because, as an inducement, he offered them £500 a year for ten years as a contribution to the cost of its subsequent upkeep.

It sounds like an odd bargain; and so it would be were it not for the income tax laws of Britain. The orphanage, being a charity, will not pay income tax on the £500 it receives each year. So, over ten years, it will receive a full £5,000. But the man who sold the property can annually deduct the £500 he is to pay before his income tax is calculated. His payment of £500 each year will, in fact, reduce his net income by no more than £60 a year, £600 over ten years. He has made his capital gain of almost £5,000, or 33% of his outlay, indirectly at the expense of the income tax authorities, but quite legitimately.

Nor can it be argued that such socialism as the government has enacted has seriously interfered with the activities of the City of London financial markets. They remain very much as they were before the war, a vast nerve center of personal relationships, whose business ties are as close and as strong as the network of telephone lines over which most of their business is done. The network has remained intact.

The Stock Exchange remains untouched. It still functions as a privately owned and managed institution. It has reformed its constitution and given the stock brokers a larger share in its management. It may have done that to avoid a harsher scrutiny from outside. It would almost certainly have done something of the kind in any case, as a result of internal pressure. As it is, it reigns supreme over the accounts and public issues of all large companies, for no individual company dares defy it. The Stock Exchange holds one trump card. It can suspend dealings or refuse to publicly quote the shares of any company which does not conform to its rules without giving any reason for its action. No company director dares face his shareholders and tell them that their shares have, through any action of his, been deprived of quotation, and so reduced in their marketability.

In a sense, the City (to use a word which, in Britain, has come to mean the sum of the financial organizations centered in the city of London) has been besieged. Some supplies have been cut off. Certain improvisations have been necessary. But the siege has never been closely pressed and nothing but the outer fortifications have been lost. The defenders stand firm, their monetary belts drawn a bit tighter because of high taxation, their amusements curtailed because some former avenues of spending have been closed off; but they remain a compact and integrated body. A few citizens of note from their ranks have negotiated with the enemy, but they feel that no one who matters has gone completely over to the other side.

Materially, the business executive has suffered some loss of income and of freedom. Death duties have made it impossible for him to accumulate a fortune which will endow his family sufficiently for them to live in similar style. But almost by definition, the business executive is a man who—in any country still primarily capitalist—will make a good income for himself, whatever the difficulties. In this respect, Britain over this five years has been a capitalist country.

The man who does deserve sympathy is the middle-class worker. His monthly salary has not increased in proportion to the increases in weekly wages. In 1938 the total income coming into the hands of private individuals in the state was divided so that 37% went to those who were paid wages, 24% to those who were paid salaries, 2% to those in the armed forces and the balance of 37% represented interest, dividends, rents, farm earnings, professional earnings and the profits of businesses in the ownership of one man. In 1948 (the 1949 figures show little change) the proportions were: wages, 45%; salaries, 23%; armed forces, 3%; interest, etc., 29%. These figures, almost in themselves, tell the story of the middle classes. Their total incomes have not fallen. It is the proportion of the national income coming into their hands that has fallen. Their loss is relative, and that is sometimes the hardest thing to stomach.

The salaried man does not possess the capital to spend in keeping up his old way of life, or to use in operations intended to produce capital profits. The little extras that his greater income once enabled him to buy are not subsidized as are food or rents. On the contrary, their prices are inflated by a purchase tax. He lives between two worlds, without the special privileges of either.

He is still better off than the man of the working class. That is not the point. He has become relatively worse off than he was. He feels that it is part of a deliberate policy, and he resents it. And the privileges he valued most, that of owning and running an automobile, and of holidays outside his own country, were hedged around by limitations, sometimes by actual prohibition. The monthly allowance of gasoline for pleasure motoring was minute. So too was the allowance of foreign currency. And the whole of the dollar area remains barred to the pleasure traveler.

In October, 1948, a Labour party leader, Mr. Arthur Greenwood, quoted a letter he had received from such an individual, commenting on Lord Woolton's triumphant announcement at the annual conference of the Conservative Party that he had received over £1,000,000 in gifts to the party to enable it to fight the Labour Party more effectively at the election:

If you are really interested in how Lord Woolton got his million, I, who was a keen Labour supporter for many years . . . can give you one hint. I myself alone know of sums totalling almost £500, including my own donation, sent to Lord Woolton purely out of fury and hatred for a Government which demonstrably out of petty spite has robbed the middle classes of their petrol.

That letter contains the true bitterness of a minority that believes itself both despised and persecuted.

But to return to the first question: are people better or worse off?

A government has two duties to its citizens. It has an obligation to provide efficient machinery for performing those functions that its citizens have handed over to it. It has also an obligation to carry out the political and economic program which the majority of its citizens want it to follow, but—and this is a test of its fundamental decency more than of its democracy—with proper regard to the views and interests of the minority.

It is impossible to draw a clear line between these two functions. Perhaps in Britain, the government department that has least to do with politics, generally so-called, is the Post Office, but even the Post Office must make some political decisions. For instance, when it fixes the postage rates for its mails, or whether it is planned to run at a loss or a profit, or just to cover the costs of operation. Today in Britain, the Ministry of Health, because of its housing responsibilities, is most definitely a political ministry. Bricks and mortar are not political, but the number and size of houses to be built, and where and by whom, and at what prices they may be sold—if at all, or let, if at all—are all political decisions, and all matters on which Mr. Aneurin Bevan, as Minister of Health, has in these five years laid down and enforced the most definite rules, for political reasons.

The remainder of this section is about the machinery of government and government departments, particularly those portions of it overhauled and changed by the Labour Government. All this machinery is designed to help and protect the individual, and on balance it does it well. But these chapters do not fully answer the question with which this chapter began.

The substance of the letter with which this chapter started is that the average worker in Britain is living in a fool's paradise, that all he has gained since 1938, in more food, more security, more apparent control, is not so much an illusion as a temporary phenomenon which he has not earned and which therefore will pass away as the wheel spins. That, I feel, is too crude a view, and ignores the reality, for instance, of the increases in production that have in fact taken place, of the permanent changes that have been made in the balance of economic power and privilege between the classes. It ignores, too, the inherent momentum and resilience of every closely knit civilization.

None the less, this basic question cannot be answered by adding and subtracting figures, by paper rights to pensions, or holidays with pay, all the gains that gladden the heart of the trade-union official, and occupy so many columns of the speeches of cabinet ministers. A puff of the trade winds may blow a million men out of employment, a vote in the United States Congress may snip a score of points from a standard of living.

This section of the book displays, I hope, some of the factors that go into the final answer. The book as a whole will provide the data on which the reader himself can give the final answer—if he is bold enough to believe that there is a final answer to be given.

CHAPTER IX

Agriculture

Of all major industries, agriculture has undergone the greatest transformation during the last ten years. The description "Cinderella Story" is, for once, apposite; save that the Prince Charming is rather a blurred figure in the story, and some of his methods have been remarkably crude. But the Labour Government can lay no claim to being the Fairy Godmother. What it has done amounts to no more than a strenuous effort to prevent the clock from ever again striking twelve. Aided by world affairs, the clock for the farmer is certainly still some way from midnight, if in fact it is moving at all.

What does a farmer in Britain get, in terms of money, out of being a farmer? Information on the financial results of farming is hard to come by; farmers tend to talk about their losses freely enough, but keep the conversation well away from details during those times when they are doing well. But over the years, some facts have been extracted by various institutions.

It is easy enough to record the changes in the prices of farm products. The following are the average prices in Britain of certain prime commodities in 1931 and in 1947 and 1948, the low and the high of the price curve for farm products.

Commodity	\multicolumn{6}{c}{*Average price for the year*}
	\multicolumn{2}{c}{*1931*}	\multicolumn{2}{c}{*1947*}	\multicolumn{2}{c}{*1948*}
	s.	*d.*	*s.*	*d.*	*s.*	*d.*
Wheat (per cwt)	5.	9.	19	11	23	8*
Barley (per cwt)	8	10	24	1	27	7
Potatoes (per ton)	133		181	10	201	11†
Sugar beet (per ton)	42	4	111	2	108	8
Fat cattle (per live cwt)	44	11	89	11	98	8
Fat sheep (per lb. deadweight)		11	1	11	2	2
Bacon pigs (per 20 lbs deadweight)	11	3	31	10	35	1

* This price includes a government subsidy in the form of an acreage payment.
† Provisional figure

Between 1931 and 1947, the prices for home–produced cereals almost tripled, and prices for live stock more than doubled. Only potatoes showed less than a 50% rise.

These figures give one side of the farmer's finances, his receipts from sales. How did he fare on expenditures? Did his actual profit increase?

With regard to that, information is more scarce. But some figures exist. The Cambridge School of Agriculture has made various investigations into the actual budgets of forty separate farm holdings, in the east of England, with an average acreage of 134. These surveys were made both for 1931, and for 1943 when farming was at its war-time peak. The figures for the two separate years are not directly comparable because the samples do not necessarily include all the same farms, and almost certainly do not include all the same farmers. Probably too, the samples were not extensive enough to provide a true average but, taking into account all these qualifications, the figures do show the trend with reasonable accuracy.

District		Net Income per 100 acres farmed	
		1931	1943
Central Norfolk (light loam soil)		£–46	£505
North Essex		£–61	£551
South Essex	clay soils	£ 86	£448
South Cambridgeshire		£–11	£531

A detailed breakdown of the figures for 1943 is given in the appendix for this chapter, along with other tables concerned with farm income. In these figures the cost of the farmer's own time is not included as an expense, and the result is plainly shown in the fall of the profit earned per acre as the cost of hired labor per acre increases. The figures also show the relative stability in Britain of dairy farming. None the less, it is clear that in 1949, an average farmer holding some 200 acres could feed and house himself and his family, and hope at the end of the year to have made a profit of some £500. In 1931, in most districts of England his year's work would have left him poorer than when he started. It is against this background of increased financial stability that the farmer's reactions to wartime control and the postwar agricultural program must be judged.

The farmer in Britain produces for the home market. He is not an exporter. He rarely distributes his own produce. His principal requirement is stability, stability in the tenure of his land, stability in the methods by which his produce is collected and distributed, stability in the prices he receives. On occasion, a farmer may cater to a special market and so obtain a special price, as with early potatoes or the first strawberries of the summer, but the bulk of the crop and livestock produced by the average farmer is sold subject to normal conditions, at normal times of the year and in free competition with others in the same markets. Specialization is the exception.

The prewar depression in agriculture was caused by two factors: the inability of the world in general to find some method which would enable mankind to buy the total crop produced in the world; and the converse, the fact that the average consumer did not receive sufficient money to buy all the farm produce he and his family could physically have consumed. The effect of the second factor was direct; the effect of the first was indirect. The first hit the farmer in Britain in the form of the imports of foreign produce, sometimes subsidized by foreign governments, directly competitive with his own wares and made available at prices which were occasionally below his cost of production.

Mankind, at the outbreak of war, had failed to solve the first problem. In Britain, some attempts had been made to deal with foreign supplies, mainly by marketing plans and import restrictions, intended to reduce home prices and to protect the home market from external competition.

Farmers in Britain are not naturally co-operative in marketing or in any other activity concerning their trade organization. As early as 1922, a government committee, under the chairmanship of Lord Linlithgow, had reported that producer "co-operation can perform beyond dispute an undoubted and invaluable economic service." It was not until 1931 that any legislation authorizing the setting up of marketing programs was passed, and then mainly because the average farmer was looking for protection, both from foreign competition and the bargaining power created by those distributors in his trade who had organized themselves into powerful monopolies. If he could obtain sufficient protection in the form of subsidies, or by statutory limitations on supplies from abroad, he was content. He preferred to do without a marketing board.

The main Agricultural Marketing Acts were passed between 1931 and 1933. They were voluntary; it was left to the farming organizations to initiate action under them. Any group of producers could propose to the Minister of Agriculture a marketing plan for a particular farm product. Then followed various advertisements and inquiries, and a poll of all the producers of that commodity. If the plan received the approval of two-thirds—both in number and in productive capacity—of the producers voting, the minister could initiate an order making the program binding on everyone. Even then, this order required the approval of both Houses of Parliament before it came into full effect.

One act decreed that marketing plans should follow one of two alternative patterns, or a combination of both. Under one, a trading plan, the marketing board or organization set up under the scheme bought up the whole of a particular crop or product from all producers, marketed it and divided the net proceeds among the producers. Under the other type, a regulating plan, the marketing board made regulations as to the quality, grading, packaging and pricing of the commodity, which gave it as much or more power as if it had purchased the whole crop outright. Each program gave the marketing board powers which effectively prevented any producer not registering from independently trading in its commodity.

Marketing boards were boards of producers. Distributors and consumers had no direct voice in their operation, although it was customary to set up advisory councils to represent their interests. They also nominated boards, the original board being nominated by the Minister. Vacancies thereafter were generally filled by election from among the producers working with the board but, inevitably, leading figures in the agricultural organization behind the plan had the best chance of election.

The major marketing plans introduced before the war were:

Commodity	Promoters	Percentage of voters in favor	Date of introduction
Milk........	National Farmers Union.	96%	October, 1933.
Hops........	"	94%	September, 1932.
Potatoes......	"	90%	March, 1934.
Pigs..........	"	99%	
Bacon........	Bacon Section of Food Manufacturers Association.	69% (92% of productive capacity)	September, 1933.

The plans for milk and hops covered England alone. The remainder covered all of Britain.

The milk marketing program is the most significant, if only because of the importance of the commodity it handled. As its organization developed, the board purchased all milk as it left the farm, and sold it at differing prices for consumption or manufacturing. In consultation with the National Farmers Union and the retail distributing organizations, it fixed the prices of milk at the farm, and sold it to the wholesale and retail distributors. The board succeeded, between 1933 and 1938, in increasing the price received by the producer, in increasing the general consumption of milk by improving the facilities for distribution, both technical and administrative, and in improving the quality of the product by insisting on a high and universal standard of cleanliness and hygiene on each farm. In 1939, aided by government subsidy, it also sponsored the production and consumption of tubercule-free and quality milk. Production of milk rose from 1,270,000,000 imperial gallons in 1933 to 1,330,000,000 in 1938; liquid sales rose from 643,000,000 to 767,000,000 gallons and the weighted average price per gallon—taking summer and winter prices into account—from 13.99d. to 16.25d.

But the hop marketing plan is more typical of the ideas originally behind the conception of such programs. The yield of hops per acre in Britain varies considerably from year to year. Hops are grown for a single market, that of the brewer, but because the cost of hops in brewing beer represents a low proportion of the total cost of beer (about 1%), a rise in the price of hops does not reduce the demand. There were consequently wide fluctuations in price. In 1928 and 1929, the area under hops was almost 24,000 acres. The 1928 crop was 242,000 cwts. at an average price of £10.5.0. per cwt. The 1929 crop was 359,000 cwts. at an average price of only £3. 10. 0. per cwt. In other words, the total cash value of the 1928 crop was £2,600,000, and the 1929 crop (about 50% greater in weight) no more than £1,615,000. After 1932, the hops marketing plan stabilized the acreage under hops at about 18,500, and the price per cwt. at about £8. 10. 0. The board has powers to prevent any addition to the acreage planted. It used them, and was able to maintain the price at a reasonably high and remunerative level.

In addition to marketing plans along these lines, the government set up, between 1932 and 1939, certain "Commodity Commissions." The main functions of these commissions was to secure minimum prices for the commodities they governed. The minimum prices were in part maintained by government subsidies and in part by money raised through levies on importers. The commodities covered by these commissions were wheat (the Wheat Commission also administered subsidies for oats and barley), sugar (the Sugar Commission supervised a large-scale reorganization of the British sugar beet refining industry, based on a considerable government subsidy, and also fixed the price for sugar beet as between the producer and the refiner), and livestock. The Livestock Commission was made responsible both for subsidy payments to breeders of fat cattle, and supervised all branches of the trade, including slaughtering. These commissions were headed by independent chairmen, but their members were usually drawn from men with knowledge of the trade.

The general picture at the outbreak of war was a patchwork, each farmer being affected by these same governmental bodies and statutory restrictions if he produced certain commodities. For his milk and hops, he had virtually a guaranteed market, and a price that was quite adequate if he were efficient in his methods. For his livestock and various other crops, there were plans that helped him in marketing his product. Over the vast range of other possible activities, such as soft-fruit growing or poultry breeding, he stood on his own feet, unfettered and unaided. Already, however, appreciation of the successful operations of the Milk Marketing Board in particular was beginning to win over many farmers to the idea embodied in the boards.

The war changed everything very drastically indeed. The government was compelled to procure the growth of as much food as possible within Britain, and to do so it was prepared to use every variety of method, from systems of differential prices for various crops, designed to influence a farmer to produce the most needed commodity, to plain straightforward directions that such and such a field must be planted with such and such a crop. The farmer was assured of a market and guaranteed a price, provided he grew what was wanted. This was something new. Previously, a farmer had been free to make his own decisions, his own successes and mistakes, with only his creditors to account to if he finally failed. Now, the Ministry of Food said what food was needed and the Ministry of Agriculture did all it could to see that it was grown.

The Ministry of Agriculture came, bearing gifts. It supplied the farmer with machinery. It set up county pools of tractors and farm equipment. It supplied labor, in the form of prisoners-of-war. It supplied technical aids of every kind, from fertilizers to local demonstrations of the solutions to farming problems. Land drainage was tackled comprehensively. The ministry fought to keep the War Office and the Air Ministry from being too greedy about the land they needed for operations or training. But, equally, it issued orders to the farmer.

It issued them through an organization it built up during the war, the County War Emergency Agricultural Committees, one for each administrative county, and because mistakes in handling the farmer could have been most damaging to the war effort, a great deal of thought went into the constitution and methods of these committees. The ministry made certain that the men who constituted them were practical, selected from the best known of the local farmers and landowners. Their importance now is that these committees form the basis on which the Agriculture Act of 1947 has been built.

Two things stand out in sharp contrast from the wartime years. The Ministry of Food, responsible for distribution, relied almost entirely for its system of controls and allocations on the various boards and commissions, trade associations and trade groupings, that had existed before the war. It used them as its agents and guaranteed them their commissions and profits, although the circumstances which justified the payment of commissions and profits altered completely during the war. The Ministry of Agriculture was compelled to start something new. It built up this system of executive committees for the supervision of farming itself. As a result, at the end of the war, the distributive side of the industry struggled, with all the strength and persistency of a coiled spring, to return to its prewar methods and freedoms. The producing side of the industry was faced with the need to decide whether to keep this new system or return to the old limbo of the farming world. It was compelled to face an issue and decide.

This may account for the fact that whereas the Agriculture Act of 1947 deals comprehensively with most aspects of farming as a producing industry and is itself the product of a general agreement within that industry, four years went by before the Government even began to formulate a policy for the distributive side of the industry, and even then the industry had reached no agreement over the lines which any changes should follow.

The record of the Labour Government over farming is mainly an account of the Agriculture Act of 1947, the one major act of that Government which even Conservatives in the House of Lords were prepared to support.

It would be a little facile to describe the Agriculture Act of 1947 as "revolutionary." Farmers in the United States might use that word against an act which seems to subject the individual farmer to "direction" by a body of officials, an act which makes him liable to be dispossessed of his holding, whether he owns or rents it, if these officials think he has farmed badly. Yet in other parts of the world, the act would be dubbed "reactionary." Otherwise, why so much regard for the rights of a landowner, why these rules giving him rights to compensation if his tenant farms the land badly, and the right to claim increased rents for money which he spends for improving his land?

The act can more properly be called a bargain. It is the result of a long series of negotiations in which the Minister of Agriculture, the National Farmers Union, the trade unions for the agricultural workers and various individuals took part. The terms of the bargain were roughly these: the Government undertook to maintain some element of continuing stability over the quantities of commodities required from farms, and over their prices. The farming community undertook to see that the land of Britain would in the future be farmed efficiently and well, and that each acre would produce its proper share of the total required. The same bargain was repeated in another way. While he respected this obligation to farm his land well, the individual farmer, even if only a tenant of his holding, was given a much greater security of tenure than ever he had possessed previously. The whole basis of the act is the reverse of Marxism, for it strengthens the individual farmer in the possession of his land.

The first part of the act contains the first half of the bargain, providing guaranteed prices and assured markets for about 70% of the total produce of an average mixed farm. Every February—more frequently if required—the Minister of Agriculture will meet with the representatives of the farming community and work out with them what commodities the country needs and the prices they should bring. After this annual conference, each farmer knows in general terms what the demands from home markets will be and, in detail, the actual prices his cereals, fat stock, milk and eggs should command for one year ahead; and also the minimum prices, and conditions that will govern their sale, for two to four years ahead.

The information will be given as a guide. It will not dictate what each farmer will or will not produce. But it will naturally influence his decisions. The prices which the Government will fix will be adjusted to encourage production of those commodities of which there is a general shortage, and to discourage the excessive planting of those commodities threatened with a surplus. So far, vegetable produce, seeds, wool and table poultry alone are outside the scope of the act.

Part I of the act is a skeleton. It provides the machinery by which government plans for agricultural production can be carried out. It obviously does not provide the plans themselves, for these must change from year to year. But the act does guarantee that the farmer be consulted before these plans are finalized.

The second part of the act deals with good husbandry and good estate management. Section 9 imposes on the owner of agricultural land, whether he rents it or farms it himself, an obligation corresponding to that which the tenant farmer has borne since 1923. It provides that owners of agricultural land shall manage their acreage in accordance with the rules of good estate management, as well as providing that the occupants shall farm their land in accordance with the rules of good husbandry.

The rules of husbandry are detailed. There is a general provision that an occupant must maintain a reasonable standard of efficient production regarding type of produce, quality and quantity, and that he must so manage his holding that this standard can be maintained in the future. Following this are detailed rules for particular cases, including obligations to keep the land fertile and free from pest infestation, to keep stock, to preserve harvested crops, and to undertake necessary works of maintenance and repair.

The rules of good estate management are not so positively defined. The act states that an owner fulfills his responsibilities if the management of his land is adequate—in view of its character and situation—to enable a reasonably skillful farmer to maintain efficient quality and quantity production. The act does not allow a landowner to plead lack of money as an excuse for failing to do necessary work or to install necessary equipment. By implication, if he has insufficient capital to run the land well, he should sell it and hand the job over to someone else.

If owner or occupant fails in his obligations, the Ministry of Agriculture is the authority responsible for removing him. To do this, it uses the system worked out during the war, based on the County Agricultural Committees. Acting through a committee, the minister makes a "supervision" order in respect to the land badly farmed. That gives the area committee power to supervise it. If either the owner or occupant objects he can raise "representations," or objections. If the supervision order stands after a detailed investigation, the minister has the power to direct how the land shall be run, or to dispossess the occupant and, if he is also the owner, he can be compelled to sell his land to the minister. No person can be dispossessed unless he has refused to comply with a specific "direction," or been under supervision for over 12 months and has still not remedied his failings. Any person threatened with dispossession can appeal to a special tribunal, the Agricultural Land Tribunal, consisting of three members of the County Agricultural Committee with a practicing lawyer as chairman.

Part III of the act governs the relationship between owner and tenant. One purpose is to make certain that the tenant receives compensation in money for any permanent improvements he makes in the land he farms, and to give the owner a proper return, by way of increased rent, on any permanent improvements he himself makes. All these rights are set out in great detail in the act. In addition, an owner can claim damages in money from an outgoing tenant for any permanent damage caused to the land as a result of his bad farming.

It is in this part of the act that the tenant farmer is given security. Before the war, the only security a tenant farmer possessed, outside the terms of his tenancy agreement, was the fact that his landlord was compelled to pay him compensation for disturbance when he terminated the tenancy, as well as compensation for any improvements made by the tenant. By wartime regulation, a man who bought land subject to an agricultural tenancy after September 3, 1939, could not end any tenancy of that land without the consent of the Minister of Agriculture, which was not easy to obtain. Those regulations continued after the war. Under the 1947 act, any owner of agricultural land may give a termination notice to his tenant, but in every case the tenant may immediately ask that the minister's consent be obtained before the notice becomes operative. In other words, the tenant can defend himself against eviction.

The consent of the minister is not necessary when the tenant farmer has been guilty of some bad farming practice. Otherwise, it will not be given unless the owner can satisfy the minister that one of five different conditions exists, of which the two most important are that greater hardship will be inflicted on the owner by keeping him out than on the tenant by dispossessing him, or that a change of tenant is desirable from the point of view of good estate management or good husbandry.

The remaining sections of this part of the act deal with the conditions of an agriculture tenancy, rent and disputes to be settled by arbitration.

Part IV covers smallholdings, a well-established feature of British agriculture and agricultural legislation. A smallholding is one of 50 acres or less, or between 50 and 75 acres if the annual rent is not more than 150. They came into existence as a part of plans for resettling World War I veterans or, during the depression, the permanently unemployed. In each case the government gave assistance in the shape of capital and equipment. Smallholdings were by no means a complete success.

The general purpose of this part of the act is to state the conditions under which local authorities may establish smallholdings and to make certain that only men who are likely to take to farming are given a tenancy and the essential assistance with which to start.

Farming cannot be run by red tape. The men with official responsibilities, and the men given power to dispossess farmers or owners, must be men who know the job. They must have other qualities, too, but knowledge of farming is first on the list.

In this case, the war has left a good legacy behind. For six years, farmers in Britain have lived in an atmosphere which encouraged them to accept help and co-operation from officials, because those officials had real help and co-operation to offer in the shape of equipment, fertilizers, seeds and man-power from prisoners-of-war. Farmer and official learned by practical experience how to work together.

The central cog in this administrative machine remains the County Agricultural Executive Committee, a separate one for each administrative county, each consisting of twelve members. Of the twelve members, five are nominated directly by the central government, and the other seven are selected by the Minister of Agriculture from panels of names submitted by the organizations representing farmers, owners and farm workers in each county. Each member will hold office for three years and one-third of the committee will retire each year. Of those directly appointed, each will have some special qualification; for example, one may be a local government councillor, another a scientific expert of some kind.

Here is a profile of the twelve members of one County Committee. Of these twelve men, six are working farmers, three are landowners in the area, one is chairman of the local branch of the National Farmers Union, another is an official of the Transport and General Workers Union in charge of an area containing 78,000 members, and the last is a surveyor whose professional practice is mainly concerned with agricultural properties. Six of the twelve are members of some local authority within the area.

The chairman is a farmer, aged 64. He farms in partnership a comparatively small farm of 93½ acres, mostly arable, which has a herd of 60 pigs as its main livestock, and 20 bullocks. He also has an interest in a semi-truck gardening holding of 230 acres in another part of the county. The remaining farmers have varied holdings. One, aged 58, is the son of a farmer who failed to survive the depression and wet summer of 1903. At thirteen, he went to work, lived with a farmer as part of the family and saved enough to buy a 70-acre farm of his own just before the first world war. He still farms that land (he has increased the holding to 175 acres) as a dairy farmer with a herd of 50–60 dairy cows giving an average daily yield of 100–120 gallons. He is chairman of the development committee of his local authority.

The farmer with the largest holding farms in partnership six farms totaling 2,370 acres. The farming is principally arable, the main crops being potatoes, sugar beet, grain, peas and roots. The livestock comprises about 500 pigs, 1,000 sheep (400 breeding ewes) and 130 head of fattening and store cattle. He has devised a practical method for weed disinfestation, later adopted by the ministry. The acreage farmed by the remainder ranges from 1,101 acres down to 365, from truck gardening to general mixed farms.

The landowners are all men who have experience in public affairs, mainly local. One, however, was a member of the Wheat Commission. The National Farmers Union chairman has been a member of that group for nineteen years, the trade unionist an official of his union for even longer. At 36 the surveyor is the youngest member. He had a distinguished war record, mainly in the Middle East, and now commands a local artillery regiment of the Territorial Army. All of them, of course, are part-time members of the committee; that is the rule for each committee.

These men are the judges and the jury of their fellow farmers in a county of an area of 722,209 acres, of which 696,955 are under crops or grass and 25,254 are rough grazing; in which there are 8,617 separate holdings, 2,600 of them under five acres in extent.

I will not attempt to describe in detail here the government's policy for what is produced by the farmer. The objective pursued is simple; it is to obtain from the soil of Britain more of the crops and commodities that are now imported from other countries, particularly those which need dollars for their purchase. The instrument used to obtain that objective is money, money used either to provide a guaranteed price for certain produce or used in the form of subsidies. Each subsidy may either be paid directly to the farmer, such as a payment of a fixed sum for each acre that he plants with a particular crop, or indirectly, such as a payment to a particular trade to enable the farmer to buy a commodity he needs below the normal price. What crops are encouraged, and to what extent, is obviously a changing business, governed by world prices and supplies, and by weather and home conditions. That involves a yearly plan which must be recast each spring.

The Agriculture Act of 1947 is a piece of legislation designed to provide a stable background against which all this can take place. The assistant secretary of the National Farmers Union summed up the official farm view of the act in an article that he wrote in 1947, shortly after the passage of the act:

It is very largely a non-controversial piece of legislation and does rectify a number of problems left outstanding by the 1923 Act. But . . . two conclusions stand out clearly from the new Act. First, the State is in the farming and management of land for good or ill. Secondly, the Act does not, and cannot, provide a policy for British agriculture. It merely provides the necessary machinery for implementing a policy which must, if the Act is to work, command the confidence and support of all concerned in the industry, whether practically or professionally, both in times of shortage and of plenty.

The remarkable thing about the agriculture acts of 1947 and 1948, and the policy of which they form the statutory expression, is that there is nothing socialistic about either. The government's policy proceeded on the assumption that if it were possible to make farming a secure and profitable industry, increased efficiency and a greater total output would automatically follow. That may prove to be true. Equally, it is unlikely to prove to be the end of the argument. Farming has been given a charter. That charter itself may turn out to be too rigid for an industry which must change as it develops, just as its own products change as they develop.

I do not feel competent to judge between the differing points of view. If greater production is needed from the land of Britain, is the farmer to be cajoled, is he to be left alone inside a fenced ring, or is he to be chased around with a big stick? Here are extracts from two letters to the *Times,* both from farmers—neither, I should guess, socialists—the first in November, 1949, the second in January, 1950:

. . . the Agriculture Act of 1947 . . . ossified the farming industry, giving complete security to bad farmers and preventing new blood from entering the industry. At the same time, by an expensive policy of palliatives, it has put a premium on lack of initiative and enterprise and . . . has removed the essential incentives to hard work, efficiency and investment.

The Agriculture Act, 1947, and the Agricultural Holdings Act, 1948, extend virtual security of tenure for life to tenant farmers. This privilege was presumably granted because the tenant farmer is a valuable component of our farming system. The ironic fact [is] that these Acts in practice menace the whole conception of tenant farming. . . . The main danger lies in the following trends:—1. Where tenancies have fallen vacant, nowadays a rare event, landlords tend to take the farms into their own management rather than lose control of their land again for an unknown period by granting a new tenancy. 2. Tenant farmers tend only to relinquish their statutory right to possession if they are given as consideration a lump-sum payment amounting to as much as 14 years' rent. This money, however, is not easily found by a young man anxious to farm as a tenant. He should, moreover, invest what he has in stock and machinery and not in subsidising the comfortable old age of a retiring farmer whose landlord is willing to let the young man in. If the vacating tenant has been a good farmer he has no need of a present of 14 years' rent at the end of the day; if he has been a bad one he does not deserve it. To obtain the tenancy of a farm is these days almost impossible. . . .

CHAPTER X

Food and Rationing

I suppose the commonest questions over food are:

1. Is Britain worse fed than before the war?
2. Is rationing necessary?
3. How is it operated?
4. Is state control over food in Britain there to stay?
5. Does the system work well or not?
6. How does the ordinary housewife manage?

And I think it easiest to answer them as specific questions.

1. Britain is better fed than before the war, in the sense that more food is eaten and most families have more to eat. What really governs the consumption of food is not the amount that a man can eat, but the amount that he can afford to eat.

In 1931, there were 2,707,000 unemployed in Britain, nearly a quarter of the working population, almost all living on a weekly un-employment benefit. In consequence, their food consumption was arbitrarily limited by their lack of money. For the whole period from 1945 to 1950 well over a million more people were at work than in 1939 and, in consequence, a million people were buying more food. The food is still there for them to buy.

A very great proportion of the small income is spent on food—in fact, the smaller the income the greater the proportion spent on food, for food is always priority number one. When a man's weekly wage rises from bare subsistence level to no more than five pounds, most of the increase is spent on food.

Perhaps the fairest generalization to make is this: More people in Britain are eating food in greater quantities than they did before the war. For the small income family, the variety in diet is about the

166

same. A smaller number of people in Britain are eating about the same quantity of food, but of a more restricted variety than they once enjoyed. A very few people are eating less food. Egalitarianism is at its most pronounced over food.

In the appendix for this chapter are tables of basic weekly rations and a detailed discussion of the increases and decreases of food consumption in Britain.

The most noticeable thing about today's situation in Britain is not the reduction in the volume of food available but the vast change in the balance of the varieties available. A great deal more starch is eaten, and a great deal less protein. The people most irked by the situation are those who could afford variety before the war and who could still afford it now if variety were available.

2. Is rationing essential?

There are various answers to this.

The basic idea behind rationing is that when supplies are short, available amounts should be shared equally. If this idea is accepted, the rationing of those commodities which are very short (e.g. butter) is essential, provided it is possible.

There are definite limits to the effective rationing of food, because there are limits to the self-discipline which human beings will impose on themselves, and there are limits to the capacity to enforce regulations. Under existing regulations a pig-breeder in Britain may kill one pig per year for his own consumption, and even then he needs a license from his local authority to do so legally. I would not like to guess at how many pigs are killed without a license.

The reasons why rationing could not be extended to every commodity in short supply are best given by the Ministry of Food itself, in its explanation of why home-produced fruits and vegetables were never rationed and why, over these, even price control was abandoned. As set out in a ministry publication the reasons were:

(a) Price control levels out prices, but always at their highest permitted level.
(b) The consumer pays the same price for good and bad quality.
(c) Distributive movement is restricted.
(d) Price control encourages dishonesty.
(e) It also deters imports, particularly of perishable goods.

(f) Home growers have no incentive to select and grade their produce nor to improve cultivation.

(g) Consumers gain no benefit when there is a seasonal glut.

(h) Demand is always artificially restricted by the high price and as a result there are large unmarketable surpluses.

Some of these arguments—or, rather, statements of fact—apply to other commodities as well. How, then, has the ministry been able to make any rationing system possible?

It is possible in Britain because the bulk of rationed commodities in really short supply are imported, and importation gives the government unrivaled physical control of supplies. The Ministry of Food controls the purchase, the shipment and the distribution. This has two effects. It ensures a minimum distribution everywhere. It also gives the ministry a really effective weapon against any retailer who breaks the rationing laws; it can withhold from him a big enough proportion of his supplies to damage his business, and that sanction is infinitely more potent than any criminal proceeding would be.

Rationing necessitates bulk-buying overseas by the state and a strict regime at home if it is to be at all effective in operation. The majority of people in Britain would, I think, say that it has been worth it.

Sometimes other considerations affect rationing; the rationing of bread in the summer of 1947 is an example. Bread rationing was imposed on the insistence of Mr. Ernest Bevin and rather against the inclinations of Mr. Strachey, the Food Minister. Mr. Bevin mistrusted the capacity of the French authorities to collect and control the 1947 French wheat harvest. The strength of the French black market was such that Mr. Bevin feared that the amount of wheat from any year's harvest actually passing under the control of the French authorities would be disappointingly small. He thought that Britain should install, and keep in existence, a system of rationing which might ultimately be of service in helping the French government in its task of keeping the French people supplied with reasonably priced bread. Only in 1948, when the declared French harvest of wheat was well above the previous year's declared crop, did Mr.

Bevin believe that the undeclared part of the harvest was sufficient to keep the farmer happy.

Similarly with Germany. There the wheat available for the normal market in 1947 looked as if it would be below the essential minimum. Again, it was essential for Britain to have the means of supporting the German authorities in their task of feeding the population. Mr. Ernest Bevin was proved right by events.

The Opposition was perfectly right when it said, during most of 1948, that by and large bread rationing was not operative. It was not essential in most cases to surrender a bread coupon to buy a loaf, nor did the Ministry of Food carry out anything like a complete check of the bread units surrendered in retail shops. On the other hand, in Britain the very existence of a rationing system does operate as a check on waste. Inhabitants of other countries may not believe this, but it is true. And, paradoxically enough, this elimination of waste was the one factor which made airtight bread rationing unnecessary. Assuming that the waste of bread did not increase beyond that low level, Britain could—on existing stocks and future prospects of wheat supplies—have abandoned bread rationing much earlier than she did.

To be frank, the average inhabitant of this country would have been human enough to resent putting up with controls simply for the sake of foreigners, had it been put to him as bluntly as that. Hence the vagueness of the government when pressed to abandon bread rationing earlier than it did. But those were considerations that no government could have afforded to ignore.

3. How is the system operated?

A ration book is issued once a year. The ration book works two ways. With most commodities, the holder of a ration book registers with a particular supplier and obtains all of that commodity from the one store. (There are various administrative devices to cover temporary absences from the neighborhood.) In this way, supplies to each establishment can be regulated by the number of ration-book holders registered with that store. The store is responsible for the fair allocation of the supplies it receives.

A few articles, such as soap, are available in fixed quantities each month to each holder of a ration book, but the buyer is free to purchase in any shop. This, of course, is only possible with nonperishable articles, where it is not necessary to closely regulate the supplies going to each outlet.

Until 1950, there was also a "points" system in operation. The ration book contained a fixed number of "points" coupons, 24 for each rationing period of four weeks. These coupons were a kind of currency. Certain kinds of food in short supply, but not absolutely essential, were "placed on points," which meant that points must be given for them, but the housewife could vary her purchases. The number of points to be surrendered to buy any one food was fixed by regulation, and the rate could be changed at the end of any four-week period. The customer had both freedom to decide how to spend the points and freedom to spend them in any shop. They were almost as flexible as money, except that they were not transferable.

The articles on points are such things as breakfast cereals, cookies (because of their fat content) and most canned goods, from grapefruit to canned salmon (because they are imported).

In order to work well, the points system depends upon a reasonable supply of all these articles. It is exasperating to be given points to spend on individual preferences, only to find shortages prevent exercising the preference. Another objection to points is that they create a feeling of frustration. For example, to see a can of boned turkey in a store is encouraging, but not so encouraging when the point value is 48, which means that an individual could buy a can of turkey once every eight weeks—and he could afford nothing else on points in the same period.

The main advantage of the system is that it makes scarce supplies go further, and discourages the storekeeper from showing favoritism by keeping all the attractive scarcities for his best customers.

4.   Has state control over food in Britain come to stay?

I think the answer to this must be "yes," in respect to some commodities. I have given the arguments for rationing in time of shortage. I think these arguments hold good for the majority of people and no party would risk abandoning them entirely.

Another important factor is the absolute need for Britain to buy more of her imported food outside the hard currency area, a state of affairs likely to last for some time. In 1938, 40% of Britain's food came from the sterling area, 33% from Europe and "soft" currency areas and 27% from Canada, the United States, Argentina—hard currency areas. The war reversed that pattern, and even as late as 1947 the figures were still 35%, 18% and 47% respectively. But the following year, the figures were much closer to the prewar pattern: 46%, 29% and 25%. That process continues as Europe's production rises again. In 1949, supplies of butter from Denmark were double the 1948 figure, of bacon more than two-and-a-half times that figure. Poland, too, is supplying more bacon, and has become Britain's second largest supplier. On the other hand, imports of bacon from Canada fell from over 100,000 tons to below 20,000 tons.

It is for reasons of currency problems that Britain is not free to allow her merchants to buy anywhere in the world, and that fact alone makes a policy of bulk-purchasing an attractive one to a government. Such a policy can also be defended on the ground that it increases the stability of the producer's position. It has its dangers when it results in a tendency, on the part of the government buyer, to try to control the distribution of what he buys.

Yet the area over which this government control extends must shrink, if only because government control is associated with ideas of shortage, and is unpopular on that account. Any government would feel that it could gain more political advantage by relaxing control than by extending it. It is significant that the tempo of release from controls in Britain quickened in the six months before the 1950 election. Equally, there are definite practical limits to the capacity of a democratic regime to enforce regulations on such a necessity as food in times of peace.

None the less, the British system has proved to be reasonably workable and flexible. It has had nearly ten years of operation. Mistakes have been made and lessons have been learned. Some activities provoked that final excuse, "Oh, well, it does do its job reasonably well!" While the job has to be done—by which I mean while the public accepts the fact—people will accept such a system at least as a tolerable instrument.

5. Does the system work well or not?

Most of this question has already been answered.

One important advantage obtained from the system is the administrative power it gives to a government to make certain that "welfare" foods are available for those who need them, available both in quantity and price. It is these welfare foods that have played such a big part in the improvement of general health, particularly among children.

Welfare foods are those vital nutritional elements needed by children and expectant and nursing mothers. Both expectant and nursing mothers need, and get, additional supplies of milk and fruit juices at below cost price. In addition, for example, a child under five is entitled to an extra packet of dried eggs every eight weeks. The ration book is now an essential part of the machinery by which these additional supplies are allocated and distributed. Indeed, if any system involving welfare foods were to continue, some equivalent of the ration book would be needed.

All this is machinery, routine, and any government department ought to be able to devise and operate a system of this kind. Judged on that level, the Ministry of Food emerges well enough. It has managed to find enough food to feed Britain. It has had good advice, which it has usually taken. Whether it could have operated more efficiently or not, no one can say for certain at this stage. As a distributive machine, it has given rise to few complaints of inequality in allocation. As an administrative machine, it started in 1939 with an excellent system, and the various ministers have had sense enough to continue it virtually unchanged.

There are two complaints that can legitimately be made against the ministry. Lack of frankness is one. Its record over the groundnut plan in East Africa is described elsewhere, but that has not been the only occasion on which the Minister of Food has used the argument of "public policy" to avoid giving any publicity to his mistakes as a buyer. And who would assume that any minister could avoid making some mistakes? Lack of political courage is another complaint. Throughout the five years, the ministry did maintain its regulation providing that not more than five shillings can be charged for any meal served in a restaurant. The regulation, of course, has not prevented the restaurateur from collecting more than five shillings per head for the meals he has served, nor the public from paying more.

Again, the Ministry has shirked its opportunity to improve the efficiency of the food distribution systems in Britain. Five years after the end of the war, it is still paying wholesalers commissions for handling food which they can buy only from one source and can sell only to fixed recipients, and that simply because they were in that business before the war. It has not restored freedom to trade, nor has it eliminated those who serve no useful function in trade. It has been a vast protective cloak for efficiency and inefficiency alike.

The difficulties in the way of price control over the retail sale of perishable fruit, for example, is a short summary of the ministry's own experiences. Having failed in one way to secure its ends—a full distribution of fresh fruit and vegetables for sale at prices fair to both grower and consumer—the ministry lost heart and made little further effort. These marketing problems are in the border area between the ministries of Food and Agriculture, and both have sidestepped effective action.

And, being a ministry, it has spewed out forms. The owner of a solitary pig will have to fill out some ten different forms in connection with the life and death of that animal. Need one say more?

6.   How does the ordinary housewife manage?

A working-class family of four or more, living in a heavy industrial area, fares comparatively well. Four ration books will buy a reasonable quantity and variety. The man probably has a midday hot meal in his factory canteen five days a week. The children get hot midday meals, and milk, at school. These meals are "off the ration"; that is, no deduction is made for them from ration books. The housewife probably deals at the same store for most of her supplies. She knows the manager and the assistants. Her worst ordeal will be having to queue when buying fish and fresh vegetables, because the supplies come in daily and at the same time, and every housewife turns up for them at once. There are also queues for fancy cakes, because the demand for these usually exceeds supply. Still, some housewives like queues. At least in that way they are certain of an audience.

The most unfortunate person is the single white-collar girl living in her own apartment. One ration will not buy enough food in sufficient variety for every meal in her own home. It is unlikely that there will be an office canteen, so, for her midday meal she will have to eat poorly and expensively in a cafeteria. She can only shop on Saturdays, when the best has already gone to the housewife. Rationing to her is a nightmare.

There are local variations. Food is more plentiful in Scotland, and more varied in the coal-mining areas. Some ports get extra supplies of imported fruit because a particular cargo may not be sufficient for wide distribution. On the other hand, the agricultural worker is often worse off because he cannot grow meat, and he has no canteen facilities for a hot midday meal off the ration.

The housewife's worst enemy is monotony in diet. In this respect, many housewives are their enemy's best ally.

Planning and Housing

The *Saturday Evening Post* for August 21, 1948, contained an article, "Rumpled Angel of the Slums," on Father Carmelo Tranchese, a member of the Society of Jesus and a parish priest in the slum area of San Antonio, Texas. When Father Tranchese first went to his parish in 1932, 12,000 people were crowded into one square mile of dilapidated, ill-planned buildings lacking most of the amenities of civilized life.

In 1933, Father Tranchese determined to procure a public housing project for his parishioners and was successful in obtaining the President's signature approving a $4,000,000 project. But the very idea of this proposal brought down on his head a virulent campaign of opposition from the property owners. They were threatened with the loss of income from the slum properties and, not unnaturally, the men drawing such dividends wanted desperately to preserve their status quo. Yet the local housing authority managed to obtain 30 acres of the worst slums on which the owners had set a price of $1,200,000. Nathan Straus, head of the National Housing Authority, canceled the deal in disgust, but Father Tranchese, by means of a personal appeal to Mrs. Eleanor Roosevelt, eventually secured the sum of $12,000,000 on behalf of San Antonio's blighted area. Today more than 1,000 new units have replaced the slums.

Slums comparable to those in San Antonio must exist all over the world. They certainly still exist in some parts of England and Scotland. But this method of getting rid of them does not seem entirely satisfactory. Not every President has a wife like Mrs. Roosevelt; not every appeal by a parish priest is answered. Nor are there enough Father TMBancheses to go around.

In Britain, housing, town planning and public health—all the public responsibilities involved in the story of Father Tranchese

—are completely interwoven. The first town planning legislation was part of a housing act; so onward until, in 1949, a housing act declared that the provision of housing for every class of the community was a public responsibility. These subjects must be considered together and, since the planning of an area should proceed construction, let planning come first.

Town and country planning stems from three distinct sets of social ideas. The first and oldest is that any community is entitled to insist that its people are guarded against avoidable ill-health. Prior to 1840, mankind was not persuaded that bad sanitation, impure water and sunless houses were in themselves causes of a high death rate. Housing was a matter of crude economics, and failure to build the cheapest kind of house for the lowest paid class of worker was economic suicide for the man undertaking it. As a result, this was the kind of house built in the new industrial centers of Britain. The results can still be seen in some sections of London and Birmingham and Manchester.

In the end, the doctors found the causes of cholera and typhus epidemics in the cities. The engineers, particularly the hydraulic engineers, applied this information in new construction. The doctor and the engineer worked hand in hand, and as a result the Englishman, when he came to build a new house, found that he had lost one freedom—he had to provide water and a water closet. It took almost forty years of combat before Parliament ordered that all town landlords must install such conveniences in existing houses. The landmarks of the period are the Public Health Acts of 1848 and 1875.

The impulse that had brought improvements in sanitation for the individual house continued in a broader channel. Parliament had already decided that no more unsanitary houses should be built. It followed this with the Housing for the Working Classes Act, 1890, which attempted, gradually—too gradually many thought—to tear down the worst of the existing unsanitary and overcrowded houses. Some cities, Birmingham for example, had already displayed considerable local initiative in clearing bad areas with their own local resources. Others were less energetic. The culmination of this process was the Housing Act, 1936; but throughout the two decades between wars the tempo of the improvement accelerated. Local authorities were given power to acquire, by right of eminent domain, the sites of their worst slums. Payment to the owner of an unsanitary house was based on the commercial value of the cleared site. They were given specific housing subsidies, based on the number of families that they rehoused. And, in the process of destroying the worst of the old slums, the local authorities could hardly have avoided replacing them by apartment houses and cottages that were infinitely better in design, plan and convenience.

To this story, the Labour Government has added one more chapter, the Housing Act, 1949, a chapter completely in line with the earlier tradition. The 1949 act had two objects. The first was to remove from the Housing Act of 1936 the requirement that a local housing authority was only concerned with housing for the "working classes." Since the passing of the 1949 Act, a housing authority must, in making its plans, take into account "the housing conditions and the housing needs of all members of the community." Its second object was to provide means and inducements sufficient to bring the old, oversize town houses back into effective use. These structures, built for a generation that relied on an unlimited supply of domestic labor, are useless as houses today unless their internal arrangements are radically changed; left to normal economic forces, they degenerate into dingy lodging and apartment houses. This act enables a local authority to make improvement grants to private owners of such houses, the only string attached to the grant being an obligation to accept, for twenty years, control over the rents that may be charged.

The next strand in the completed fabric comes from a very different source, a book first published in the United States. Today, Bellamy's *Looking Backward* is a work of fiction which has the nightmarish quality of a vision of egalitarian robot life. But Bellamy's book struck sharply into the imagination of a London shorthand writer named Ebenezer Howard, one of those curious individuals who like to develop working models. Howard was seized with the idea of inventing a completely new town. He had spent some years in the United States, where the idea of inventing new towns was not so revolutionary as it was in Britain. He felt compelled to plan the new town as a working model, even to the extent of finding out how it could pay for itself. In 1898, he published the result of his researches, a book called *Garden Cities of To-day*.

Howard faced up to the main problems of town development. Ideally, any town should be a nicely adjusted mixture of houses, factories, shops and open spaces. But the experience of existing towns showed that it was nothing of the kind. It was just a confused jumble. Areas in which people tended to herd together, as in shopping centers and factories, were always to be found in the middle of the town; the open spaces inevitably seemed to be pushed farther and farther towards the perimeter. Yet there was a lot to be said for having most of the factories on the perimeter and at least some of the open spaces in the middle.

The superficial explanation for the present situation is that land at the center of a town is always more valuable than land on its outskirts. Therefore, it is more profitable to build the big shops and factories near the center. But, said Howard, that may be true of an existing town. Need it be true of a new town? Suppose the builder were to buy all the land—undeveloped land needed—for the entire site of his town, in one operation? Each acre of it would, for him, have no more value than any other acre. Therefore, he could afford to place his open spaces wherever they were most convenient. What gives value to land in a town is the way it is used, and the number of people who use it. If the one authority controls the growth of the town, it can not only control where every activity is carried on, but control as well every change in land values within the same area. It is the activity that creates the value, not the value that creates the activity.

Howard created two new towns in Britain, Letchworth and Welwyn Garden City. Letchworth was started in 1905, Welwyn Garden City in 1920. The layout of each is a balance of open space, industrial area, shopping center and housing. Letchworth has a population of just over 20,000, Welwyn Garden City of 18,000. Letchworth had the more shaky start. It was difficult, in 1905, to persuade the established British industrialist to set up plant and equipment on a site which was, after all, only an experiment based on the dream of a shorthand writer. It was so much easier to build the factory where the working population already existed, rather than rely upon the factory to attract a new working population to it. But both experiments succeeded; in both cases it was American capital which did a great deal to help, for an American concern establishing a factory in Britain had no local associations to pull it towards one existing locality or another. (For example, an important factory in Letchworth is the Irvine Parachute concern, in Welwyn a United States grinding wheel company.)

The cardinal feature of Howard's plan remains. In each townsite 5,000 acres of land was purchased by a single company. Each company owned the land and rented it on generally long lease. Each company was a commercial enterprise, in the sense that its stockholders expected to derive commercial and expanding revenues from the total area they owned. But to them, financially, it was a matter of indifference which acre produced the greater earnings. They could, therefore, permit the layout of the whole town to be governed by financial considerations not based on individual sites.

The importance of the Letchworth experiment lay in the fact that because it was new, because it was an experiment, it gave architects a chance to plan a town as a whole. There was a stimulus in being able to decide where the schools, the factories, the open spaces should be, in being unfettered by existing vested interests and objections. Letchworth was not only a financial experiment, it was also an aesthetic experiment. As the town gradually grew and paper plans became bricks and mortar, it provided an example of what an industrial town could be made to look like. Here was a town in which a great many people found it pleasant to live. It is significant that the first town planning act in Britain was passed in 1909.

The town planning legislation of 1909 was almost a postscript to a housing act. It was voluntary, not compulsory. It was negative in its effect; a local authority could only say "yes" or "no" to the ideas of others, and it was rigid in conception. But it was a new departure. It gave the local authorities of towns the power to "zone" undeveloped land in the immediate vicinity, to say that certain activities should not be carried on in certain areas. It meant that the power of the local authority did not stop short of control over each individual building. It extended that power over related groups of buildings. Gradually, in 1919, 1923, and 1932, the scope of the town-planning acts was extended, and planning for the larger towns became compulsory. But it was not until 1943 that the duty to make a development plan for its own area was imposed upon every local authority in Britain, and so upon every acre of soil.

The 1943 act could hardly escape being, for the moment, a dead letter, for the only actual building undertaken during the war was for war purposes and such buildings were expressly—and inevitably —exempted from peacetime planning regulation. In 1944, another planning act was passed, with the important innovation that Parliament provided a subsidy from public money, for the first time, toward the cost of replanning and rebuilding a whole section of a town. That was the state of planning when the Labour Government came into office.

The third strand in the final fabric again is woven from practical considerations and requirements. Since employment determines not only where people live but also how they live, you are inevitably drawn into consideration of the place in which they live once you begin to concern yourself in people's employment. In 1930, for example, the pressure that compelled anyone to start some positive action on this problem was the spectacle of thousands of men and women out of work, the cost of keeping them alive in idleness, and the political consequences that would follow from their inevitable revolt against a system that imposed this fate upon them.

The positive action, at the start, was individual and individualistic. One of the towns most badly hit by the 1930 slump was Jarrow, a shipbuilding town in the north of England. It was "adopted" by a wealthy individual, an M.P., Sir John Jarvis. He endeavored to organize alternative sources of work for a town in which 80% of the working population could find no employment. One man cannot move economic mountains, but these pioneer efforts were followed by government action.

An act, called the Special Areas Act, was passed in 1934. The "Special Areas" were four in central Scotland, South Wales, West Cumberland and the northeast coast, in which unemployment was particularly high. These areas had a total population of about 4,000,000 people, and in 1932, 820,000 of them, 38% of their insured population, were out of work, as compared with 19% for the rest of Britain.

They were out of work because heavy industries, coal mining, steel manufacture and shipbuilding were concentrated in these areas. In these "Special Areas," 50% of the insured workers were engaged in those industries, and the slump in world trade had reduced demand for their products more heavily than for those of any other industry. The consequences affected the entire area. The level of spending fell and everyone suffered, at least to the extent of being under-employed even if the job remained nominally open.

There were two simple answers to that state of affairs. One was to move the people out; the other was to move new, more prosperous industries in. The first had its disadvantages. The British family is not mobile as a family, because it values its home and it is never easy to move a whole family, dependents included, all at once. What happened was that younger and more active individuals did set out for other parts of the country, mainly to Southeast England. No exact figures are available but between 1921 and 1937 over half a million people moved into the Greater London area alone, and between 1931 and 1939, 160,000 migrated from South Wales and 130,000 from the Northeastern counties. In any case, organized migration in the thirties would have had most unfortunate consequences, for in 1939 the heavy industries were needed again, and they were in the areas least vulnerable to attack by aircraft. If twice as many people had been moved out in 1934, twice as many would have had to be moved back in 1940.

The organizations set up under the Special Areas Act started, tentatively enough, in 1934 to influence industrialists to establish branch factories or, better still, to move their whole undertakings, lock, stock and barrel, into these areas of high unemployment. Only persuasion and a series of minor inducements were used, in part financial, in part by the provision of new factories and services readied by government organizations. The most noticeable decision taken was that to organize government trading estates. These were areas in which a government agency built and provided factories, roads, power and transport facilities, almost all the capital equipment needed to start a new factory. Individual factories were then leased to individual undertakings, and the labor they needed was ready and waiting to work. By 1939, some 12,000 people were employed in these factories; many more were working on the construction of new ones.

The war restored the fortunes of the special areas. Even by 1939, 150,000 more people were working there than had been at work in 1937. Employment rose, but obviously, the wartime expansion of these industries could only be temporary. What would happen after May, 1945?

It is a complicated picture, when one recapitulates. The drive behind physical planning comes from the demands of the public health expert that houses have sunlight and sanitation, and that there be facilities for recreation near at hand. It comes from the demands of the ordinary man for precisely the same things, because that is how he wants his family to live. Coupled with these are the problems of industry and of strategy, of what can be described as the effects of history and geography on the individual's chances of work.

The first set of considerations is met by the housing and the planning acts, the second by postwar legislation dealing with the special areas and the new towns.

So far as the planning of the future layout of towns and country areas is concerned, the Labour Government's Town and Country Planning Act of 1947 is no more than an extension of the earlier planning legislation. Its revolutionary contents—and they are revolutionary in the true sense of the word—are those in which it tackles the problem of the cost of land.

It is not easy to compress into a few words a description of the problem and of its solution under the terms of this Act. It springs from the fact that English law considers an owner of land to have the right to do what he likes with it, and if his rights are in any way abridged, he must be compensated for his loss.

Imagine a town, surrounded by 10,000 acres of land suitable for building, which in the past has grown at the rate of 100 acres a year. If the growth of that town is to be controlled, the local authority must in effect be able to decide which 100 acres shall be built on in each year, and therefore which of the remaining 9,900 acres shall not be built on. But, under the former law, the owner of every acre on which building was prohibited or deferred would be entitled to immediate compensation for the loss of his right to build at once, although in fact he had lost no more than 1/100 of a chance that his 100 acres would be the next to be bought by a builder. In other words, to plan a town in detail, its council was faced with the prospect of compensating, at once, the owner of every building plot within possible building distance of the edge of existing built-up areas. And for that, before 1944, the central government offered no financial assistance for planning as such.

The cost was prohibitive, and planning on this scale was thus out of the question. The 1947 act starts on the assumption that land, as such, has two commercial values; its value while it continues to be used for its existing purpose, and its value if and when used for another purpose. Commonly, the second is greater than the first. For example, land near a town used for agriculture may be worth £150 an acre. When used for building, it may be worth £300 an acre. The 1947 act does not interfere with a man's rights to sell his land freely for its existing use. It takes away from him his right to get a higher price because his land has a potentially different use. Before anyone may change the use made of his land, that is, develop it, he must pay the state a development charge equal to the difference between its value when developed and its value when used as before. If there is no change in value, there is no development charge to pay.

To meet the claims for monetary loss faced by those people who already own land which has an appreciable additional development value, the act sets up a fund of £300,000,000 out of which all their claims are ultimately to be settled. But first those claims have to be calculated and assessed. In the meantime, the development charge provisions are in force.

The second main object of the act was to secure control over the future development of Britain. That is done by the direct method of requiring any owner of land who desires to change its use to obtain the consent of the local authority before he does so.

Certain "common-form" changes can be carried out without the need for such consent—changes not involving an increase in size by more than 10%, for example, or changes in agricultural land for agricultural purposes—but the conversion of a single house into one or more separate apartments does require approval.

Incidentally, anyone in Britain who desires to build his own house today must first:

1) Get his plans approved by the local authority on two counts; one, as to the kind of house construction and layout he intends to employ; second, as to the kind of building to be allowed on the particular plot of land he owns.

2) Get his "development charge" fixed and paid.
3) Get permission to employ materials and labor on the actual work itself.

It is not surprising that private building remains one of the most difficult things anyone can possibly contemplate undertaking.

The third important function of the act is to give the necessary legal power to local authorities to condemn whole areas of existing property which they want to replan and rebuild because of obsolete design or bad layout. This power is voluntary. The local authority must initiate action, its proposals must be approved by the Ministry of Town and Country Planning and the Minister is almost certain to order a local public inquiry to be held if there is any serious opposition to the proposal by any of the landowners directly affected.

Local authorities are also given general powers to acquire by compulsory sale old buildings worthy of preservation, or stretches of land, such as woodland, which are part of the locality or amenities of the neighborhood. Even more important is the fact that the act makes it compulsory for each local authority to survey its area within three years of July, 1948, and to decide how it wants that area to grow or change in the future. Thereafter, that survey must be repeated every five years. The charge of rigidity in planning is at last removed.

The major criticism to date of the 1947 act has been directed at its financial provisions. They are deeply resented by the majority of landowners because they deprive him of the benefit of the gradual appreciation in the capital value of his land, which he had come to regard as automatic and therefore ordained by nature. The landowner is reluctant to accept no more than the "existing use" value of his land, even though he may have a right to claim a portion of the £300,000,000 compensation fund for his lost development rights. Many landowners have held back their land from the market, hoping that political changes may alter this state of affairs. A landowner is not compelled to sell his land to a private individual. If he does decide to sell, there is no ceiling to the price that he may ask. But the willing buyer is faced with the fact that since July, 1948, when the act came into force, he may be asked to pay a high price for the land and be compelled to pay a development charge in addition when he starts to build.

The act has tended to force up the effective cost of land to a prospective developer when he buys land by private agreement from a private owner. The only remedy he has is to ask the Central Land Board, the authority set up by the act to assess and levy development charges, to buy the land at its "existing use" value, which the board has power to do. To the end of 1949, the board had done so in only eleven cases. However, the act has brought a considerable reduction in the cost of housing when constructed by a local housing authority, for a public authority can buy land at compulsory sale, and may not pay for it more than its "existing use" value.

Yet this liability for development charge can only apply to a small proportion of the total land in Britain, that in and around towns. Likewise, the general reduction in the cost of land for building has provided the first promise of a solution to a problem that has beset every kind of planning project for decades past. The problem that still faces the Government is whether to modify the act at all.

There are good arguments to support the claim that it is unfair to compel a landowner to pay out a development charge before he is given compensation for the loss of an earlier and legal right, but this is no more than a problem of the transition from one system to another. The real question is still unanswered. Before 1948, any development of land was a concern of both landowner and land developer. (They might be the same individual, but in Britain, certainly in the building of houses for sale before the war, they usually were not.) Both co-operated and both benefitted. The effect of the 1947 act has been to destroy any financial incentive for the landowner actively to encourage the development of his land. The effects of that have still to be seen. It may be that the land developer alone will provide all the drive needed for private building, and that local authorities will provide all the drive needed to keep up the supply of dwelling houses for the majority of the population. The Labour party would claim that the answer is "yes." The Conservative party has usually made sounds indistinct enough to be politically safe, but suggesting a preference for "no." By common consent, the added powers that the act gives to local authorities are accepted as useful and desirable.

If it is desirable to hand over to a community and its local council the right to shape its own future in a democratic way, it is foolish to be halfhearted in giving the legal powers essential for the task. The effect of the act is, designedly, a long-term one. No one expects that Britain can be rebuilt in one lifetime. Very rarely do people actively revolt against physical surroundings to which they have become accustomed. None the less, they expect change to be an improvement. But, if the appearance of Britian is not to be finally wrecked by the spread of houses with the increase of transportation, something like this act was essential. Britain is too small to be divided up into neglected areas balanced by a series of national parks. What needs preserving in Britain is the view at the end of the trolley line, for the simple reason that there are so many trolley lines or their equivalents. That is the main justification for the act.

Nor should it be looked at in isolation. The social theories and pressures that produced that act were identical with those behind the National Parks and Access to the Countryside Act of 1949.

National parks are an idea from the United States. The first national park was Yellowstone Park, established in 1872. In Britain the idea has been talked about for a long time. During the war, the Government appointed a committee to look into the whole question and its report was published in 1945. The 1949 act is based in the main on recommendations of that report.

The act is comprehensive. It established a National Parks Commission and it is on the commission's recommendations that national parks will be defined. The test is that they shall be areas of natural beauty that provide opportunities for open air recreation. It also sets up a Nature Conservancy, to protect wild life in areas not necessarily part of a park. It clarifies both law and procedure with regard to public rights of way over open country, and it gives local authorities the power and the obligation to secure public access to land not under active use various purposes. But the noteworthy part of the act is that its social philosophy is identical with that of the 1947 planning act.

The ownership of land, so this philosophy asserts, is not merely a matter of private rights and privileges. Every inhabitant of a country has some rights in the land of that country. One object implicit in both acts is the need to provide a code of law capable of holding a balance between the private and exclusive right to throw up a fence, and the public and general right to free access where it will cause no harm or material damage.

It is time now to return to the other side of the problem. Town and country planning suggests to the mind of many people mainly a matter of families and houses. Development areas, the building of new towns, the associated ideas start from the other end of the scale. These projects seem to be concerned with industry as a whole, with regions not towns, with thousands of buildings and hundreds of thousands of people. But the two approaches meet in the middle. The individual leaves his home to work in industry. The hundreds of thousands who work in industry each return to a home at night.

The "development area" was tackled by the wartime Coalition Government, before the election of 1945, when it passed the Distribution of Industry Act. That act changed the name "Special Area" to "Development Area," placed the regions directly under the Board of Trade and increased their areas. The act made more flexible the machinery by which they were created and administered, and considerably increased the powers of the Board of Trade to provide factories, finance and services.

A great deal of quiet unobtrusive work has been done by the Board of Trade under this act. Take the town of Wrexham, declared a development area under the 1945 act. The district around Wrexham, on the borders of England and North Wales, contained a small coalfield, but by 1939 the field was almost worked out. The best seams had gone, flooding was an increasing problem, and many of the pits had closed. Unemployment was high and there was no alternative employment for the mineworkers, and no work at all for the women. In 1940, the government built one of its largest munitions factories in this area, employing, at its peak, 10,000 people, of whom 6,200 were women. As a result, in June, 1945, only 444 men and women were unemployed, compared with 4,682 in 1937. The factory closed and by December of that year the unemployment figure had climbed back to 4,940.

The solution was found in this way. The factory had been built in a series of small units spread over a wide area. Under the terms of the act, the Government converted each unit into a separate factory, and

offered them for individual lease. Those factories are gradually being taken. By June, 1948, 1,531 people, 5½% of the insured population of the area, were still unemployed but the figure was falling, and
the factories derived from the munition factory were capable, when
fully occupied, of employing all the labor available in the district.

In another area, West Cumberland, the full solution is nearer. In
1937, 26% of the insured population was out of work; in 1948,
only three per cent.

One-third more people were working, seventeen new factories had
been completed and still more were under construction. In addition, a diversity of work had been created in the area, sufficient to
prevent the worst effects of a decline in the demand for heavy goods,
previously the exclusive products of the area. The total cost of all
the plans and the work already undertaken will be approximately
£38,000,000.

The 1945 act is voluntary. It gives the Board of Trade very many
powers to persuade and attract, but no powers to compel. When the
original bill was before Parliament, the Labour party—in opposition on this issue—argued that the Board of Trade should be given
compulsory powers to forbid the erection of new factories outside
the development areas. The Government preferred to be without
powers of compulsion. As a result, Section 9 of the act compels anyone proposing to build a new factory, containing more than 10,000
square feet of floor space, merely to notify the Board of Trade before
work is started. But the arguments of that debate now have an
academic ring. There is compulsion. Under other regulations, no
new building construction at all may be started without a license
from the Ministry of Works, and it has been impossible to obtain
such a license without the backing of some government department.
The two departments which have had most influence with the
Ministry of Works have been the Ministry of Supply and the Board
of Trade. The test for granting any such building license has not
only been the location for the factory, but also the nature of the
product, and manufacture for export has been the strongest card that
any industrialist planning a new factory could play. Section 9 of the
Distribution of Industry Act may have looked admirable on paper.
It has meant very little in practice.

There remains the final ingredient, the New Towns Act, 1946, and both town and country planning and the distribution of industry come together in the ideas behind that act. The New Towns Act is intended to do exactly what its title suggests, to create a number of completely new towns in Britain, complete towns, not dormitory suburbs.

There are two reasons why this attempt is being made. One applies to London alone, and is an alternative to the continuing growth of London. Some 10,000,000 people, one-quarter of the whole population of England and Wales, live in the geographical area properly described as London. This London stretches in most directions for at least twenty miles from its central point, suburb beyond suburb. Its communications are overburdened, its local government organization is a fantastic patchwork; to an outside mind it is a monstrosity, and yet it has continued to grow, steadily and remorselessly. It is a crowning example of the inertia of people and of the compelling power of a man's work.

The new towns around London will consist of a series of separate communities some thirty to forty miles from London's center, each to contain from 40,000 to 60,000 people, each built so that houses and factories become available at the same time. In that way, it is hoped, sufficient people and industry will be drained off to check the tide of London's outward swelling. About a half-dozen of these communities are already planned and under construction. Some are expansions of an existing small town, like Hemel Hempstead in Hertfordshire; others are based on no more than an existing village, such as Harlow, in Essex, a locality once very well known to some of the bomb groups of the U.S. Army Air Force.

The Letchworth and Welwyn experiments provided the experience on which these new towns are being planned, but there are these differences. Letchworth and Welwyn were built by private capital, trading companies under private control and intended to earn dividends and capital gain. They had no more social responsibility than that possessed by their individual directors (which proved in fact considerable). They had greater difficulties but were more free to feel their way out. The new towns are financed by government money intended to earn no more than its interest and sinking fund payments, and an immediate dividend is not expected. Letchworth and Welwyn owe their existence, and their locations, to the chance that their promoters were able to buy through private agreement the land on which they stand. The new towns acquire all the land within their boundaries by compulsory purchase. Letchworth and Welwyn were operated by two companies with no powers beyond those possessed by all trading companies. The new towns have governing bodies which are in part trading concerns and in part the equivalent of municipal authorities. Welwyn provides a case of child swallowing parent, for the original garden city company has been taken over by a development corporation established under the act, the better to marry the town with its older but more disorganized neighbor, Hatfield.

Those new towns are part of the relief for London. Others are being established for other reasons. Glenrothes is a new town in Scotland. It comes into existence because—as indicated earlier—it is to be the central town in a new coalfield now being opened up in that area. Aycliffe, in Durham, grows from a vast wartime munition plant, too costly and too well-equipped to be abandoned, too remote to attract labor once the powers of compulsion had ended. It is now to be made attractive enough to revive on its own merits. A third is Basildon, in Essex. Basildon is the name of one part of a district that is very little better than a shanty town, between the East End of London and the sea, a shanty town without form, without amenities or very much in the way of main drainage. It was felt that the whole area could best be pulled together and tidied up by a new town development corporation.

How, in concrete terms, does a new town development corporation go to work? Company X makes, let us say, fire extinguishers in an old factory in a London suburb. It has grown gradually, and now has a payroll of some 80 people, the majority unskilled. It has outgrown its present rented factory, and its management knows that it must move if it is to continue to grow. On investigation, there are snags in the way of every proposed move. To buy a larger factory in the same area would tie up a great deal of its working capital. The local branch of the Ministry of Works says that it has instructions not to grant any more licenses to build factories anywhere in the Greater London area. In the end, the management hears about the new towns organization, where the authorities can and will build both factories and houses, and rent them. Edged along that particular road by this set of circumstances, the management contacts the development corporation of one of the new towns near London, and lays its problem before it.

At the same time, the officials of each new town organization have been discussing the local labor and housing situation with the labor exchanges, and local authorities in the areas of London they are designed to relieve. As they begin to interest Company X in their new town, they are able to offer these London suburbs work and houses for the many families still waiting for new homes. These proposals are passed on, by the labor exchanges and the local councils, to individuals who have already said they would consider work outside of London, if it carried with it the chance of a new house. So, with an inevitable percentage of failures, the new town signs up both employers and labor, keeping supply roughly balanced with the known demand. The motives that drive each group to the new town are mixed. There is a certain amount of "negative direction" about it. If Company X and its existing workers were quite free to choose, they would probably vote for a new factory and a new house within five minutes of where they already are. But there is no positive compulsion about the move and, as Letchworth and Welwyn have shown over the last forty years, once the move has taken place, the experiment will probably succeed.

There is something very British about the whole approach. Some people would move about a country, in search of work, even in search of no more than change, without requiring very much pressure to start them out. Not so the British. They will move—they have moved all over the globe—but they find it easier to make a decision to emigrate 10,000 miles than they do move 200 miles. In some countries, no official would dream of wasting time trying to persuade people to go where the authorities wanted them to be. An order would be issued, and that order would be obeyed. This building of new towns is a mixture of public and private enterprise, and as an experiment is one of the most interesting going on in Britain at the present time.

This has taken us a long way from the question of how the authorities in Britain would deal with the situation that faced Father Tranchese in San Antonio.

A local authority in Britain—acting in its capacity either as health or housing authority—had the power, under the pre-war housing acts, to condemn any slum property that needed clearing and re-building. It now has, under the Town and Country Planning Act of 1947, power to comdemn in the interests of the town as a whole any area which needs complete demolition. Any such proposal would need ministerial confirmation, and there would almost certainly be a public inquiry before any compulsory purchase order was made. At that inquiry the owners of the property would have the right to state their case. But, if conditions were comparable to those in the San Antonio area, there isn't much doubt that the compulsory pur-chase order would be made as a matter of course, and the local au-thority would be given a grant of public money towards the total cost of reconstruction.

The price of the land would be dealt with too. As long ago as 1919, Parliament (and this has nothing to do with socialism, for the 1919 Parliament was certainly far from socialistic) passed an act called the Acquisition of Land Act, to provide a means of determining the price of land which any official authority had power to purchase by compulsion. If the seller and the buyer cannot agree on a price, the price of land to be acquired is fixed by an official arbitrator, a sur-veyor, at the "amount which the land, if sold in the open market by a willing seller, might be expected to realise." The operative words are "by a willing seller." An unwilling seller cannot hold up anyone to ransom by demanding a price high enough to change his unwill-ingness into willingness.

As with Father Tranchese, someone would have to start the campaign. But, having started it moving, they would have a pretty effective mechanism for carrying the whole operation through to successful conclusion.

Finally, we come to housing. It is very difficult to estimate housing needs in any country, and for a very simple reason. The desire for a separate dwelling may be frustrated by an inability to pay for it. The demand for houses, then, is a product of two independent and vari-able factors, the number of persons of an age likely to wish to occupy a separate dwelling, and the number among them who have either capital or income sufficient to maintain a separate dwelling.

The pressure to acquire a separate dwelling varies. It will be strongest in the married couple with young children, and the majority of these will have the means with which to pay at least the rent of one. From this group, the curve of pressure will diminish, sharply among those who are younger and unmarried, less sharply among those who are older. Young unmarried men or women would perhaps like to have a separate home before marriage were their means large enough to afford such a luxury. Without such an income, they are tolerably content to live with their parents or in a rooming house. The elderly widower or widow would probably very much prefer a separate apartment to living with a married son or daughter. Their problem is to find the income to pay for it. In short, the demand for separate dwellings is an elastic one, and one very difficult to plot from any set of statistics.

The difficulties in Britain were worked out in *Estimating House Needs* by Alexander Block, published in 1947. He contrasts two sets of figures. The first is an estimate made by Lord Simon (then Sir E.D. Simon), an expert on local housing problems, in 1933. He calculated that in Britain in 1931 there was a shortage of 830,000 dwellings, that the increase in the number of families desiring houses between 1931 and 1941 would be 750,000, and thereafter the number of families would expand by 195,000 before becoming stationary, owing to the fall in population. As against this, the Registrar-General, in his housing report based on the 1931 census, estimated that no more than 771,000 additional houses would be required between 1931 and 1941 to take care of the additional families needing separate houses.

What, in fact, happened to housing between 1931 and 1941? Between April 1, 1931, and March 31, 1939, it is estimated that 2,500,-000 new houses were built, as compared with 1,616,000 between 1921 and 1931. (The estimate is based, for the most part, on concrete figures.) Allowing for wastage—that is, houses demolished or converted to some nonhousing purpose—the net increase in dwellings between 1931 and 1939 was 2,182,000 compared with 1,421,000 between 1921 and 1931. On the face of it, it would seem that the housing problem in Britain had been more than half solved by 1939.

A committee which investigated the question of the statutory limitation of rent increases in 1937 reported that the scarcity of certain classes of houses was still so great that it would not recommend that the rents of houses be released from control. The large towns reported similarly on the number of applicants still seeking houses in their areas.

A further factor is the gradual change in the age of the population of Britain. That is shown from the following estimate published in the Beveridge Report in 1942:

POPULATION OF GREAT BRITAIN BY AGE GROUP, 1901–1971

(Figures in millions)

Year.	Total Population	Under 15.	Per cent of total	Men 15–64 Women 15–59	Per cent of total	Men 65 and over Women 60 and over	Per cent of total
1901	37	12	32.5	23	61.3	2	6.2
1911	41	13	30.8	25	62.4	3	6.7
1921	43	12	27.9	27	64.2	3	7.8
1931	45	11	24.2	30	66.2	4	9.6
1941	47	10	20.6	31	67.5	6	12.0
1951	48	9	19.1	32	66.4	7	14.5
1961	47	8	17.9	31	65.1	8	17.1
1971	46	8	16.5	29	62.6	10	20.8

One conclusion to be drawn from this is obvious. In 1901, 32.5% of the total population could not possibly have needed a separate dwelling, because they were still under the age of 15 years. In 1951, that percentage will have fallen to 19.1% of the population.

Another variable is the house itself. At some stage or other, a house becomes worn out. The useful age of a house varies considerably. So does the individual view as to when a particular structure should be discarded and replaced. There are some 12,400,000 houses in Britain, and 3,400,000 of them are over 85 years old. In 1935, a Conservative M.P., a surveyor by profession, estimated that no fewer than 4,600,000 houses in Britain should be pulled down at once on account of their age. In 1938, the Government's plan to demolish all houses that were then considered to be slums included no

more than 300,000 individual dwellings. The truth must lie somewhere between these two figures; if the life of a habitable house is
taken to be 80 years, the estimate of the Conservative seems to be the
more sound.

All this may sound too vague. It might be thought that in a remote corner of some government office, an individual would have
been set to the task of making an official estimate of the number of
new buildings needed. Maybe some individual has done just that,
but if he has, his calculation has not been published. For five years,
the Ministry of Health has built as many houses as it could persuade
local authorities to undertake, in the belief that it was unlikely to
produce too many. The official reply I received to my inquiry ran:

> I write in reply to your letter of the 17th August to say that the outstand-
> ing demand for new houses can only be assessed by examining the local
> situation and finding out how many families still have no home of their
> own, the number and make up of the families who are waiting for homes,
> and the number who have applied to more than one local authority . . .
> The long-term programme must also include new housing for those who
> are now living in unfit homes that ought to be demolished and it will,
> therefore, be necessary in due course to ask local authorities to survey the
> local conditions and to ascertain the needs in respect of slums and over-
> crowding.

What, in fact, did Mr. Aneurin Bevan, when he became Minister
of Health, propose to do about housing? He started from two assumptions. The first was that what the majority of people needed
were new houses which they could rent rather than buy. The second
was that private enterprise would not build houses to rent. As a result, he decided upon three steps. The first was to encourage local
authorities to devote all their efforts towards the building of houses
to rent. The second was to prohibit the erection of houses by builders, either for speculative sale or under contract for an intending
owner-occupier, save when licensed by the authority. He directed
these authorities to issue these licenses only when there was a surplus
of building–labor and material available in their neighborhood. To
that he imposed, as an additional deterrent to private building, a
ceiling on the total cost of any house built for private sale or occupation.

His first argument does not need much evidence in its support. Only a small number of people can put down in cash even ten per cent of the cost of a new house (now running from £1,350 to £1,500 each) and at the same time furnish it. Further, they are not commonly to be found among the young married couples, the veterans, the men and women who want to make a start in married life. Mr. Bevan was consistent. He had been put into office, so he said, to house the working classes and that he intended to do.

The second assumption is also reasonably easy to prove. In the four years following World War I, 1919–1924, when private enter prise in housing competed on even terms with local authorities, only 275,000 houses altogether were built, of which local authorities built 171,003, while in the last full year before the war, of the 359,656 houses built, 265,058 were built for sale.

The private builder must act on the assumption that he will sell the house he has built. The businesses of house-building and house-owning are quite distinct, and need quite different financial structures. In Britain, the majority of building concerns are small, employing no more than twenty men, and possessing only limited capital. They rely on the sale of a completed house to finance the building of the next. They cannot afford to lock up their capital in rented houses, even if the return on their money were attractive which, usually, it is not.

Nor are there a sufficient number of investment organizations to undertake that operation. The large blocks of apartment houses in London are owned by investment companies, rarely the small single house. Nor do building societies help. They exist to finance the purchase by installments of property by the owner-occupier. They do not themselves invest in the ownership of rented property.

Mr. Bevan, if he meant to pursue his policy of providing rented houses to its logical end, was compelled either to rely on the existing local councils, or to create an entirely new system for the construction, finance and management of residential properties in every parish in the Kingdom. Local authorities may have their defects; a new creation would have been only too likely to possess the same defects and to have developed new ones of its own.

That was Mr. Bevan's view, and he has stuck to it through thick and thin. It has attracted middle-class resentment. For that he was prepared. He was not building for the people with money. He has encountered technical difficulties of one kind and another; his grasp on administrative details is not so strong as his grasp on policy. There are 1,470 local authorities, of all sizes, of varying degrees of efficiency, with very different resources available in their respective areas. All have been authorized, indeed, compelled to build houses for renting to the inhabitants of their areas, and to refuse licenses to build to most of those who wanted to build their own houses on their own land. The policy of leaving building to them has produced (after a bad period of disorganization in 1946 and 1947) a reasonably steady flow of houses to let.

Here is a summary of the houses built in Britain between 1945 and the end of 1949:

Period	New Permanent Houses	Temporary Houses	Conversions & Adaptations	Repair of war-damaged property	Temporary Huts	Service Camps	Requisitioned Properties (net)	TOTAL
			England and Wales					
1945	1,445	8,939	8,606	60,817	2,822		15,078	97,707
1946	51,090	70,931	35,994	46,420	658	9,241	10,233	224,567
1947	127,541	34,351	35,027	19,774		4,967	2,464	224,124
1948	206,405	10,746	27,273	9,799		5,541	−1,447	258,517
1949	171,780	3	13,555	4,844	−439	1,734	−2,505	187,974
TOTALS	558,261	124,970	120,455	141,654	3,041	21,483	24,023	993,887
			Scotland					
1945 to 1949	65,086	32,176		13,170				110,432

That gives a grand total of 1,104,319 housing units completed in the period.

Of the new houses completed, 471,645 have been built by local authorities, 100,522 by private builders for private owners, and the remainder by housing associations, government departments for their own employees, and so on. In addition, some 39,000 houses, totally wrecked by bombing, have been rebuilt on their former sites. The building industry has been kept in full employment, but it has not been expanded and it has not worked so hard.

All these problems can best be seen through the eyes of one particular authority and locality. Canterbury, for example. It is one of the old, historic cities in England, the seat of the Archbishopric, the shrine of St. Augustine, and for that reason one of the cities the German *Luftwaffe* punished as much as possible. Politically, it is middle class and Conservative, not a city in which one would expect to find the majority predisposed to co-operate with Mr. Bevan for party reasons.

Before the war it contained some 24,390 people living in 7,000 houses, and 730 of these houses were totally destroyed by bombing. Another 850 were seriously damaged and nearly all the remainder received some damage, perhaps slight, but involving time, money and labor in repair. Before the war, the city council had estimated that some 100 houses were needed each year for the natural growth of the population. Virtually none was built during the war. This was the problem that faced the city authorities in 1945, when the local councillors found that it was for no one but them to solve.

War damage was not the only cause for Canterbury's concern over housing. A great deal of Canterbury is old, not only the cathedral. There are terraces of four-room houses, centuries old, unsanitary by modern standards, overcrowded, and waiting for a return to reasonably normal conditions before demolition. And that demolition program was bound to wait, too, for new houses to be built.

Canterbury presents another interesting phenomenon, a town's revolt against too much planning. By 1944, the *Luftwaffe* was no longer much more than a vague threat, and the City Council was considering the future of its city. The councillors had called in an expert in town planning, and he had prepared a plan which included the compulsory acquisition by the council of some 200 acres of land within its boundaries, including some 75 acres of land in the center of the city. That plan was made possible under the terms of the Town and Country Planning Act, 1944, which authorized the local authority of a town, in which war damage was extensive, to acquire the entire area in which the damaged were centered. It was a most comprehensive plan and, if carried through, it would have considerably altered the appearance of Canterbury. Possibly that was why the majority of the inhabitants of Canterbury did not like it. In the municipal elections of October, 1945, a citizens' association opposed to this plan, defeated all the local councillors who had supported it, and won the twelve vacant seats on the council. It was a resounding victory for the antiplanners. Still, the problem of building new houses, planned or unplanned, remained.

The new chairman of the housing committee of the Council was a Mr. T. E. Carling, a wine and spirit merchant, who had been in business in the city for over twenty-one years. He had fought the election as an Independent, opposed to the old council's plan. Having disposed of one plan, he had to work out another.

In five years, the City Council of Canterbury, spurred by Mr. Carling's determination and the professional guidance of a newly appointed city architect, has acquired by compulsion 122 acres of undeveloped land for building. It has also prepared a new, less ambitious, but still comprehensive plan for the developed sections of the city, which will involve in the end the purchase of some 31 acres of land, including 10 acres of the war-damaged area. It has completed 227 brick houses and has another 265 under construction. It has erected 200 steel houses and 74 aluminum houses (reasonably permanent), and 263 Quonset huts and 138 concrete temporary bungalows. These were all completed by 1948. It has also completely rebuilt 94 partially destroyed houses and has another 24 under construction. In that way, it has provided separate homes for 998 families.

Private builders, under license from the council as agents for the Ministry of Works, have built 86 houses in the same period and are at work on another 14. (Doubtless the private builders would have liked those figures to be larger.)

These results are relatively as good as any in the country. Yet they have not solved Canterbury's housing problems. The new houses have not done much more than restore the accommodation lost during the war. They do not provide houses for the total increase in population, or for those whose houses are unfit for further use. In

1946, the list of people awaiting houses was 1,800. At the end of 1949, the list still contained 1,300 names. Even so, such a building program has meant that Canterbury has used to the full its force of building contractors.

The experience of Canterbury illustrates two other points that have plagued or perplexed every housing authority. The first is the method of allocating priorities among those who apply for houses to rent.

At first, the council adopted a system, popular as a theory at the end of the war, which had the merit of seeming on paper to be extremely fair. A committee of the council drew up a list of factors to be taken into consideration in determining priorities: length of war service, whether married or not, size of family, present circumstances, and so on. Points were allotted for each separate item. Those who scored the largest number of points went to the head of the list. The United States Army adopted a similar plan in deciding priorities for release at the end of the war.

But the system did not work very well. It was too complicated. Too many applicants failed to understand it, or, if they did, failed to accept this kind of impersonal assessment of what they knew to be their legitimate claims, with the result that they ceased to believe that such a system could be fair. Once they felt that, they began to suspect that some people were getting houses by favoritism. No system can stand up once suspicion is aroused, however wrongly.

Under the revised system adopted in Canterbury the applicants are divided into these groups:

1. Those living in Canterbury.
2. Those working in Canterbury.
3. Those living and working outside Canterbury.

Once assigned to their basic group, applicants are further divided into sub-groups based on the size of the family. Finally, each applicant in a sub-group is arranged in categories, under headings such as these: present overcrowding; whether former home was destroyed by bombing; whether medical considerations exist which call for better housing; whether there is domestic friction, and so on; all the varying social troubles on which housing conditions have such a profound influence.

When this is completed, a sub-committee of the council considers each applicant personally, with a personal interview, and makes its own decision as to the priority to be given him. The decisions are made by elected councillors, not by council functionaries. In short, the council has changed from automatic selection by points to a modified form of personal selection.

The other illustration provided by Canterbury's experience is a financial one. These are the rents of Canterbury's postwar houses:

Rents per week	*Permanent Houses*	*Temporary Houses*
Rent of majority of houses...........	£1.5.3.	18/10
Highest rent paid..................	1.7.7.	18/10
Lowest rent paid..................	1.1.7.	17/10

These rents are subsidized. For the year ending March 31, 1948, the government subsidy to Canterbury Council for its postwar houses was £4,224. In addition, the "rates," or local finances of the city, were called upon to provide another £1,408, approximately the yield of a rate of 1½d. to the pound on the total annual assessment of the city. But the amount of this particular subsidy is exceptional, in that it covers sums paid out during the year for houses in course of construction and not, therefore, income producing. None the less, as a rough estimate, each house built in by the council Canterbury since the war will need about a ten-shilling–a–week subsidy if its present rent is to stay unchanged.

Under the Housing Act of 1946, the official subsidy available for each house built by a local authority is £22. per annum, of which the government furnishes £16. 10. 0. and the local authority £5. 10. 0. The Ministry of Health has, during this period, refused to disclose detailed figures of housing costs throughout the country. Yet it is clear that the size of the actual subsidy per house may be greater than that contemplated by the act, particularly in areas of high cost, such as London. The accounts of the London County Council for the half year from January to June, 1949, showed that the actual deficit on 3,424 houses was £14. 12. 2. per house for that period. Figures obtained by the *Economist,* and published in January, 1950, showed that only two, out of nine boroughs from which the paper obtained statistics, were operating their postwar housing accounts without a deficit. In the case of one town, the average weekly rent charged was £1. 5. 5., in the case of the other, £1. 10. 0. The economic rent of a postwar house would seem to be between £1. 6. 0 and £1. 10. 0 per week, depending on location.

The cost of new housing is still a major problem, both absolutely and relatively. In 1938, 2.6% of the national income was spent in housing construction. In 1947, 2.4% of the national income was spent in producing no more than 56% of the number of houses built in 1938. A typical house built by a local authority in 1938 cost £380. In 1948 it cost £1,242—and there was no appreciable decline in costs for 1949. These figures cover the cost of the structure alone. By the time the cost of the land is added in, and the cost of the roadways and equivalent amenities, the total cost of the dwelling to the local authority is more likely to be between £1,500 and £1,600. From the figures obtained by the *Economist,* the lowest all-inclusive price was £1,366, the highest £1,825. Sir Thomas Bennett, who was Controller of Temporary Housing at the Ministry of Works during the war, furnished in November, 1949, his estimate of the average cost of a local-authority house, an even higher figure, £1,899.

Part of the additional cost is due to the fact that the standard house since the war has been bigger and better equipped than its predecessor. Its floor space has increased from about 800 square feet to about 1,050 square feet. According to a Ministry of Health inquiry into housing costs made in 1948, the increase in the size of the house accounts for some £200 of its additional cost, and the higher standard of fittings for another £125. But the main item has been the increased cost of the labor employed. On the house costing £1,242, labor has added £297 to the total bill, of which £96 is due to increased wage rates and £75 to the improvement in the house itself (which naturally enough needs more work in its construction and fitting). But £126 of this increased cost is due to what can only be described as a decline in the productivity of labor itself.

The 1948 inquiry was concerned with the figures of 1947, and it is reasonable to suppose that productivity has increased since then. None the less, the report of the 1948 committee on these increased costs, and its views on their causes, have still a good deal of relevance. The causes it suggested were:

1. Shortage of materials, with resulting delays, hold-ups and frustrations on the job itself.
2. Shortage of labor, leading to uneconomic working on the site.
3. Reduction in the "quality" of labor, due to the war, and to wartime methods of payment on a cost-plus basis.
4. Disorganization of the industry owing to excessive demands placed upon it.
5. Lack of individual effort and of more effective incentives to stimulate individual effort.
6. The extremely bad weather in the early part of 1947.

Cause 6 is about the only one for which everyone in the building industry and the Ministry of Health has a perfect alibi.

As in Canterbury, so all over Britain; the housing problem is not yet solved. There are still young people who want to get married and have children in a home of their own, and who find it impossible to find that home. There are still old people reluctant to face the last years of their lives as lodgers in the home of a son or a daughter–in–law, and who still hope that they will find an apartment of their own. There are still houses which are unfit for habitation, but which are still inhabited because there is as yet nothing better to offer to their present occupants.

Mr. Bevan has left many unsolved problems in his wake. The strict economists complain of the proportion of national capital investment devoted to housing. Those who are alarmed at the size of the subsidies now being paid, and likely to be paid, demand that government expenditure on housing must be cut (although their cries diminished in intensity as the election came nearer). Those who have had sufficient money to build homes of their own to their own design (more elegant than is possible under the present price ceiling), have complained of a policy that prevents them from making a start. Yet Mr. Bevan pursued his way for five years with a consistency of purpose, if not of method, unique among his cabinet colleagues and, while doing so, was able to confound his critics in every housing debate in Parliament.

By the end of 1949, he was able to announce that the millionth house, new or reconstructed since the war, had been made available for occupancy. As the *Economist* said of his policy in its survey of housing policy at the beginning of 1950, "It has been erratic, expensive and, in some respects, unjust. But judged by the paramount test, that of numbers of dwellings completed, it has succeeded." One cannot quite escape the conviction that none of the alternative plans for a housing policy, on paper so balanced and just, so free from all the defects that critics have seen in those actually in operation, would have produced quite so many actual homes for quite so many of the people who needed them most.

In five years, Mr. Bevan caught up with the damage and dislocation caused by the war. Roughly, some 470,000 houses were lost during the war. Since 1939, an additional million new families have been actively seeking a separate dwelling. By the end of 1950, that basic need, some 1,400,000 to 1,500,000 new dwellings, should have been satisfied.

The problems of the next five years are of a different nature. It is defensible—as an arrangement to operate during an emergency—to subsidize new housing on this scale, and by these rough and ready methods. Yet it is increasingly evident that the man who has the new and more convenient home is paying less for it than the man who still lives in an unsubsidized and less convenient house. The first problem is financial, to bring some sort of justice into this medley of differing rent systems and subsidy systems. That will require political courage, for some rents should go up. The second problem is to make a start on slum clearance. For ten years no house has been closed purely for sanitary reasons. Those that were on the borderline in 1939 are now well past it. A great many more have crossed it. The third problem is to improve the productivity of the building industry itself.

CHAPTER XII

Insurance and Health Service

National Insurance—the welfare state. By now, the inhabitants of Britain are sometimes inclined to think that they are considered by the rest of the world—at least, by the United States—as the inventors and sole proprietors of this experiment in social legislation, with all the opprobrium and praise, if any, that goes with such intrepidity. Someone has described it as a vast system for maintaining those who don't want to work at the expense of those who must; contrariwise, the most important development in the relations between the individual and the community that this century has seen.

That's as may be. Certainly Britain did not invent all the developments in social insurance. Certainly the Labour party did not give birth to all the ideas that now form a part of it. More than two centuries ago, Daniel Defoe suggested that the government should set up a compulsory "pensions office" to which all would subscribe, and from which all would draw their pensions. In the last quarter of the eighteenth century, the Reverend John Acland of Devon, a noted social reformer, put forward a parallel proposal. The Poor Law Commission of 1832–34 was in favor of a nationally organized plan for public assistance; it was the kind of proposal that appealed to Jeremy Bentham's tidy mind. The network of friendly societies (which, from 1911 on, were incorporated in the national insurance program under the name of "Approved Societies") were an early nineteenth-century creation and came into existence because thousands of staunch individualists preferred to provide co-operatively against the starvation that might follow accident or sickness rather than accept the "charity" of the community's poor law system.

Compensation for injury at work was first established by a Conservative Government in 1897. Old age pensions began in 1909, originating from a Liberal Government. Mr. Churchill, then a Liberal cabinet minister, first introduced state payments to cover some forms of unemployment in 1911; they were extended by a coalition government in 1920. All parties, all shades of political thought, have edged the machine of social insurance further and further along the road to universal application.

Britain's existing plans are based primarily on the monumental Beveridge Report of 1942. The work of casting those plans into legislative and administrative shape began immediately afterward, and continued throughout the war. The general outline was completed in 1944, the work of the wartime Coalition Government. The general election of 1945 was fought on the assumption that whatever party was returned would introduce bills to convert the project into a working operation. With respect to the national health plan itself, Mr. Willink, a Conservative Minister of Health, had begun negotiations with the medical profession before the election of 1945. Indeed, in many ways Mr. Willink, in the proposals he originated in 1944, would have treated the medical profession rather more severely than did Mr. Bevan three years later. Probably, however, he would have been more polite to them, at least at first, before his temper was provoked too far.

The national insurance plan contains these elements:

1. Insurance against loss of income through unemployment (the individual being able and willing to work, but unable to find it).
2. Insurance against loss of income through illness or accident (the individual being unable to work for physical reasons).
3. Pensions for those too old to work.

To these, certain additional benefits have been grafted on, such as family allowances, maternity benefit and a death grant. Substantially, all these main forms of social insurance existed before the war. What the Labour party has done is to consolidate them into the one program and extend the amount and range of the benefits provided.

Another social project is the Legal Aid and Advice plan, established by an act of that name passed in 1949. Under this act, legal advice centers are in the course of being set up in each locality under the control of the Law Society—the body responsible for the internal management of the solicitors' branch of the legal profession. At these centers any applicant with an income below a certain level will be able to obtain free legal advice on his problems from a practicing lawyer. Further, if a local committee of lawyers thinks that the applicant has a cause for legal action, the applicant's case will be taken over by a local solicitor and the state will pay him 85% of the fee he would normally receive for the work.

Finally, there is national assistance, governed by the National Assistance Act, 1947, which might be called a residuary program, replacing the centuries-old Poor Law. This provides an applicant—regardless of his social history—with a weekly cash payment sufficient (with what he has already), to insure that he does not die of either starvation or exposure, to put it crudely.

The whole plan is complex. One point of departure is to divide the program into those sections which are intended, basically, to be self-supporting, and those which are intended to be mainly state-aided. The first are really insurance plans. The state is the underwriter. It fixes a weekly contribution which, actuarily, should cover the total cost of both benefits and administration. It then makes it compulsory for everyone to enter the plan and make the prescribed payments. The other sections of the program are not insurance in that sense. They are a social service, the provision of some form of assistance which the state thinks everyone should have whether he can pay for it or not, although the potential beneficiary may be required to make some contribution to it.

The major items in the insurance category are:

1. The Industrial Injuries Scheme. This replaces the former liability of each employer to pay weekly compensation to his workmen injured on the job, by a national program under which the injured workman is compensated by a state-operated organization. It is intended to be wholly self-supporting, by means of weekly payments from both employer and employee.
2. The National Insurance Scheme. This provides a weekly payment to the contributor when he is out of work or sick, plus a pension on reaching a certain age or on retirement from work. It also includes a pension for the contributor's widow, payments for any infant children after the death of the contributor, and a fixed grant for the birth of each child, and for the contributor's death. It is intended to be partly self-support-

ing, in the form of weekly contributions from the whole of the working population.

The items of social service are:

1. The National Health Service. This makes full medical, surgical and hospital treatment (plus dental and optical treatment) available to everyone without individual payment. The cost falls on the general finances of the state, except the small charge for doctors' prescriptions imposed at the end of 1949.
2. The Family Allowance Scheme. This provides for a weekly payment to thé mother for each child under sixteen, except the first. The full cost is borne by the state.
3. National Assistance. This, too, is to be a state liability.

Industrial Accidents

The plan originated under the Workman's Compensation Act of 1897 and remained in existence until 1948. The 1897 act, as amended from time to time, imposed on every employer the liability to make weekly payments to any man in his employment who met with an accident "arising out of and in the course of his employment"—a deceptively straight-forward phrase. Payments were to be made to any man earning less than £400 a year, as long as he was disabled. The full cost was borne by the employer and, as a rule, he insured himself against the risk.

The change made in 1948 transferred some of the burden of this risk from the employer to the workman, little else. For each person employed, over the age of 18, the weekly contribution paid to the state is 8d. (women 6d.), half of which is paid by the employer, half by the workman. The new act does not alter substantially the conditions under which a workman becomes entitled to claim the weekly benefit.

Socially speaking, the advantage of the change is that it amalgamates supervision and treatment of those suffering from industrial accidents with the general health service of the country. It increases the medical facilities available to the injured man, and relieves him of the risk of having to take legal proceedings against a hostile insurance company, to enforce his rights.

National Insurance.

The National Insurance Scheme embraces everyone in Britain, male and female, who is old enough to leave school (now fifteen, but to become sixteen) and under the pensionable age (which is 65 in the case of a man and 60 in the case of a woman) with the exception of those who earn less than £104 a year and certain married women. Those included in the plan are in it by statute; they cannot contract out.

On entry, the individual is classed into one of three groups, based on his work, and the rates of contribution vary according to group. Groups and rates are:

	MEN			WOMEN		
	Paid by	*Paid by*		*Paid by*	*Paid by*	
AGE	*Employee*	*Employer*	TOTAL	*Employee*	*Employer*	TOTAL
18 and over	4s.11d.	4s.2d.	9s.1d.	3s.10d.	3s.3d.	7s.1d.
Under 18	2s.10½d.	2s.5½d.	5s.4d.	2s.4d.	1s.11d.	4s.3d.

Class 1. (Employed Persons)

Class 2. (Self-Employed Persons)

MEN		*WOMEN*	
18 and over..............	4s.8d.	18 and over...........	3s.8d.
Under 18................	2s.9d.	Under 18..............	2s.3d.

Class 3. (Non-Employed Persons)

MEN		*WOMEN*	
18 and over..............	4s.8d.	18 and over...........	3s.8d.
Under 18................	2s.9d.	Under 18..............	2s.3d.

Contributions are paid by National Insurance stamps which are stuck on a National Insurance card every week.

The benefits covered are:

SICKNESS BENEFIT

MATERNITY BENEFIT   UNEMPLOYMENT BENEFIT

Maternity Grant   GUARDIAN'S ALLOWANCE
Maternity Allowance   (Allowance to person support-
Attendance Allowance   ing an orphaned child.)

WIDOW'S BENEFIT   RETIREMENT PENSION

Widow's Allowance
Widowed Mother's Allowance   DEATH GRANT
Widow's Pension

With the exception of the death grant, the full program had come
into operation by July 5, 1948. The death grant was passed a year
later.

Those in the first group are entitled to all the benefits, the second
group to all except unemployment benefit, and the third to all except unemployment and sickness benefits and the maternity allowance.

The only people of working age who do not have to pay the weekly
contribution are:

1. People drawing unemployment or sickness benefit, so long as they continue to draw it.
2. Those engaged in a course of full-time study or apprenticeship.
3. Those earning less than £104 a year.
4. Those drawing the widows' benefit.

In general, married women do not come directly under the plan;
they receive their benefit as the wife of a contributor. But a married
woman who was on July 5, 1948, insured under the old plan can
continue on as a member and draw benefits in her own right instead
of as a wife.

The unemployment benefit, summarized, is:

1. Single man or woman over 18:   26s. a week
2. Man and wife: 42s. a week
3. Man, wife and one child: 49s. 6. a week.

Unemployment benefit is payable for not more than six consecutive months at a time, with further extensions under certain conditions. On the other hand, once anyone has completed three years' contributions, sickness benefit for any permanent incapacity is payable indefinitely until pension age is reached.

The widow's allowance or pension varies according to circumstances. It starts at 36s. a week, which lasts for thirteen weeks (43s.6d. if there is a child at school). It continues as an allowance of 33s.6d. a week if there is a child at school; otherwise it stops after the 13 weeks. If the widow is over fifty and has been married for more than ten years, at the end of the thirteen weeks, the allowance becomes a continuous pension of 26s. a week until she is 60, when it merges in the retirement pension. Earnings up to 30s. a week effect no deduction in pensions. The pension is correspondingly reduced for any earnings in excess of this figure.

There is also an allowance payable to the person caring for an orphan. It is 12s. a week. This replaces the allowance of 7s.6d. which had been payable since 1936, under an act of that year.

The retirement pension is payable at 65 for men (60 for women directly insured) and is a weekly payment of 26s. An essential condition is the previous payment of three years of normal weekly contributions. If a man at retiring age continues at work, the start of his pension is postponed until he does retire, and his ultimate pension is correspondingly increased.

The maternity benefit is a single payment of £4. on the birth of each child, plus a weekly allowance of £1. for the four weeks following the birth. The death grant is a single payment of £20. That was the law to come into operation from and after July, 1948.

The man reputed to have drawn the largest sum for benefit under the plan is Mr. Leslie Franklyn, of Plymouth, Devon, during the time he was unemployed in 1949. Mr. Franklyn is a carpenter, the father of sixteen children, eleven of whom were under the age of sixteen, and he drew £7.4.6d. a week. This was made up as follows:

Family Allowance:

11 children at 5s. per head per week...................... £2.15. .

Unemployment Benefit, at rate applicable to married

man with one child...................................... 2.09.6.

National Assistance Board grant, to cover balance of

cost of maintenance of whole family........................ 2. . .

Total benefit..£7. 4.6.

His weekly budget, or where the money went, is as follows:

Rent.. £1.02.10.

Food... 2. 5. 0.

Milk... 18. .

Clothes.. 1.10. .

Fuel and Light....................................... 10. .

Insurance, etc....................................... 8.11.

Miscellaneous.. 9.10.

Total Expenses....................................... 7. 3. 9.

Mr. Franklyn's record is beaten in one respect; there is a man in Liverpool who draws 5s. a week for thirteen of his sixteen children. Fortunately he is employed.

The cost of the plan is bound to be considerable. When the National Insurance Bill was introduced, the government published its actuary's estimate of what the financial burden would be and on whom it would fall. This estimate appears in the appendix to this chapter.

It is misleading to think of the plan primarily as one imposing fresh burdens on the community as a whole. Usually, a man out of work, a man crippled or sick, is kept alive by somebody. In Britain, he has not, legally, been allowed to starve since the Poor Law was set up in A.D. 1601. Over these 300 years the arguments have always been over the standard of living to be given, and the amount contributed in return. Who should provide the money for his support? His immediate neighbors in his own locality—in Britain, the parish —or his relatives? Charity—money given by those who can and will spare it? Should he be compelled to make some provision himself for the future? If so, in what way and how much? So the argument progresses, until it reaches the contributions a man can make to his own future support. Should these be supplemented by money taken from those whose incomes are sufficient to enable them to live, in reasonable comfort, after they have paid their state and local taxes?

The National Insurance Acts say "yes" to both these questions. A man must make some provision for himself and his dependents. That he does by means of his weekly contribution while at work. Industry, as such, is required to add to that. The balance is made up by those whose incomes are large enough to be taxed.

The burden has, in part, been shifted from one shoulder to another. It is possible that the scheme may enable some old and some sick people to live longer than they otherwise would have done. It certainly should enable them to live in somewhat greater comfort. In so far as it does that, it increases the economic burden on those who are fit and working. Otherwise, the plan is primarily a social readjustment.

Family Allowances

There is very little that need be said about this by way of explanation. The underlying idea has been pretty thoroughly canvassed, in all countries. The British plan is not an innovation of the Labour Government; the act establishing it was passed by the Coalition Government before the 1945 election.

A mother is entitled to draw five shillings a week for each child under sixteen, except the first in the family. She receives that sum weekly by presenting a card at her local post office. She is not required to account, either to the state or her husband, for how the money is spent.

By July, 1949, the number of families receiving the benefit was 2,900,000 and the number of children covered by it, 4,600,000.

Current Cost

The current cost of these services is about four times as large as the amount spent on equivalent services, where they existed, before the war. They can be summarized:

PAYMENTS MADE TO PARTICULAR GROUPS OR FOR PARTICULAR
SOCIAL PURPOSES

(Figures in millions of pounds)

	Calendar Years		Financial Year 1949/50 (Estimate)
	1938	1948	
1. Social Security Payments:			
Family Allowances................		59	60
Insurances *.....................	124	333	385
War and industrial injuries *.......	38	85	100
National Assistance...............	105	75	85
	267	552	630
2. Subsidies towards —			
Milk and Food for Mothers }	1	{ 36	37
etc. }		{ 6	8
TOTALS......	268	594	675

*General Subsidies (receivable by community
generally regardless of needs).*

3.			
Food...........................		428	428
Agriculture.....................	14	19	25
Other (excluding housing)........		43	7
	14	490	460

(Figures collated by *The Times*)

* NOTE: The figures for 1948 and 1949 include certain payments which were
made by the state when in 1938 corresponding payments (e.g. compensation for industrial accidents) were made through nonstate
channels.

The Times, in publishing these figures, made the following points:
Were food subsidies to be abolished altogether, an individual wish-
ing to consume the same food would have to smoke only fifteen
fewer cigarettes a week to balance his personal budget. On the other
hand, a married man with three children, earning £5. a week and

receiving 10s. family allowance, would probably find his food bill increased by as much as 15s. in the week, and an old couple with only the 42s. a week retirement allowance would need another 5s. or 6s. simply to keep alive. These figures support the argument that the subsidy element in a social security program can only be a rough and very extravagant form of social justice.

Two matters remain to be dealt with in greater detail. One is the National Health Service, because it has at all times aroused great controversy, and the other is the Legal Aid program because, superficially, it looks like a direct assault on the freedom and independence of the law. To take the second first:

Legal Aid

In essence, the legal aid plan is a program by which lawyers in private practice may be paid by the state for work they do for a private individual, if that individual cannot himself pay the bill. (And it is worth bearing in mind that, in Britain, all the fees payable to a solicitor are governed by statute, and that it is illegal for a solicitor to be paid by being given a share in what is recovered by his work.) The principle of that is as old as Magna Carta: "to none will we sell to none will we deny justice." Lack of means can result in a denial of justice.

The scheme embodied in the 1949 act is based on earlier experience going back to the first charitable legal aid bureaus, some of which were well over fifty years old, to the Poor Persons Rules of the High Court, in operation from 1914, under which lawyers gave free service to men and women with incomes below £200 a year, and to the wartime experiences of the Legal Aid plans operated in all three of the armed services under the control of the Law Society. All this experience was embodied in a plan prepared by the secretary of the Law Society, and approved by a government committee, known as the Rushcliffe Committee, appointed in 1944.

The keystone of the plan is decentralization and local control. The Law Society supervises what is done, but the work itself is performed by local solicitors in local practice, holding no government appointment and drawing no government salary. It is they who decide what applicant should be helped, and how. There is hardly a civil servant in the whole plan.

What gives the private citizen his major element of protection from political interference is the independence of the Law Society itself. The Law Society consists only of practicing lawyers who have always maintained for themselves a strong independence from the executive. It is the Law Society which grants the individual solicitor his license to practice, and which can revoke that license if he is guilty of professional misconduct. The society has been in existence for some 125 years, and its members are filled with a vast determination to keep clear of goverment domination. If the plan is to be criticized at all, a more solid ground for doing so is that it gives the legal profession a much firmer grasp on the strings that control all its activities. In effect, the profession can be said to have secured a government subsidy towards its continuing existence (it is estimated that the cost to the public will be some £8,000,000 a year, most of which will go into the pockets of the lawyers) without having to give up the substance of control over its own activities.

The Health Service

The bill to establish the National Health Service was introduced into the House of Commons by Mr. Aneurin Bevan in March, 1946. Mr. Bevan had the benefit of the early drafts and of the earlier discussions between his predecessor and his officials, on the one side, and the doctors and their organizations (of which the major one is the British Medical Association, the B.M.A.), on the other. But Mr. Bevan had his own ideas, his own variations on the general policy, and his own personality. Also, he was dealing with a profession with strong traditions and a strong corporate sense. Inevitably, there was considerable scope for disagreement and argument. Neither side lost many opportunities for both.

The health service proposals in the government's bill involved three main projects:

1. The grouping together of all public hospitals under regional boards set up by and responsible to the Minister of Health. This would liquidate the independent entity of many voluntary hospitals, and remove from the control of existing local authorities many others.
2. The transfer of administrative work carried out by the approved societies to the newly created Ministry of National Insurance. That would involve the disappearance of a peculiarly British institution, the volun-

tary collecting society, which collected weekly sums from thousands and paid sick benefits to them in illness.

3. The extension of the right to free medical treatment to the whole population, with resulting vast changes in the whole organization of the medical profession.

The government—and this was not a one-party decision—desired to remove, once and for all, the barrier that money creates between the individual and full medical treatment. Health, it was felt, is a national concern. Every form of medical and hospital service should be so organized that the best possible professional treatment is available to everyone, regardless of his means, and without imposing on him any financial burden that he cannot carry.

To quote from a pamphlet, published by the Ministry of Health in 1949, at the end of the first year of operation of the program, in the section headed "Why a Change was Needed":

Looking at the old Health Services as a whole, it is not difficult to see why a new scheme was needed . . . Although insured workers could get medical treatment free, their wives and children could not. . . . For many middle-class people excluded from compulsory and voluntary schemes a serious illness in the family could be ruinously expensive. . . . Specialists and consultants in order to make a living—for they have hardly ever been paid for their work in voluntary hospitals—were obliged to charge their patients heavy fees, and to settle in towns and districts where people able to afford those fees were numerous. Over wide areas of the country this made it difficult for any but the wealthy patients to obtain their services.

In general, the medical profession supported these objectives. Some of them did not like all their implications. They feared that they would become a "state service." The dangerous implication, in their eyes, was that under such a plan, the paymaster of the medical profession would change, and they were shrewdly aware that it is the paymaster who, in the end, is boss.

By tradition, the relationship between doctor and patient is a personal one, in all its aspects, including how much the patient pays. If medical attention became a state concern, then the contract would no longer be personal to doctor and patient. There would be a third party, the state (in whatever form it operated), paying the bill, and thus having a status vis-à-vis the doctor that it never had before. So claimed the B.M.A.

That, of course, was not entirely true for the majority of the profession. Since 1911, there had been in Britain some form of health insurance under which the state paid doctors for the services they rendered to insured persons, those within the program. But that covered only a part of the population, and the general practitioner, because he could take private patients and make what bargain he liked with them, had been able to think of himself as free from state control.

The course of events in 1948 was this. After two years of negotiation and argument, by the end of 1947, the ministry's final proposals were, in outline:

1. The doctor was free to join the health service or not, in whole or in part. But he might not charge fees to patients on his list of insured persons, whom he had accepted as "national health" patients.
2. On entering the health service he would receive as remuneration a basic annual salary of £300, plus a per capita fee for each person on his list of patients. (It was intended that the maximum on one doctor's list would be 4,000.) The amount of the per capita fee would depend on the number of doctors, and the number of people included in the scheme. In general, it was designed to produce for the doctor with, let us say, 3,000 patients on his list, between £2,375 and £2,700 per annum (plus the fixed £300).
3. The doctor could, for professional misconduct, be debarred from further service in the plan, but only by decision of a statutory tribunal, and with a right of appeal from that tribunal to the Minister of Health.

There were two important future restrictions on the profession. Doctors were to be debarred from buying or selling that portion of the goodwill in future practices which arose from health service patients. To compensate for that loss, the state proposed to set up a fund from which the capital values of existing partnerships would be repaid to the doctor losing by the change. A doctor might also be prevented from opening new consultation rooms for health service patients where a local committee considered the existing medical facilities adequate for the population. He might be "negatively directed" to areas where there was a shortage of doctors, the direction taking the form of an additional monetary payment (discretionary), for which 1% of the total national receipts (estimated at about £40,000,000 annually) had been reserved.

Specialists had greater freedom. The ministry agreed that there should be a proportion of beds in each public hospital reserved for private patients, and that for some of these there would be no limit to the fees chargeable by the specialist. On the whole, under the service, the specialist might expect to lose some of the uncertainties of his early days in practice, but likewise some of the higher rewards at the end of it. However, he escaped the imposition of any absolute ceiling on the amount he could make.

The main points to which the B.M.A. objected were:

1. The existence of any guaranteed minimum salary (the £300 per annum). That, they said, was the opening wedge of the state.
2. The uncertainty of the position of buying and selling practices, and of the allocation of the compensation fund set up to meet actual losses by doctors as a result.
3. The absence of any right to appeal to the courts in cases where the statutory tribunal debars doctors from further practice within the plan.

Among the medical profession, particularly among the older members, there was a great deal of uneasiness over the proposals, not so much about the details as about the risk they saw of the whole plan gradually edging their profession into a state medical service, subject to rigid control in all matters; control, moreover, exercised by civil servants or worse (if there is anything worse). Some such possibilities were inherent in any plan. Some of the fears were fanned by semi-political arguments on both sides.

Younger members of the profession were less alarmed. Many of them had spent some years in the armed forces under the most rigid of systems, and had seen that it was not the system but the men in it that determined both its humanity and efficiency. But they were in a minority, and a valid criticism was that the minister had pushed the program forward too fast, that it would have been better to wait until the profession contained a higher percentage of physicians and nurses who saw the way things were going, and who still were content to serve under a government-operated system.

Another valid criticism was that the success of the plan to some extent depended upon the establishment of local health centers where the families could be treated and studied as units. Only by this means could the level of treatment be raised, and the gulf between the treatment given to the paying patient and the "free" patient be closed. But health centers required buildings, and the provision of new buildings was ruled out. As a result, many doctors felt it would be impossible for them to give their former private patients as good service as before.

At this stage the B.M.A. was very much on the defensive. Its leaders had been driven this far more by pressure of public opinion, both lay and professional, than by its own convictions. The reactions of the public were not so sharply defined. People thought the financial terms for the doctors generous, and £300 a year out of a probable £3,000 did not seem to them very much of a ball and chain. They sympathized with the doctors on the question of the right of appeal to the courts (for sentimental reasons—a right to appeal to the courts has a fine old English sound). They would have lost no sleep over a disappearance of the doctor's right to sell goodwill, for they knew that what the doctors called "goodwill" was, often enough, no more than the public's inertia. But the people, too, were uneasy over the whole plan, again about something the ministry had ignored.

What the public wanted was the substance of the old personal relationship between doctor and patient. They could, as they so often had to, dispense with the trimmings. And the point is that the doctor is to many families their father confessor, their psychological support, as well as the dispenser of colored bottles. What they did not want—and would not stomach—was the doctor who said, directly or by implication, "It's six now and my shift is over. Dr. Jones will take over. I've left him my notes."

That was the background to the B.M.A. plebiscite in February, 1948. The results showed that 17,037 general practitioners disapproved of the scheme and only 2,500 approved, a decisive majority against. The B.M.A. was very pleased at this support. Its view was that here was proof of what the entire profession thought. It was now for Mr. Bevan to make fresh proposals, if he wanted any doctors, as well as patients, in his plan.

Then followed a period of less public negotiation, in which the president of the Royal College of Physicians played some part. The upshot of that was that the minister gave a definite assurance in the

Commons in April that a full-time, salaried, state medical service would not be introduced under the existing act. He also agreed that the basic salary of £300 should only be mandatory for new entrants into the profession, and then only for their first three years in practice. After that, each doctor would decide for himself whether to accept £300 plus a lower capitation fee or a large capitation fee and no minimum salary.

Mr. Bevan did not give way on two of the other objections raised by the B.M.A. He did not agree that doctors should retain the right to buy and sell the goodwill of insurance practices, nor did he agree to alter the procedure by which a complaint against a doctor was investigated.

On this statement, the B.M.A. promised to hold another plebiscite later in April, 1948, and, after what looked like a disagreement in their council, added that if 13,000 or more general practitioners still disapproved the B.M.A. would advise all practitioners to remain out when the plan came into operation.

The result of the April plebiscite was that based on a smaller poll (18,227 compared with 19,537 in February), 8,639 general practitioners were now satisfied and the number who disapproved had fallen to 9,558. The B.M.A. kept its word and advised the general practitioners to join the plan. Most of them did, many of the 9,558 perhaps reluctantly, some fearing that their private practices would fade away completely after July, others with misgivings, but prepared to try to make the·program work.

So a National Health Service did come into operation on July 5, 1948. It did leave the doctor free to join or not, or to work partly in the service and partly in private practice. It left the individual equally free to use the service or not, or to use it in part (as, for example, for hospital treatment) while continuing to employ and pay his private dentist. The Ministry of Health could honestly say that there was no sort of compulsion about the whole plan, except— not a point emphasized by the ministry—the relentless economic pressure on the individual to avoid paying twice for the medical treatment, once in his taxes and once in fees to a doctor in private practice.

There was also the dental profession. In Britain it is represented by two professional associations, one of which accepted the minister's proposals on behalf of its members, while the other did not. As a result, the plan started with about half the dentists in and half out.

Quite a number of those dentists who came into the scheme did very well. Their association had made certain that, as previously, the scale of payments for dental work was based on the work done for the patient, not on a capitation basis. Some dentists earned gross incomes, in the first year, of remarkable size for a professional man— £10,000 in the year was not uncommon. But that is to anticipate. The dental associations were not thinking in those happy terms while their negotiations with the Ministry of Health were in progress.

All that the doctors had said the dentists repeated, not perhaps so frequently but even more loudly. They had an additional grievance. There had at least never been any suggestion that a doctor's prescription should be checked by a civil servant before the druggist was allowed to make it up. Regarding dental treatment, however, where the work to be done exceeded a certain limit of cost, the dentist was bound to obtain the approval of the ministry before starting on it. Otherwise, the authorities would be free to decline to pay his bill.

On the face of it, that appeared a considerable imposition, but there was another side to it. The dental profession, to be candid, lacks some of the traditions of the medical profession. Free dental treatment for persons insured under the former national health acts was introduced after World War I, and it proved an enormous financial boon to the profession. Not all dentists could resist temptation to profit by it financially. Case after case came to light of dentists who proposed extraction of every tooth in a patient's head when conservative work on half a dozen teeth would have restored the patient's health and comfort. There is no doubt that some dentists lacked skill in conservative work and, when faced with a difficult tooth, advised pulling it out because that was the only solution they personally could tackle.

The approved societies, which then were paying the bill and had only limited funds with which to provide dental treatment, became increasingly cautious, and their reaction was to require that estimates for large-scale jobs, involving multiple extractions, be referred to them for prior approval. The Ministry of Health maintained a service of independent dental practitioners to whom any dispute over treatment could be referred for adjudication. This system was carried into the new health service; it would be pleasant, but reckless, to assume that no need for it still existed.

How is the health plan working? Jerkily, and with all the difficulties that might be expected. Doctors are overworked. Many people needing treatment, who before could not have paid for it, are now visiting doctors with no imposed financial hesitations, to their eventual benefit. Some, no doubt, who need no treatment whatsoever—except the adult equivalent of a sharp slap—are also visiting doctors with financial impunity, and to the detriment of those who are genuinely sick. From July 5 onward, there was a flood of patients, and many doctors felt somewhat submerged in it.

That has its serious dangers. The doctor with an overcrowded office cannot give proper personal treatment to every case confined to bed at home, and those, after all, are the more serious. Instead, he tends to order the sick patient into a hospital, where he knows that at least he will be under observation. That again diminishes the chances that every hospital patient will be given the best care.

Hospitals are more overcrowded than they were, and still almost as understaffed. The plain fact is that the National Health Service Act, of itself, neither created any more doctors nor conjured out of the earth any more hospital accommodations. In so far as most doctors were, before the act came into operation, working to capacity, the additional burden thrown on the existing facilities could only have resulted in some fall in the quality of the service available to those using it.

An American specialist, visiting London in August, 1948, put the professional case against the plan as a whole as concisely as it can be put. He said that, in his view, the risk created by the new program was that the whole standard of medical treatment in Britain would be reduced to the level of that formerly available for the insured person, and that the new service would hamstring any hope of raising the level of treatment for the insured person up to that formerly given to the best paying patients. Is that true, as a long-term view?

In the fall of 1949, *The Practitioner,* a journal of the medical profession and not noticeably prone to support for the government, published a survey it had made within the profession of reactions to the first year of the service in operation. There were criticisms enough.

Older people still prefer the former regime, if they can afford it: ". . . in some districts, the few (doctors) who remained out of the scheme became more busy than before. . . . As seems inevitable in the process of nationalisation, the number of officials in the hospitals has increased." But it is clear enough from this survey that the basic structure of the system is effective and that in its operation it is not inevitably wrecking the traditions of the profession. One surgeon wrote: "The fundamental difficulty . . . is that the attempt has been made by legislation to give uniformity and exact definition to a system that has grown slowly." Yet those customs and traditions of the profession have been strong enough to make the plan work; the fears of the profession that it would be controlled from above and by laymen, instead of from within, have proved to be unfounded.

The impact of the scheme on the dental services as a whole was sharp and, in some aspects, more dangerous to public health. Dentists, whether working for approved society members or a patient paying directly, had always received an individual fee for an individual job. Unlike the doctor, the only limit to the amount a dentist could earn in the year was his inclination to work hard and his ability to work fast, and fast work in dentistry is not necessarily good work.

Before the war, the ministry had been building up a separate dental service for children and for expectant mothers. That service was staffed by dentists paid a salary on a fixed scale. The two systems of remuneration existed side by side, and managed to do so largely because the amount of money available in the hands of approved societies for the payment of dental benefit was limited. Equally with the medical profession, in July, 1948, the supply of qualified dentists fell short in numbers of the number needed to treat everyone who wished dental treatment once it was available by the simple process of walking into a dentist's office.

The inevitable happened. It was the salaried service that broke down. The school dentists deserted the salaried field for the field of free enterprise. And, to quote *The Practitioner* survey again, this breakdown "is regarded by the whole profession as the greatest and most tragic failure of the new Health service. Although it may be politically expedient, it is nevertheless scientifically wrong, as well as economically unsound, to provide dentures for octogenarians while allowing the teeth of the rising generation to be neglected."

The national health service as a whole is expensive. Parts of it are defective. Almost all of it is capable of abuse. The element of political dogma injected during its process of formation has not yet worked itself out. For its completion, it needs the expenditure of a great deal more capital money, particularly in the provision of health centers, the halfway house between the doctor's office and the hospital. Any one of these difficulties may wreck it. But I do not think they will. I think it will take a generation to establish it well, but I believe that the doctors themselves would prefer—and will manage —to remold it into a better service for health.

One solid argument remains; far-reaching schemes of this kind that are postponed for a year or so because of practical difficulties, somehow never seem to start at all. Water never seems to become warmer while you hesitate on the brink and shiver. A wider front in the attack on disease has been opened.

I think the final answer to the whole problem will depend on something that was hardly discussed in public at all, throughout all these negotiations and experiments. The new system may in the end weed out the doctor who used his profession for his own aggrandisement. If it replaces him by a man who thinks the system more important than the patient (or even as important) the change will be for the worse. The only person who should be a doctor is the person with an intense interest in other human beings. Too few have done any thinking on how these—and only these—men and women can be attracted into the profession.

CHAPTER XIII

Unemployment and Rehabilitation

Here are four cases from the records of the Reading Labour Exchange, Reading being a town in Berkshire some 40 miles west of London, with a prewar population of about 100,000 people.

One Friday evening in September, 1943, four Canadian soldiers, waiting outside a military camp, stopped a passing taxi driven by a man called Tom Peyton. They said they had 48 hours leave, and that they wanted to spend the weekend at Brighton on the South Coast, a favorite resort of Canadians, and a run of some 45 miles. There was nothing unusual in the request. Peyton quoted them a figure; they agreed and got inside. When they were nearly there, and passing through a wood, the four men signaled Peyton to stop. As he drew up, his passengers sprang out, grabbed him and carried him bodily into the wood. There they beat him up, left him unconscious and drove off in the taxi. Later, the four men were traced and sentenced to long prison terms. But what of the taxi driver?

They had disposed of Peyton, so they thought, by kicking him. They wore heavy army boots with steel toe-plates and cleats. It is hard to say if they intended to kill him outright or merely leave him unconscious and unable to do anything in time to interrupt their weekend. Whatever their intention, the injuries kept Peyton in hospital for eighteen months and left him permanently crippled. He was 35 and a healthy man, which is probably why he survived.

When he came out of hospital, he had a permanently injured spine; he was in constant pain and, when walking, he was only able to move his feet six inches at a time, and that with the aid of two canes. In a sense, he was a war casualty. In a sense, it was just bad luck that he happened to have encountered these four savages who

226

thought attempted murder the easier way out of paying a taxi fare. But there's no glory in being crippled that way. At 37, what does one do to start again?

Whatever had been broken inside Peyton's body, it hadn't been his spirit. As soon as he could move about at home, he began to experiment to find in what new way he could earn a living and keep his wife and child. He could never move far from his home again, let alone drive a car. He found an answer pretty quickly. One result of the war had been to put a premium on new shoes, and so on those who could repair old ones. Peyton started mending shoes for his neighbors and their children. It wasn't an ideal job for a crippled man. Shoe repairing involves standing most of the time, but Peyton liked it because it was a job he had discovered himself, right away, and the one at which he had started to earn a living again, free from charity. He had the use of his hands and arms. He contrived a high stool which gave his legs some relief. He was earning a living, and he had back his self-respect.

The officials at the labor exchange saw all this when Peyton came onto their books, as he was bound to come as a disabled man. The hospital that discharged him reported his name and the circumstances to the area labor exchange as a matter of routine. The Disablement Relief Officer called on Peyton at home, and discussed his plans with him. He made no attempt to dissuade Peyton from the line he had himself chosen. Instead, he arranged for him to take a course in boot and shoe repairing at a Ministry of Labour training center. Peyton accepted the course, particularly when he knew that he would be learning side-by-side with perfectly able-bodied men. He was determined not to be a "case." He was determined to become a normal boot and shoe repairer, capable of standing up, economically and technically, with the best men in the trade.

Peyton was one of the center's most memorable cases, so the manager told me, and not because of what they taught him but because of his spirit in going through with it. He was never free from pain while he was there. They improved the stool against which he could half-sit, half-lean. (Other trainees, in the carpentry section, made one for him to keep.) And there he learned the whole trade, how a shoe is built up, how you use the tools and machines and so give new life to an old pair of uppers. The instructor made certain that

Peyton could earn his living that way, so far as skill went. Peyton had all the rest.

Before the war, Andrew Moore was an assistant in a general store in East London. When the war broke out, he was the same age as Peyton, married, with a delicate wife. He was undersized, timid, ordinary, never likely to make a big success at his job, always the man who could successfully sell you a shirt or a tie, if you wanted one, and leave it at that. Still, he had so far been capable of earning enough to keep his wife and himself alive.

The war closed down his job in 1940. Sales of shirts were falling, and Moore was not the kind of man any management would put itself out to keep. The only job he could think of was civil defense, and for the winter of 1940–41 he served as an air raid warden during the worst of the bombing of London. The effect on him was cumulative. He said afterwards that it kind of screwed him up to a higher and higher tension, so that in the end he could never relax at all, even in quiet periods. The strain manifested itself in the form of gastric ulcers. He struggled on until, in April, 1941, his own house was destroyed by a bomb. All anyone could do for him then was to evacuate him and his wife into the country, fifty miles from London, and hope that he could keep himself by working on a farm. There was no difficulty then in finding a job of some kind on a farm.

A farmer did hire Moore and gave him and his wife a cottage fifteen miles from Reading, about four miles from the nearest village. As he wasn't physically much good, the farmer had him taught tractor driving, and at first his stomach condition improved. He had a job which he could just about manage; the country air and food was better than he had ever had before; he was free from the anxiety of air raids, and he was doing his bit to help win the war. For four years life was bearable, but in 1946 his wife fell ill again. She had never taken to the country, and the remoteness of their cottage depressed her. The war was over and she wanted to get back to London. And that—plus the tractor driving—brought on his gastric ulcers again.

Moore was desperate. There was no hope of going back to his old job. The shop had gone and that part of East London was still a waste of grass-grown plots where the foundations of hundreds of destroyed houses still stood. His wife would not stay in the country. He had no particular skill, no confidence that he could acquire any. The farmer would fire him as soon as better men from the forces came back. He wanted a quiet job in London, where his wife would have some interest in life, some neighbors with whom to gossip. But what could he do? He went to talk to the officials in the labor exchange. So far a pretty undistinguished story.

As he talked, he played nervously with a carved piece of wood and, when asked what it was, he explained a little shamefacedly that when the raids in London in 1940 were heavy, he got out a knife and a piece of wood and carved out dogs' heads—Airedales they always were—because the effort of concentrating on the carving dimmed in his mind the threat from bombs. Very conventional heads, but well done of their kind.

After Moore had left, the man at the labor exchange rang up his opposite number in an exchange in London, and asked him for a list of small shops in the West End of London which make and sell fancy knick-knacks like lampshades and pipe racks and salt holders. When that came through, he asked Moore to call, and told him to go and show his carvings in these shops to see if any of them would offer him a job. A week later Moore came back, excited but worried. One firm would like to take him on, but what about a house in London? The officials explained to him that as a former civil defense worker, and because his own house had been destroyed by bombing, he had certain priorities in the allocation of new houses being built in London. A month later Moore and his wife moved into a flat in North London.

Six months later, Moore wrote a very glowing letter of thanks to the official, and announced that his wife was very much better and that he had been made manager of the workroom, where the lampshades and the dogs' heads and salt holders were made.

Another success story; one that would sound much better if Moore had fixed it up all on his own initiative. But, like a great many others, initiative was just what he lacked. If no one had bothered with him, he would have drifted into a hospital, and in the end he would have been a liability to somebody, state or family, for the rest of his life. Instead, he is supporting himself and his wife, and paying his share of taxes.

Joe Harman was blinded in the 1914–1918 war, and for the next 25 years lived with his sister and her husband, doing nothing, supported by his war pension. Then the sister's husband died and there wasn't enough money to keep the home together. Joe had to think about work.

The trouble about Joe was that he was surly and outspoken and his personal habits were bad. He spat frequently, which some other people are inclined to resent. But he was active and quick minded, very independent, and he was quite accustomed to being blind.

He went to the employment exchange because he wanted to work. He didn't expect them to find him any. It was a last resort, but he was willing to give anything, even a government department, a try. The man he saw thought over his case for some time. Then he remembered an employer in Reading who had told him about one job he had in his factory which he could never fill for long. Everyone, man or woman, said it was too monotonous. It was a machine-minding job, and it consisted of fitting a half-finished product into a hand press, and then bringing the press down on it. It required a certain delicacy of touch, and you could earn good money if you could stand it. The problem was, could it be done by a blind man? He took Joe along to see.

Joe sat at the machine and asked the foreman to explain it to him. His hands curved over the mechanism and the pieces he had to handle. It was as though his fingers were seeing what had to be done. Then he started, slowly at first, but without mistakes. After a quarter of an hour he said, "I'll stay."

A fortnight later, the employer rang up the labor exchange and thanked them for sending Joe along. There had been only one difficulty. Two of the girls working alongside Joe had objected to his habit of spitting. They had moved the girls, not Joe.

Finally, there was the case of the Miles Aircraft Company.

The Miles Aircraft Company started expansion for rearmament work about 1936. Its main factory and airfield are close to Reading, and its wartime production was enormous. It continued production on a considerable scale after the war ended and, in July, 1947, it was still employing 5,097 people, in the ratio of about eight men to one woman. It was in that month that the number of layoffs began to mount, for it was then that the financial difficulties leading to its final collapse first began to worry the management. By the end of the year, the company was in serious difficulties, and by the first quarter of 1948 it was out of aircraft manufacture entirely.

At first, Reading was not greatly affected. The concern at its peak had drawn labor from an area of 25 to 30 miles around. For war purposes, it had profitted the management to provide special transport for workers to and from their homes, and when the management began to check over their avoidable running costs, the men and women from those areas were the first to be discharged. The re-employment problems of these people did not fall on the Reading exchange. But Reading had to meet the second wave of dismissals. By January 21, 1948, 972 Miles workers living in the Reading area had lost their jobs, and 760 of them had been placed in other work. Even by April, only 102 of those discharged had remained unemployed for more than two weeks. By July 31, 1948, the total of discharges had been 1,503 men and 207 women over the six months. Fifteen hundred of them had found other work, the biggest single job which the Reading exchange had tackled.

But the Miles affair was not a 100% success story. In Reading, there has existed for over a century a firm of woodworkers that has built up a reputation for ship and hotel fittings of the highest quality. The firm has handled contracts to provide the internal fittings for ships of most of the major British steamship lines. Before the war, a craftsman there, skilled in working on every kind of hard wood, could expect to earn £5 to £6 a week. When Miles expanded, from 1936 onwards, it offered work on aircraft frames to skilled woodworkers, and many switched to Miles, partly to earn better wages (up to £10 to £12 a week), partly because of the patriotic impulse to make aircraft. In 1947 and 1948, most of these men were discharged from the Miles works, ten years older and, what was much worse, no longer the skilled men they had once been.

For ten years, they had been working in soft woods, generally on one or two standardized operations. They had lost their touch and craft on hard woods. Some were glad to get back into their old jobs in the old firm, with loss of ten years' seniority and a considerable cut in earnings. Some were resentful and expected something as good as the Miles job had been. Some had become foremen and had given away their tool sets, confident that they had finished with work at the bench forever. The fortunate ones were those who got back into their former jobs of ten years back.

The British Ministry of Labour exists to supply industry with labor it needs, not to supply men with work. It can only place men in existing vacancies. It cannot, save for the seriously disabled, create jobs for men to do. There is that limit to its responsibility, and all its officials must in the end apply that test to everything they try to do.

But let us continue with the Reading Labour Exchange, for Reading is a fair enough example of a British "Middletown." It is in the center of an area which is primarily agricultural, but the town itself contains a number of light industries. During the war it was used as an evacuation area for London, and its population grew to about 140,000. Now the population has shrunk back to about 110,000, and from that figure it is likely to grow rather than diminish.

To British ears, the sound of the name Reading means biscuits. Huntley and Palmer has made biscuits in Reading for a long time: it is one of the seven largest employers of labor in town. The others comprise two light engineering concerns; the Reading Co-operative Society, a general distributive store; and three public authorities, the Reading Borough Council, the Administrative Council and the Agricultural Committee of the county, the latter two of which have their principal offices in Reading. Reading is the seat of the Berkshire County government, and there are regional offices of a number of government departments.

Among the secondary industries, building and civil engineering, printing and the distributive trades predominate, plus, of course, agriculture outside the actual town area itself. Reading is a city of mixed industries and mixed occupations, from a small concern making hand-sewn footwear to the principal county distributor of agricultural machinery.

These are the figures of its industrial population as of July 31, 1948:

	Employed	*Self-Employed*	*Non-Employed*	TOTAL
Men	42,111	2,208	754	45,073
Women	18,473	295	1,469	20,237
Juveniles (those under 18)	5,081	4	20	5,105
	65,665	2,507	2,243	70,415

The number of "non-employed" may be misleading. The numbers of those "non-employed" seeking work through the official employment exchange were: Men, 545; Women, 285; Juveniles, 3.

Reading is, then, fortunate. Of its total working population only slightly more than one in a hundred at any one time are actively in search of employment. The Labour Exchange records show that on the average, during the first half of 1948, about 800 men were placed every month.

A labour exchange is a business organization, run by a manager. He is a civil servant. On certain points of policy, and on certain matters involving the expenditure of public money, such as sending men for training courses, he is subject to control from a regional office of his ministry. Otherwise, he is a manager and he is expected to run his exchange flexibly and efficiently.

In Reading, he has a main building, modern but in a back street (no doubt to save the cost of a main road site), in which his administrative departments and the men's section are housed. The women's and juveniles' sections are in another building and he has a third office, one in the center of the town where the "Resettlement Advice Office" was set up.

The main volume of the work of any exchange is the finding of unskilled and semi-skilled men for local industry. Consequently, the organization of the office is built upon two registers, a register of those men seeking work and a register of those employers seeking labor. The officials in the exchange try to find out what each employer in this district needs, and to submit to him men who seem fit for the job he has to offer. The exchange does not interfere with the individual employer's right to hire or fire his own men.

The simplest cases run on these lines: a builder is starting work on a new contract, and he puts in what is called an "order" for 20 bricklayers. The order is passed to the clerk in charge of the section of the register containing the names of unemployed bricklayers. The clerk sends a card to each man with details of the job. Each applicant goes to the employer and either he or the employer reports the result.

Similarly, a man seeking work goes to the exchange. The man carries his ministry card which shows his industrial history. The exchange also has a file which shows what employment he has had. (If he moves from one district to another, his file follows him when he reports to the exchange in his new district.) The clerk looks up the list of orders for vacancies in his trade, and gives him details of any that exist. Armed with that information, he goes off to look for a specific job. If there is none available, his name is noted and he is given a time to report back at weekly intervals. While in this position, he is probably entitled to his weekly unemployment benefit.

With skilled and some semi-skilled employments, there is considerable variation in the method of finding and filling jobs. For instance, on Clydeside in the shipbuilding area, the local exchange is extensively used for all trades. An employer gives an order for so many riveters or electricians, and they come to him through the exchange. In the printing and automotive trades, nearly all skilled employment is found through the trade unions. The exchange is only used when a man's union cannot suggest where he will find work, which means that the chances of finding work are poor.

The department for women runs in very much the same way.

Clearly, the chief task for any labor exchange manager is to see that his card indexes of jobs and of men who can fill them are kept up to date, and are efficiently handled. It is these records which handle the volume of his work. But they do not by any means perform the whole task.

One essential requirement is that the manager should do all that he can to make local employers and employees aware of the full services his exchange provides. That has become progressively easier. In the days of prewar depression, many exchanges were no more than places for paying out weekly unemployment money to men and women who were losing all hope of ever finding work again. Employers did not need to call up an exchange to find a man, because there were a score of men for each vacancy. They ceased to think of an exchange as a place which could provide a man they needed and had failed to find for themselves.

The war changed that. The exchange was the determining factor by which most men entered the armed services, or war work—and for most men and women either one or the other was compulsory. The exchange became the office of the National Labour Officer, and each employer was compelled to obtain his consent before he engaged or fired any men. There was almost complete direction of all labor, channeled through this one office. And, perhaps unexpectedly, it improved the opinion that both employers and employees held of the exchange and its officials, very largely because both learned a good deal more about them.

Every exchange manager has several committees which meet regularly in his office. Each consists of voluntary members from the locality, employers, trade unionists, clergy, social workers and so on. The three most important are the Employment Committee, the Youth Employment Committee and the Disabled Employment Committee. They exist to inform the manager on local conditions and local problems. In exchange, he tells the committee what he has done, what he will do, what he would like to do, and what he can't do. In addition, most exchange managers regularly talk to the local chambers of commerce, trade councils and Rotary Club meetings, sometimes on general topics, sometimes on specific problems. A manager can become as much an accepted figure of the locality as the managers of banks.

One of the assistant managers at Reading was formerly in the R.A.F. on a long-service enlistment. He entered the service as a fitter, was commissioned, and finished the war as a technical staff officer. Then he exchanged that job for one in the Ministry of Labour. He told me that it has taken about two years for him to come to know Reading really well. Now he can tell you how many power lathes there are in the area, their brand-names, their location and what job they do. He can tell you what concerns have closed shops. (It's no good sending a non-union man there if there is an alternative position to offer him.) He has a very good idea of what contracts most firms expect to get, and when they fail to get them. (Both are important as guides to future shortages, or surpluses, of men in those trades.) He probably has a very good idea of the capabilities of each concern, and of its record as an employer. He works on the assumption that if you want to help a man find the right employee, you must know both him and his establishment. Only then can you hope to eliminate most of the mistakes.

He feels similarly about the men on the books of the exchange, particularly the minority who, for some reason or other, are difficult to place. At first, he says, the exchange tries to place a man in his normal trade. In certain circumstances—where a man can no longer support himself in his old trade but might improve his earning power if he were taught a new one—the exchange can arrange for him to be trained, free, in some new trade. Much depends on the individual, on his capabilities and his eagerness to help himself. The exchange does not exist to provide a man the job or the pay he thinks he should have. If circumstances in his old trade have changed, and a man must adjust himself to that hard fact, generally they give him about six weeks in which to do so. Thereafter, if he refuses to look for a job he could handle—even though it is inferior to his last—he finds that he has lost his right to unemployment pay. Even in a labor exchange, starvation must be a club.

Disabled men are always handled individually, and each exchange has a special officer assigned to take care of them. In fact, all disabled men and women go on a special register. In 1944 Parliament passed the Disabled Persons (Employment) Act. Its purpose is clear enough from its title. Any person over sixteen who is substantially handicapped in employment because of any ailment, wound, injury, deformity or natural disability, is entitled to be placed on the special register. It does not matter how or when the disability was caused. The only test is whether or not it imposes a substantial handicap in getting or keeping suitable work.

The effects of the act are these:

1. The person with the disability may claim special training free of cost.
2. Three per cent of the staff of each firm employing more than twenty workers must be from the local register of disabled persons.
3. Certain occupations (at the moment attendants in parking lots and in electric passenger elevators) are reserved exclusively for persons from the disabled registers.
4. The government has set up, and maintains by grant, factories and establishments solely for the employment of those so disabled that they could never hope to earn a living in a competitive market.

In Reading and district, the area covered by the exchange, there are 3,872 men and women on the disabled persons' register; on June 30, 1948, 203 of them were unplaced. Peyton, Moore and Harman are not exceptions, but on the whole, luck was on their side. They each encountered an official who was both conscientious and imaginative. They had also some personal quality which helped. Two hundred of the others have not been so fortunate.

The responsible officer at Reading told me of another case he placed during the war. The man was about fifty. His father had been wealthy; the son had never been compelled to work. In his youth he had driven racing cars, and had drifted through the usual car business, selling on commission, doing well in good times, unemployed when they were bad. He had never married. He lived at home, suffering from the consequences of disapproval from his father because he never made good, but having the sympathy from his mother, who thought it a shame that he should have to soil his hands at work. When the father died, enough money had been left to enable him to continue this completely unsatisfactory existence.

The war came and he had to register at the exchange, ready for work of national importance. He did so quite willingly and quite hopelessly. By this time he had developed a mild neurosis from his frustrations. It took the form of excessive cleanliness. After any contact with the outside world, he would feel compelled to go and wash his hands.

In the end, his problem was solved with ease. He was sent to a laundry, as a checker in the department which sorts out the completed wash. He wore a clean overall every day. He handled nothing but newly washed clothes. He was supremely happy. He is still there and his neurosis is very much improved.

On the whole, the disabled war veterans recover the most successfully. After blindness or the loss of one or more limbs, there is a grim period of readjustment, when the victims are intensely apprehensive about the loss of capacity, and resentful of the fact that it has happened to them. The vast majority of them recover, once they are given a chance to gain a fresh skill. Their personalities are often strengthened by the fight they have got to put up to do so. If retrained, they are generally all right.

Much less fortunate are those whose brains are damaged. Something has gone—they may be incapable of any sort of concentration —and they are horribly aware of what they have lost. It requires great spirit for them to rebuild with a hope of any sort of independence. Reading has one case like that, a brilliant young parachute officer who was shot in the head while parachuting into Normandy on D-Day, 1944. After two years of hard work, he can count up to ten again; and they've found him a job.

Then there are the group of neurotics, and the men with such permanent disabilities as latent tuberculosis, or epilepsy. There are some things they can do. The difficulty is to find enough jobs of that kind to go around.

Finally, there are those whose incapacities will always deny them economic independence, and yet who are not completely helpless. It is an act of charity to find them what work they can do. It would be folly to expect a commercial undertaking to be able, unaided, to carry the burden of their limitations. For them the government has two separate plans.

The first involves the building of ten special factories, all in South Wales. They will be leased to commercial enterprises which undertake to employ men suffering, for example, from pneumoconiosis (stone-dust in the lungs) or other forms of partial disability. In order to qualify, the firms must employ at least half their payroll from the disabled list. In exchange, the firms receive a rebate of half the normal rent of the factory. For those who were so badly injured they can never compete commercially (it is estimated that between 5,000 and 7,000 badly injured men can do some form of productive work), the government has established a separate corporation, the Disabled Persons Employment Corporation, which will employ them and pay them the standard union wage for the job, whatever their output. The corporation will sell the products and, if there is a trading loss each year—as is probable—the government will make it up. This is the "Re-employ" Scheme.

The remaining section of the exchange deals with juveniles, those under eighteen years. The raising of the school-leaving age from fourteen to fifteen became effective in Britain in September, 1947, with the result that the succeeding twelve months were an isolated stretch with very few children leaving school. Responsibility for juvenile employment may be taken over by the Education Authority of the area, as is the case in Reading. If not, it falls on the local labour exchange. Because Reading Exchange escapes full responsibility, here are some details from a smaller exchange, in Midhurst, Sussex.

Midhurst is only 40 miles from London, but it still continues to be a fairly isolated district. The territory covered by this exchange is about fifteen by twelve miles, mostly broken country, where lumber is as important a local industry as agriculture. Very few skilled mechanical trades are employed in Midhurst.

There is only one high school in the area, a secondary school for boys in the town. The nearest county high school, for boys and girls, is at Chichester. For the rest there are the normal primary schools. How do the juveniles find jobs?

The answer is, naturally enough, a patchwork. The boys tend to follow the occupations of their fathers, but with a greater drift towards mechanical or clerical work and away from agriculture. (The manager of the local exchange believes that you can predict whether a boy will go into a town job or a country job by whether he makes friends with town boys or country boys while he is at school.) The girls follow their parents. They often go to the same job, even in the same place, that their mothers held before they married. The mother knows the shopkeeper, for example, and she places her daughter in the shop before the girl has left school. In short, most juveniles find jobs through their parents. The labour exchange comes into the picture in two ways.

The first consists of offering advice to the children, and to their parents, in the child's last term at school. As a matter of routine, the exchange manager visits every school in his district (there are 22 of them) towards the end of each term. The child is there, the parents are there—or are invited—and the teachers are there. The manager tells the children the kind of jobs that are available in the district, and what he can do to help place them. He discusses each child's bent with parents and teacher, and he tries roughly to fit the child to the job. He claims, in fact, that he gives them the kind of advice he would give his own children (he has four).

A child remains a juvenile, in the eyes of the Ministry of Labour, until he reaches 18. Until then, he has a different type of employment card, pays a different rate of weekly contribution and is under different regulations while at work. The juvenile is on a separate register at the exchange. His employment and changes of employment, are watched. He is invited to informal gatherings at the exchange, where he can raise any problems he has. There is a special officer detailed to watch over juveniles to try to discover why one changes his job so often, to see if another can be found a job better suited to his talents. The general idea is to settle the juvenile at the start, to help him to find the job which will give him a steady trade, or a good basic experience at the beginning, when he has time on his side, and while he and his family can best tolerate a low wage during training.

The manager at Midhurst is a family man. He was formerly a surveyor and lived for some time in Australia. He likes to know what is going on in the town. "If you talk sense to people," he said, "if they see you are out to help, they'll bring their problems to you. I've brought up my own four sons, and I reckon I know enough to help most folks.

"Take the case of Sally Green. She was a bright kid at school—she finished at Chichester County School. I saw her when she left, and in the end I found her a job at an Admiralty signal establishment, just outside my area. She learned signaling and cipher work, was given a commission in the Women's Naval Service and now she is doing very well indeed. She took her chance properly.

"What I hate to see is a young chap following his father's trade just because he can earn good money at it straightaway. There's a coffinmaker in Midhurst who wants an apprentice—thirty bob a week, maybe, till he's trained, but after that a steady, skilled trade that's never likely to die out. And yet a man who's been a general laborer all his life will want his son to follow him at that when he's seventeen or eighteen instead of giving him a chance to learn coffin making. Result, the son'll never earn more than £4. 10s. a week, or its equivalent, and yet he could, with a bit of encouragement from his parents, learn a trade where, in the end, he could earn twice as much, and probably be a master man."

Of course, it makes a difference where you are born. Some cities have built up fine systems of training and part-time education for juveniles. If you are an exceptional child, a great many educational doors are opened for you. But the acid test of a system is what it can do for the average child born in the country, who belongs to the country, who probably will be happier if he can find a job in the surroundings he knows, a job which will give him skill, confidence and security for his working life. In an urban country like Britain, it is easy to think of the country areas as full of blind-alley occupations, with far fewer of the opportunities that come easily to the town child.

Midhurst is an answer to that. You're not driven back to a town for work, nor compelled to stay and accept whatever happens to be available. There's freedom of choice.

It is possible to write out a long list of specialized services provided by the Ministry of Labour. I would like to describe just three more.

The average labour exchange deals with the normal skilled, semi-skilled and unskilled workers, whose rates of pay may perhaps ultimately reach a ceiling of from £8 to £10 a week. Above that is a group which is much smaller in number, but just as varied in occupation, the managers and technicians. It includes the accountant and the chemist, the production engineer and the sales director, some with technical qualifications, others with personal qualifications which may lift them into the £1000 a year or more class. For these, there are the appointments department, and the technical and scientific register of the ministry.

The departments can properly be described as employment agencies pure and simple. The routine of registration for work is carried out by the local exchanges. But any man may put his name down in an exchange as seeking a higher-grade appointment; so may any exchange that comes across a man who it thinks could hold down such a job. In that case, the name goes into the card index of the appointments department, or of the technical and scientific register. The first deals with men whose qualifications are mainly for business, the second with men who are primarily scientists, technologists, professional engineers, or who are surveyors or architects.

The appointments department maintains fourteen offices at key points over Britain. Each is connected to the others by teletype and each, at a fixed time every day, transmits to all the others the details of the men and the jobs it has on offer. The department cannot move unless it is given details of what jobs are available, but in this respect it is not surely passive. It has a considerable ability for selling itself and its service to employers, either by direct contact or by offering its services to those who advertise vacancies for those posts the department exists to fill.

The office system can be very simply described. Every possible variety of job is given a code number. That code number, and experience and qualifications of each applicant, are recorded on a card. (If a man has two capacities his card is duplicated.) At each office, an official is in charge of up to 100 or so cards of individual men with roughly the same qualifications (for example, 100 accountants). That official daily sees the records of all jobs available for accountants, and he passes on to the prospective employers the names of about half a dozen men who seem capable of filling the job. The employer can make his arrangements as to how and when he interviews an applicant, if at all. All he must do is notify the department if he fills the vacancy, and whom he has given the job. He pays nothing for the department's services, nor does the applicant.

The word in the last paragraph that begs a lot of questions is "qualifications." It is one thing to write down a man's experience. How do you arrive at his qualifications, which include so much of pure human personality?

That is done by interview, based on a standardized technique, largely worked out during the war. A man's industrial personality can be assessed by reference to his basic preferences in relation to people, ideas or things. By a series of carefully framed questions (which have been tried out pretty exhaustively), any individual can, in these times, be assessed. He is given a range of ten points; his pattern may be People 5, Ideas 3, Things 2; he will be a misfit if he drifts, or is pushed into, let us say, a job in a routine industrial chemistry laboratory.

This kind of test is of the greatest value for men and women without industrial experience, those leaving school or college or the services. By the time a man reaches thirty, he has usually found a type of job which suits him or, less frequently, has adjusted himself to the job he has trained for. He does not need grading in this way. But when he is interviewed—and every man seeking an appointment through the department is interviewed—the man who talks to him has this kind of classification system in mind. His object is to arrive at as accurate a picture of the man as possible, so that he can describe him to the prospective employer, and thus avoid sending the employer the wrong kind of man.

That is not always easy, for employers frequently are vague in disclosing some of the vital details of the job they are offering. They hesitate to commit themselves. One concern asked for a production manager, and said it was prepared to pay £1250 a year salary. The department passed details of this job over to a man who had said he wanted between £1250 and £1500. The applicant went for an interview, but without much enthusiasm. He was received by the full board and they talked for an hour. The board liked the applicant and the applicant liked the board, and the job. At the end of it all they offered him £1500 a year. He shook his head and smiled deprecatingly. "The job's worth more than that." A quarter of an hour later he walked out with the job at a salary of £2300 a year. Because of their original hesitation, the concern might very well have missed that man.

The appointments service can guarantee no one a job, nor can it guarantee to find the ideal man for any vacant job. It cannot prevent men losing jobs it has found for them, nor does it compel an employer to keep a man for any minimum length of time. But it does own the biggest card index of men and vacancies in the country, and it does its best to insure that its card index is intelligently run. It is of enormous value to the man with ability but few connections. It can tell a man of the opportunities which might otherwise skip his door on their way down his street.

Training centers are intended to teach a man a new industrial job. A man cannot go there just because he thinks he would like a change; for one thing, the capacity of the centers is limited. While at a center a man is paid a weekly allowance roughly equivalent to a reasonable wage, so that he and his family can keep alive during the non-earning period. A man who wants to take a course at a training center must satisfy the local labour exchange that there is some reason, beyond his control, which prevents him from ever making a living again at his former trade—it may be anything from an amputation to an anxiety neurosis. In addition, he can only be trained in a trade which suffers from a shortage of men, and the numbers for each course at all training centers are worked out by the ministry in conjunction with the trade unions of those industries, to make certain that surpluses are not being built up by government action.

Take one training center, at Whaddon near London, as a specimen. It was set up before the war; during the war it worked to capacity, training men and women for war industries. It started out after the war with large numbers of men training for the building trades, and now its activity is well below peak. At the start of 1947, there were over 600 men in the center, of which 150 were disabled. The others were men released from the forces. In mid-1948 there were under 300, but the figure of 150 disabled was about the same.

In 1947, 475 men passed through the center. Three hundred and sixty-four were placed in jobs as soon as they left, 58 more within a fortnight of leaving. Twenty-seven were not physically fit to go through the whole course, eleven left of their own accord before the end (there is no compulsion for anyone to stay, nor penalty if he leaves), four were not mentally able to absorb the training needed for their courses and two were discharged for misconduct. The others failed to qualify at the end.

Government training has nothing to do with socialism. I watched one man of about fifty who was learning the basic elements of wood–working and cabinet-making. He was an engineer's traveler who had developed spinal T.B., with the result that he couldn't walk any longer. He had planned to set up a small toy-making shop at home and build up a business of his own. He had come to the government training center to learn the elements of the trade, so that he would at least know what his men were doing and how well they were doing it.

"It's all one to us," the manager said. "Our job is to get them to work again; never mind who employs them."

Then there is rehabilitation. Rehabilitation really precedes the work done at a training center. The job of the rehabilitation center (now at Egham, Surrey) is to try to make an injured or disabled man capable of learning a new trade.

The first concern is to make the man physically fit—as fit as he can be—for physical recovery is the foundation on which confidence can be rebuilt. From the start, each trainee mixes with the rest of the men, which is an admirable method of stripping from him the feeling that his injury, and the personal disaster it has brought to his former life, are unique. He begins to feel less sorry for himself. It is only when he has begun to find his mental bearings, and to improve his physical condition, that he is given the chance to work out for himself the kind of occupation he will in future be able to tackle with confidence. He may find a new way of doing his old trade. He may get a clue as to what new trade would suit him very well. The ministry's own handbook puts it simply enough, "When a man leaves Egham . . . he knows, with certainty and confidence, just what he is capable of . . . Either he will go at once to work which is waiting for him, or he will set off to a further course of specialized training, without any of the awkwardness of a first approach to something new and strange. At Egham, he will have broken the ice. He can take the plunge with confidence, because he knows, now, just what to expect, and what he is capable of accomplishing."

It is too easy to become sentimental over the injured, equally easy to dismiss all attempts to help men to find jobs as sentimentality. The plain hard economic facts that lie behind all that Britain does through its Minister of Labour are these: the first is that Britain is short of men, and dares not allow even a man with a capacity no more than 25% of normal to remain idle. The second is that the more highly complex a civilization becomes, the smaller is the proportion of men and women who are at work actually producing something new. If Britain wants social security and free education, it must make even its disabled contribute to new production. If these two facts were otherwise, the drive behind all this activity would be much less.

But that is only half the story. The other half is that these efforts do produce results, and so increase the sum of human happiness and contentment. The average man can be helped to find the right job, and is glad when that happens. The cripple does prefer to be taken out of the category of those who litter up the home or the infirmary in idleness, and is instead converted into a man who gets a sizeable pay envelope each week, and earns it.

Yet it is necessary for all this to be organized. No individual can create his own labour exchange or his own Egham rehabilitation center; and it would be useless to him if he could. Part of the cure is the communal life. Part of the service is the fact that it is available to everyone. All these things are not charity. They are part of the common man's rights, just as much so as the right to join a union.

This feeling works both ways. In the end, the most impressive thing about any of the ministry's activities is the quality of the men whom they have found, and trained, to run them. These men are both realistic and competent. They do not expect 100% success every time. They are concerned if their organizations fail to produce the percentage of successes they know they should produce. Their interest is in men, in men who are or can be made normal functioning individuals, men who they feel should accept all these services naturally, and use them to the full as of right. Their confidence in themselves, and in the men they work for, breeds a like confidence on the other side. If these things were charities, if they were handed out as rewards or privileges, this atmosphere would be gone, and so too would half their effectiveness. These men deal in confidence; they have it themselves and they foster it in others. Confidence is the basis of all their skill. Charity destroys confidence in its recipient. A man flinches when he is made to feel he needs charity; he cringes when there is a risk of its being taken away.

Of course mistakes are made. The officials are part of a civil service organization; the civil service, like the currency, has suffered from continuous inflation over the last ten years, and everyone riding on an inflationary band wagon finds it extremely hard to face the practical consequences of a change in policy.

But the Ministry of Labour organizations have at least this advantage. They have grown slowly, and many of the lessons were learned a long time ago, and as a result of comparatively small–scale experiments. What exists now has been tested by experience, the experience of adjusting the whole industrial machine of the country to a war.

I claim that the importance of this ministry's work, as with the national health service, is that it is getting rid of charity. In social questions, I believe that charity is as dangerous a motivation as pity. In the authorized version of the Bible, charity is used as the equivalent of love, a mixture of compassion and tenderness, of service and brotherly help. When has love been expressed in terms of money? And yet today charity is adorned with every known form of monetary symbol. The charitable man, by common definition, is the man who gives most money; so often he is the man who gives nothing else.

It is often said that a community is only healthy when the people in it think their obligations as important as their rights. And that is true enough of the people who have acquired plenty of rights and are in a position to shed plenty of obligations. But if a community is to mean anything to the men at the bottom, they must be convinced then that their rights are as inherent in the system as their obligations.

PART IV

THE LABOUR GOVERNMENT AND SOCIETY

CHAPTER XIV

The Press

The Labour Government's relations with the press, throughout the five years, have been uneasy even when they have not been downright bad. Some members of the government have continually spoken as though they had not forgiven the press for failing both to prophesy and to welcome their victory in 1945. And that attitude has persisted. In the House of Commons, as late as the end of October, 1949, Mr. Aneurin Bevan made a venomous attack on what he described as "an obscure provincial paper" (in fact, one of the oldest papers in the West of England) for reporting a statement by a local councillor on what Mr. Bevan himself had said on the future form of local government in England. However, Mr. Bevan himself was dealt with in a short but powerful editorial in *The Manchester Guardian*:

What a strange man Mr. Aneurin Bevan is! Whenever he is confronted with a statement from a newspaper he turns round and says it must be 'invented.' A man must have malevolence in his own soul to be so ready to impute malevolence to others. The *Hereford Times* and *Berrow's Worcester Journal* reported a speech by the Labour Mayor of Hereford at his city council meeting. Mr. Bevan's immediate comment is that 'there is no limit to the capacity of the British Press to invent stories'. . . . It never seemed to dawn on his twisted mind that the report might be an accurate account of what someone had said. He did not like it; therefore the newspapers must have invented it. It is fortunate for the country's traditions of decency that we have not many such people as Mr. Aneurin Bevan in public life.

Mr. Bevan once described the press of Britain as "the most prostituted Press in the world." Is that a fair description?

The national periodicals which have a definite political orientation can be divided into three groups, the daily morning papers, the Sunday papers and the weeklies.

The weekly periodicals are a group, of which the constituent members have by now recognizable characteristics, almost recognizable personalities. The *Economist* is the bluff business man, disclaiming any political prejudices but having, shall we say, certain fundamental habits of political thought. It resembles the man whose commonest utterance is, "Well, as I always say, . . ." It is solid, knowledgeable, very positive in its opinions and read by practically everyone who has influence or responsibility. Despite its title, politics and public affairs are covered quite as extensively as business and economics. It has strong links with the United States, and represents in Britain an American liberal point of view.

Tribune is the young man of the family, radical, impatient, too logical, short-tempered with those who think more slowly or more conservatively. It is a left-wing paper, responsible but not too highbrow. Its main appeal is to the intelligent young trade unionist.

The third masculine paper is *Spectator,* which has some of the qualities of the university tutor and the family lawyer; aware of the problems of life, but rather at second hand. The advice it offers is always sound, but likely to be submerged in the general chatter going on around.

The leaders in what must be called the female side of the group are *The New Statesman* and *Time and Tide. The New Statesman* is the middle-aged spinster don from Cambridge, acid, witty, clearsighted and yet, because of her celibacy, too often waspish and querulous. *Time and Tide* is avowedly feminine. It was founded by a woman, Viscountess Rhondda, and it is largely run by women; even some of the male contributors whom it attracts display a certain feminine streak. It too is spinsterish, but rather more hearty. Its spiritual home is the village, near enough to London to receive the mighty at weekends, but none the less convinced that women's clubs and the state of the postmistress's temper are equally important.

The circulation of these weeklies ranges from 30,000 to 60,000, their price from 6d. to 1s. They are published at the end of the week; in consequence they are the weekend reading in a country where there are no Sunday supplements. All make their appeal first to the mind, then to the emotions. They deal in comment and interpretation, rather than in straight news. Their public is the politically conscious public of Britain, of every party.

All of them are independent of any of the major daily newspapers. *The Economist* is part of a financial group, headed by Mr. Brendan Bracken, Conservative M.P., which owns *The Financial Times,* but the tie is not one governing policy and no editor of *The Economist* has ever written, or even felt any effective pressure to write, anything other than what his conscience dictates. In fact, the constitution of the company guarantees him freedom. Lady Rhondda, too, is a capitalist, but by inheritance rather than choice. Her paper is colored by her views, but a weekly exists to have views. Over *Tribune,* it is Mr. Aneurin Bevan himself who is believed to have the greatest influence. His wife, Miss Jennie Lee, M.P., a politician in her own right, has been a member of the editorial board, and the present joint editor is Mr. Michael Foot, M.P. Mr. Kingsley Martin edits *The New Statesman and Nation,* and Mr. R. H. S. Crossman, M.P., is the principal editorial writer. Its ancestry connects it with the Fabian Society (the Webbs as well as Mr. Bernard Shaw were among those who provided the original capital in 1913), but it has never regarded itself as anyone's handmaiden. *Tribune* is sometimes rude about trade unions. *The New Statesman* is rarely polite about Mr. Ernest Bevin.

Picture Post is another weekly which should be included in the list, although it bears no superficial resemblance to any of those described above. Founded in 1938, its inspiration, so far as format is concerned, clearly was *Life.* It believes emphatically that one picture is worth at least a thousand words, and is controlled by Mr. Edward Hulton, himself the son of a former newspaper owner, but a newspaper owner whose kingdom (although not his fortune) was dispersed before his family had a chance to take it over. *Picture Post* inclines to the left, but the inclination is clearly the result of one man's personal make-up. There is nothing doctrinaire or organizational about it. *Picture Post* has a very much larger circulation than that of any of the more serious political weeklies. The total of its influence may be considerable, because its layout frequently has the sharpness achieved by the good advertising agent.

The Labour Government should have had no reason to fear the serious political weeklies, despite the fact that their influence is far wider than their circulation figures would indicate. Two of them,

Tribune and *The New Statesman and Nation,* could be counted to be generally on their side. The others would be critical but fair. In any case, their public is an informed public. On politics, their readers know where they stand. They would not be swayed by misleading comment; politically, they are too mature. But the daily press is different.

It is not easy for anyone living in a country to give an objective view of his country's press. As with his country's beer, he is conditioned to take it and like it, and his recollections of other recipes become dimmed by years of abstinence. But some attempt must be made. The dailies:

The Times: A paper with an influence out of all proportion to its circulation. *The Times* is not a governmental organ, but all governments have seen that it is kept well informed. Politically independent, but favoring an empiric approach to the problems of government. Its outstanding qualities are the range of its coverage and the uniform excellence of its writing. There is no typical reader of *The Times.*

Manchester Guardian: Obtains an influence almost equivalent to *The Times* on a smaller circulation, but the circulation has grown of late. Devoted to Manchester and foreign affairs. Liberal, humanitarian and possessing a sense of humor. A newspaper that has humanized a tradition without traditionalizing its humanity.

Daily Express: Technically Britain's most arresting paper. Its typical reader would be an intelligent commercial traveler. Its politics are those of its proprietor, Lord Beaverbrook, which means that they are never socialist, always conservative and sometimes liberal. Keynote: private enterprise, with emphasis on the word "enterprise."

Daily Mirror: A tabloid, but a British one. Typical reader, the young housewife of the lower middle classes. Its politics are leftist, but theory is avoided. It is an expert on the human interest angle. It is the paper about which the *Daily Express* is the most uneasy, as it is the one popular paper which does not employ a variation of the formula used by the *Daily Express* in its layout and news presentation.

Daily Mail: Very like the *Daily Express,* occasionally better but rarely substantially different. It is angled more to catch the feminine interest, and its typical reader would be the wife of the intelligent commercial traveler. Controlled by Lord Rothermere, and its politics his: private enterprise with emphasis on the word "private."

Daily Herald: Like the *Daily Express* in form, but not in substance. Owned by Odhams Press, Limited, and the Trades Union Congress in almost equal shares; it is not one of those children who inherits the best of both parents. Reads as though written by jaded professionals. Typical reader, the trade union branch secretary.

News Chronicle: By ancestry a survival of Victorian days, when some capitalists believed that they had a mission to do good to the industrial classes. Officially liberal, but with general left-wing sympathies. If the *Daily Herald* is produced by jaded professionals, the *News Chronicle* is produced by brilliant amateurs. Typical reader, a young schoolmaster.

Daily Graphic: Although being groomed for stardom by its proprietor, Lord Kemsley, it is still an ineffective rival of the *Daily Mirror.* Politics: patriarchal conservatism. It has two typical readers: the middle-aged housewife who doesn't know it isn't the *Daily Mirror,* and the young white-collar secretary who is rather proud of having found a more respectable alternative.

Daily Telegraph: The poor man's *Times.* A paper of which Mr. Neville Chamberlain would have approved. Controlled by Lord Camrose, brother of Lord Kemsley, and equally conservative but less patriarchal. Typical reader, the middle-aged, second-grade civil servant.

Daily Worker: A paper for the faithful. Very uneven in its writing; occasionally brilliant, frequently the reverse. Read by communists as an act of faith, by others as an act of duty. Controlled by a democratic committee nominated by the Executive of the Communist Party.

The Sunday papers—which are very different from American Sunday papers in that they are no bigger than daily papers—have no supplements and can, in fact, be read in their entirety during the course of a single Sunday. The following have no weekday counterparts:

The *News of the World:* Claims to have the largest circulation of any newspaper in the world. Its certified net sales during the half year ending December 31, 1949, showed a net weekly sale of 8,428,113 copies a week. Contents, one-third sex, one-third sport, one-third everything else. The "everything else" is well informed and fairly, if simply, written.

The Observer: Owned by the Astor family, who have converted it into a public trust. Progressively conservative. Gives the impression of consisting entirely of special articles by special correspondents.

Reynolds News: Owned by the Co-operative Movement. Generally left wing but not as tied to the Labour Party's apron-strings as is the *Daily Herald.* Always prepared to make a valiant attempt to be "popular."

The remaining Sunday papers are, substantially, Sunday editions of their weekday counterparts. The *Sunday Times* is the *Daily Telegraph* dressed up for a day of rest; that is, given a greater literary flavor and using more words to spread the same political message. The *Sunday Express* is the *Daily Express* in more boisterous form, thus containing even less news for the tired commercial traveler, while the *Sunday Pictorial* enables the *Daily Mirror* to give sex a final weekly twirl. The *Daily Mail* on Sunday is the *Sunday Dispatch.* The *Sunday Graphic* is only too like the *Daily Graphic,* and *The People* is the *Daily Herald* produced without such close T.U.C. supervision. The *Times,* the *Manchester Guardian,* the *News Chronicle* and the *Daily Worker* have no Sunday counterparts.

In the thirties, the national press in Britain had become grouped into six major combines. On a 2,000,000 daily circulation, the net return from sales is £1,500,000 a year. In 1938, the average daily would be costing some £2,750,000 a year to produce, and it would be spending up to another £500,000 a year on direct sales promotion. It was left to advertising to fill that gap in revenue, and to provide the profit, and as the dividend records of the newspaper groups show, advertising succeeded. One estimate is that in 1938 nearly £21,000,000 was spent in newspaper advertising (by 1942 the figure had fallen to £9,000,000). Of the £21,000,000, advertisements for food and drink provided one-quarter, household equipment and stores £4,500,000, patent medicines £3,250,000, and clothing a mere £1,250,000.

The budget was completely dislocated by the war. For one thing, the circulation of London newspapers rose, from some ten million to between fourteen and fifteen million daily. The reduction in size of each newspaper was enormous—from sixteen to four pages—and with that, advertising revenue fell, despite increased rates, from sheer impossibility to print enough advertisements to equal the prewar income.

Yet newspapers became more profitable. They needed less staff. Even though the cost of newsprint rose fourfold, the weight of newsprint used in each issue of a postwar daily paper was only one-fifth the weight of its prewar counterpart, and newsprint is bought by weight, and newspaper transportation costs are based on weight. In short, a well-run newspaper in 1948 and 1949 could make as much profit out of four pages under postwar conditions of competition as it had ten years before from a sixteen-page paper. The uncertain elements in the situation were the gradual increase of staff as men returned from the services, the continued upward curve of all costs, and the possibility that at any time the increased sales would suddenly shrink to a prewar level.

But this is to anticipate. The question that concerned the Government more and more, as 1946 progressed, was what influence all these papers had on their readers, the ordinary voter, man and woman.

On the government side there were two considerations, one narrowly partisan, the other more disinterested. The four most powerful newspaper groups, Beaverbrook, Rothermore, Kemsley and Camrose, were bound to be ranged against any socialist administration, and for political reasons the Government would have liked to limit their power. But for nonpartisan reasons, many people also felt that it was dangerous for four men to have the right and the opportunity to carry their views, and nothing but their views, into nearly 7,000,000 minds. The Government couldn't quite hope that everyone who voted for it would at once abandon the *Daily Express* and the *Daily Mail* for the *Daily Mirror* and the *Daily Herald,* but it would have been rather relieved to see that happen.

What influence have these papers?

First, a note on their circulation. The British press is truly national; that is, London and Edinburgh, Wales and Cornwall, read substantially the same papers at breakfast every morning, even though it may be printed in London, Manchester or Glasgow. Two out of every three of the men whose daily decisions, large and small, shape the course of events in Britain read *The Times* at some time during the day. They may not read it all. They probably do not read it exclusively. Few of them take their politics directly from it. But it does supply them with the bulk of the information they have concerning affairs of which they have not direct knowledge. As a result, they are as well informed as any corresponding group of men elsewhere in the world.

That statement is based on observation. The results of a more elaborate method of finding out who reads what paper are embodied in a "Readership Survey" made by the Hulton Press, Limited, in 1948, a survey based on readership as distinct from circulation.

Their calculations, based on a sample survey, give the following results:

ESTIMATED ACTUAL NUMBER OF READERS OF THE MORE IMPORTANT PERIODICALS

(Estimated Population aged 16 and over — 36,000,000)

Number who read: —	*(in thousands)*
NEWS OF THE WORLD	17,950
RADIO TIMES	16,480
PEOPLE	11,580
SUNDAY PICTORIAL	9,950
DAILY EXPRESS	9,320
DAILY MIRROR	8,730
PICTURE POST	8,160
SUNDAY EXPRESS	6,880
DAILY MAIL	4,980
DAILY HERALD	4,620
SUNDAY DISPATCH	4,560
NEWS CHRONICLE	3,690
SUNDAY GRAPHIC	2,520
DAILY TELEGRAPH	2,250
SUNDAY TIMES	1,410
OBSERVER	1,060

One interesting point about this list is that it shows the considerable attraction of the radio, since the *Radio Times* is substantially no more than a detailed account of the three B.B.C. programs for the current week.

The Hulton survey contains various breakdowns of the main statistics. (It even gives an estimate of the number of the caged-bird sellers who read each publication.) The two most relevant ones are those that give the extent to which different types of periodicals are read:

Morning Newspapers:

(Figures in per cent)	Men	Housewives
Reading no National daily......................	17.8	27.2
Reading no daily paper at all...................	8.3	16.2
Reading one only.............................	64.6	65.0
Reading two..................................	20.9	15.7
Reading three or more........................	6.2	3.1
Total reading any National daily................	82.2	72.6

Sunday Newspapers:

	Men	Housewives
Reading no National paper.....................	8.2	14.5
Reading no paper at all.......................	5.8	9.6
Reading one only.............................	27.8	32.4
Reading two..................................	37.2	34.7
Reading three or more........................	29.2	23.3
Total reading any National paper...............	91.8	85.5

In brief, nine out of every ten households will read some daily newspaper, four out of every five will read one of the national newspapers, but the political views of the provincial paper will be less sharply angled than those of the national paper.

But surveys or no surveys, what is important is that these papers will form only part of the mechanism by which these households obtain the information on which they build up their views and make their decisions, political and otherwise. The other channels of information are the radio—used as a source of information far more by the middle and lower classes than by higher groups—conversations at work, in pubs and socially, and finally, to a lesser extent, the cinema. Their interests outside the home and their work are wide enough for them to tend to regard the popular daily as a source of entertainment rather than one of instruction or political guidance. In home affairs, the direct political influence of the penny paper is small. The reader has too many other sources which act as checks.

But the press possesses a considerable indirect influence in the field of foreign affairs, and the basis of that influence is the fact that it can give or withhold information, not otherwise obtainable, concerning other countries. It can also mislead. In part, this is an inevitable result of lack of space. The average paper cannot afford to devote more than, say 3,000 words each week to general information on the United States—even less for other countries. To give an accurate picture of any country in 3,000 words a week is hard in any circumstances. To fit them into the general news standards of a morning paper of bits and pieces makes the task almost impossible.

Food and clothes are always major news topics. A correspondent reports that he has seen a shop window in New York full of silk stockings or that he has eaten a five-course dinner in Paris. Immediately, the superficial reader (and, after all, she is the average) has a mental picture of every woman in America dressed in all the things that she herself lacks, and of the average family in France living on unrationed food in a land of plenty. The most conscientious of foreign correspondents can hardly avoid that kind of misrepresentation and, if he is encouraged by his managing editor to send only one kind of story, which is not unknown, the resulting picture is completely false. It is possible to understand the Soviet view that it is better to keep all foreign correspondents out than allow them to deceive their readers by condensed reports of untypical instances.

That was the background to the Government's reactions on the problem of the press, and its relations with it. From Mr. Aneurin Bevan's utterances, it is not unreasonable to suppose that he for one would have liked to see the press overhauled and purged; "prostitution" is not a word which carries with it even a hint of approval. From his actions, it is equally safe to assume that Mr. Attlee himself was indifferent to the question. He has never behaved as though he credited the press, or any form of publicity, with the slightest political influence. On the other hand, Mr. Herbert Morrison has always been acutely aware of the press. He has shown commendable skill in manipulating as good a press as possible for his policies, and a certain degree of petulance when he failed. There must, then, have been quite a substantial element in the Cabinet in favor of positive action in one form or another.

The recent history of Argentina has shown that there are a great many different ways of securing a reasonably uniform and approving press, all of which stop short of direct control or censorship. In Britain, one simple way would have been through limitation of newsprint. A substantial portion of the newsprint used by papers is imported from North America. Shortage of dollars explains the present size of the normal issue. Would it not have been possible for the Government, unobtrusively, to have made certain that the "co-operative" publications did rather better in the allocation of these limited supplies than did the others?

It would; happily, the Government did nothing of the kind. It did not, so to speak, dope any of the horses in the race. But it did do what it could to increase the stake-money, to continue the simile. It took this step in the autumn of 1946. Until then, circulations of the leading dailies had been virtually frozen by the method of allowing each newspaper a fixed quantity of newsprint based on its earlier circulation. In September, 1946, the government announced that it would release additional newsprint to newspapers, but only to the extent needed to print the additional copies which they actually sold each day. Possibly the Government hoped that the sales of those papers that supported it would show the biggest rises. If so, it was disappointed; the circulation of the *Daily Herald* did not respond noticeably to this stimulus. That of the *Daily Mirror* did, but few would suggest that the reason for this lay in any greater support for socialism, or the Labour Government, displayed by the management.

An alternative method of affecting change is to appoint a Royal Commission of inquiry. A Royal Commission, in Britain, has the power to compel the attendance of witnesses, to take their evidence under oath, and to investigate the books and records of any undertaking. An inquiry by Royal Commission, it might have been thought—and here it is possible to imagine Mr. Herbert Morrison thinking along these lines—would prove to the electorate as a whole that these press combines were octopuses strangling news at its source, distorting everything to give it a party—worse, an anti-Government—bias. A Royal Commission might well build up a public demand that something should be done about the press. Better still, it might even discover and suggest some way in which something could be done about the press.

The history of the demand for an inquiry into the press begins with an agitation at the annual conference of the National Union of Journalists, the newspapermen's trade union, at Eastertime, 1946. There was on the agenda a resolution pressing for a Government inquiry into the monopolistic tendencies of the press in Britain, the kind of resolution that invariably appears on the agenda of that kind of conference, usually to be carried with a great deal of enthusiasm and little debate and then dropped, unwanted and unnoticed until the following year, into the limbo of pious resolutions. This resolution was carried, and Mr. Haydn Davies, a journalist M.P., duly put down a question in the Commons, asking if the Prime Minister would consider doing anything about it. The Prime Minister duly replied that he had no intention of doing anything of the kind, and there the matter seemed to end, true to form.

But it was resurrected during the summer of 1946, partly in speeches by Mr. Herbert Morrison and Sir Hartley Shawcross, the Attorney-General (who indulged in a series of alternate accusations of and apologies to the Press Lords, which delighted the Conservative Press), and partly in another resolution in the Commons by Mr. Haydn Davies. This resolution was supported by some 100 other M.P.'s.

Again the agitation seemed to peter out, but this time it proved to possess more than its usual powers of recuperation. The summer resolution received no more than lukewarm support from the Government. Yet in October, 1946, a fresh resolution asking for an investigation appeared on the Commons agenda, in a form which closely foreshadowed the terms on which the inquiry was set up. The Government left the resolution to a free vote, but that did not, apparently, affect its trust in its followers to divine its wishes. Clearly, at some point between June and October, someone had persuaded the Cabinet that a press commission would be a good thing. What was not clear was why the Cabinet was so anxious to have such an investigation, when only a month or so previously it had decided that the matter was not urgent and, in any case, of doubtful political advantage.

Any journalist may exaggerate the political reactions to anything that looks like an attack on the liberty of the press. Most people in Britain, when they thought of the subject at all, were vaguely suspicious of the combines that controlled so great a proportion of the popular dailies, and would not fly into any paroxysm of fear or resentment if those combines were curbed. But, equally, they were not convinced that free expression of opinion was impossible. Ninety percent of readers could still find some daily that reflected their habits of thought. What disquieted so many people about the appointment of the Royal Commission was not so much what was being done, as the way in which it was being done. It looked horribly like a snap decision by Mr. Herbert Morrison in an irritated moment, and good rarely comes from snap decisions.

The theory of the snap decision was not upset by subsequent events. The motion for the appointment of the Royal Commission was passed in the Commons in October 29, 1946. The commission was not appointed until March 26, 1947, five months later. The delay may have been partially due to the difficulty of getting the right people to become members of it, but five months is a long time. It left the impression of a certain half-hearted casualness about the whole affair.

The chairman finally chosen for the commission was Sir David Ross, a man of sixty-nine, Provost of Oriel College, Oxford, whose connection with public affairs had until then been confined to work on various public arbitration tribunals. There were sixteen other members, three of them women. They included one ex-editor (of the distinguished but Scottish daily, *The Scotsman*), a journalist, a Baptist minister, the inevitable trade-union secretary, and Mr. J. B. Priestley. Mr. Priestley did not stay the course; he resigned.

The terms of reference were "with the object of furthering the free expression of opinion throughout the Press with the greatest practical accuracy in the presentation of news, to enquire into the control management and ownership of the newspaper and periodical press and news agencies, including the financial structure and monopolistic tendencies in control, and to make recommendations thereon." The great ship was launched.

The commission held its first meeting on April 30, 1947. Between then and June, 1948, it held 48 meetings, each of them lasting the greater part of a day. Of these meetings, 38 were devoted in whole or in part to hearing oral evidence. Oral evidence was heard from representatives of 47 corporate bodies, principally newspaper owning companies, and from 37 individual witnesses. The commission spent about 150 hours in hearings.

The commission sent out five questionnaires addressed respectively to newspaper owning companies and their associations, journalists associations, news agencies, advertisers and advertising agents and their associations. Replies to one or other of these questionnaires were received from 157 groups. In addition, the commission asked 53 undertakings to supply balance sheets and profit and loss accounts and certain other statistical material covering the period 1937–46. Nineteen individuals and nine organizations submitted formal written evidence other than by way of reply to a questionnaire. The newspaper proprietors and their editors gave evidence. So did the representatives of the National Union of Journalists, and the men who had originally alleged that the investigation was necessary. And over all these proceedings crept a thin veil of boredom. The evidence tendered to the commission was not only longwinded, it was also very very dull.

The final report of the commission was not very much better. It provided a certain amount of entertaining reading, in an appendix which examined in detail how various newspapers had reacted to various items of news, and displayed for all to see how headlines can vary according to a paper's political orientation. But it is never really necessary to set up a Royal Commission to prove the obvious, unless the commission is intended to be no more than a sop to some vociferous minority.

What did the Royal Commission establish? It established who owns the newspapers of Britain (in that it was forestalled by a newspaper proprietor himself, Lord Camrose, with his book *British Newspapers and their Controllers*, published in July, 1947). It established that a small number of men own more than one newspaper. It established that the proprietors of newspapers expect their undertakings to show a trading profit on the year. It also pointed out that these proprietors like to exercise some of the normal functions of management, and to place in charge of their properties men who accept their responsibilities as managers of commercial undertakings, and who are not determined to write views directly contrary to those held by the proprietor himself. Everyone knew all that before the commission was ever appointed.

The commission also established that the press in Britain is free from any external pressures strong enough to distort its presentation of news. As the final report said, "The policy of the Press is dictated neither by the advertisers, nor by the Government, nor by any outside financial interests. It is the policy of those who own and control the Press." Does this concentration of ownership then prejudice of itself the free expression of opinion or the accurate presentation of news? "No," said the commission, on page 176 of its report.

Then what did the commission find to be wrong with the press? It came a little more definite when it discussed, tentatively, that vast area that lies between truth and falsehood. A paragraph in a newspaper can contain no false statement and yet leave a false impression at the end. No one expects a newspaper proprietor to print an editorial advocating views that he holds in abhorrence; one would expect that everyone is entitled to assume that the proprietor will not apply the same habits in his decisions about news content.

The commission had this to say: "Partisanship is present in some degree in all the papers. . . . The Press is part of our political machinery, which is essentially partisan. But partisanship can and does on occasion lead to a degree of selection and colouring of news which can only be regarded as excessive."

How did the commission propose to meet that danger? The best it could do was to recommend that the press establish a general council of the press consisting, in the main, of men in the profession, with no more than 20% of lay members, and that the objects of the general council should be to safeguard the freedom of the press, and to encourage the growth of the sense of public responsibility and public service among all people engaged in the profession of journalism. That is not a strong recommendation. It bears some signs of being the result of a compromise within the commission itself. But at least it faces the fact, almost entirely ignored by the protesting journalists of the Labour party, that the present-day weakness of the press more properly lies at the door of the journalists than at that of the proprietor. Bias in news is largely a matter of day-to-day presentation, and there the deciding factor most frequently is the routine sub-editor, not his chief nor his proprietor.

The truest criticism of the press of Britain today, one that was hardly voiced by the journalist critics of the newspaper proprietors in their evidence before the commission, is that too many newspapers are trivial. Some papers, their proprietors, editors and sub-editors, seem to have given up the struggle to compress news and world information into four pages of newsprint. Instead, they have turned their publications to entertainment. They have exchanged influence for circulation.

There are various causes. The fashion appeals to many readers. It fits in with the circumstances under which many of them read their daily papers. It is easier to fill a four-page paper with a multitude of trivialities than it is to compress the news of the world into the same space, let alone explain it in a way that makes it readable. Some journalists are more concerned with impressing other journalists in Fleet Street than they are with informing their readers. But there is more to it than that.

One reason is that the working journalist is too acute a barometer of the mental climate of his time. He lives in a world in which propaganda is destroying the efficacy of the one tool he uses, language. Words like "democracy" and "freedom" no longer have a fixed meaning. To understand what is meant when they are used, it is necessary to know the origin of the publication in which they appear. The journalist is expected to write in black and white, when he knows that the news is almost certainly no more than some shade of gray. His world of certainties has shrunk, so that now he can believe only what he himself can see and hear; even about this he cannot be certain of the explanation. To be trivial is better than being pompous. But that trouble is world wide. It does not explain all the failings of the press in Britain.

Another reason for the shortcomings of the press in Britain can be found in the British law of libel, as applied to newspapers. The press commission had a good deal to say on why newspapers do not publish political views with which they do not agree; much less on why newspapers do not publish facts and comments with which they agree but which the laws of libel deter them from printing.

British newspapers today are small. They deal with events, political, sport, sex and crime, in concentrated form. But one thing is left out: comment on people. There is a little social gossip, rather more publicity from the entertainment world, and that is all. The reporter, the sub-editor, the editor, are often frightened to publish what they know to be true, frightened to state a belief that they honestly hold, because a defective law of libel may make them pay for their sense of duty. No British newspaper could have described accurately the activities of Mr. Sidney Stanley while they were in progress and before the Lynskey Tribunal started to unravel them. It could not even publish a "profile" written with the frankness attained by the *New Yorker*.

The basis of the law of libel in England is the common-law right of every man not to be held up to the hatred, ridicule or contempt of his fellows as a result of a false statement made about him by some other party. The law of defamation has made valiant attempts to keep pace with a rapidly changing civilization, but it has failed, and failed particularly where newspapers are concerned.

As the law stands, a newspaper has various defenses open to it when sued for libel. It can set out to "justify" the statement complained of; that is, prove that the statement was absolutely true. But if the published words were wrong in one single fact, that defense will almost certainly fail. It can plead "fair comment," that is, that the comment made was based on opinions honestly held. But again, if any fact mentioned in the same context as the comment was incorrect, that defense may fail, because the courts have held that opinions apparently based on even a single mistaken fact cannot be said to be "fair comment." The newspaper may plead, where the libel is contained in a report of some event, that the occasion is a "privileged" one. But only what is said in Parliament or in a current law case is absolutely privileged. In all other cases, the privilege is said to be "qualified," and qualified privilege is no defense if the person libeled proves that the writer or the publisher was motivated by "malice." What editor can check every motive in the head of every contributor?

That is a skeleton of the law of libel as it applies to newspapers; it closely resembles the game of snakes and ladders. A twist of luck may defeat almost any defense. When, in 1939, the *Daily Express* published the fact that a certain Mr. Y. of Camberwell, had been convicted of bigamy (which was true), how was the subeditor who passed on the paragraph to know that there were two Mr. Y's in Camberwell, with identical names but not identical habits? The non-bigamous Mr. Y. recovered damages.

Every newspaper runs a similar risk any time it publishes a simple statement of fact. Statement of fact is one thing; socially, statement of opinion, or comment, is the more important. There the question is, on what occasions the right of the public to information should override the rights of the individual to personal privacy. Comment is as much the function of a newspaper as the supply of news, yet in Britain it is more difficult for a newspaper to comment adversely on the activities of a man with a bad record than on one whose record is good. The law has come to tie its hands in this way largely by a mesh of small legal rules and decisions, but none the less effectively for that.

In whose interests? It is hard to see that any legitimate interest is protected, but undoubtedly the men who would be most loath to see any change are the larger figures in public life. The vicious and un-scrupulous man has reason to be thankful for every cloak he can drape about himself, and in that he is, not designedly but effectively, assisted by the public figure who resents any adverse comment on himself, the man who wants his cake to remain whole while he is eating it. Public life provides him with its rewards for what he sur-renders. He cannot at the same time claim all the privileges of pri-vacy enjoyed by the anonymous.

Even this does not, I suggest, reach the heart of the matter. It may add to the cynicism, and so to the irresponsibility, of the professional journalist. It is not the positive cause of his too-frequent inadequacy. That comes from the tyranny of the large circulation.

It is estimated that to launch and establish a new London daily newspaper with national circulation would cost today some £2,000,-000. A newspaper selling at 1d., as the popular dailies do, cannot cover its costs from its circulation revenue. It must depend on its revenue from advertisers for a good deal more than its profit. It fol-lows, paradoxically, that the greater the circulation of a penny pa-per, the greater the loss to be made good by the advertising depart-ment. This can be done, as the advertising revenue increases with the circulation, but the system has its penalties.

When its circulation reaches the millions, the popular daily paper ceases to be an individual production, even a team production. It be-comes a formula. Certain characteristics have been present while cir-culation expanded. Therefore, those characteristics induced the in-crease in circulation. Therefore, those characteristics must not be changed. They are the formula for success and therefore sacred. The steps in this argument may be founded on false logic, but what proprietorial board dares risk making a change in that formula when so much is at stake?

Again, the formula must be comprehensive. A newspaper with a daily circulation of 300,000 can fairly believe that its readers have some characteristics in common, and that they share a common and a positive acceptance of the paper's standards of emphasis and presentation. The newspaper with a circulation ten times as great dares not assume that its readers have anything in common, save an interest in sex and crime. It must therefore provide something for everybody, and act on the assumption that only sex or crime provide stories strong enough to hold every reader's interest for a whole column devoted to one story.

The law of libel could be changed by a single act of Parliament. It will take a great deal more to free newspapers from the fetters of their own success, for they must fight hard to stay successful, and while they succeed, politics and world affairs must be made "entertaining" to every single one of the three or four million readers.

The press commission was appointed because the Government was fearful of the reader only in his capacity as voter, and it never entirely escaped from the atmosphere in which it had been conceived. Yet, at the end of all this hubbub, of what had the Government been frightened? Had it expected the conservative press to become non-partisan, just because the Labour party had won an election? Did it feel that, as a Government of honest idealists striving to take one and all to the Promised Land, it was exempt from criticism? Was it afraid that the complications of the nationalizing processes were so intense that it could never expect to see a fair explanation from a political opponent? Or was it just humanly riled when some writer guessed where the corn was and stamped hard on that spot?

Probably it has been a mixture of all these feelings. Some sections of the press have been unfair intermittently, and in a few cases continually. For instance, over the dock strike in the summer of 1948, it was obviously partisan for some conservative papers to drive themselves into a fit of righteous indignation at the Minister of Labour's presence in San Francisco, when the slightest touch of responsibility would have convinced them that, from a national point of view, it was more important for the minister to try to produce results from an international conference than it was for him to flutter around the trade unions and the strikers in London, bleating about government nonintervention in dock strikes. But always, somewhere in the press there is someone talking sense, and talking fairly. There are all sorts of ways in which the press could be improved, and be made more responsible, but to hint that all would be well if every newspaper in London were a duplicate of the *Daily Herald* is hardly one of them.

To sigh for a press that is always fair to a government is, in fact, to ask for a press which has been regimented out of its diversity, and that happens only in one kind of state. The press of Britain is still free to make political mistakes without going to prison for them, and I for one rate that freedom pretty high.

When owning a newspaper ceases to be big business, and becomes rather smaller business, the press will be free. In the meantime, quite a number of periodicals have evaded that prison, and entertaining they are.

CHAPTER XV

Business and Management

Dogmatic statements are pleasant to make, for they give one a gratifying internal glow of assurance. But they fall into two categories. We may say that Florida is warmer than Alaska. We may say, just as confidently, that British industry is not so efficient as industry in the United States. But there is this difference between these two statements. The first can be proved or disproved exactly. We can check up the records and thereafter be both dogmatic and accurate. The second statement cannot be proved in the same way. People who make it are relying upon experience, observation and judgment, all of which are human, and fallible, measuring apparatuses.

Again, comparison between like and like is easy. Wherever the sun shines, the methods of collecting and measuring its heat and duration are subject to an international uniformity of standard. A thousand bricks in Britain are very like a thousand bricks anywhere in the United States. But how can anyone compare two differing yards of woolen fabric? The whole point may be that they are intended to be different.

But there are methods of comparison. In 1948, the Cambridge University Press published, for the National Institute of Economic and Social Research, a study of productivity in British and American manufacturing industry, prepared by Dr. Lazlo Rostas, based on prewar conditions and prewar research. Dr. Rostas does not ignore any of the commonly advanced arguments that direct comparison is impracticable. He admits that the structure and organization of industries in the two countries are different, that even classification is a problem. All his conclusions cannot achieve anything like the literal accuracy of a comparison of rainfalls. But if they do no more than give evidence of trends, they are valuable.

What do trends show? They show that in 32 manufacturing

trades, taken in identical years (mainly 1935), the output per worker in Britain and the United States was in a ratio of 100 to 216, that the industries in which the United States led were those making packing materials and durable mass-produced consumption goods (e.g. automobiles and radios) where the ratio was 100 to 300–400, while the trade in which the comparable output was nearest equality was the building materials trade. About the best industry, from the British point of view, was the cement manufacturing industry, where a British figure of 100 would be met by a figure of 110 in the United States. It still maintains that advantage.

But one does not need to rely solely upon an economist for proof of that proposition? A productivity team from the steel industry, which toured the United States in the early part of 1949, committed itself to the same view. Productivity in the steel industry in the United States now is some 75% to 100% above that in Britain. Why?

This book is not a technical survey. It is about people and ideas. So let me say at the outset that I do not want to leave the impression, by not talking overmuch about technical equipment, that all that is wrong can be attributed to people, that the equipment they have is all right, judged by any standard. That is not so. For instance, by United States standards Britain is pitifully short of electric power and power tools. In every industry, if more power were available, the total of production would expand at once. The present shortage of power is a consequence of the war. Britain could not build a bombing fleet and additional generating stations at the same time. Likewise, while Britain must export, and so long as the world clamors for her heavy engineering goods, she cannot give the home market a first priority on those supplies. It is essential to bear in mind that however many people may become convinced of the need for higher productivity, there are physical limits to what they can do about it at this moment.

Yet the problem of people is still the more important. If they had unlimited power, would they use it without restraint to produce more? Why was it that, before the war, when there was no physical obstacle in the way of expanding the supply of power, when there were well over a million unemployed to provide the labor, the rate of productivity in Britain was still below that of the United States? One cause is that industry itself has tended to become "limitation minded," which is a variation of a comment made by an American to a visiting British industrialist: "You look at manufacturing operations as an opportunity to afford employment. We examine them to find to what extent we can do without labor." Limitation in output of everything not directly needed for military operations was a condition of industrial life in Britain during the war, and it has left its mark. But with some, the inclination to think and act in those terms was already there.

The British confectionery trade, like others in 1948, was still subject to control. It depends for its product almost entirely on imported raw materials, and so control can easily be exercised by strict allocation of such raw materials as the government decides to import. These supplies are divided among the existing firms in the industry, on the basis of their prewar consumption of each, and the system was coupled with an understanding (to put it no higher) within the trade that the distributing side would refrain from any great degree of competition. The industry, in short, had become noncompetitive.

In September, 1947, a leading figure in the trade, in a letter to *The Economist,* likened the industry to a circus parade of horses—it having ceased to be a race—in which the relative position of each horse was determined by events outside its own control, and each horse was assured of a stall and a good evening meal at the end of the day.

He continued: "There are three ways in which an industry like this can be operated. The first is the present circus, consisting only of these horses which were running in 1939; except as a very temporary measure, such a system cannot be supported. Private enterprise working in a closed shop is indefensible. Secondly, some form of nationalised organisation would still require a circus, but clearly it would not require 190 horses [the number of prewar firms in the trade]. Fifty good ones would probably suffice. And, thirdly, effective competitive enterprise. The industry has always assumed that it would go back to the competitive system."

Certainly, the industry had protested against controls when they were imposed. Did the industry, in 1947, agree with the statement contained in the last sentence of the letter quoted above?

A month later the *Confectionery Journal,* an organ of the trade, produced this comment on the letter. The commentator began with some figures: Production of confectionery, he said, increased from 4½ ounces per head of the population per week in 1924, to 7 ounces per head in 1939, while the average price of the product fell during the same period from 5½d. to 3d. per quarter pound. Much as the consumer might rejoice, these figures presented a different story to the manufacturer. He received from the consumer in 1939 something less than the total paid in 1924, and in exchange he had sold—been compelled to sell—55% more chocolate products.

The writer in *Confectionery Journal* went on: "Effective competitive enterprise in this instance meant a tremendous struggle for extra business, which in the long run left the industry as a whole not a halfpenny the richer . . . We see no point in increasing turnover if the only result is to be a harassed industry, subject to increasing unemployment and a return anything but commensurate with the increased work involved."

I do not think the case for and against unrestricted competition within an industry in Britain can be put more clearly than it is in the original letter and the subsequent comment.

These views are not held in the confectionery trade alone. In May, 1948, official control of the price at which bricks could be sold was removed, and the industry returned to the benefits of internal competition. The secretary of the Midland Federation of Brick and Tile Manufacturers commented: "The removal of the minimum price structure in the Order was gravely premature at a time when confidence had declined almost to zero in the ultimate rehabilitation of the brick industry to pre-war level."

The same point arose when an official committee investigated the distributive trades for building materials and commodities. The committee found that the industry was dominated by a series of price rings, and recommended that action should be taken to restore competition. But, as the *Financial Times* said by way of comment, "The committee offers no opinion how the . . . measures are to be imposed on a group who, in fact, do not want to compete and (whatever rules are made) are determined not to."

The trouble is that limitation of supplies can make for too easy a life within the trades involved. True, there is a ceiling to profits, for there is a limit to possible sales. But there is also a floor to profits because a restricted output in a period of inflationary demand usually sells itself; certainly it reduces the element of competition among firms in the same trade.

On the first charge, there is some evidence in support.

What are the criticisms usually leveled against individual managements? They can really be summarized under one heading: too much rigidity. They are too rigid in their trade organizations. Too many firms prefer an easier life within a trade-wide price-fixing system, to the more strenuous world of acute competition among all units within the trade. The class structure is too rigid. Too few employers look for talent among their workers or encourage it when found. Management is too rigid to appreciate where co-operation will help and not hinder, where common research, marketing and a host of other things will pay better dividends to every participant.

This second charge, so far as it affects the quality of management, can be put in another way. Do industries attract the right men into them? Is British industry dominated by the eldest-son-of-the-founder type of management? Is it that the men who direct Britain's major concerns lack the sense of urgency that actual ownership should give? For so long now, trade union speakers have said that industry was governed by men who owed their position only to the possession of money or the accident of birth. They have said it so often that even other people have come to believe it.

The facts, certainly true of some of the major industrial concerns, are these.

In the case of Britain's largest industrial company, Imperial Chemical Industries, Ltd., there are 191,000 individual holdings of shares. No single individual owns as much as one per cent of the £50,000,000 of ordinary capital. In fact, no individual, in distinction to holdings in the name of trust corporations or other companies likely to be nominees for multiple beneficial interests, appears as holding as much as one one-hundredth part of the capital. Only two investors, neither of them directors, approach this figure. One, Sir Felix J. M. Brunner, holds 47,896 ordinary (common) shares; the other, Mrs. Constance Goetze, holds 43,000 ordinary and 10,448 preference (preferred) shares.

Among the directors, Mr. John Rogers has the largest holding appearing in his own name, with 13,069 ordinary shares. The chairman, Lord McGowan, appears in the latest share register as the holder of only 1,935 ordinary shares. Many of the directors merely hold the necessary qualification for office of 1000 shares. In all, the 22 directors of the company hold 66,781 ordinary shares out of 50,-000,000 shares outstanding. With this holding, these 22 men control the destinies of an industrial company whose assets, at the end of 1947, totaled £161,000,000. By way of remuneration, they received for the year a total of £268,177.

There are a number of large shareholders who are obviously nominees for some other person. The largest holding in the name of a nominee is one of 2,792,516 ordinary shares, generally believed to represent the financial stake held in the company by the Brussels chemical firm of Salvay et Cie. The next largest shareholder in this company is an insurance company, the Prudential Assurance Company which holds 360,363 ordinary and 336,891 preference shares.

The oil undertaking, Shell Transport and Trading Co., provides another example of the same kind. It has an issued capital of £57,000,000. Its directors hold only one-tenth of one per cent of the equity capital, 39,139 ordinary shares out of a total of 38,594,177. There are 127,000 shareholders on the register, and no one of these is, apparently, in a position to exert a decisive influence on the control of the company. The largest shareholder (excluding a group holding of all shares held in France, a result of currency difficulties) is the Bank of Scotland, with a holding of 1,600,000 ordinary shares.

Of course, there are exceptions. One existed in Lever Brothers and Unilever, Limited, which has £70,081,000 of issued capital and is largely an Anglo-Dutch concern. A substantial section of the business was built up by the first Lord Leverhulme and his son, the second Viscount, remained a large shareholder all his life. Altogether, Lord Leverhulme was, at his death in 1949, interested in 5,273,742 of the ordinary shares worth, in 1948, well over £12,000,000. But for the rest, this company follows the same pattern. None of the other directors holds more than 4,000 ordinary shares. The largest individual holding, after that of Lord Leverhulme, was also in the name of the Prudential Assurance Company, Ltd.

Another is to be found in Rootes Motors, Ltd., one of the major automobile manufacturing concerns in Britain. That business has been built up almost from zero, from 1917 onwards, by the two brothers Rootes (with financial aid from the ubiquitous Prudential Assurance Co., Ltd.) so that in 1949, out of a total ordinary stock of £1,000,000, divided into 5,000,000 shares, Sir William Rootes owned or controlled 1,910,105, Sir Reginald Rootes 951,835 and the Prudential Assurance Co., Ltd., 1,229,376. The annual average of the combined profits of the business for the twelve financial years which ended on July 31, 1949, was £954,586.

These are the facts from some industries. In each of them, save one, the leading men have worked their way to the top without the aid of either a large inheritance of money or powerful family backing. There are, of course, men in authority who owe their influence to possessions other than their own inherent abilities; they do not control the major industrial concerns.

In fact, it is the smaller businesses which more frequently display the dangers and disadvantages of inefficient or unimaginative management. To quote from a letter from a correspondent to the editor of *The Observer*, published in November, 1948, regarding a "small and prosperous but inefficient manufacturing concern" stated: "The firm is engaged on work of vital imporance to the home and export markets. The management is in the hands of one director and the methods of handling and manufacture are at least thirty years behind the times. The factory buildings are dilapidated and the office accommodation is inadequate. No joint consultation between management and worker exists. The order book is full and with a minimum reorganisation the output could be doubled. . . ."

Another alleged handicap to industry in Britain is government interference. This argument is used by those who ascribe to it the general weakness in British industry which they claim exists. It is also used by men in control of industry to account for what they feel is their own comparative lack of success. Of course, some government control is still inevitable, at least to British minds. To quote Mr. Oliver Lyttelton, a Conservative M.P., Coalition Minister of Supply, and a determined opponent of socialism: "Any Government, whatever its political complexion, is bound to concern itself with the affairs of industry in 1948." But is that control or interference carried too far in practice?

I feel that most of the arguments against government activities are implicit in the following two quotations. The first concerns the case of the Nigerian railway engines and is from the report of the Select Committee on Estimates on the colonial estimates for 1948:

As far back as October, 1943, the Ministry of Production had received from the Crown Agents [the purchasing agents in Britain for all colonial governments] a list of Colonial railway requirements for 1945 which included eleven main line locomotives for Nigeria, and in the following July these locomotives were given a place in the United Kingdom programme of production for 1945. In November 1944 the order was allocated by the Ministry of Supply to a manufacturer whose works were not capable of making engines of the required design, and it was not until August 1945 that a suitable manufacturer was found.

At the same time, the Nigerian Government asked for the order to be increased to twenty engines. It now became a question whether the Nigerian order could be placed in the United Kingdom programme of production for 1946. The Colonial Office, supported by the Ministry of Food, strongly urged the Nigerian claim, on account of the importance of moving not only the groundnut crop from the Northern Provinces, but also the palm products. At this point it was discovered that the firm finally selected to carry out the Nigerian order had begun work on an order of between fifty and sixty-four engines for the London and North Eastern Railway, which had never been authorised in the official programme of production, and that it was too late to stop it. As a result, the Nigerian order was put back for delivery to August 1947. The twenty engines were eventually shipped on May 12th, 1948.

In the meantime, in June 1947, fourteen engines arrived from Canada, thirteen months after the placing of the order.

The second is from the speech of Lord Trent, Chairman of the company, at the annual general meeting of Boots Pure Drug Co., Ltd., in 1948.

No less a person than the Permanent Secretary of the Board of Trade [Sir John Henry Woods] has expressed his fears whether the central machine of government can stand for long a continuance of the present pressures. In 1938, he points out, the Board of Trade had 60 administrative officers in a staff of 2,400. Today the staff number 15,000 and there are 400 people taking decisions, with all important questions passing through a "super bottleneck" of fifteen under-secretaries, via two second secretaries to the Permanent Secretary and through him to the President.

How can the decisions of 400 people possibly be kept from conflicting with one another? Sir John Woods' comment on this is: "We may spend so much time on being sure of keeping in step that we hardly advance at all." He goes further. He says that he has thought for some time that many controls are too detailed and that they delay and hamper industry unnecessarily. "But," he goes on, "neither I nor any of my senior colleagues can possibly find the time to examine in the necessary detail the many controls which the Board of Trade administers . . . In other words we know that there is something of great importance to be investigated, but we have not the necessary time.

. . . A business is run successfully on the basis of those who take decisions being kept in day-to-day touch with all the relevant facts and figures. Indeed, the whole system of Government control is founded on the assumption that the State is in a better position than an industry to know all the relevant facts and figures. In practice, however, it comes to this, that State Departments take their decisions on the basis of statistics and reports, but by the time all the statistics and all the reports they need have been collated and digested they are inevitably too out of date to be of any value.

But "government interference" is too loose a phrase to describe anything accurately. First, there is "interference" which consists of imposing on industry certain standards of conduct which are accepted by the majority without question. Just as a legal code prescribes punishments for fraudulent bankruptcies, so a factory code provides punishments for failure to take proper safety precautions. The difference is that the law does not investigate a crime before it has taken place, while a factory inspector can and does investigate a factory both before and after any accident there. The idea behind this kind of interference cannot be attacked.

Then, again, some interference comes as a by-product of some other activity or responsibility for a government. For example, the government's fiscal policy inevitably introduces distortions into the patterns of trade and distribution, by causing departures from what used to be considered "normal" (if the word "normal" has any meaning now). A sudden increase in the tax on beer and cigarettes may cut consumption of each and leave a manufacturer powerless to prevent a sudden drop in sales, however he may try. Individual trades may find that an increasing supply of quite a different commodity will divert trade from their own products into quite other channels (the radio trades, the better class stores, the publishing businesses, all provided examples of that tendency in 1948). All these possibilities add to the general uncertainties that face every business enterprise, but they very much resemble the constantly occurring changes in public taste and demand.

The "interference" of which industry complains most bitterly is that which is clearly prompted by a political motive, but even there the issue is not clear-cut. The rationing of steel, for instance, already described, the rationing of food; the motive is political but is that the whole story? What is a government to do if an essential commodity is scarce?

The real justification for the imposition of any such form of control, certainly in the eyes of a Labour Government, is that it prevents money from buying priority. It enables the small man, the small concern, to get its share. It is easy enough to see how that operated with respect to food. The logical end of uncontrolled food distribution in times of scarcity was to be seen in Western Germany in 1946 and 1947. The farmer, the producer, held back his produce to await the best bid he could get for it. The best bids, of course, came from the black market. No honest man could afford to work a full week at his job, because he was compelled to spend some time each week either shopping on the black market or in direct barter with a farmer.

But the basic elements in that situation are equally true where other commodities are concerned. When supplies are scarce, the business with a big bank roll does not buy for its present needs alone. It bids for all the scarce commodities it can find and hoards them. It uses its money to build up its stock reserves, and if in doing so, it squeezes the small man out of business, it sheds no tear. Quite apart from any sympathy for the small man, that result can be damaging to total production, which depends as much on the small man's contribution as it does on production from the larger concern.

The political question, in Britain, amounts to this. All governments must have some political considerations in their minds when they take political action. In Britain, the Labour Government has thought and acted in the terms of two mutually contradictory political slogans: "Fair Shares for All" and "The Worker must come First." Food rationing, clothes rationing, candy rationing, all spring from the first of these slogans. The discrimination against the building of houses for private ownership is an example of the second.

I am not suggesting that all that the Government did to insure equality of distribution was effective. Planning, if the word means anything at all, means the arrangement of present actions to avoid anticipated future difficulties. Too often, the Government abandoned planning for control as a lazy way out, for all that control involves is the saying of "No." But "Fair Shares for All" has, I think, an appeal that the other slogan lacks.

Yet government interference has its converse in government aid. Regarding that, I would like to contrast the growth of two industries in Britain, the one old and the other new. I think that the age of each is significant. You would expect the old one to be the more rigid, and it is. You would expect the new to be more alive and vigorous, and it is. The older industry is the British machine-tool trade, the younger the gas turbine industry.

All national machine-tool industries suffer from fluctuations. These industries are of paramount importance in war. Their importance under peace conditions is apt, officially, to be underrated, and to that the British industry is no exception. But at least the British industry can rise to the occasion. Of the 459,000 machine tools installed in factories and shops in Britain during the war, 73% were provided by the British industry, 14½% were purchased for cash from the United States and only 12½% were supplied by the United States under Lend-Lease.

Quantitatively speaking, the machine-tool trade in Britain is not in the first order of importance. In 1935, there were 123 separate concerns in it, employing 21,000 people. By 1938, the number of employees had risen to about 27,000. In 1947, there were 224 concerns and the industry employed 35,900 employees. But in its peak year, 1942, it produced 95,800 machine tools of various kinds, of a total value of £43,000,000. In 1948, the level of production was running at about £25,000,000 yearly, and it exported about 60% of its products (the export figure for 1948 was £15,708,000). It ranks very high on the list of industries which add value to a raw material by their work upon it. Although, numerically, about one-third of all the workers in the industry work in concerns employing over 750 employees, the greater number of individual concerns fall within the group employing between twenty-five and forty-nine workers.

It is estimated that there are about 873,000 machine tools in

Britain, and that in 1947 the home industry was producing new ones at the rate of 35,000 a year. The 1949 figure was much better, estimated in the trade to be at the annual rate of £34,000,000 in value.

What are the factors which held it back in 1946 and 1947?

There were shortages, for steel for machine tools was not among the five major priorities for steel dictated by the cabinet. The industry consumes about 140,000 tons of iron and steel a year, 54,000 tons of steel and 86,000 tons of cast–iron. Steel shortage has been more of an inconvenience than a positive limitation. Time is wasted getting it, but most energetic concerns have been able to secure the supplies they have needed. The most acute shortages were, first, foundry products, contributed in part by a shortage of cast-iron, in part by the uneven standard of the foundries themselves. For that, the machine–tool industry is itself partly to blame. It has taken too little interest in pushing development and rationalization in the foundries that serve it.

The second shortage is in the supply of electric motors and ball and roller bearings, for which the industry has less direct responsibility, although there again its own passivity has consumed valuable time.

With respect to ball and roller bearings, the industry is a victim of a larger menace, the monopolistic tendencies of the ball-bearing industry throughout Europe. That industry is one of the few which have been able to build up an effective international cartel, largely directed from Sweden, with the result that the ball-bearing manufacturers have for a long time been able to insure that output did not exceed demand; and of that the converse is that manufacturing capacity is always kept below actual demand. For small and fractional horsepower motors, the industry had to wait its turn with all other consumers. In 1946 and 1947, the supply of small motors in Britain was well below demand.

The effect of these shortages on the machine–tool industry itself is to be seen in the lower productivity rate in the industry (35,000 employees in 1948 were producing approximately the same volume of output as 27,000 in 1938), in its gradual loss of skilled labor, and in the inordinate delay in deliveries.

The machine–tool trade mentions these circumstances in its own defense when criticized. But it is apt to overlook other equally significant facts. At the end of the war, the British Government had some 220,000 surplus machine tools. The disposal of surplus was well-organized, and fair prices were charged for those sold. Between 1945 and the middle of 1948, approximately 200,000 of these machines were sold, for a total price of £43,000,000, and very few of them were exported. In short, industry in general showed itself capable of absorbing this stock of used machines without wrecking the home demand for new ones. True, many of these sales were paper transactions for machines already installed and in use. Many represented overdue replacements for the war period, but it does look as though the industrial users could and would absorb a larger output of new machine tools than it did prewar, provided prices and delivery terms were reasonable. The machine–tool industry has not developed its home market so well as it might.

Today, in machine tools, it is the United States and Switzerland which are thought of as the major competitors of Britain. That is true for certain classes of machines—heavy presses, and the like— which the United States alone can make economically because of the demand from its home market, and of the most delicate instruments which have grown out of the Swiss watch-making industry. But, for the common run of machine tools, the United States manufacturers do not sell at prices lower than those which their British counterparts can reach. And at the moment the volume of American overseas sales is limited by the dollar shortage.

Britain has a good market for machine tools in Europe, India, Africa and Australasia, throughout the Commonwealth, in fact. In Europe, the French market has been dead for two years, and the Scandinavian market affected by currency difficulties. In 1947, Palestine imported machine tools to the value of £169,618, a substantial section of the whole Middle East demand. That market may be recovered. In all these markets, there are local industries which make the simpler machine tools. What they now need, and what Britain should be able to supply, are the machine tools which make machine tools, the implements of local precision industries.

Since the war, both Sweden and Czechoslovakia have increased their exports to the rest of Europe, but the outstanding feature of the postwar export market has been the absence of competition from Germany. In 1938, Germany provided 74% of Europe's machine-tool requirements, the United States 21% and Great Britain 5%. Germany has not exported machine tools since the war, but the agreed level for her industry is 66% of its prewar output. German manufacturers are now free to take the export chances that exist, and 1949 saw a rebirth of their trade. And nothing that the machine tool industry in Britain can do will stop Germany from beginning to export again, for the pressures to allow German exports are far too strong.

The British manufacturers have had four years in which to jump into the position once occupied by Germany. They have not done it. They have reasons and excuses for their failure, but they have not done all that they might have done to help themselves. They have a year's backlog of orders for the export market, and that is not good enough.

They could have made their machine–tool exhibition (the first postwar exhibition at Olympia in London, in August, 1948) an annual event. Instead, they postponed their next exhibition until 1952. They could have built up new forms of co-operative export agency. They could have compelled those who supply their castings and components to provide a better service. They could have done more to tackle the shortage in electric motors when that troubled them, and could have designed more machines to meet what some of them still think of as eccentric foreign demands. There is a great deal which they could have done and which they have not done.

The substance of the criticism that can be leveled against the industry is that it assumes that competition must be accompanied by secrecy. It lives in a nineteenth-century world, because its organization is still nineteenth century in structure. As an industry, it has little powers of co-operation, save for the organization of political pressure, largely negative in intention. Each manufacturer assumes that he can only lose by letting a competitor know the truth about his activities and future plans.

That might be an argument difficult to counter if the example of the American industry did not show that the reverse was a more beneficial policy for such a trade. There are no signs yet that the British industry is prepared even to think of adopting the American plan of pooling information and of inducing its customers to publicize their needs and requirements in detail. Never in Britain has there been a conference of machine-tool makers, designers and the users of their products, such as is a regular feature of General Motors' relations with the American trade.

For that, the blame must be laid at the door of the leaders of the industry. Such a policy requires imagination and of that they do not possess enough.

The industry cannot be criticized for the quality or design of its products. In 1948, a British manufacturing concern produced an electronically controlled milling machine which provided a combination of infinitely variable spindle speeds, with infinitely variable feeds under full automatic control, the first of its kinds in the world. It provided a range of spindle speeds from 100 to 3000 rpm, regulated by a single dial operating a rheostat. By this means, the load on the spindle determines the power supplied to it, rather than the reverse. Coupled with that was an automatic, hydraulically operated table feed, giving a fast approach to the cutter, a slow feed and a fast return. Operating the machine was a matter of push-button control. Its whole production was a remarkable triumph of co-operation between the machine–tool designer and the electronic specialist.

Where the industry fails is in the basic tasks of an industry, as distinguished from those of the individual firm; that is, in the successful general exploitation of individual capacity to design and produce. But again it would be wrong to say that this is a common failing in Britain. On the contrary, it is precisely in this that some British industries have excelled. The gas-turbine industry is one of these. Before going on to that, look for a moment at the development of radar in Britain.

Radar comes high on the British list of essential operational research, because it provided a means of preventing an invasion, just as the wooden ship and the Martello tower were in the first line of defense against Napoleon. The first use of radar equipment in the world took place in 1934, in Britain, when Sir Edward Appleton used the reflection of a radio wave to determine the height of the "Heaviside Layer," and found it to be sixty miles above the surface of the earth. In February, 1935, the first special radar equipment, specifically designed and used to plot the position of an aircraft, was put into operation at Daventry, in England. By March, 1936, the first radar towers, 240 feet high, had been erected on the East coast of Britain and from the station they served, the course of an aircraft flying at 1,500 feet 75 miles away was plotted. By September, 1939, the whole of the East and most of the South coasts of Britain were defended by a complete radar watch, covering all the English channel and most of the southern half of the North Sea. From then on, progress was continuous and, of course, by 1941 it had become a joint Anglo-American project.

Parallel progress in Germany suffered many of the faults which exist today in the machine–tool industry in Britain. In 1940, the German General Staff thought it had won the war and issued an order forbidding work on any scientific or development project which could not produce results of military use within six months. That was a major mistake in itself, for time lost by dropping research and development can rarely be regained. In 1942, they revised that order, but they did not revise their methods. They still went through the old performance. First, the operational staff prepared detailed specifications. Then, these specifications were put out for bids among competing firms of civilian manufacturers. Finally, one firm was selected and awarded a contract to produce the equipment required. And the result frequently was a waste of resources by the overlapping work done by the two or more competing firms in preparing to bid, and the production of a piece of equipment which was beautifully made, but which was just not quite right for its intended function because the men who had made it had not been helped to visualize its operational use.

The story of the development of the gas turbine in Britain shows that it is possible for a government to aid private industry and private enterprise. It also shows one of the best methods by which this can be done.

The development of the gas turbine could provide a number of morals for those who like to draw morals from real-life stories. The gas turbine was developed in Britain mainly by the initiative and drive of one man and the individuals he gathered around him. He has declared that "as every engineer knows, it is always the work of the team." The first money provided, to develop a working engine from the original drawings, was found by a private investment banker, for what must have been, then, a pure speculation,

yet the whole conception of the idea is based on the technical training that the state gave freely to the originator. "Of my twenty-one
and a half years service I have spent ten under training, mostly engineering."

The first patent for a gas turbine was taken out by an Englishman,
John Barber, in 1791. Theoretically, it was an admirable design,
but constructional difficulties in that period of material development prevented it from going further. The first gas turbine engine was built by a German in 1872, but again, the general lack
of knowledge of aerodynamics at that time prevented it from being
a feasible power unit. The use ot steam turbines, using axial-flow
compressors, began with Sir Charles Parsons in 1884, and continued
with a development of the gas turbine for static installations. The
particular contribution of Frank Whittle, now Air-Commodore Sir
Frank Whittle, was the application of the gas turbine to jet propulsion, which meant that the engine must be light enough to travel in
an aircraft. In invention, timing means a great deal.

Frank Whittle was born in 1907 in Coventry. He went to a state
secondary school and won a scholarship to Leamington College
where his career was, in his own words, "not particularly noteworthy." At the age of sixteen, he enlisted in the R.A.F. as an aircraft apprentice, and the first trade he learned was that of metal rig-
ger. The training period was three years, and he finished it among
the first six in 600, and was awarded a scholarship to the R.A.F. College at Cranwell. He spent another two years there under instruction, and was awarded a prize for aeronautical science when he left.
Then followed another eighteen months of operational duty with
a fighter squadron, after which he was sent for training as an instructor. It was during this course that he filed his first patent application
covering the use of gas turbines for jet propulsion. The year was
1930.

The principal of the turbine is, basically, identical with that of
the windmill, pressure of a gas on a surface, set obliquely to the
direction of the flow of the gas, in order to produce a rotary movement (the process, of course, can be reversed, so that the rotary
movement produces pressure in the surrounding gas). Its cycle of
operations is similar to those of every internal combustion engine,
compression, heating, expansion. A major difference is that in the

turbine the process is continuous, not interrupted, and the engine uses the last phase, the expansion, to give the propulsive effort.

But the construction of an aeronautical engine embodying these features is a task of very considerable magnitude, for success depends upon the high speed, high temperature, complete and instantaneous combustion, and on maximum efficiency from every part, so that the design for the shape of each conduit is as important as efficiency of each moving bearing. Whittle's first patent in 1930 was based primarily on his theoretical calculations for the ideal mechanism for such an operation. Production of the thing itself had to wait.

In 1932, Whittle started an officer's engineering course. The course normally lasted two years but his papers in the entrance examination were good enough to exempt him from the first year's lectures. At the end of the first year, he obtained a mark of distinction in every theoretical subject. Special arrangements were made by the Air Ministry for him to go on to Cambridge University to take the mechanical sciences tripos. He went up in 1934, at the age of twenty-seven. He took a two-year course and obtained first-class honors.

Between 1930 and 1934, he had made spasmodic efforts to interest either the Air Ministry or private industry in his patent, and had failed. In Jaunary, 1935, he failed to pay the renewal fee on the patent and it lapsed. In May, 1935, two former service friends suggested trying to obtain enough money from private sources to finance the invention. The investment banker they approached obtained a consulting engineer's report, which was favorable, and agreed to advance up to £3,000 in consequence. The original company, Power Jets Ltd., was formed in March, 1936, and an order was given to the British Thomson-Houston Co., at Rugby to make the first actual engine.

This time, the Air Ministry did display considerably more interest. They made arrangements for Whittle to stay at Cambridge for an additional year and, after the first engine had run, they also met a part of the expenses of the actual project. By the end of his postgraduate year, the experimental engine was making successful test runs and thereafter, until 1941, Power Jets Limited operated continuously under ministry contracts. Until the middle of 1940, about 55%

of the finance it used was found by its promoters, and the remainder by the ministry. In 1940, the Ministry of Aircraft Production took over responsibility for all aircraft production and development, which meant that the company operated only on Government account. In 1944, the Government bought complete ownership of Power Jets Limited. By then the total spent on development (but including the building of a complete factory) was on the order of £400,000.

Of course, experimental work for the departments was not confined to Power Jets Limited. The Royal Aeronautical Establishment initiated an experimental line of its own, which went on in parallel. The present arrangement, dating from July, 1946, is that all experimental work on gas-turbine technology is carried on by a specially created Government establishment, the National Gas Turbine Establishment, which took over from the other two. All the commercial assets resulting from that work, including patents, are held by a limited company, Power Jets (Research and Development) Limited, wholly government owned but operating on commercial lines. The Power Jets Company now owns some 2,000 patents or patent applications, in some fifteen different countries, and is actively engaged in fostering their commercial use and development wherever possible, on a royalty basis.

The importance of gas-turbine development lies in the fact that gas turbine itself is a prime mover potentially more efficient, more flexible in operation, and more varied in its possible applications, than any yet devised. In addition, because its component phases of operation, compression, combustion, and expansion are separate sections of the whole machine, the search towards the improvement of each opens up new fields for the use of each, either singly or in conjunction.

It is not necessary to say much about the first. The gas turbine for aeronautical engines has already established itself; so, too, have gas turbines at the other end of the scale, heavy installations for power generation and railroad traction. The intermediate weights and uses are in course of development now.

The second development has far wider possibilities. The compressor unit alone is capable of use in a vast range of industrial processes, from heating and refrigeration to all kinds of liquid and gas evaporation and atomization. Improved methods of combustion have equally wide applications in smelting, for example, but parallel with this is the development of metals capable of withstanding high stress at high temperature. The efficiency of the turbine improves with increased temperature of the gaseous mixture flowing through it. Before 1939, the materials available were only able to withstand a temperature up to 550°C. Work by the Mond Nickel Co. produced nickel alloys, first "Nimonic 75," later "Nimonic 80," which should work under temperatures approaching 700°C. By 1950, it is estimated that 850°C. may be the ceiling. Advance continues, because there is behind it the pressure of an actual use ready and waiting. Demands for higher working temperature result in demands for metals capable of resisting increasing loads without "creep." With the expansion stage are allied developments towards better heat regeneration and heat recuperation which increase efficiency, and reduce costs. The implications of gas-turbine technology are far wider than the present applications of the existing machines.

At the moment, Britain leads the field in general research, and in practical work on aero gas turbines, which means on all turbines of the lighter types and uses. Switzerland leads the field in practical work on heavier installations. The American industry is partly derivative, partly progressing along certain isolated lines of practical application. The value to Britain of the aero gas turbine and of the aircraft industry allied to it, in exports alone, must by now exceed £15,000,000 a year.

The emergence of the British industry is due, I would suggest, to a combination of causes and habits of thought that are well developed in Britain, if they are allowed freedom to form the right pattern. Every nation is capable of throwing up personalities such as Frank Whittle; the real test is what use a country makes of them. It may be an accident that Whittle joined the R.A.F., but it cannot be an accident that the system in that service picked him out from the mass of apprentice recruits and provided him with the training without which his talents would have been largely wasted.

Again, the gas turbine in Britain has progressed through a curious compound of private initiative and state enterprise. Power Jets Limited, owed its early financial backing to private and public finance in almost equal shares. It is the result of a working partnership of state and private industry which has brought benefits to both. But what is even more important is that the state, once its interest had been won, did not insist on submerging the private enterprise element in the undertaking. Over gas–turbine technology, the state has assumed responsibility for the basic research, which is the only sure foundation for every extension of practical application. It has left the commercial exploitation of the products of that research to an organization, the existing Power Jets Company, which is still in mind and activity a commercial concern. There is no doctrinaire logic about this method of approach, but it does produce results.

The Swiss firms have done excellent work in industrial gas-turbine development, but they appear to have based their development on steam turbine practice. In this they are very skilled, but in the long run this may prove to have retarded their progress. Switzerland is in the happy position of having actual operating gas turbines "in the shop window" now; there simply has not been time since the war for British firms to design and construct comparable machines. But the enormous resources for research and development built up in Britain during the war will have been turned to good effect when their results are fully embodied in British industrial plants.

In the United States, it would appear that there is little or no coordination or technical exchange between one firm and another. That may be part of the American way of life; it looks not unlike the methods of prewar German industry. Despite the enormous manufacturing potential of the U.S.A., these highly competitive methods of business can prove to be a brake, rather than an accelerator to development. Co-operation does not rule out competition.

There is a middle way. Radar, for instance, began as a government project, but from the first, it was the men of the services, as the ultimate users, who came to watch the experiments in operation, and who helped to prevent development from becoming a preserve of any one firm. The Telecommunications Research Establishment grew from these experiments, and a characteristic of that organization was that its directors expected admirals and generals, pilots and anti-aircraft gunnery officers, to sit in at the weekly conferences and to pool their experience with the knowledge of the experts.

A pilot would say what could and could not be done with an aircraft, a production manager would say what could or could not be done on the production line. A fighting man would raise for expert solution a problem that he could, perhaps, hardly define in words. The experts would take his idea, explain it to the man himself and then find the answer.

Development of industry in both war and peace has a common basis. In each case, it is an expression of a nation's powers and determination. A scientific worker is not merely a superior workman, to be told what to do and, sometimes, how to do it. He is an expression of a nation's most profound thought, grappling with every problem, be it how to make equipment or how to use it. He can only give his best if he has mental freedom to think of every consideration that can affect the possible solution.

It is not that he cannot be drilled. It is that he loses a great deal of his value if he is drilled. It is not that he cannot "compete," in the business sense. It is that he loses a great deal of his value if he is compelled to think primarily in these terms.

Britain, during the war, achieved scientific pre-eminence because instructively her men and women adapted themselves to the kind of working organization necessary to achieve it. This the Germans and the Japanese failed to do. With the gas turbine, she is achieving a parallel success because development by any individual commercial firm (of which there is a good deal) is based upon a pool of knowledge and technique, co-operatively produced by every interest concerned. The gas-turbine industry has succeeded under these conditions. I would argue that the machine–tool industry is lagging behind because, being old and set, it has not so far applied a similar form of development to itself.

As a footnote, and lest anyone should think that British industry is unaware of its problems and of the lines along which a solution must be sought, let me quote again from the report of the steel-foundry productivity team, published by the Anglo-American Council on Productivity in 1949:

High productivity is a touchstone of industrial conduct. Traditional practice is all too frequently a euphemism for obstinacy, trade custom for pig-headedness. Neither traditional practice nor trade custom has an export value. High productivity has . . . Neither precedent nor procedure can stave off starvation.

Today, there are in Britain increasing numbers and groups of these determined and experienced men, drawn from both sides in industry, who are consciously intent on seeing that this test is applied to every process with which they are concerned.

CHAPTER XVI

Trade Unions and Trade Unionists

So far, we have dealt with problems that are primarily problems of management. Not that I think these problems are only the concern of management; on the contrary, management has a greater chance of finding answers if it can enlist the co-operation of everyone with ideas and an interest in their solution. But it is the responsibility of management to make the decisions, and give the orders. Prior consultation, prior explanation, may make it easier to give the right orders, may make it easier to get co-operation in having the orders carried out. They do not alter the essential fact that at some stage, some one person or group of persons must accept responsibility for a course of action and must thereafter see that it is followed. There is a boundary between direction and operation, and no organization has yet escaped this fact.

But what of the situation on the other side of the fence, among those who have to do what they are told if production is to be maintained? If production is less than it might be, how much is their fault? Is labor, as it is called, interested co-operatively? Is it submissive and passive, or is it obstructive and arrogant? Here, right away we are mixed up with the trade unions, for trade unions are, more rightly than wrongly, looked upon as the outward manifestation of the whole world of labor. Do the trade unions as organizations, and trade-union leaders as individuals pull their weight, or is it true that they are restrictionist in outlook, afraid of high output, afraid to make capitalism work well because they have a vested interest in trouble?

I would say this, after many talks with people in industry, at all levels. There is, in Britain, enough evidence now to convince anyone that a real and a positive trend towards co-operation in industry exists. And by co-operation, I mean a realization that output must be increased, that increased output can only follow joint understanding by management and men of the problems they have to tackle, and a joint willingness to look for practical solutions to those problems fair to both sides.

That may appear a cautious, even a flat, statement. None the less, I believe it indicates a state of affairs of fundamental importance. A trend may sound vague enough, but if it is possible to see accurately a trend in ideas, there are few bounds that one can set to the extent of its influence. The period between the wars was a one of decay in British society, of decay in industrial relations, in confidence, and in hope. That period was bound to end. It could have been succeeded by one of increasing conflict between the owning and non-owning classes. If, instead, it is being altered into a period in which co-operation between those classes is deliberately sought by both of them, then Britain has avoided one great pitfall.

So far this trend is more apparent in the top levels of industry, among the chiefs of the larger undertakings and among the men at the top of the trade unions. Joint consultation in industry, functioning as a necessity during the war, has had, among other things, an educational effect on all who have taken part in it. The employers' side, through such bodies as the Institute of Industrial Management and the Administrative Staff College, is trying to carry that lesson right down their chain of command. The trade-union side moves more slowly, but the education process is beginning, helped considerably by contact with American trade-union leaders. Yet I say "beginning" advisedly. I don't think that events could completely reverse this process, but they could give it some nasty knocks.

The major criticism, I feel, to be made of trade-union leadership is almost a complement of this increase in willingness to make joint consultation work. It is that the leaders of each trade union are too prone to assume that the industry in which they are interested must always be considered an expanding one in point of numbers of men employed, never one in which those numbers may be bound to fall. Everyone can produce stories of men who, when their manual job is replaced by a machine, expect to be guaranteed the same wage for watching the machine at work. That reaction, in a few individuals, can make a funny story. The story ceases to be funny when the spirit creeps in to a whole industry, as it has on a large scale among railway men, for instance. A great deal of the ferment among railway men during 1949 was due to their fear of losing jobs to machines. It is a very real fear for them, but technological unemployment in some industries is bound to become a very real fact. Too many union leaders have shied away from that unpleasant fact. They have used their power and their influence to convert the idea of full employment into the dogma of perpetual employment in your present job.

Is the scene no more than a study in applied but blinkered harmony? Of course not. But first, what is the strength of the trade-union movement in Britain?

The number of trade unionists has continued to rise throughout the five years. By the end of 1948, the date of the last official figures available, they totaled 9,301,000; 7,632,000 men and 1,669,000 women, the highest number ever. So had union funds increased, totaling £54,000,000 as compared with just over £20,000,000 in 1938. Of these men and women, all but some 1,364,000 were in the 187 industrial unions affiliated to the Trades Union Congress. Two-thirds of the total membership of all unions were in the 17 largest individual unions, all affiliated to the TUC. Yet there were 400 minor unions with under 1,000 members. In short, about three out of every four men at work are trade unionists, and the urge to become one has increased over these years, not diminished. And what kind of movement do they find themselves in?

The first comment any observer feels that he must make about the British trade-union movement is that there seem to be few men of outstanding quality left among the leaders. Politics obviously have drawn off some, Mr. Ernest Bevin for instance. Nationalized industry secured others, such as Lord Citrine in the Electricity Authority and Mr. John Cliff in transport, but these withdrawals leave behind few men of anything like the same caliber within the trade-union movement itself. The government's early plans for the iron and steel industry were handicapped by the fact that it could find no single individual within the trade unions representing the industry who it could claim had both the technical knowledge and the executive skill to take charge of a nationalized concern. The same state of affairs arose in the transport world. The largest railway union is the National Union of Railwaymen. It includes all but the engine crews, the shopmen and the office staffs, who have their own unions. The majority of other workers in the industry, road transport, docks and canals, are organized in the Transport and General Workers' Union. Mr. John Cliff was a T. & G.W.U. man who joined the London Passenger Transport Board when it was set up in 1933. When the rest of the industry came to be nationalized, the man chosen to head the Railways Executive was Sir Eustace Missenden, from the management side. Sir Eustace might have become a trade-union official. He entered the industry as a boy of sixteen without influence or formal training. But he climbed the other ladder, that of management.

Two of the men prominent in the trade union world in 1949—and who had avoided too many entanglements with any other world—were Mr. James Bowman, Vice-President of the Mineworkers' Union, and Mr. J. B. Figgins, General Secretary of the National Union of Railwaymen. They are contrasting personalities, and they illustrate the virtues and defects of trade union leadership today.

Both are between fifty and sixty, Figgins the elder. Both entered the industries, whose workers they now lead, at sixteen—Bowman had the longer practical experience. Both see the world through the eyes of a trade unionist. There the resemblance ends.

Bowman is a man of lucid mind and speech, with a sharp sense of humor and of proportion (very much the same thing, of course). He is a Northumbrian, and after service in the Royal Marines during World War I went back to the pit, later to become secretary of the Northumberland Miners' Association. He planned very many of the details of the final amalgamation of the miners' unions. He planned, too, the basis of the plan, adopted by the Coal Board in 1947, for increasing the rate of recruitment into the industry. He remains completely trade unionist and a socialist. He was very reluctant to surrender his union's right to claim wage increases as part of the TUC plan in 1949. Equally, he is capable of telling the delegates at an annual conference, again as he did in 1949, that they must not think of their problems in what he described as a miner's vacuum. He has seen a problem against a wider background.

Figgins was born in Ayrshire, in southern Scotland, and he became first a signalman and later a ticket-collector before his union became his career. In World War I, he was a conscientious objector.

His progress to the general secretaryship of his union was slow and aided by chance. In 1942, he failed to secure election as Assistant Secretary; the following year the man who was elected died suddenly and he succeeded him. He became General Secretary in 1947, when his predecessor was appointed to the board of the Transport Commission. It was then that Figgins took over the conduct of his union's wage claims for its 460,000 members.

At least he was persistent. A claim for a general wage increase of £1 a week was rejected in 1947; instead the court of inquiry awarded a rise of 7s.6d. a week. In 1948, he returned to the charge with a claim for the remaining 12s.6d. a week. That was rejected by the National Arbitration Tribunal, which meant, under the terms of the general agreement between union and management, that the claim could not be repeated. Instead, early in 1948, Figgins, this time without the agreement of the two other unions representing railway workers, produced a variation, a claim for a 10s. a week general increase, plus extra overtime rates for weekend working. The management explained that the railways were not earning sufficient to pay anything of the kind. Figgins' reply was a complaint that the management had refused to give the workers the right amount of control in the operation of the railways themselves. Then followed the unofficial slowdown movements and the Sunday token strikes, about both of which the union gave the impression that its heart was not in any of the official rebukes it felt bound to give. After a period during which the Minister of Labour fluttered around unhappily, Figgins agreed to allow this final claim to go before a special conciliation board. It appeared to those closest to him that he expected an award of at least 5s. a week increase. He had already rejected, almost contemptuously, a management offer of a 2s.6d. a week increase for the lowest paid members of the union.

The result of the conciliation board's decision reached Figgins at the annual conference of the TUC at Bridlington, early in September, just after he had accepted the TUC plan for no further wage demands. The board's decision was an outright rejection of the union's claim. An observer, possibly an unkind observer, of whom there seem to be a number around Mr. Figgins, said that Mr. Figgins looked rather like a barrage balloon struck by lightning.

Figgins is the kind of trade-union leader who makes one feel that he believes *"L'état c'est l'union,"* and *"L'union c'est moi."*

Why this scarcity of real leadership among the unions? After all, innate talent is spread in a fairly uniform way. The explanation must be that the trade union recruits the wrong kind of man for a big executive position, and even more important, gives him when young the wrong kind of training for such a post. As a rule, the trade-union official starts his career in one of two ways. He may be picked from the bench because some official in his branch thinks that he would make a useful assistant. He may agitate among his fellow workers, have himself elected as a shop steward, increase the area of his authority, and finally induce or compel the union organizing that trade or shop to take him in as an official. In either case, this means that he has some gift for impromptu oratory and enough ambition to want to climb out of the average level. It also implies, as a rule, that he has no belief that he will ever climb up the other ladder into the managerial ranks. It can imply that he has sincerity as well as ambition. But, in fact, the aspirant enters a bureaucracy.

He develops his talents for fast talking and superficial good fellowship. During his formative years, he is the equivalent of a ward leader; his world is a world of small things, petty disputes, such as widows' pensions and compensation for industrial injuries, combined with an interest in the more manipulative side of local politics. At forty, he may be an important man in his area. If he is, he is fully conscious of the fact. From forty-five to fifty, he may be considered as a parliamentary candidate for one of his union's kept seats. So, between fifty and fifty-five, he may become an M.P., and for the first time he enters a different world. The immediate reaction of some trade-union M.P.s is to make the House of Commons bar as much like their accustomed public house as possible. They have lost their capacity to change. Men like that are not cabinet ministers, nor are they executive chiefs of a major industry, nationalized or not.

The trade-union movement remains a collection of individuals, individual men and individual unions. Some union leaders themselves have not worked for over twenty years in the trades they claim to represent. Some do retain contact with the thoughts and spirit of the men who work in their industry, and some retain their sincerity and desire to give public service. Some become Labour party politicians, more become pure negotiators, capable of dealing with a dispute when it happens, though much less capable of original thought on how to avoid disputes; still less on how to improve the productive capacity of the individual man in their trades. A few men drift leftward; more allow themselves to think that nationalization is something which gives them a chance to exchange a £750-a-year union appointment for one worth from three to five times as much in a nationalized body. Some drift completely from their moorings, and finish up as the subject of a full-dress judicial inquiry into allegations of bribery. The trade-union movement sometimes looks as though it was in the position of having power without the capacity to bear the responsibility.

Yet, because it is untrue to generalize, it is equally untrue to dismiss all union leaders as men living in their own pasts and attempting to make the present and the future fit into that conception of things.

After all, in these five years, Britain has been remarkably free from industrial unrest. The comparative figures for working days lost each year as a result of strikes or lockouts, are:

1920.......26,568,000	1935.......1,955,000	1945.......2,835,000
1921.......85,872,000	1936.......1,829,000	1946.......2,158,000
1922.......19,850,000	1937.......3,413,000	1947.......2,435,000

(Figures in thousands of man-days)

The contrast between 1945–47 and 1920–22 is of real significance. The worker in Britain, even if he has not worked as hard as previously—which is arguable—has certainly worked with much less voluntary interruption than during the period after the earlier war.

But there are still strikes, unofficial strikes, rarely very serious, but always news while they happen.

There are two kinds of industrial dispute. The first is that which affects trade as a whole. It may arise over rates of pay, conditions of work, the length of the work week, or even a minor detail, such as payment for free time lost in long-distance telephoning back to a distant office for further orders (a point in dispute in one of the un-official transport strikes). The essential feature of that kind of dis-pute is that it relates to all the men doing similar jobs in the same industry. Thus, its settlement must be negotiated on a national level, so that any agreed terms can be universally applied. That is as im-portant to each employer as it is to each man, and clearly a fairly complex machine is necessary to make the whole operation possible.

The other species of dispute is that which is peculiar to one par-ticular factory, or district. A frequent cause of trouble is when a managment fires a man because of his political activity. His fellow-workers call that victimization and usually demand his reinstate-ment. To the man's fellow-workers, reinstatement may become a burning issue. To everyone else in the industry, on both sides, it has no urgency at all—possibly not even very much interest.

Both employers' associations and unions in Britain have, over the last fifty years, built up an elaborate conciliation machine to deal with the disputes involving national issues. The organization is usu-ally on a three-tier basis, local, area, and national, each with joint committees and a well-established procedure. It works well, given time; which is just what the urgency of the dispute in the single factory does not give it.

In one quarter of 1946, one union had reported to it by branches what were claimed to be three cases of individual victimization. In two cases, the other employees in the factories concerned staged an immediate—and of course, unofficial—sit-down strike. In the third, the union put the dispute into the conciliation machine. In the first two cases, the man involved was reinstated by his employers; in the third, he was not. In that case, the dispute reached the highest level of the conciliation machine only after a delay of six months. And, pending the hearing, of course the man was still out of work and his workmates were steadily becoming more and more disillusioned with the efficacy of conciliation.

This one union, in 1946, referred altogether 96 minor disputes to the central body of that industry for mediation. In 49 of them the union's complaint was rejected. Only in six was a settlement made which was approved by the union. Twenty-nine were adjourned and the remainder, for one reason or another, were not adjudicated. Each one of those 49 cases would have justified the union, on paper, in calling an "official" strike. They did not do so as they did not consider that any of them were serious enough to warrant it.

During 1948 and 1949, a high proportion of the unofficial strikes took place in the transport industry. Those strikes had two causes, the particularly unwieldy nature of the conciliation machinery in the road transport industry, and the dilatory methods of the union concerned in making use of that machinery.

The transport industry was unionized late in the day. Unionism has spread through it very largely only in the last ten or twelve years. When the road transport industry was first placed under a limited form of public control, in 1932, there was no effective union organization to negotiate a reasonable national agreement with the employers. On the other hand, the government felt that something must be done to regulate wages and conditions of work among the men, as well as to regulate the management of the industry. The first attempt at control was to attach conditions concerning pay and conditions of work to the operating license of each employer. But that did not work out in practice. Accordingly, in 1938, the Road Haulage Wages Act was passed.

That act set up the Central and Area Wages Boards and specified that their wage awards should be binding on the whole industry. The central board is a vast affair, consisting of 24 members from areas appointed by the Minister of Transport, another 36 appointed respectively by employers and unions in equal numbers, and three (or five) "independent" members, again appointed by the minister. The board has managed to settle major questions without trouble, but every dispute, large or small, has to pass to and fro between area board and central board for discussion, and, not unnaturally, opportunities for delay—even if none is desired—are considerable.

The basic criticism of the Transport and General Workers' Union comes to this. The act of 1938 provided that employers and unions concerned could, together, if they so liked, work out their own simplified procedure for settling disputes; the Transport and General Workers' Union failed to make any attempt to do that between 1938 and 1948. It may have been difficult, but it was not impossible, for under the pressure of one unofficial strike in 1948, a new conciliation machine for a section of the industry was worked out, agreed to by both sides and set in motion, all in less than a week. It is fairly clear that this union was not in close touch with the men it was supposed to represent. As a result, it came in for some public criticism on that score.

The Transport and General Workers' Union looks after a great many trades. It has ten sections, each representing a trade, ranging from dock workers through transport to clerical grades. It had a membership of about 1,323,679 at the end of 1948 and considerable funds. Its last financial report (that for the year ending December 31, 1948) shows that its total income from members in that year was £2,061,473, of which £1,988,656 came from contributions (a decrease of £45,934 from 1947, but the 1947 results showed an increase of £302,000 over 1946).

Out of this vast income, the union paid out some £287,326 in benefits (only 12½% of its total income), and added £746,665 (36% of its total income) to its reserve, bringing its accumulated general fund to £5,476,813. Expenses absorbed £1,110,787, of which salaries are the largest item at £576,460. The report does not contain any total figure of the number of officials on the union payroll but whatever else the union may be, it is clearly a considerable employer itself.

Is it democratic? Not particularly. The main avenues by which its members can influence its policy are through its biennial general conference, and through area conferences for each trade section, held every three months. The general secretary (who, because Mr. Ernest Bevin designed the constitution of the union, occupied an office of considerable power) is elected, and so is the general executive council. All other officials are appointed by or through the executive. But the union is by no means immune from influence by its members, and its constitution is certainly more democratic than some. The major union in the iron and steel trades, for example, has no provision for any general meeting of its members or their delegates.

The most solid of the charges against this particular union is its size. It is too big and too comprehensive to be able to give the workers in each of the trades it represents the feeling that their affairs are having the detailed attention they have a right to expect. But that size is the result of a deliberate policy, originated by Mr. Bevin, when he became secretary of the amalgamation 25 years ago and pursued with his customary determination throughout his period of office. While his influence and that of his pupils among the officials remains, that policy is not likely to be reversed. On the contrary, it is defended by the union officials. In the August, 1948, issue of the union's publication, Mr. Arthur Deakin, the General Secretary, said, "The larger union is at an advantage. . . . It has greater bargaining power. Its finances are less a cause for anxiety . . . It has a bigger field of available talent . . . Administrative costs are relatively lower. . . ." He finished with the claim that in 1947 his union negotiated over 500 separate agreements.

But this form of growth, and these delays in the machinery for conciliation, give the Communist party in Britain its best opportunities. In Britain, the political activities of the party are a secondary concern at the moment, and in the foreseeable future. They bring publicity and a certain amount of money. They are a platform. Their effect generally is extremely small and the party itself is well aware of that. Its main interest is in the industrial world.

The Communist Party of Great Britain has a membership of some 40,000, of which over half are in London. For some time past, it has been concentrating its efforts on four major concerns, the Mineworkers, the Electrical Trades Union, the Transport and General Workers, and the Railway men. In the Mineworkers, it is past the peak of its influence; the same is probably true of the Railway men. In the ETU, it is at its peak. In the T & GW Union it has probably been checked at a point rather below that to which it would have risen had the course of external affairs not focused so much attention on what it was doing.

Fifteen years ago, Mr. Papworth, of the London Busmen's section of the T & GW Union, a Communist, was a rebel union member barred by his union's executive and known chiefly for his interest in unofficial strikes. In 1948, he was a member of the executive, along with seven other party members, the Communists holding eight out of 37 seats in this body. This was a measure of their penetration into the union, and of the time it takes to do it. At the end of 1949, the union took steps to ban all Communists from official positions. It will not, of course, be completely effective, but it is a considerable check to the Communist party.

Trade unions are always in this difficulty. They are, in origin, a negative response to competitive capitalism. They sprang from a resistance by the workers to the individual capitalist's desire to increase his profits by cutting his wage bill. The earliest and most effective weapon was a strike, a strike intended to compel an individual employer to change his ways. Another is limitation of output, spreading the available work among the maximum number of men. But both these weapons have now become too dangerous to use, particularly against a state monopoly of a capitalistic organization such as the National Coal Board. For one thing, there is no multiplicity of employers who can be played off one against another.

But that is the least of the obstacles. The nationalized industry is something different in kind from the individual employer. It is part of the state, and therefore part of the machinery by which the very strikers themselves live. Every man at work, including the miner, is able to see clearly enough already that a national strike of mine workers would wreck all his own standards of life. The strike method is therefore far too dangerous to the union and to the working class to be employed with its old freedom on a national scale.

The communist state has its own answer to that, as the workers in Czechoslovakia are finding out. It is compulsory labor, backed by the prison, the labor camp and, as an ultimate sanction, the firing squad. The argument of the socialist element in the Labour party was that socialism could work out an alternative approach to these apparent flaws in both capitalist and communist economics, as practiced. It may be a good or bad argument; it is certainly an unproved one as yet, for the trade unions have been reluctant to try it out.

Take a concrete case of an industry, the textile industry, faced with the call, the need, and the opportunity to increase its output. Lancashire is struggling to recapture its former export trade. One of the ways in which that can be achieved is by increased output from the existing machines, and one of the ways in which increased output can be achieved is by recasting the tasks and routines of the men and women in the weaving sheds and spinning mills. The battle over that began after the war, but was greatly intensified in 1948.

It is an individual battle, with individual mills as the first array of objectives. The Cotton Board, being advisory, can only coax. It cannot compel. The union leaders are of two minds and can only advance slowly towards co-operation with those managements that are themselves progressive. In 1949, they had certainly not reached a state of unanimity of mind in which they could or would bring pressure to bear on unprogressive managements. On the contrary, they were so afraid of positive action that they shied away from it on quite flimsy pretexts; as, for example, that the *Manchester Guardian,* their local paper, was trying to drive them too fast along that road.

Spectacular results were obtained in individual cases. In one concern, the increases in output were, in cardroom 40%, in spinning rooms 77%, and in the weaving sheds no less than 80%. All this had resulted in an increase in earnings of 27% and a decrease in direct labor costs of 22%. But only in some areas was this idea of "redeployment" of men and women permitted by the unions at all. The area in which the unions agreed contained some 14,000,000 spindles, about half of the total in Lancashire. Only a few concerns out of a total of 450 have yet begun actively to apply scientific techniques to the arrangement of tasks and processes in their works. Part may be a fault of management. Certainly part of the cause lies at the door of unions.

A major barrier to more rapid action—the practical barrier, in distinction from the barriers against innovations that do exist in men's minds—is the existence of a vast network of trade agreements in the Lancashire textile trades which govern the rate of pay for every process and labor classification. These agreements are the pride of the old-fashioned trade unionist's heart. They represent the result of generations of battles with employers. Each has its own history of conflict, success, failure or compromise. To the union leader, their very existence is a guarantee against exploitation; on the management side, it is an insurance against labor disputes. Lancashire men keep their word. When the full terms of a bargain between employer and union are written down in black and white, there is no room left for dispute and, therefore, infinitely less chance of a stoppage. Yet if "redeployment" is to be effective, many of these agreements will have to be scrapped. They provide that certain things must be done in certain ways, and it is precisely that that must be changed.

But the major political problem of the five years, as they developed, has been the freezing of wages and personal incomes.

The TUC resembles the Security Council of the United Nations. It is an association of sovereign bodies, each possessing some power of veto. If it is hard for the executive body of a single union to agree on a policy for one industry, it is considerably more difficult for 187 unions to agree on a common policy regarding problems that extend beyond the limits of industry altogether. The TUC can seem to be speaking with one voice, when that voice is no more than the sum of 187 common protests or 187 common demands. Yet during the fall of 1949, the TUC did develop something new; it almost became a tree-climbing fish. It seemed to develop both a corporate point of view and a national policy. True, it was clearly still a fish. But it was living out of water.

One of the fears commonly held, when the Labour party took office, was that for the first time in history a British government would be under the control of an organization not responsible to Parliament. Labour ministers, it was said, would be appointed by their party's executive. They would need to seek permission to serve as such, they would at all times be subject to the dictates of an anonymous caucus. And, when the influence of the TUC was added, "Goodbye," said the critics, "to parliamentary government as it once was in Britain." In fact, nothing of the kind happened.

At first, the situation seemed to be almost an exact reverse. In 1945, the TUC had one political aim in the forefront of its mind, the repeal of the Trades Dispute Act of 1927, an ambition which corresponds to the giving of a V-sign back to Mr. Churchill, a principal advocate of the 1927 act after the 1926 general strike. That done, the trade-union movement sat back and waited for the Government to produce the rest of an industrial policy. After all, the Labour party was its child, the intellectual of the family. The TUC knew what it wanted done. The Labour Government would explain how to do it.

Which, of course, that Government did. It had a complete set of policies. Nationalization and full employment between them would solve every ill. So the armies set out, with flags. But gradually the colors changed. By 1949, the two branches of the labor movement had almost reversed roles. It was the Government which knew what ought to be done, but it was the Government that was waiting for the TUC to tell it how to do it.

The difficulty in which the Government found itself, during its last two years of office, was that it had piled up too many contradictions among its plans for its own comfort. It wished to maintain full employment in as many industries as possible, to increase the number of people at work in industries producing goods easily sold abroad, and at the same time it wished to avoid using any of its powers for the compulsory direction of labor. Equally, it wished to make certain that every worker had a living wage, that every worker had a wage incentive sufficient to induce him to higher output, and at the same time it desired to bring down the total cost of production in Britain, in which the largest element, of course, is wages. Politically, it may be desirable for any government to be able to point to a record of full employment for five years. Economically, it is even more essential that the community shall be offered some reward for greater production or some deterrent for falling production, or both. But it is not possible to maintain forever such a set of assorted objectives in a state of equilibrium. Sooner or later something will snap. In its dilemma the government was compelled to turn to the trade-union movement for help.

It is worth stating again that a trade union is still an association of men and women working in a particular industry who have combined to improve their wages and conditions of work in that industry. During the five years of Labour Government, the bulk of the trade unions in Britain had not attempted, in their corporate capacity, to step out of that role. Individual trade unionists had become individual politicians, just as they had become individual members of the board of this nationalized industry or that, and as individuals they could escape, to a greater or lesser extent, from their earlier training and environment. But only one major union, the National Union of Railwaymen, had claimed that the union, as such, should be given the right to take part in the function of management and in the operation of its industry. In general, each union had pursued its traditional policy of looking after its own men and women in its own industry in its own way.

Judged by every trade-union tradition, in a state of full employment the action to be expected from every trade union would be to say to employers on behalf of its members, "If labor is scarce, it is reasonable to ask you to pay more for what you have." Equally— like Mr. John L. Lewis, and provided the union felt secure enough —it might well add, "What our people produce is so important that you dare not refuse us anything we ask, provided we leave you just enough to stay in business." By that tradition, a union could be expected to say to its members, "The more skill each individual has, the more pay we will get for that man." All these things the Government asked the trade-union movement not to do.

This should be put quite plainly. The government asked the unions to drop their century-old way of thinking, their century-old relationship vis-à-vis the employers. It asked the unions not to exploit their position, not to use this contrived state of full employment to start another cycle of temporary wage gains. In a sense, it asked the unions to share with it the responsibility of government, of convincing the average man that an additional pound a week in wages would, in the end, do him more harm than good.

It took the general council of the TUC a long time to make up its mind to agree to this. It took the general council a long time to persuade the majority of the individual affiliated unions to follow its lead. But in the end, the council resolved both to support the Government's request, and to make its decision as effective as possible.

The statement of policy that the general council of the TUC issued in November, 1949, is, therefore, an important document. It contained eight points:

1. This was a general reiteration of the gravity of the country's economic position and a call for "vigorous restraint upon all increases of wages, salaries and dividends."
2. In this, the TUC opposed any statutory regulation of wages, and declared that wage negotiations and the fixing of wages must remain trade union responsibilities.
3. The general council went as far as it could go to tell unions to follow its advice, "unions must pay regard to the realities of the economic situation . . . and act loyally in conformity with the policy now recommended by the general council."
4. A saving clause to permit some wage increases for the lowest paid workers (the wage which the general council had in mind as the

criterion of a "lowest paid worker" was £4.12.6. a week, but no figure was publicly announced).

5. This was the operative clause. In it, the general council specifically recommended no wage increases while the standard index of retail prices, the semi-official measuring rod, did not move outside the limits of 106 and 118 (when the statement was published the current figure stood at 112). If it did, the declaration of policy would no longer be binding. In any case, the whole position would be reviewed on January 1, 1951. An important feature of this clause was that the truce was also to apply to those industries in which there was an existing agreement that wages would automatically rise and fall as this retail price index figure moved.

6. & 7. General promises by the general council to do what it could to increase productivity and to extend systems of payments-by-results.

8. A promise to the unions to keep the whole situation under constant review.

To obtain such a statement of policy, the government was compelled to promise the TUC that it would not introduce any further stimulating or depressive factors into the retail prices index. Equally, it was compelled to reassure the TUC that it honestly believed the index figure would not rise above 118 in the coming twelve months. The Government also promised that it would increase the profits tax on the distributed profits of companies. (It is worth noting that the general council's statement called for restraint in any increases in dividends, not profits.) But despite these inducements, it is impossible not to recognize that the TUC did take a remarkably courageous step when it pledged itself to such a policy.

For one thing, it was asking certain unions, and through them some 3,000,000 trade unionists, to forego wage increases to which they were then entitled under existing agreements. The boot and shoe workers, the blast-furnacemen, the building trade workers all had agreements which provided for these automatic increases in wages. The building trade workers were placed in the most difficult position, for their national agreement provides that wage rates are reviewed every February. As a result, they were asked to surrender any chance of a wage increase in February, 1950, based on a twelve months' change in the cost of living.

Again, the trade-union leaders were only too well aware that this declaration of policy would be hotly attacked by every Communist, big and little, in trade union ranks, and that the attack would be directed at the leaders themselves, as "pseudo-socialists." Every trade-union leader must feel that, although he may claim to lead his union members and to have their confidence, outright abandonment of all wage claims is a hard thing for him to explain away, just as defeat is for any general. And what trade-union leader lightly risks his personal popularity and influence?

It may be said that the trade-union leaders were shrewd enough to see that they stood to lose more by a defeat of a Labour Government than they did by agreeing to this policy. That is only half the truth, but it implies a good measure of political sagacity. The other half of the truth is this. By November, 1949, the leaders of the major trade unions had come to accept another loyalty in addition to their traditional loyalty to union members. They had come to see that they too must carry some of the burdens of the state, and some of the responsibility for the political policy of their chosen instrument, the Labour party.

I would like to pay a respectful tribute to the courage of that decision.

The effectiveness of that decision is another matter. The policy of the general council was put to a special conference of executives of affiliated trade unions in January, 1950, and it was carried, but only by a narrow margin. On a card vote, there were 4,263,000 votes for and 3,606,000 against. The ETU, under Communist influence, was always opposed to any policy of official wage stabilization. So were the Railwaymen and the Shipbuilding and Engineering Confederation. The Mineworkers' Union took a vote from its branches, and the branches refused to follow their executive in support of the general council. Nor did the unions with sliding-scale agreements accept the surrender of their existing rights.

None the less, the policy statement of November, 1949, remains a landmark. It is the first occasion on which trade unionists, as such, accepted from a government the need for a national wage policy, and produced a body of men capable of working out an agreed policy in response to that demand.

CHAPTER XVII

The Commonwealth

You can argue that Britain has lost three empires. The first was in continental Europe, but that went when the English kings failed to hold France, during the fourteenth and fifteenth centuries. George Washington, coupling his name in this connection with that of King George III, broke up the second. The third disintegrated between 1900 and 1940. What are the chances of building a fourth? This fourth would certainly have to include Western Europe. I remember an Italian politician, with a dry turn of wit, saying to me, "And why not? You English have a natural genius for the creation of empires." Or has the spell been broken, the talent lost? What has happened to the old empire, the product of Queen Victoria's day, an empire that still lives on in the imagination of so many (among whom it is difficult to say whether Americans or British predominate).

Eire was the first to go. Field Marshal Smuts, by the sheer force of his personality, held South Africa formally within the Empire until the day came, in 1948, when he lost his premiership of the Union. Burma slipped away quickly, apparently into internal chaos. India hovered on the brink, not so much of complete independence —for all the dominions have real independence—as of complete severance of the nominal tie. Pakistan, to show she was not India, celebrated her freedom by conciliatory gestures to Britain. But were they anything more than gestures?

Australia and New Zealand, among the dominions, seem to value their links with Britain as much as before. So does Canada, despite the very much greater difficulties in her way. Ceylon is still present, and there are still the colonies, in all their infinite variety of status, from those that have virtually complete self-government, like Southern Rhodesia, those that have legislative or consultative councils,

315

as in East and West Africa and the West Indies, to those that have a British governor and no frills, as in Fiji.

The past and the future of the British Commonwealth are, of course, fine subjects for endless speculation. Those parts of the Commonwealth which stem directly and naturally from Britain itself can accept with equal ease one pattern of a Commonwealth relationship, one which is flexible, largely unwritten, depending more upon usage and tradition than upon statute. Those which do not, those which, like Eire, are peopled by a different race with a different history, prefer a more specific and defined relationship. What Eire wanted in 1922 was "external association" with the Commonwealth. Failing to get it, she has cast off the links one by one.

Three new dominions have been created, all consisting of peoples of separate races and traditions. "External association" certainly defines the relation between Britain and India and Pakistan. If Burma could have been offered membership in a union of nations only "externally associated," if she had understood that the Commonwealth could mean that, would she then have decided on nominal independence? To what extent have the separatist tendencies in South Africa—and to a lesser extent, in Canada—been due to the existence within these territories of a mass of people who are not British in origin and still not British in thought or speech?

But let us take each in turn.

Ireland has changed, as the result of its general election in 1948 showed. The generation that Mr. Costello represents did not fight in the General Post Office in Dublin, 1916. But some of its elder relatives did, which may account both for Mr. Costello's acceptance of a new trade agreement with Britain, and the grim determination of his Foreign Minister, Mr. McBride, to sever the last formal link between Eire and the British Crown, the use of the name of the King of England in the appointment of Eire's foreign representatives.

Eire went through a wartime experience common to all unoccupied neutrals, a state of internal prosperity despite the almost complete collapse of overseas trade. Individually, her people might favor the cause of the Allies. Officially, they were told they could do nothing in aid of it, and, indeed, the risks of any departure from strict neutrality were considerable in 1940. So Eire remained isolated and a little decayed, living on horseback in the age of the jeep and, like Sweden and Switzerland, a little smug in her isolation. No nation can escape all of the evils inherent in a total world war, masked as they may be, and those that creep in through neutrality are often the most corrupting.

By 1948, Eire was very conscious that she was part of Western Europe, and that another war might not spare her. But, in her view, any close tie with Britain was impossible while partition remained, and Northern Ireland (Ulster) was separated from the rest of Eire.

Mr. de Valera's views on Ulster and partition had grown into an obsession. There was only one way in which the deadlock could be resolved for him, a complete surrender by the Northern Ireland Government. The emotional content of the situation demanded nothing less. Mr. Costello was prepared to try a fresh approach. True, in any settlement with Northern Ireland, Belfast must become subject, in some way, to Dublin, but limits and definitions, when penned by an Irishman, can become things of most flexible meanings. The essential thing would be to make a start. Once the boundary between Eire and Northern Ireland had ceased to be a national frontier, the common sense of both people would prevent it from ever becoming that again.

So far as Britain was concerned, the Labour Government was no longer a government which could only see Ulster through a red-white-and-blue mist. The ruling regime in Northern Ireland is, after all, Conservative, and old-fashioned Conservative at that, and some of the Conservative M.P.s from Ulster have bitter and wicked tongues. The British Government's view of Northern Ireland can be summed up in the words of the Victorian poet:

> Thou shalt not kill, but needst not strive
> Officiously to keep alive.

Mr. de Valera had always looked westward for support, to the United States; indeed no Irishman can fail to do that. But times had changed. The emotional appeal from Irish politicians at home to Irish politicians in America no longer seemed to have the same potency. By 1948, the men of influence in the United States were military men, notoriously blind to the nuances of political opinion in foreign countries. Could it be, the Irish politicians thought—unbelievingly—that they regarded the whole of Ireland as no more than a single European base? As such, the island has some disadvantages, when compared with Great Britain. It lacks ports and industrial facilities, but militarily, the general staff in Washington no longer seemed to attach so much importance to the existing ports and industrial facilities in the British Isles. In any new war, the expectation of their working life might be very short. There was Ireland, a geographical unity on any military map.

So in July, 1948, when engaged in selling food to Britain, Mr. Costello raised this other question. He was not a de Valera, he hinted. He could be trusted to do something to save Ulster's face. What did Mr. Attlee propose to do to help him?

Mr. Attlee certainly saw some practical difficulties. One was the question of the Commonwealth, nationality and loyalty to the British Crown. Ulster was loyal to the Crown; its leaders said so at least once a month. What about Eire, which regarded the Commonwealth as an "external association" and the Crown's nominal rule over Eire as an anachronism on the point of being tidied up and stowed away in the history books? The House of Lords had been very difficult about this question of the definition and status of British subjects, during the July debates on the British Nationality Bill, almost as though some of the Conservative peers had had news of what was in the wind. What could Mr. Costello do to help him with that?

One difficulty, of course, was that there is not one Ulster but at least three. One is the Ulster of the Northern Ireland Government, rigid, self-perpetuating and extremely loath to exchange the realities of virtual independence for a place as a provincial local government authority. Then there are the Ulster Roman Catholics, exiles from all the government posts that matter, embittered by twenty-five years of mild persecution. There is also a labor movement in Northern Ireland, more deeply split than its English counterpart, consisting of a right wing of old-world trade unionists, and a left wing of marked Communist complexion.

And presumably, somewhere about—as in most countries—there is a large body of men and women who do not much care for politics at all, but is interested in regular employment and low taxation (if those things can ever go together again).

The British Crown is still a barrier between a united Ireland, if only because northern and southern Irish use it both to mask and to fortify the real obstacles in the way of their union. Northern Ireland will not give up the Crown; Eire will not accept it. The very fact that it arouses an emotion is a convenience to the politicians. It saves them from having to justify themselves by argument.

Ireland remains tied by her old dilemma, unable to escape from trading with Britain, even if she desired to, unable to forget her wrongs and seek, like India, a new relationship intended to make the best of both political worlds. She waits upon world events, because her rulers have trained their people not to think about them save in emotional terms.

Eire's decision to quit the Commonwealth is like a floating log deciding that it will quit the whirlpool. It's just the kind of decision any prudent log should make.

In the long run, India and the states on the Indian Ocean will likely prove most directly and permanently affected by the election in 1945 of a Government headed by Mr. Attlee rather than Mr. Churchill. Mr. Attlee was determined to give India independence; Mr. Churchill was not. The issue between them was as clear-cut as that, and it was Mr. Attlee's view that prevailed.

All the negotiations and proposals during the three years were over ways of carrying that determination into effect with the greatest advantage to both sides. They were not about the end to be achieved. When the Cripps Mission to India in 1942 failed, Mr. Attlee made up his mind that India needed independence, and he stuck to that thereafter.

The first important step taken by the Labour Government after its accession to office was to send to India a cabinet mission, headed by Lord Addison, to work out a long-term plan by which the independence of India could be achieved. The most important result of that mission was not its actual negotiations in India, but the fact that its members succeeded in convincing the majority of Indian leaders, for the first time, that a British Government did intend to give them their independence. Thereafter, the outstanding struggle in India was internal, between Moslem and Hindu. There were a score or more of additional complexities, ranging from the future of British trade interests to decisions on India's sterling balances, but all of them, even those which were once of paramount importance, were eclipsed by the racial problem. By the end of 1946, that situation was essentially a conflict between the Congress Party and the Moslem League to obtain, from the outset, as much power as possible under any new Indian constitution and accordingly, each attempted to deflect any attempts by the other to gain positions of tactical importance.

The long-term plan for the whole of India, worked out by the British cabinet mission earlier in 1946, provided for a three-tiered constitution, with an All-India Federal Government at the top (though with powers over a very restricted field), a series of provincial governments at the lowest level, and on the second tier, three groups of provinces (one certainly Hindu, one very probably Moslem, and the third, consisting of Bengal and Assam, undetermined). The group was to have some federal powers over all the provinces within its borders. This plan was perhaps clumsy, but it did come from an agreement among the politicians who would operate it, a vital step. It was embodied in a document issued by the cabinet mission on May 16, 1946, and it was accepted and signed by all the major Indian political groups, Hindu and Moslem.

The signed agreement did not remain an agreement in fact for very long. By the end of 1946, the Hindus and the Moslems were in conflict over the interpretation of two clauses in the document.

The document provided that the next stage should be the setting up of an All-India Cabinet (which was done, and the Moslems joined) followed by the calling of a Constituent Assembly, convened for December, 1946. The Moslems declined to participate in any such assembly while this point of interpretation was in dispute. The Hindus, with reluctance, but with a considerable degree of statesmanship, proposed as a next step that the document should be submitted to the Indian Federal Court for interpretation, and that they would accept the court's ruling and operate the constitution accordingly. The Moslems (which meant Mr. Jinnah) did not accept that proposal. They seemed to be drawing back to their earlier stand; reluctance to join with the Hindus in constitution-making at all. Then came a violent outbreak of communal rioting in Bihar and at once the Moslems said that the implications of this were so serious that attempts at constitution-making must be suspended until law and order were completely re-established, by the British, of course.

These conferences convinced the men of India—rather earlier, in fact, than they convinced the people of Britain—that on this question Mr. Attlee was determined to pursue the course he had set steadfastly and without check until the end of what he regarded as inevitable was reached. To a man of a different cast of mind, there was everything about the situation to give reason to pause. It was obvious by then that the agreement between Hindu and Moslem had never been real, that consciously or unconsciously, it had been based on the illusion that the British would never get out of India. Not only that, there was clear enough evidence, from other places besides Bihar, that the final withdrawal of the British Raj would be followed immediately by bloodshed of a horrible and ecstatic kind, and on a considerable scale. These considerations did not move Mr. Attlee or his cabinet. They did not accept the notion that the past traditions of British rule in India carried any present obligations binding on the successors in the business. Even if India shied at the responsibilities of independence, independence she still should have.

The original date fixed for the institution of Indian independence had been June, 1948. Mr. Attlee advanced it by one year. The original plan had been to leave Viscount Wavell as Viceroy until the changeover was complete, but Lord Wavell, who knew India well, hesitated at all its implications. He was accordingly replaced by a new Viceroy whom Mr. Attlee could hope would see, in his own speed and brilliance, the best hope of wringing both success and prestige from a most difficult situation. He selected Lord Mountbatten and, for his purpose, the selection could not have been better.

The two dominions came formally into existence in August, 1947. India and Pakistan were placed in the hands of men who could have no claim to being aggrieved by Britain. They had been given precisely what they asked for. Disconcerting as that might be, difficult and unexpected as that situation might appear to any statesman, it is not one which can ever call for public repining.

The immediate problem facing the two new dominions was racial. The boundaries between them, drawn by the British with the same determined speed, left in one area—the Punjab—an explosive mixture of Moslems, Hindus and Sikhs. The other danger spots were Hyderabad, Kashmir and Jungagadh. In Hyderabad and Junga-gadh, Moslem princes ruled over peoples of which the majority were Hindus. In Kashmir, it was the prince who was Hindu, the people mainly Moslem.

The Indian dominion government struck at once in Jungagadh, just as soon as the ruling prince made an attempt to attach to his state the Dominion of Pakistan. A considerable show of force, a local demonstration that can only have been partially spontaneous, and India had dealt with that weak spot. Jungagadh became part of the Dominion of India willy nilly, and that was that.

With the Punjab, the dominion governments had, at first, shown a desire to make common-sense arrangements about irrigation systems and power supplies. They were powerless—or indisposed—to compel their peoples to display an equivalent restraint among them-selves. There followed the massacres of August, 1947, the grim spec-tacles of mass murder and mass flight, with no possible choice for the common man save that between flight or death, often no more choice than as to where death would come. Massacres like that are part of India's history; but they had not been the first result else-where of a grant of dominion status.

Kashmir was a problem of the same order, if not on the same scale. Kashmir is a frontier state in the northwest. Being on the frontier, it had been, during British rule, something of an artificial state in the sense that the British authorities had always been prepared to intervene to check any disintegrating influence. As soon as Britain left, Hindus, Moslems and Sikhs were bound to attempt to claim their own, and probably more.

Take one example of the difficulties that arose as soon as fighting started in Kashmir, in the fall of 1947.

In April, 1948, the State Department in Washington decided that no more arms or warlike equipment should be supplied either to Pakistan or India until the Kashmir dispute was settled. On the face of it, this looked like intelligent anticipation, in the form of a meas-ure designed to limit any conflict over Kashmir by the simple means of cutting off supplies. In fact, it was nothing of the kind.

All ordnance factories in what was formerly British India were located in what is now the Dominion of India. There were none in

Pakistan. Similarly, all wartime reserves of army equipment, including stores taken over from the United States Army, were located in India, with one exception, the stores of engineer equipment, which were at Lahore, in Pakistan. The result was that Pakistan, on its creation, possessed neither reserves of war equipment nor the means of providing them from her own resources.

That situation was dealt with by the Joint Defence Council, which included representatives from both dominions and was presided over by the Governor-General of India. Its decision was that, from these reserves, up to some half million tons of ordnance stores should be transferred from the depots in India to Pakistan, the basis of division between the two dominions being roughly 70–30. That was the intention. The communal riots prevented the actual transfer of any substantial portion of these stores to Pakistan, for after the middle of August, 1947, there was almost a complete breakdown in railway communication—certainly for freight—between the two dominions.

Pakistan, thereafter, was left with a military force devoid of essential replacements. Most of its armored vehicles were of American manufacture, and replacements could only come either from these stores in India or from the United States, and that the State Department ruled out. On the other hand, India possessed not only her share of the wartime reserves, she was in effective possession of those allocated to Pakistan as well.

It would be idle to imagine that Pakistan could accept this situation, particularly while India retained her supplies. The Pakistan authorities were nervous about Indian intentions; they were even more nervous about Sikh intentions with regard to the Western Punjab. They were bound to seek some source of supply. If the doors of the United States were closed, they would ask Britain. If Britain failed to produce what Pakistan considered to be necessities, where else could she turn save Soviet Russia? Was it likely that the U.S.S.R. would fail to seize any chance of gaining goodwill in the Moslem world, even if her intentions were no more than to embarrass Britain and the United States?

In the end, Pakistan was given her supplies from British and American sources. And, of course, she used some of them in Kashmir.

The United Nations Commission has produced an uneasy truce over Kashmir. It has not brought about anything that has even begun to look like peace. India claims that the Hindu ruler of Kashmir acceded to India, and so settled once and for all the legality of Kashmir's status. "Pakistan is a robber and an aggressor," Pandit Nehru has said. The people of Kashmir are to be allowed to decide for themselves, of course, to which dominion they will belong, but only if there is no interference from Pakistan. And interference by India? That is quite different. India, and her troops, are in Kashmir by legal right. So the argument continues within its closed circle.

The Dominion of India, within the geographical limits of the sub-continent of India, has embarked upon a policy that is predominantly expansive; the speed and the anxiety with which India took over the 562 princely states, for example, are evidence enough of this. Such an incorporation, and consolidation, was inevitable—indeed desirable—but the history of the Jungagadh, Kashmir and Hyderabad states shows that the intention behind it was rigorous and ruthless. The Dominion of India contains about 35,000,000 Moslems, yet communal differences had to take second place to the immediate urgency of the establishment of regimes subject to the central government. Kashmir has not been so easily swallowed. Hyderabad presented fewer difficulties for India, in that 85% of some 17,000,000 people were Hindus ruled by a minority, in the main Moslems. India had no difficulty at all in hearing such an audible cry from fellow Hindus.

Had Hindu and Moslem, India and Pakistan, been anxious to arrange a compromise, it would have been easy enough to do so. The Nazim of Hyderabad made constitutional proposals to the Indian Dominion Government which, while not meeting the full text of its specific demands, did concede the substance. But India regarded a compromise settlement as the least desirable alternative. It was necessary to show quite clearly where mastery lay, and military action provided the simplest way of teaching that lesson. And from India's point of view, that decision was right. A negotiated settlement would have been no settlement at all. There was no native tradition in either country strong enough to have given it binding force.

Clearly these two "dominions" in the Commonwealth are of a kind quite different from those state structures to which the word was originally applied, the colonies, mainly of British extraction, which had gradually built up a democratic society capable of self-government. Mr. Jinnah underlined one difference at the very outset in 1947, when he made it clear that he intended to be the governor-general of the new Dominion of Pakistan. Aside from the question of whether he had verbally agreed that at the start the two new dominions should have a common governor-general, who should be Lord Mountbatten (and there is a good deal of evidence that he had so agreed), Mr. Jinnah clearly was not the kind of governor-general that Dominions were accustomed to have. By British constitutional usage, a governor-general in a dominion is not an active politician. He is a political adviser to, and often a political arbiter between, the leading politicians of the country. He is an instrument—not a negative one, but again not a policy-making one—in the machinery by which the largest political party governs. Mr. Jinnah could be nothing like this; the idea would be alien to his mind. He was the leader of Pakistan. He intended to be at least three-quarters of the government of Pakistan. And so he was while he lived.

Pakistan faced another set of circumstances. It first had to create the machinery of state, and policies are of little use without the machinery with which to carry them out. Most of Pakistan's actions over its first year can be traced to this circumstance. It was groups of the people of Pakistan who led their government into Kashmir, and into the then half-acknowledged, half-denied military interventions. In India, it was the government which forced the pace, in Pakistan the reverse.

Pakistan is well behind India in almost every form of state apparatus and is, therefore, much more on the defensive. But having less control of her people, and particularly of the Moslem League, she is liable to be committed as a state to foolish adventures lacking a solid background of thought and preparation. Further, the Pakistan government found the resettlement of the refugees from the Punjab a considerably greater strain than did the Indian government.

The menace which hung heaviest over the heads of the Pakistan government was the latent threat of Sikh ambition. It was evident that the Sikhs were by no means reconciled to the present political divisions within the Indian continent. The territory they occupy spreads across the eastern frontier of Pakistan and the western frontier of India. They are a strong and virile people. In the political sense only, they occupy a position parallel to that held by the American Indian in the colonial wars between England and France in the eighteenth century. India, and to a lesser extent Pakistan, could each make use of their fighting and destructive capacity, provided they were certain that the Sikhs would never turn on the hand that guided them.

The two dominions watch each other with a deep suspicion. India devalues her rupee in conjunction with the pound sterling. Pakistan does nothing of the kind. Both use resources which they can ill spare—in fact, resources which should not be used for this purpose at all—in preparing to defend their own sides of this common frontier, in maintaining two divisions of men each along that line, even in planning how the rivers and watercourses of the whole Punjab can be twisted to conform to this political boundary. The Hindu leaders accepted partition in 1947 because they had come to see that with Mr. Jinnah on the other side, the alternative was no separate and independent India either. But Mr. Jinnah is dead. What is there now to hold them back from reducing Pakistan by force of arms?

Various factors. World public opinion is one. The pressure of communism from the north and east is another. The disruption that such an act would cause to the whole Commonwealth; not at all an emotional reason but a very practical one, taking into account the stability and defense of the whole of Southeast Asia. There are a great many reasons, and together they may be strong enough to persuade the government of India that war between the dominions is unthinkable. But if India does hold back, it will not be because of regard for Pakistan or because of regard for the principles of self-determination, or even out of respect for the former Pax Britannica. I do not say that in criticism of India. India is realistic in her own way, in her own time and on her own responsibility.

The point is that the West has retreated. Where once a British chain of political control stretched from Suez to Sydney, now the line eastward from Suez breaks off at the eastern end of the Persian Gulf. Ceylon and Malaya are no more than stepping stones. Eastward from Singapore, British influence merges with the new American sphere in the Pacific.

To return to the start of all this. Was Mr. Attlee right in handing

India over to the Indians in the way that he did, and at the time when he did it? Of course, many people in Britain think he was wrong. Among them are those who live in the past, and believe that the glories of Victorian imperialism could have been kept alive if it wasn't for these detestable socialists. But many others have a greater sensibility. Did not Britain owe it to the peoples of India? does not any ruling power owe it to those who have given it their allegiance, so to time its departure as to prevent such an event as the Punjab communal massacres?

That was the challenge. The Labour Government based its action on principle, on the enlightened European conception of the duties owed by a state to its alien subjects. Freedom is a desirable end. Therefore time is not a relevant factor in a political plan for freedom. The desirability of the end cannot be affected by the speed with which it is approached. Personally, I rather doubt that proposition. I feel that the Einstein theory has some political applications, too. Not that such an opinion matters. What does matter is that the Labour Government in its actions over India did represent a majority in Britain, and that that was how it approached the dissolution of Queen Victoria's former empire in India.

South Africa presents a very different, and a much more ugly scene. Substantially all that has happened in South Africa in the last forty years stems from four sets of facts. The first is that there are (on 1946 census figures) 8,923,398 non-Europeans in South Africa and only 2,335,460 Europeans. The second is that the white population is of two different origins, not speaking the same language and neither willing to give up its own tongue. The third is that Britain did not, when creating the South African Union as a British Dominion, insist on the political objective for which she had ostensibly fought the South African war of 1899. The fourth is that all the whites in South Africa are now desperately afraid of the non-whites.

The first fact requires no explanation, except the comment that the non-Europeans in South Africa include a great many Indians who are, commercially, already in direct competition with the white population. Nor does the second need elaboration.

The third fact does require amplification. The slogan which ral-

lied the Uitlanders in the Transvaal against the Boers was "No taxation without representation." What the Constitution of the South
African Union provided was no taxation of whites without representation.

The fourth fact is obvious enough. It is confirmed by all visitors
to the Union. It is unfortunately apparent in all the actions of all
the political parties in the Union.

The basic situation in South Africa has not changed fundamentally since 1895. The capital which controls the basic industries, gold
and diamonds, is still mainly British in outlook. The farmer is the
reactionary, the man who hates change, and he is still the Boer of
Dutch origin. But the circumstances of the conflict have altered, and
additional complications have been introduced.

Secondary industries in South Africa have grown by leaps and
bounds in the greenhouse of war. In 1938–39, the value of materials used in secondary industries was £98,000,000, in 1944–45
£186,000,000. The labor force employed in these industries increased from 108,734 Europeans and 172,923 non-Europeans to
115,577 and 255,660 respectively over the same period. Moreover,
a great many of the men controlling the secondary industries were
Jews or Indians. And in consequence, the farmer had an additional
competitor for native labor, besides the gold and diamond mines.

But the purchasing power of the native has hardly increased at
all. In 1936, it was estimated to be £3 per head per employed
person, and the 1943 estimate was no more than £6 per head, very
little more than is represented by the increase in the cost of living.
Since internal purchasing power increased so little, secondary industries of South Africa remained small-scale concerns, inefficient by
international standards, handicapped by a dual–color standard in
operation, mainly dependent on the purchasing power created by
the gold and diamond mines, and capable of survival only if protected by a high tariff wall. And their principal customers remained
the mining companies. In 1947, the gold mining companies spent,
mainly in South Africa, £33,000,000 on stores and equipment,
£22,000,000 in salaries and £12,000,000 in wages.

The position of the farmer vis-à-vis the industrialist had worsened. The farmer benefitted from the general improvement in
the prospects for agriculture all over the world. (For example, in

1945, the value of wool exports from the Union was £10,693,943, in 1946, £30,491,664.) But in South Africa itself, Boer farming is based on native colored labor, and for this competition had mounted. Poor as are conditions in the city labor compounds, poor as pay in industry is compared with that of the European workers (in 1940–41 the average yearly remuneration of a European in manufacture was £261, that of a non-European £60), both were much in advance of those prevailing in agriculture.

The Boer farmer is not by nature conservative in his approach to the soil. He has been inclined to take his crops and move on. Only fifteen per cent of the surface area of the Union can now yield any agricultural crop. And, as so often, comparative lack of success bred an increasing resentment among the farming communities for the towns and all they stood for, the Industrialist, the British, the Jew and the Indian.

General Smuts owed his political power in South Africa to his history as a Boer fighter, to his personal qualities as a man, as a lawyer and a politician, and to the appeal he still had to the average Boer farmer. He saw to it that the farmer had some direct benefit from his administrations. But in 1946, he lost the confidence of the country districts, and the South African electoral system gives the country districts greater relative influence than the towns.

A great many of the natives, intending to work in the mines, come south and they pass through the townships of Bethal. The 1,200 or so farmers in the district resented the fact that so much of this potential labor which they needed, passed on out of their reach. They organized round-ups, and these round-ups were based on flogging as a coercion. They carried that flogging of the natives to lengths which no Government could ignore. A hundred South African police were moved into the Bethal area, to protect the native. The white inhabitants were aghast. Protect the black man against the white? Was it for this they had returned Smuts to lead the government in Pretoria? Their reactions were shown clearly enough in the general election of 1948.

On paper, the election figures did not give the impression of a landslide in favor of the Nationalist party. There are some 1,500,000 voters in South Africa. The United party polled some 500,000, the Nationalists 400,000 and the Afrikaners and the Labour party about

60,000. It was a 78% poll. But the election result was decisive, since the Nationalists—despite their minority vote—won a majority of seats. It may prove to have been the most decisive ever fought in South Africa.

The Nationalist party is a party based on fear; as a result, its strongest urge is to do what it can to keep the native segregated in reservations away from the towns, available as labor for the farmers rather than for the industrialists but, above all, segregated, divided and supervised.

It is a party which lacks a tradition of parliamentary democracy as developed in Britain—in fact, many of its leaders have always preferred German ideas of government to those of Britain. Mr. Eric Hendrik Louw tried, during the war, to organize a boycott of those young Boers who fought in the Union's armed forces.

It is a party which dislikes foreigners—and the term foreigners includes British, Indians and Jews—and resents the idea of even nominal allegiance to the British Crown. "Britain's hands are still red with Boer blood," is one of Dr. Malan's most common expressions.

These are the motivations of its action. Expediency may control its immediate decisions, but the roots from which they spring will remain unchanged.

Whenever any events of this significance take place, there is always a tendency to minimize their possible consequences. Talk in opposition is one thing, people say. The experience of office—the responsibility of actual government—there are a great number of phrases of this kind.

"After all, they've only a minority of actual votes." Have they? The United Party polled 500,000 in 140 constituencies, the Nationalists 400,000 in 90 constituencies, of which they won 79. If they had fought 140 constituencies, would their total poll still be below that of the United Party?

"Dr. Malan is seventy-four. He's an old man, riding into power in the age of his prejudices." And if Dr. Malan were to die tomorrow, would he be replaced by men less convinced, less extreme than himself? Mr. Louw, Mr. Strydom, even Mr. Havenga of the Afrikaner party—the Foreign Minister—these men are equally determined, equally forceful, equally competent to make use of the power they have won.

"With such a strong opposition, and such a narrow margin in the Lower House . . ." But is the opposition strong? When Dr. Malan proposes to abolish the native representation in the Cape Province, does every member of the United party vote against it? When the Indians are attacked, if the Jews were attacked, would every member of the opposition fly to their defense? It is the opposition which is, in truth, the divided party.

The consequences of this shift of power are not hard to imagine. Some have already been translated into facts, such as a virtual annexation of the Southwest Africa mandated territory. A mandate implies that, in theory, there is or can be some external supervision of the administration. This is alien to the ideas of the new government. Again, considerable pressure on Britain to hand over the protectorate of Basutoland, Swaziland and Bechuanaland to the Union is already a consequence. It was bruited at the Transvaal Nationalist Conference in 1948, and Dr. Malan has since made it clear that he is only waiting for the right moment. The new Union government cannot favor any regime based on the principle that a colony is a trust for the native inhabitant.

The only brake on the Union government is economic, the fact that its advent to power checked the flow of capital money from the United Kingdom into South Africa. But the devaluation of the pound sterling, and with it South Africa's currency, lifted some of the pressure from that brake. Not only did these decisions help those dependent on the gold-mining industry, they also assisted the balance of South Africa's external trade by increasing the value of her main export by 30%.

But the most dangerous action of the Malan government can only come from its attitude towards and its actions over the colored races. Any form of parliamentary representation for the non-European was bound to disappear, as a matter of political principle; even the rudimentary rights of the Indian, and the provisions as to native representation written into the Constitution of the Cape Province. South Africa has already served notice on the Indians that she does not want them in South Africa, that she would like to get rid of them if that were possible, and that in the meantime they provide, as over the riots at Durban in 1949, something of a stalking horse in racial trouble. South Africa is becoming a microcosm of the results of the white man's conviction of racial superiority, a country which can teach, but which does not seem able to learn.

And the black men? I would rather leave that to the comments of two South Africans, in letters to the editor of *The New Statesman*:

. . . Most South Africans, whatever their party views, hold that Native policy must be based on two principles.

The first is the principle of racial individuality: that is, the right of each of the four communities of South Africa—Whites, Cape Coloured, Bantu and Indians—to survival as a distinct people, with its own culture, language and way of living. This implies the express rejection of any idea of the fusion of the four peoples into one—in other words, of the absorption of the other three peoples into the Bantu mass—and this in turn entails opposition both to miscegenation itself and to anything likely to lead to miscegenation, such as the mingling of races on familiar terms in social life.

The second principle is that of White's ascendancy, which we regard as the indispensable condition for the performance of the White man's function as guardian and propagator of the values embodied in Western civilisation. We do not derive this claim to ascendancy from any belief in the innate superiority of one race over another, but hold that it arises out of the function, which in turn arises out of the fact that the majority of the population of South Africa are still in the state of barbarism. To establish full equality under such conditions would mean transferring power to the uncivilised majority and thus entrusting the fate of civilisation to people who have not as yet accepted it. And if a civilised and an uncivilised man are really equal, what is the meaning of civilisation? . . .
Cape Town   CHARLES OULD

Sir,—When will my countrymen acquire sufficient discretion not to defend their policies outside South Africa? If only they would leave it to the extremists everyone would disbelieve them on the grounds that things could not possibly be so bad. It is when the Mr. Oulds (who, after all, are not so different from the Mr. Clarks) rise in their own defence that they really stand condemned. For it has all been said before, so often . . .

We break down tribal tradition, force the natives into the towns, leave them to rot in *pondokkies,* educate a few of them to Standard Two, leave them ill-housed and ill-fed, with no facilities for entertainment, then piously remark that they cannot have the vote because they are not civilised.

The policy of the Nationalist Government is a logical continuation of the policy laid down by Hertzog in 1936, in a Government in which many of the United Party leaders held Cabinet posts. The laws which are now being enforced with such disregard of Western values have been in the statute book for years, but only now are men like Mr. Ould (and there are many) waking up from their own complacency to find that the tradition they have been cherishing is not that of the humanists who brought European culture to its highest peak, but the other branch—the branch that makes Asiatics and Africans sometimes wonder about European culture—that of Hitler Germany.

Let us be quite frank about our White South African values. So far, we have not produced any Shakespeares or Michael Angelos . . . But we have produced some first-rate values in gold mines and farms, which could not get on for a day without cheap Native labour. Nor would our washing or cooking get done, nor our houses swept nor our children looked after. Things would be simply terrible. Quite uncivilised. . . .

THELMA GELDENHUYS

South Africa lies at one end of the vast half-circle which extends round the rim of the Indian Ocean, from Simonstown to Singapore. Halfway round lies Colombo, and to the north of Colombo are the dominions of the Indian peninsula, whose nationals in South Africa are already crying out concerning what they describe as their persecution. At the other end of the half-circle is the Malayan Federation, in which the white man is already engaged in a struggle to justify his claim that his regime can be less oppressive than that of the communist. North of the Union lies the rest of the continent of Africa itself, an essential element in the strategic defense plans for both Western Europe and the United States.

At the southern foot of Africa, there is now a state which is xenophobic, unbalanced, faced with many difficulties that its instinctive actions will only tend to inflame, a state which looks back on its European connections with distrust. The Nationalists are determined that South Africa shall live its own life, that it will cut itself off even further from the main stream of international thought and activity. In their mind, South Africa must be self-sufficient, and the white race predominant. No one from outside can help this country in its malaise, certainly not at the present time, perhaps never.

South Africa, in everything but name, is no longer a part of the Commonwealth. But she is a part of Africa. In Central Africa, the British Colonial Office is trying to carry out a native policy directly opposed to every idea for which Dr. Malan stands. Between Central Africa and the Union lie the colonies of the two Rhodesias and Nyasaland, together a vast potential source of agricultural and mineral wealth. The Union and the Colonial Office, consciously or unconsciously, are fighting for control over the future of the Rhodesias, in fact for the soul of the Rhodesias. That is the most decisive battle that will be fought in Africa in the next decade.

Those are the dominions with particular difficulties. Dominions like Australia and New Zealand faced the world in a rather more assured way.

Australia, when compared with other countries, fared well in the maintenance of internal price stabilities. Her net income from industry rose from £803,000,000 (Australian pounds) in 1938–39 to £1,280,000,000 in 1946–47, the first real postwar year. During this time the estimates for the index of wholesale prices for basic materials moved only from 1,000 to 1,488 (compared to 1,896 in Britain and 1,887 in the U.S.A.), while a weighted average of retail prices in six cities only showed movements of 1,000 to 1,309. The national income in 1948–49 was estimated to be £1,955,000,000.

Financially, too, Australia has had a remarkable postwar record. The 1946–47 budget showed a deficit. From that year onwards it has been balanced, in the year 1948–49 at the figure of £535,000,000. In addition, the government has been able to reduce taxes, redeem some of its short-term indebtedness in London, successfully convert longer term stocks held in Britain to a 3% basis, raise its expenditure on the social services to £81,000,000 a year, and between 1945 and 1949 make gifts to the United Kingdom Government totalling £35,-000,000. At the same time, Mr. Joseph Chiffley could start off his election campaign in the fall of 1949 with the boast that 720,000 more men and women were at work in June, 1949, than had been in June, 1939, and that every available worker has had a job, every new worker has had a job.

Australia has been maintained on the crest of prosperity by two things, her successful crops of wheat and wool, and the fact that the world prices for these commodities have been maintained. That, likewise, is the potential weakness in her economy.

Yet the country has its difficulties; technical, like the shortage of capital, equipment and the continuing need to import such things as oil, rubber, and tea; sociological, because there was still a shortage of labor in the industries that needed them most. The majority of fresh entrants into labor entered the secondary industries, not the primary industries which still produce two-thirds of all Australia's exports. Between 1939 and 1947, the number of men engaged in the primary industries actually fell from 562,000 to 559,000, in mining and quarrying from 71,000 to 59,000. Yet the workers engaged in manufacture rose from 694,000 to 934,000, an increase of 34%.

Australia's iron and steel industry remains a low cost producer, but her output is less than it was in 1938–39, mainly because output of good quality coal was low, and the 1949 coal strike produced a real setback to industry, because coal reserves were quite inadequate to cushion the blow. To quote an austere critic of the Australian economy, "Output of confectonery has increased, but brick production is still lagging on prewar figures."

But Australia has a great deal to take into account in any long-term assessment of her prospects. She has started on a big hydroelectric power and conservation scheme. She has set up and maintained what must, relatively, be one of the most successful immigration schemes anywhere in the world in the postwar years.

New Zealand's problems were very much the same. In the summer of 1948, the New Zealand government revalued its currency in terms of pounds sterling and, by so doing, increased her financial power to import by 25%, and reduced her receipts from her exports by the same proportion. The change was made very shortly after the completion of a series of long-term selling contracts with Britain, and the New Zealand government cannot have assumed that it could easily or quickly increase the sterling prices fixed for its produce. The basic reason for the decision must have been that the government wanted to reduce the real income of farmers. And it believed the country's need for the additional volume of foreign-made capital and consumers' goods, which could be bought with the revalued currency, so urgent as to demand an acceptance of the risks inherent in an upward revaluation of the currency, and a consequent fall in income for the agriculturalists. Again, the explanation is that it is the secondary industries which are needed to support the farmer.

I don't feel that this book is the right place for a detailed discussion of the problems of Canada. Canada too has been faced with a shortage of manpower. Canada too has revalued her currency (earlier than New Zealand, in July, 1946). But Canada's most acute difficulty after the war has sprung from quite a different set of circumstances, from the fact that her trade was tied to two different currency systems and that those systems became unhitched. Canada, in trade, is the circus rider with a foot on each of two horses in harness, the United States dollar and the British pound sterling. When the harness of sterling-dollar convertability broke, Canada was not even so well placed as the circus rider. She could not plump to stay on one horse and let the other ride.

Canada is a pastoral and agricultural country, like Australia, indeed like the United States, before she is a storehouse of minerals or a manufacturing center. But, whereas the United States exported only some 5% to 6% of her national production, Canada exported as much as between 25% to 30%. She was dependent on her customers' being able to pay for what they bought in a currency freely convertible into dollars. No country can have welcomed more the return of convertibility in 1947. No country was potentially in greater danger as a result of the collapse of the sterling-dollar convertibility arrangements in August, 1947, or by the devaluation of the pound sterling itself in September, 1949.

The difficulties of one industry alone show how desperate is the problem. The Canadian lumber industry in British Columbia was largely built up to meet the British market. Imports of British Columbian timber into Britain grew from 98,000,000 feet in 1930 to 741,000,000 feet in 1938. In that last year, 34.5% of the total import of timber into Britain, came from Canada. The proportion in the following year, the first year of the war, was 72%; in 1945, it was 46%. But in 1947 the currency shortage began to intervene. The timber order from Canada for the year ending June, 1948, was extended to run over to June, 1949, thus halving the yearly rate of supply. And, to Canadian dismay, Sir Stafford Cripps began to talk of Britain obtaining more of her supplies from the Baltic countries, a "more natural pattern" of trade. Since then there has been a series of temporary expedients, none of them calculated to reassure the Canadian farmer that the British market had a real stability for him. And, although the wheels of exports from Britain to Canada began to move, they had a governmental slowness.

The Labour Government has had an uneasy conscience about Canada, which does something to explain the outburst of bad temper over Canada from its left–wing members after the Washington Conference in 1949. Its uneasy conscience arises from the fact there is so little that any British Government can itself do to maintain the prewar volume of Canada's export trade to Britain, and yet it is extremely awkward for the United Kingdom to talk to—even to think of—dominion government in terms that can quite legitimately be used in respect to a foreign country.

Economically, Canada is bound to march in step with the United States. Politically, the non-French elements in Canada think and feel themselves to be part of the British Commonwealth, all the more stubbornly because of the French element. The Commonwealth connection gives Canada her independence from the United States, yet it may completely dislocate the present pattern of her economy. The dilemma will of course be solved, because I think the Canadian people are tough enough to stay alive, and the fact that they do stay alive will mean that they have found some solution. But someone is going to get hurt in the process, and I have a shrewd suspicion that it will be the Canadian farmer.

In point of time these paragraphs on the dominions end with the conference of Commonwealth Foreign Ministers at Colombo, Ceylon, in January, 1950. But I have the feeling that the Colombo Conference properly belongs to the start of a chapter, not the close. No conference like this had happened before, and whether one like it will ever happen again depends on what is done in the future, not on what has happened in the past.

The conference was unique in many ways. It was the first conference of the Foreign Ministers of the United Kingdom and the Dominions. It was the first Commonwealth conference to take place on territory not settled and developed by people of European origin. It was the first conference in which the three new non-European do-

minions (in terms of population) had taken part. It was the first conference where it was known beforehand that the views of the various
dominions on external affairs were at variance over matters of major importance.

But it is too soon yet to say if the conference will prove to have
been really significant—for one thing, it did not improve the relations between Indian and Pakistan. Perhaps it is a point to the credit
of any conference if it recognizes the obvious, in this case the urgent
need to raise the standard of living throughout the Far East. But no
statesman coming away from the conference explained in detail precisely how the assembled ministers had decided that was to be done,
not even how he himself thought it ought to be done.

The dominions are sovereign independent countries, responsible
for their own decisions and, like an adult child, legally capable of
any form of independent action. The colonies are not. The distinction between a colony and a dominion lies exactly here. The range
in the forms of government actually in operation throughout the colonial empire is considerable, from a benevolent dictatorship by a
team of officials (as in some of the West Indian islands) to almost
complete self-government, as in Southern Rhodesia, where about the
only power retained by the British Government is control of foreign relations. But the fact remains that for each colony, either the
Colonial Office or the Dominions Office in London accepts some degree of responsibility.

The British Colonial Empire is a vast trading concern. The British Government publishes regularly (but rather in arrears) a book
called *Statistical Abstract for the British Commonwealth,* a volume
of intense interest, if figures do not—in your mind—obscure the realities behind them. In it, the trade of each colony is set out in detail
and the last abstract, for the ten years from 1936 to 1945, is of even
greater interest because it shows the enormous changes in the patterns of trade imposed by war.

For instance, in 1936, Cyprus exported 69,131 cwts. of raisings, of
which Italy took 25,198 cwts., France 12,885 and Palestine 698. In
1944, the exported crop was 70,031 cwts., of which 44,420 cwts.
went to Egypt and 23,654 to Palestine. The value of the export had
increased from £28,000 to £184,000.

The biggest single export from Southern Rhodesia in 1936 was asbestos, to the value of £959,000. Then, the bulk of the mineral exported went to Britain, the United States taking only about one-fifth of the British total. In 1945, the weight of production was about the same, its value had increased to £1,674,000 and Australia had replaced the United States as the second largest purchaser.

In 1936, the total value of the exports of all British colonies and protectorates was £127,100,000 of which £40,900,000 (32%) went to the United Kingdom. In 1945, the value was £143,100,000 of which £53,900,000 (37%) went to the United Kingdom. The extent of dominion trade with foreign countries had increased over the same period, from £238,486,000 to £976,832,000, and the percentage of trade with Britain fallen from 45% in 1936, to 23% in 1945.

On trade, the fact that a particular territory is British influences the direction of the export trade of that area. It does not govern it absolutely. For imports into a colony, the strongest link between Britain and the colonies today is the fact that the currency used is identical, but it would be wrong to assume from that that the colonies are tied to the British market. For example, in 1936, Nigeria imported wearing apparel to the total value of £305,000. Of that £96,000 came from Britain, £139,000 of it from Japan. In 1936, Jamaica's total import of merchandise was valued at £4,922,000, of which only £1,875,-000 came from Britain. By 1945, Britain was supplying Jamaica with merchandise to the value of £1,321,000, the United States £2,-882,000 and Canada £3,943,000.

So much for trade. The pattern of administration is equally diverse. The basic framework is simple; an administrative head, usually a governor-general, but occasionally, in the smallest colonies (like some of the West Indies islands), no more than an administrator. He is assisted by a staff of which the two major branches are the Colonial Secretary's department (administration) and the Treasurer's department (finance), each expanding and breaking off into other branches as the needs of the colony require. Representation for the inhabitants usually begins with a consultative council, its members nominated by the official machine. That grows into a legislative council of nominated members; at first with a majority, then with a minority, of official members. That, in its turn, gradually changes into an elected legislative assembly with powers of control that gradually increase. By the time this assembly has complete internal responsibility, the colony is well on the way to full dominion status.

Nor is the Colonial Service itself a preserve for the people of Britain only. The total number of employees for which the Colonial Office is responsible is about 300,000. Ninety-six per cent of them are natives of the colonies, not of Britain, and to assist these men to climb to the highest positions, where most of the four per cent of British are still to be found, £1,000,000 of the Colonial Development and Welfare Fund has been set aside to provide scholarships for them.

Further, lest it be thought that this assembly of officials must inevitably be antipathetic to the normal activities of trading enterprises, here is a testimonial from the Chairman of Messrs. Booker Brothers, McConnell & Co., Ltd., one of the biggest firms of merchants trading in the Caribbean, with tentacles spread into Africa as well. It was given at the annual general meeting of his company in 1949:

. . . Much criticism is levelled nowadays at Government departments and their so-called bureaucrats. I and my colleagues can say in all sincerity that in the Colonial Office we find men of great ability and vision who are prepared at all times to discuss our many problems with us and to give invaluable assistance and advice where it is possible and proper for them to do so . . .

But these men of ability and vision give assistance and advice. They do not attempt to run things themselves.

The most ambitious scheme for any of the colonies since the war has been the "plan for the mechanical production of groundnuts in East and Central Africa," intended to increase the supply of vegetable oils available in the world, and presented to a rather skeptical public early in 1947. The plan began as an amalgam of state and private enterprise. It was fostered primarily by the Minister of Food, but the managing agent appointed for the initial stages in the territories concerned was a specially created subsidiary of the United Africa Company, Ltd., itself a subsidiary of the Unilever combine. (It was that company, incidentally, which had proposed such a scheme in March, 1946.)

In 1948, a new Government-created body, the Overseas Food Corporation, took over the enterprise, and that corporation was not only Government-created, it was Government-designed.

Basically, the detailed plan, worked out by the special mission of experts—the Wakefield Mission, as it was called, appointed in 1946 to investigate the United Africa Company's proposal—was that 3,250,000 acres of bush land in Tanganyika, Northern Rhodesia and Kenya should be cleared of trees and scrub by mechanical means and replanted with the groundnut plant, the nut of which conveniently yields about 60% of its weight in edible oil. The area to be cleared was divided up into 107 units of 30,000 acres each (eighty of the units were to be in Tanganyika), and on each, a planned system of crop cultivation and rotation would be installed, leaving only about half the area actually under groundnut cultivation at any one time. It was estimated that the whole area could be cleared by 1952 and that it would then produce some 609,834 long tons of nuts annually. The 1948 crop was to be 56,920 tons and the 1949 crop 227,676 tons (the figures were as detailed as that).

The total capital cost was estimated at £24,000,000, or £7, 9. 6d. per acre of land included in the original scheme, of which clearing operations would account for about half. The experts' plan was adopted and the Government brought its organization into action. The investigation on the first stage was held in the fall of 1949.

By the end of March, 1949, the scheme had cost £23,000,000. The 1948 planted acreage was 7,500, the 1949 acreage 49,620. The crop in 1948 was 1,566 tons of shelled groundnuts, that of the following year no more than 2,150 tons of nuts and 800 tons of sunflower seeds, an alternative oil-bearing crop. Not even a press agent could have described the project as having met with outstanding success.

Naturally, the floodgates of comment and criticism, or recrimination and counter-attack, opened on the Minister of Food, Mr. John Strachey, on the Chairman of the Overseas Food Corporation, Sir Leslie Plummer, on all concerned. Mr. Strachey dismissed two members of the board of the Food Corporation. *Picture Post* flew a reporter out to Africa to make an investigation. There was a debate in the House of Commons on the Food Corporation's report. All the unlikely and likely explanations for what had happened were produced, and some of the facts. In the end, Mr. Strachey girded up his loins, determined to plod on, expressed his complete confidence in the reconstituted board of the operating company, and promised to spend another £25,000,000 by 1954, but to have 600,000 acres under cultivation to show for it. His party, of course, gave him the necessary check—it was too near the general election to do otherwise. They would have made it a blank check had he insisted.

Some of the causes of the failure had been both unavoidable and unforeseeable. The worse setback had been a drought in the 1948–49 season which had damaged crops all over East Africa, privately as well as publicly owned. Some of the causes had been unavoidable. Shortage of the right equipment was one. When the work began, there were no suitable heavy tractor units of the right type available in Britain, and only a few new machines could be acquired in the United States. A search was made for used vehicles, and a number were picked up from U.S. Army surplus stores in the Philippines and the Middle East. Likewise the Valentine tank was adapted for use as a tractor, but these were no more than gallant efforts. Again, during 1947, a new railroad line was built from Msgala to Kongwa, 16 miles in length. The annual flood washed away part of the embankment. Part of the crop was attacked by the rosette disease.

But so much, one would have thought, could have been foreseen. Was it to be expected that adequate mechanical repair and maintenance shops and facilities could be summoned up out of the ground in East Africa ready made, and that they could be suitably manned straightaway? It is possible to establish adequate port and transportation facilities, where none existed before, in a very short time. It was done during the war, but that requires unlimited money and the highest organizational skill. One of these must have been lacking in East Africa.

The British Colonial Service has been built up on a tradition of steady but slow progress. Five–year plans were rather pushing it, in its view. It has had every excuse for this attitude of mind. Speed costs money, and the Colonial Service has never had much money to spend, not from the days, a century ago, when the home government allowed the annual sum of £4,000 for the whole cost of administering the settlement which is now the Gold Coast Colony. The criterion of a good colonial management before the war was a budget in which local expenditure did not exceed local revenue. That steady policy had produced results, if time was measured in decades. It had, for instance, built up the irrigated cotton growing in the Sudan without very much in the way of a yearly deficit. But that kind of machine is the worst possible sort with which to tackle a rush job, and never before in peacetime had any colony seen anything approaching £23,-000,000 of public money spent on it, over no more than three years.

This traditional service approach to a problem of large-scale commercial development within a colony had not escaped earlier comment from outside. In 1948, a Select Committee of the House of Commons produced a report on the Colonial Estimates with particular reference to Nigeria.

The Nigerian ten-year plan contemplated a total expenditure of £55,000,000. On that the committee made these comments: "The plan does not propound a complete strategy of development; it is merely an aggregate of proposals for spending money . . . The plan concludes with a series of appendices in which the heads of the several Departments put forward their suggestions for spending their share of the development money. That is not planning. . . ."

One cannot escape the impression that the groundnut plan was no more than an aggregation of plans for spending money. At bottom, the initial disaster to the scheme sprang from the political outlook of the ministers responsible for it. They seemed to have started from a series of false premises. First, that a scheme carried through on the basis of private enterprise must be wrong because some private profit might emerge from it. Therefore, a scheme operated on a socialist basis must be organized on lines which are quite different from the methods employed by private enterprise. Finally, good intentions are bound to make a success of any organizational methods, good, bad or indifferent.

The Select Committee on the Nigerian Estimates had had something to say on the respective roles of public and private enterprise in colonial development:

In the past, commercial enterprise has played the leading part in the economic development of Colonial territories. Without the pioneering work of the trading companies the foundations of Government could not have been laid and the services provided by Government are still maintained from the sources of revenue which commercial enterprise has developed. . . . It is plain, therefore, that the planning of Colonial development must take account of the part which private enterprise will play. . . .

. . . but private enterprise cannot play its proper part . . . so long as the belief exists among the Colonial people that it is unfairly exploiting them. There appears to be an especially strong local feeling against the United Africa Company on two grounds: first, because it is believed to have practised conditional sale of merchandise; secondly, because it draws a large annual revenue from mining royalties.

(In justice to the United Africa Company, I should add that the report of the Select Committee went on to explain that the United Africa Company had offered to surrender these rights as long ago as 1943, "in return for a capital sum, and investigators were appointed to determine the amount. Their reports are still awaited." That report was published in 1948, and a waiting period of five years reveals the other side of the coin. For an organization that could allow five years to pass by, and still assume that local opinion would remain happy and quiescent, is lacking in one attribute of importance in government, imagination.)

To attract to the management of an enterprise, the size of that set up in East Africa, the few men in the world capable of making it succeed, it is essential to offer them a high reward. In a capitalist country, that is money. In a communist country, it is power. It is equally essential to make them realize the penalties of failure. In a capitalist country, it is bankruptcy, and in a communist country, death. The Labour Government was half–hearted about the rewards, and quite unable to think of imposing any penalties, and of the two the second was the greater mistake.

The Government scheme has not been abandoned but, like a child, it will find it hard to escape from the climate of its formative years. The worst of the consequences flowing from the politics of the whole original conception is that it has made this plan for African development a political shuttlecock. It has smeared it with the mud of political in-fighting—worse, it has dragged Africa and Africa's needs into the arena of a purely British conflict. It is not so much the loss of such a considerable sum of public money. Commercial enterprises do lose money, and that money is public money—in the sense that its loss diminishes the total available for public investment, even though the loss may have fallen on the few instead of on everyone who pays taxes. The damning thing, now, is that it will be years before the Overseas Food Corporation and its results will be judged dispassionately. The chairman, if a socialist, will tend to think of every point of criticism as a political attack, to be resisted; he will think so, because it is a criticism not of his personality nor of his methods but of his politics and his political loyalties. As a result, policy becomes "confidential." It is too dangerous to tell anyone, even the public, anything. Equally, the opponents of socialism will search the cleared areas of Africa, not for groundnuts but for anti-socialist brickbats.

This reaction, even more unfortunately, will not be confined to Britain. If any American is asked to find money for the development of Africa his response may well be, "What, on the basis of the Overseas Food Corporation? Not on your life." But it will be the African life that loses most.

The world need for additional food remains. Africa is possibly the greatest potential source for an increased supply, and beyond doubt a country with every need for an increased productive output, both for domestic consumption and for increased exports and revenue. Such a plan may have been too large, and its results too uncertain, for any single trading company to sink the money required to launch it, purely as a commercial speculation. It may have been necessary for the Government to accept the risk and to refuse to be deterred by the inevitable setbacks. More food for the world would result. But it was not necessary for the Government to throw its cloak over the whole business, to say that the project must be run on the pre-ordained lines of a British Post Office, simply because it was intended to provide a public service. The answer should have been an organization like Power Jets, Ltd., but this conforms to no theory set out in any textbook on socialism or capitalism, nor is its success studied with rapture by the civil service.

It is always pitifully easy to attack a large constitutional service at work. Such a service can never be perfect and it is easy, even for an outsider, to light upon some of the imperfections, fatally easy for him to imagine that he has spotted most of them. Yet I doubt if anyone today could attack the British Colonial Service for the paramount aim it has pursued, that of creating in each colony a community which can adjust itself to, and continue to grow in a changing world. Nor can the service honestly be attacked on the balance between European and native interests which it has, in the main, fairly kept. It has not ignored what the European can offer, while it has controlled the amount he has taken. It has not idolized the native, nor lost heart over his faculty for picking up, first, the worst tricks of some of the Europeans he encounters. Aims and methods have both been fair enough, and the service in general has built up a reputation for just, honest, and disinterested administration. In areas where the population is pastoral, and basically self-contained, the administrative machine has provided all that is needed, and the system could hardly be bettered. It provides advice and assistance.

What have been its failures? They are most apparent where a colony has become involved in international trade. It is not because of the trade itself, but because of what inevitably follows that trade; the first contacts and exchanges of commerce, the increase in the native merchant and professional classes, and the growth of an often distorted form of nationalism. The service has not always accepted quickly enough the fact that its machine must become a part of the people, either by accepting the people into the machine (as Indians came into the Indian Civil Service), or by training its own white staff to cease to think as external administrators.

A tragically urgent problem in West Africa is the swollen shoot disease in the cocoa plantations. Its causes cannot be traced; there is as yet no known cure and, if unchecked, it can wreck the whole economic life of the colony because it is killing the cocoa trees by the million. Yet the committee of experts on plant diseases, which was appointed to make an investigation in October, 1948, could have been appointed six months or more before. Because nothing effective had been done, the natives began to feel that the administration had no interest in finding a cure. Because no explanation of the disease was offered, the natives were resisting what attempts were being made to cut out the diseased trees from the plantations. This was one of the causes of the riots that broke out at Accra in February, 1948.

The government appointed a committee of inquiry, the Watson Committee, to investigate these riots and the committee's report provides two examples of what might be called a lack of any feeling of urgency in the administrative mind. Criticism made by the committee was that the local administration had failed to give the native population any feeling that it was concerned about the rising prices of imported goods, or that it proposed to take any action to remedy the situation. Similarly, although an increase in the payments to ex-servicemen had apparently been "under consideration" for some time, only after the demonstration that terminated in the riots did the administration announce its intention to give the increases.

Yet, how did these criticisms come to be made? By a United Nations investigator? By someone hostile to the whole British system? On the contrary, they were made by men appointed by the British Government to comment on the activities of the government's own regime. It is not that men who write such reports as these are always right and the colonial administration always wrong. It is that Britain is responsible for both, and the political tradition is that difficulties of this kind should be thrashed out in public, in the belief that they can better be solved that way.

The Watson Committee had another important consequence. The Gold Coast Colony had been given a revised constitution in 1946, a colonial constitution in almost common form, with a majority of official members in the legislative assembly. The Watson Committee advocated changes in that constitution, changes based on what the committee felt to be a decline in the old system of tribal administration and so in the effectiveness of administration based on the old tribal organization. The Colonial Office did not accept that suggestion, nor the diagnosis which gave rise to it. The Watson Committee consisted of men from England without any long experience of the colony. It was decided to appoint yet another committee, but this time the committee appointed was something novel. Its thirty-nine members were entirely African, headed by an African judge, Judge Coussey. The only European connected with it was one of its two joint–secretaries. The Coussey Committee published its report in September, 1949.

The report is a long document and its constitutional proposals are very detailed. But these two things stand out. The members did not ask for complete self-government, although they did ask for a legislature, with two chambers, in both of which elected African members would form a majority. They also believed that their tribal organization could be changed (by making a majority of the tribal councils elected members, not members nominated by the tribal chief mainly from among his relatives) into something very like a British form of local authority, locally responsible for health, education, housing, roads and fire services. Not much more than a century ago, the white folk regarded the natives of the Gold Coast as an exportable commodity. On the average, about 10,000 men and women a year were shipped by the slavers to North America, a form of dollar export that must cause some feeling of uneasiness even now. Yet today, these people wish to stay within the British Commonwealth, and to adapt their own native institutions into a likeness of those which are native to Britain. However it is looked at, the Coussey Report is a considerable compliment to Britain.

The Victorian empire has shrunk, as other empires have shrunk. There was a day when Spain and Portugal could claim that between them they ruled all the known world outside of Europe and Asia. Empires fall if their rulers are more concerned to exploit than they are to develop.

The parts of the world for which the Government in London has direct responsibility are now confined to Africa, Malaya (the lease there is a short one) and the dotted islands and enclaves that mark the oceans of the world. Over some of these responsibility does not in practice extend to external affairs. (Can it be imagined, for instance, that Britain would or could pursue a foreign policy for Bermuda or Fiji that was directly contrary to that of the United States?) All these parts of the world are in direct need of development, and the United States must help in that development, because she cannot avoid that responsibility even if she would.

It is an immensely difficult task for Britain. A main dollar-earning export from the British colonies is rubber, and the main market for rubber is the United States. About that, to quote Sir John Hay, an expert in rubber: . . ."In 1939, under a Barter Agreement, we exchanged 90,000 tons of rubber for 600,000 bales of cotton. On the basis of present values, the same quantity of rubber is worth less than 200,000 bales of cotton. This distortion of values is not due to the free play of supply and demand; it is the outcome of American restrictive trade policy. Simultaneously with enforced restriction on the use of natural rubber in favour of America's own synthetic product, there is the maintenance, through U.S.A. Government support, of high prices for their domestic farm products, and our ability to close the dollar gap is thus rendered increasingly difficult . . ."

The most solid and practical contribution Britain can ever make to world stability, through the Commonwealth as well as directly, is to produce the raw materials and the manufactures that the world needs, at fair price and of the right qualities. Only by that means will the rest of the world be able to export to Britain the primary products, agricultural and mineral, on the sale of which their own economies are bound to depend for a very long time. It may be argued that Britain's relations with the Commonwealth are discriminatory against other nations, but the amount of discrimination existing is relatively small—much less than many people in the dominions would like. Britain has been compelled to strain the ties between the dominions and herself by denying herself dominion trade rather than allow all the damage from trade dislocation to fall upon the rest of the world, particularly upon the rest of Europe.

To those of British descent, again, the Crown means a great deal. How is any Government in Britain to break down the feelings of opposition it arouses elsewhere, and yet retain it in a form vital enough to survive with still some positive and helpful meaning?

Trade, defense, feelings of common kindred and loyalties, and their attendant difficulties, are all a part of the Commonwealth. But I believe that they are overshadowed by another with much wider implications and of infinitely greater complexities. That is the problem of race and color. It faces the whole of Western civilization. It is the one problem which Russian Communism can claim, with apparent justification, to have solved with greater success. And, whether the white peoples like it or not, there are more colored people than white in the world.

I most sincerely believe that the way of life proposed to be followed by the white races in South Africa will bring ruin and destruction on themselves and jeopardize the ideals of freedom and democracy for which the white races of the world claim that they stand. I believe that the centers of continuing friction between white and colored in Africa and Asia show that none of the white races can, at present, truthfully claim that they have a sure solution for this problem. I believe that the withdrawal of British domination from India, and the British experiments in East and West Africa, are of the highest importance to the world because they are concrete pieces of evidence on which colored men may base a hope that co-operation with whites, on a basis of equality, is ultimately possible, however difficult it is and however many the backslidings may be.

I believe that, if voluntary co-operation among colors cannot come, then the white races have not only failed in that. They will have condemned their whole civilization to an inevitable overthrow and extinction.

CHAPTER XVIII

Anglo-American Relations

I would produce as Exhibit A the following criticism of an American film shown in London in the fall of 1949. The criticism is from the *News Chronicle* of October 8:

Last week Mr. Humphrey Bogart found his soul as a night club proprietor, which moved me to award that profession second place for general democratic glamour. A little thought, however, has caused a slight adjustment of the award.

Here is my list of those callings wherein, according to Hollywood, the American dream of male success materialises in all fullness and glory. In order of precedence they are: gambler, show producer, advertising agent, night club operator, orchestra leader.

In the crowd, well below these symbolistic figures, come reporters, private detectives, undercover men, crooners, piano concerto players, war heroes, composers, plain and fancy business men, plain and fancy racketeers, etc., etc., etc. Creatures of glamour certainly, but lacking the fundamental nerve, insouciance, freedom and solid glamour of the big five.

Any Number Can Play . . . is the gambler's apotheosis. Its hero, Charley Kyng (Clark Gable), is surely the American model man, iron nerved, uxorious and white through and through. The gambling joint where his worshipping home-loving underlings wear black ties and jackets and striped trousers, is run with more decorum than a reception at the White House. And Charley can't bear to see his clients suffer and will stake them or give them their car fare home when they are cleaned out. . . .

Charley's model son is the only person in the film who doesn't love him. He is ashamed of his father's profession. To this surly pugnosed young man—whose hoarse voice and lack of manners mark him as the ideal collegiate type—Charley desperately explains that all American business is gambling and that it's something to be a clean gambler.

But it is not until he sees Charley stake everything on one throw of the dice and beat off a couple of gunmen that the pristine nature of Charley's patriotism becomes manifest to him. One manly loving look between them and the film has made its great testament.

There is, shall we say, a certain tart flavor about that review. The critic—although he is writing for a popular morning paper—has clearly a sophisticated public in mind. But he does say some of the things I myself have so often found myself wanting to say concerning trends apparent in American life, this taste for cruelty and violence, this blindness to social implications, this conviction that it is not necessary for anyone under the age of thirty to show the faintest consideration towards anyone else, unless some direct self-interest is involved. Can all American children be the spoiled little brats one sees in the movies?

That is the thought which should bring one up with a round turn. People outside America are not necessarily seeing the people of America as they are. They are seeing them as Hollywood portrays them. What is much more important, they have no means whatsoever of checking that impression against reality. It is now nearly five years since the majority of people in Britain had much personal contact with Americans, and those memories are fading. It is Hollywood that provides the current impression, and that every week. I am not suggesting that people in Britain continually brood over the American scene, any more than the majority of people in the United States have any interest in what goes on in Britain. But at least people in Britain regularly see something which calls itself America. If they were asked to think of the United States their minds would be full of movie stills.

Official visitors from the United States move in restricted circles. Members of the administration, senators, newspaper editors and an occasional film star; they come, they make a rapid tour of places within easy reach of the Savoy or the Dorchester in London, and they return home. Some talk when they get back, some make pronouncements, others give interviews, but space prevents very much of that from being reported at any revealing length in the press of this country. The fact remains that the majority of people here do not see them, or hear them, while they are here and do not know what they say or think or do when they get back home. The ordinary visitor is still a phenomenon. It is difficult to think that he can be representative. The average man must depend for what he knows about America upon films, B.B.C. commentaries, his newspaper and what public men here say about the place. What are his reactions to the American scene?

Inevitably, the result is a curious and very inconsistent patchwork. The United States is a land of rich people and highly paid workmen, all with automobiles. They are well fed and want still more food. A great deal of public life is corrupt. Americans are either sentimental, or crude or both. They are arrogant and kind-hearted, ignorant and well-intentioned, wasteful and hard-working. They seem to despise politics, and yet spend half their lives in political agitation of one kind or another. They have powerful unions, yet the average trade unionist seems to vote only for the old political parties. Everybody seems to be equal, and yet rudeness is almost a social custom.

That is the main motif of the medley. Another layer of opinion is better informed, but still hardly up-to-date in its judgments. To them the prototype of all good Americans is the late President Roosevelt; what Mr. Churchill is to Americans, Mr. Roosevelt is to the British. He was a man who understood other countries, who could be patient and yet act decisively in a crisis. They can neither see nor feel at first hand any of the enmities that he aroused, any more than Americans can see or feel the enmities that Mr. Churchill aroused. Mr. Roosevelt understood the world, people think, and if he had not died, he would somehow have straightened things out much better than his successors have succeeded in doing.

It is the people who think this way who were the most uneasy about the American loan. They felt that it would tend to weaken the Commonwealth and poison Anglo-American relations. About trade, they feel, in a vague way, that the Americans are unfair; they are more ruthless and don't even apologize for it. They are inconsistent when inconsistency is to their advantage, and do not blush when it is pointed out. They play to win; they go into training, and they think hard over every possible move in the game. To them, too, America is a mixture of the very attractive and the very repellent. If only the United States had some historical background. There is a dreadful arrogance about this attitude. It lives on, and nothing will change it. When a king abdicates, he gives up his throne but he never ceases to think of himself as king. When a British Foreign

Office representative speaks so easily and confidently to the United Nations for, say, the Sudanese, he is distressed if he has to explain his right to represent them. Surely everyone can see that British rule in the Sudan must be better than handing the place over to the Egyptians? Surely no one could have taken Zionist propaganda seriously? Britain has sent her best men to govern India and Palestine and the colonies generally. Does one have to explain further?

Men in the labor movement do not think quite along those lines, except in so far as their thinking is done for them by men who do. The Labour party judges the United States by the standard of labor relations. The British Labour party has grown up with an historic belief that unrestricted capitalistic enterprise must—cannot help— exploiting its workers. It is so long since Britain's economy expanded at the rate of the American that, in Britain, the possibility that a worker might welcome, and benefit from that expansion is visualized with the greatest difficulty. If an American workman believes that he too will be boss, then the more fool he. The United States, the socialist is apt to think, has such a lot to learn—and yet its people have so very many of the right ideas. They do not put on airs. They think in terms of equality.

So much for the generalizations. Over these five years there have been four specific causes for Anglo-American discord: differing economic beliefs and practices; the trading disequilibrium between the dollar and sterling areas; political questions within Europe, notably over Germany; and Palestine.

Palestine is past history, save for its scars. Friction over the dollar gap had, by the end of 1949, been largely eliminated through the sincerity and understanding of Americans themselves, although it would be stupid to pretend that the trouble itself is cured. Germany, and Germany's position in Europe, are matters which are working themselves out rapidly, with the result that the problem itself is changing and will continue to change. The difference between American capitalism and British socialism remains. I would like to discuss the first three here and now. The fourth—well, again, this whole book is one aspect of the fourth.

This is no place to embark on a history of Palestine, or even of the British mandate over Palestine, but a convenient starting point in history, as well as in policy, is the report of the 1937 Peel Commission. Over the last fifteen years there have been three major reports on Palestine:

(a) The Peel Commission, whose report was published in July, 1937.
(b) The Woodhead Commission, whose report was published in October, 1938.
(c) The Anglo-American Committee of Enquiry, whose report was published in April, 1946.

Of these Commissions, the Peel Commission advocated partition; the other two rejected this solution.

The Peel Commission report is the most comprehensive, studied and valuable. The Woodhead Commission was a technical one, appointed ostensibly to work out a partition scheme as advocated by the Peel Commission, and it finished up by rejecting partition on the grounds of impracticability, rather to the relief of the government of the day. The Peel report is 300 pages long and it must carry increasing respect simply because so many of its prophecies were proved right by events.

It did not suggest that partition was either theoretically desirable or practically free from difficulty. On the contrary, it emphasized the reverse. It said, without too many of the usual qualifications, that the system operating under the mandate would fail, that the conflict between Jew and Arab would deepen, and that partition was the only possible way to avoid a completely repressive regime on the part of the Palestine Government. And in fact, the existing regime, however disinterested its aims, had—by the end of the mandate—become completely repressive.

The conclusions in the report were admirably succinct: "An irrepressible conflict has arisen between two national communities . . . There is no common ground between them . . . They differ in religion and language. Their cultural and social life, their ways of thought and conduct, are as incompatible as their national aspirations. . . . In these circumstances to maintain that Palestinian citizenship has any moral meaning is a mischievous pretence. Neither Arab nor Jew has any sense of service to a single State. This conflict was inherent in the situation from the start. . . . The estranging force of conditions inside Palestine is growing every year . . . for internal and external reasons, it seems probable that the situation, bad as it is now, will grow worse. The conflict will go on, the gulf between Arabs and Jews widen."

The report continued to discuss whether peace, order and good government in Palestine could be maintained without repression, and came to the conclusion that they could not. What, then, was the solution? "Manifestly, the problem cannot be solved by giving either the Arabs or the Jews all they want. . . . We do not think that any fair-minded statesman would suppose, now the hope of harmony between the races has proved untenable, that Britain ought to hand over to Arab rule 400,000 Jews or that, if the Jews should become a majority, a million or so Arabs should be handed over to their rule. But while neither race can justly rule all Palestine, we can see no reason why, if it were practicable, each race should not rule part of it . . . There is little moral value in maintaining the political unity of Palestine at the cost of perpetual hatred, strife and bloodshed." As for the practical difficulties—"We do not underestimate them. They cannot be brushed aside. Nevertheless, when one faces up to them, those difficulties do not seem so insuperable as the difficulties inherent in the continuance of the mandate or in any other alternative arrangement which has been proposed to use or which we ourselves could devise. Partition seems to offer at least a chance of ultimate peace. We can see none in any other plan."

All that was written in 1937. The pity of it is that no action was taken on it at the time.

In 1939, the Jewish population of the world was estimated to be 17,000,000, with 10,000,000 in Europe, 5,375,000 in North and South America (4,641,124 in the United States in 1941), 830,000 in Asia, 600,000 in Africa and 33,000 in Australia. By 1946, the 10,000,000 in Europe had sunk to 4,500,000, of which 2,665,000 (as compared with 3,550,000 in 1939) were in USSR. The pre-war 3,351,000 in Poland were no more than 80,000; in Holland, 150,000 had been reduced to 30,000; in Czechoslovakia, 315,000 to 65,000; in France, 320,000 to 180,000. There were 109,000 (out of 275,000) left in Germany and Austria, but the majority of these were displaced persons from other countries occupying camps as aliens in a land they feared. Only in Britain had the figure increased from 340,000 to 350,000. European Jewry had, in that time, lost its best men, women and children. American Zionism, with its membership of 1,000,000 out of the 4,500,000 in the United States, assumed the leadership of world Jewry.

The war brought an Indian summer of peace to Palestine, an interlude between the Arab revolt of 1938 and the war which followed the end of the mandate. Those were the days when the Jews organized brigades to fight in the British Army. Those were the days when the Middle East Supply Centre existed, under Commander Jackson (now of the United Nations), the Australian who organized the whole economic life of that area with a staff of 400 men, a man who could make Americans, British and Russians work together in cooperation, a fact which now seems quite fabulous. What the world lost when the United States and Britain allowed MESC to be closed down can still only dimly be glimpsed. With a little drive and goodwill it could have been built up as the nucleus of a real Middle East federation, too valuable for racial conflicts to kill completely. That death, I think, must be chalked up to American interests, and more to their ideological dislike of that kind of organization than to any practical objection to the work it was doing.

But with the end of the war and termination of pressures and controls, there was really only one question left about Palestine. All plans for Palestine could be classified by the one test: did they involve partition? And that problem itself, in practical politics, came to mean this: did the plans involve the handing over to a Jewish authority the right to decide how many Jewish immigrants should be admitted? Details in plans and proposals might vary, from major points, such as the boundaries of the territory over which a Jewish authority would have this control down to those of minor importance, such as customs regulations between one territory and another. By the end of 1946, the unrestricted right of immigration, even over ten square miles, would have been partition. Communal autonomy, and a paper plan for a federal state, if unaccompanied by this, was not.

Throughout the whole period there were in Britain opposing schools of thought over almost every aspect of the future of Palestine. On strategy, one school held that a first-class base in the Eastern Mediterranean was an absolute necessity for Britain and, through Britain, for the Western powers and that once the right to stay in Egypt was gone, Palestine provided the only alternative. Therefore,

Britain must maintain some rights over Palestine soil. The other school maintained that with air warfare, the whole strategic picture in the Eastern Mediterranean had altered and that permanent bases could be sited farther away from the center, the Middle East oilfields.

Another school of thought maintained that it was essential for Britain at all costs (although it is very unlikely that the costs were accurately counted) to retain the goodwill of the Arab world. Consequently, while human sympathy and American susceptibilities required that Jewish claims should be advanced as far as possible, it should be made clear to the Jews what the ultimate limits were. The other school held that the Jews were in Palestine to stay and that it was possible, and desirable, to make the Arabs realize that fact. They believed that the Arab had a predisposition to accept the accomplished fact, and that he should be confronted with it at the earliest possible moment.

This conflict persisted within the Labour party, and equally within the Opposition, throughout the whole period to the end of the mandate. The Foreign Office view was pro-Arab. It believed that it was both unjust and impolitic to dispossess Arabs of territory in Palestine simply to make room for an independent Jewish state, just as it would have been unjust and impolitic to dispossess, say, Mexicans of a portion of their territory to resettle Jews in the new world. To that view Mr. Bevin subscribed, with a slight touch of anti-Semitism added.

The left wing of the Labour party felt that the balance lay the other way. Its vote against Mr. Bevin in the fall of 1946 was not based solely on its opposition to his views on Palestine, but this played a considerable part, because it was the most vivid issue in the left-wing mind at that moment, and the one most canvassed.

But this must be said about both policies; they were based on the reality of the Middle East situation, which is oil. Whatever the maneuvering, wherever the skirmishes and battles might be fought, the aim of both the USSR and the United States is control of the Middle East oil, and the aim of Britain is a regime in the Middle East which will allow her to draw the oil to which she already has commercial rights. Further, Britain at least remembered that if you wish to exploit a country's resources you must pay some regard to the interests and aims and susceptibilities of the people who inhabit and live in that country.

No such tribute can be paid to American policy. Assume, for the moment, that American Zionism had not existed as an organized force. There are good grounds for asserting that European Jews would have been content with something less than an independent sovereign state of Israel. They would have found some way of living with the Arabs, as Israel will find a way of living with Jordan. The debate at the vital Basle Conference of Jews in 1946 shows that, without the intervention of American Zionist passion, the remaining delegates would have empowered their executives to work out a solution with the British Government, and the internal pressures within Britain would have produced a solution which secured a home for the Jews not based on the eviction of some 350,000 Arab inhabitants of Palestine. And that might have produced a Jewish state whose foundation stone was free from the blood of Count Bernadotte, among others.

Such a solution would have satisfied American commercial interests as well. One can say this about American oil interests: they have the instinct of every big business to be ruthless whenever, and for so long as it is possible to be ruthless but make concessions when there is no other way of attaining their desired ends. They are consistent and direct. It is possible to see what they want and to make terms with them that will hold. That much certainly cannot be said for the American Zionists; still less for those who allowed their actions to be swayed by the Zionist screams.

By the end of 1946, opinion in Britain had become exasperated by what was heard from the United States. It was not American Army sergeants who were being hanged in Palestinian orchards. It was not the American Zionists who were suffering in D.P. camps in Europe, or were under canvas in Cyprus. If the majority of them were to visit Palestine, it would be as comfortable tourists, not in unseaworthy derelicts salvaged by greedy Greek and Italian shipowners. American Zionism seemed to feel itself inspired to throw lighted matches without coming in direct contact with the flame.

As an article in the January, 1947, *New Statesman* said of Rabbi Silver: ". . . he is fighting for the principle that the Jew who pays the shekel must call the tune. For him and his colleagues . . . the

Palestinian Jews are not a nation but colonists, who must obey the instructions of World Jewry, which means, in effect, the American Zionists. At Basle, he played the role of a George III who was not going to tolerate any Boston tea-parties in Tel-Aviv."

Had Palestine been Alaska, and the headquarters of World Zionism London, the comments of American papers and politicians on the activities of a British Rabbi Silver would have seared asbestos.

But, despite all that, there is more excuse for a Jew than for a gentile. The Jew was governed, was possessed, by emotions of the utmost depth and strength. Those might produce results which, to a gentile, looked fantastic, unreal, ruthless and cruel. But they were real. Not even that much can be said of those who, non-Jewish themselves, were swayed or intimidated by this Jewish campaign.

The British could at least respect an American who said, "I don't know much about all this but I'm willing to join in and learn." They did not care for those who said, "I'm not willing to join in and learn, but we've got to have oil; otherwise we can't fight the Russians. And we've got to have a Jewish state. Otherwise, our party might fail to carry New York State. And you've got to fix it so that we get both."

Not that this provides any defense for British policy over Palestine. I believe events will continue to prove Mr. Bevin and his advisers to have been wrong in their assessments of the relative strength of Jew and Arab. That is in itself a condemnation of any policy. I believe, too, that they lacked the moral courage to make whatever policy they had effective. And that is poor statesmanship.

Mr. Bevin could be desperately obstinate and clumsy. For example, his action in shipping back to Germany the Jews in their immigrant ships in July, 1947, was indefensible. True, he did not start with that intention. It was first planned that the immigrants should be disembarked at Marseilles, but they refused to land. There followed that grimly comic scene near Marseille, the launches circling the three transports, the French rabbis offering the hospitality of France, the Hagannah loudspeakers saying "Stay on board," and the inevitable gathering of journalists who must, to those wandering Jews, have seemed horribly like vultures, appearing only at the most desperate moments. And the final scenes in Hamburg, the elaborate precautions, the military drills and instructions, all to bring back some thousands of Jews to a land whose very name must have filled them with terror.

But British policy had this much contact with reality. All along, Mr. Bevin's theme has been that no lasting peaceful settlement in Palestine will result until Jew and Arab reach an agreement for a joint way of life. He may have failed to use all his opportunities but he was trying for something worth while. Israel has still to make its final terms of living together with the Arab states.

The British mandate came to an end in May 15, 1948. During its thirty years of existence it had seen the following progress.

The settled population had increased from 649,948 in 1923 to 1,743,484 in 1945; roads from 280 miles to 2,660 miles. In the six years between 1939 and 1945, the number of people carried by road transport had trebled.

In 1921, revenue (in Palestine pounds) was £1,136,951 and ordinary expenditure £1,259,587. In 1946, revenue was £39,148,325 and ordinary expenditure £1,259,587. In 1926, imports were valued at £6,594,098 and exports £1,308,333; in 1938 the corresponding figures were £11,356,963 and £5,020,368. Receipts from income tax jumped from £196,674 in 1941 to £2,995,288 in 1947, from customs and excise from £2,338,381 in 1938 to £7,047,198 in 1946.

Between 1943 and 1945, the number of schools increased from 1,514 to 1,682 and the number of pupils from 176,446 to 216,317. There were 2,909 beds in hospitals and government expenditure on health and education in 1946 at £2,585,512 and £709,103 respectively were just over double what they had been ten years before. In the 1945 accounts there appears for the first time an item of £240,-213 in social services and in 1946 £12,016 on town planning. The following year, more was spent on social services than on the cost of running the Customs and Excise Department.

That was the background to this racial conflict. As is so often the case, the background made considerably more attractive a picture than the human figures in the foreground.

Israel is now a sovereign independent state, and the affairs of the Palestine mandate authority are only a matter of history, an era of history, one may guess, unlikely to be a compulsory subject in the schools of Israel for quite a time. The problems of the lands that once were Palestine and of the people in them, have changed. With the possible exception of East Prussia and Silesia, it is difficult to think of any territory which has changed so completely in less than two years. Yet, to the rest of the world, Israel must be just another state in the Middle East, no more and no less. Her birth has altered the nature of the forces in the Middle East, their strength and so the resulting balance; but the fixed points around which the whole of the Middle East revolves are the oilfields of the Persian Gulf and Iraq. None of these is in the hands of Israel.

The midwives to the birth of Israel were grotesquely inept, but inept or skilled, their task was bound to be of short duration. Their quarrels are no longer important, nor are arguments about those quarrels.

This is not the place, equally, to attempt a history of Germany, but it is emphatically the place to comment on the morass that still opens up where Germany and her future relations with Europe are concerned.

There is what may be called a European view about Germany, which is this: The German people have a great many specific qualities which are admirable in themselves. They are in general hard-working and honest, methodical and patient, capable of great devotion to a cause. But those qualities do not necessarily add up to a trustworthy whole. For very nearly a hundred years, the German peoples have insisted on regarding themselves and their "race" as the dominant nation in Europe, and they have in consequence proceeded with a ruthless and almost insane logic, and with a complete contempt for the other peoples, to do their best to dominate Europe. What has damned Germans in European eyes is not so much the foul cruelty of the few but the complacent assumption of every German that he is entitled to have the rest of Europe working for him as slaves.

This feeling of distrust is still there. It is at its strongest in those Slav countries where the Germans treated the inhabitants as sub-human, expendable fodder. But it is strong in every country which was occupied by the Germans. It explains the participation of Norway and Denmark in the North Atlantic Treaty, and the absence of Sweden.

This feeling, too, is a key to a great deal of what has happened in Eastern Europe. The prison in which Czechoslovakia and Poland are confined is called communism, but the warder at the gates is fear, fear of Germany. It is possible to argue that Stalin, with a purely Eastern cunning, encouraged the Czechs to drive out the Sudeten Germans and the Poles to seize the Oder-Niesse frontier line with the purpose of impressing on those two peoples the fear of a later German anger, and so of making them dependent on Russia, from whom they would never dare to struggle free.

Germany, to Europe, is basically an emotional and political problem, as the Negro is a political and emotional problem to the men and women of the southern states of America. Yet the United States, in the mouths of so many of its representatives or seeming representatives, has seemed to think of Germany solely in terms of strategy and economics. Western Germany is a drain upon the dollars of the American citizen, so let her industries be restored and expanded as rapidly as possible, in order that she may carry her own burdens with her own exports and pay her way. Western Germany needs new capital equipment to become efficient and competitive with the rest of the world. So forget where and how Germany squandered the fruits of her peoples' work during the thirties. Build her up again with American capital participation. Set the individual industrialist free to look for his own profit where he can find it—that's a sure guarantee of peace and security. And every page of recent European history laughs in the face of such political naïveté. Every dead G.I. shipped home to his native town is evidence of the risk that is being taken when that policy is in the ascendant.

Britain was not occupied by German troops, with the result that reactions are less strong in Britain than in continental Europe and the British Foreign Office is sometimes an ally of those Americans who try to argue France out of her traditional fears.

Thirty years ago, German industry was likewise to be controlled by Allied forces, of whom America was one. The controls vanished and German industry was revived, largely by American money, with results of which Europe is still only too conscious. Foreign capital, anyone's foreign capital, of itself was not sufficient to control the German industrialist once he was on his feet, and most Europeans have a shrewd suspicion that the Germans have a considerable capacity for seeing, from time to time, on which side their bread is buttered.

Nor was confidence in American consistency of policy helped by some of the curious maneuvers over Spain in 1948. Admittedly, touring senators are not the government of the United States, but people in Europe can be forgiven for believing that United States army generals are closely connected with it. After some of the episodes in 1948, it is only too easy to imagine an army staff conference poring over the map of Europe and someone saying, "It would be mighty useful to have a few airfields in Spain—easy flying time to anywhere in Europe, from Copenhagen to Vienna. See if you can fix up a deal."

Of course, there is no easy answer to all this. Of course, Dr. Adenauer is not hell-bent for destruction. Of course, the High Commission is not unaware of the problem, but the outburst from Germans of all parties over dismantling during the German election campaign of 1949 was equally a part of the German way of thinking.

In November, 1949, Mr. McCloy said: "The Germans have not by any means been reborn. In view of this outburst of nationalism, it's fair to say that if we—the Western Powers—do not give the Adenauer Government reasonable support, we will encourage the extreme nationalists."

There is the dilemma, and there it remains. It will not be solved in economic terms alone nor in military terms alone. Above all it will not be solved in anti-communist terms alone.

All of which must have been clear to the State Department, for no observer can escape the impression that the entirely different results achieved over the handling of economic relations between the United States and Europe, particularly Britain, during 1949 by the State Department sprang from a real appreciation of the situation. Anglo-American economic relations at the end of 1949 were better than they had been at any time since the end of lend-lease, and that with every opportunity during 1949 for them to have gone wrong.

By the end of 1948, the average socialist in Britain, without special connections or responsibilities, was thinking of Anglo-American economic relations with a certain amount of complacency. Like Mr. Mayhew, a junior minister at the Foreign Office, he felt that foreign observers were shortsighted—where they were not outright malicious

—when they queried the reality of Britain's postwar recovery. The country had attained an over-all balance of trade, if invisible exports were taken into account. The dollar difficulties were real enough but —and there men were apt to allow their thinking to become a little cloudy—some combination of increased empire production, increased exports to America and reduced imports from America would produce the required answer by 1952. If the gap was not quite bridged—well, no doubt some alternative to Marshall Aid would be forthcoming. In any case, 1952 was after the next general election and that, in politics, is what matters.

Nor had the American scene, in 1948, been an encouraging spectacle. Aside from the antics of the Committee on Un-American Activities—not at all an ideal diversion to those watching from outside—the special session of Congress in the summer had seemed to find all the elected representatives of a vast and powerful people fighting madly to avoid any action or decision which might upset a single business interest. It led to a feeling of bewilderment and, in some quarters, of a mild contempt. Was this the zenith of "free enterprise" and constitutional freedom?

Again, in 1948, there was the crisis over Berlin, and Americans do like to make noises in times of crisis, noises of protest, of excitement, which have something of the sound of a million radio commentators talking against a background of a thousand Benny Goodmans. Yet, many people in Britain thought: who had the atom bombs and where will most of them be dropped? The attitude toward the whole experiment at Bikini of the observers and of the goats on the target ships was bound to be at variance.

In those circumstances, it was possible for a Government supporter in Britain to resent criticism—expressed or implied—from outside, on the grounds that it was clearly ill-founded and therefore must be partisan. Did the evidence not show that under this peculiarly British and admirable form of socialism Britain had in fact achieved a remarkable degree of internal stability? This attitude of mind had one by-product. It made both Government supporters and the Opposition conscious of criticism. Government supporters looked for it with the touchy pride of a parent detecting criticism in the not-quite-fulsome-enough praise of his offspring. Government opponents looked for it to reinforce their convictions, their hopes, that all this internal prosperity was only an illusion, or at least founded on sand.

But the scene changed in the spring of 1949. An American business recession was one thing; it could hardly surprise a good socialist. An American recession in the purchase of goods and raw materials from Europe and from European possessions was quite another. The dollar problem suddenly became the dollar crisis. It became shockingly clear that the foreigner didn't trust the pound sterling as much as Sir Stafford Cripps said he should, and that his trust or mistrust made quite an appreciable difference to the stability of the internal regime.

There were very great dangers to Anglo-American relations in this sudden change in the color of the landscape. It would have been very easy for both countries to have slid into a protracted and deepening campaign of mutual recrimination. Instead, this period of mutual recrimination, during July and August, 1949, never became very much more than a release of steam before the job of finding some remedy was tackled. After the Washington Conference of September, 1949, it was clear enough that Anglo-American relations had been improved by the events of the year, not damaged by them.

Some credit for that must go to the British Government. Its record over international economical obligations, though not brilliant, was not discreditable. It had held Britain fast to a regimen of internal austerity as a guiding principle; no one could seriously believe that the majority of people accepted that from choice. Britain had lived soberly within its actual means, even though those means did include a proportion of gift money. It had paid out perhaps more of its assets than it should in the partial redemption of its war and pre-war debts. The government had struggled hard to reconcile the principle of "Fair Shares for All" with exhortations to those who could increase exports to the dollar area—resembling a maiden aunt encouraging a small boy to pull his younger brother out of the stream, but not to wet his feet in the process. And it had endeavored to keep any note of hysteria from creeping into its voice when it talked of the dollar gap, which in itself kept down recrimination, along with a good deal else.

But much more positive credit should go to those American and Canadian politicians and officials who were handling their end of the situation. It was useless to attempt to keep their public quiet. Their problem was to keep a skeptical public and a vociferous collection of congressmen from making it impossible for the small still voice of reason to be heard, to convince enough people in North America that all this good American money was not being poured into the waste lands; above all to convert a negative approach into a positive one; to couple the drive engendered by a fear of communisim to the constructive task of building European unity. The impression they left on those who came into contact with them was of men desperately concerned that things should come out right. The decision in which they should have most pride, announced immediately after the conclusion of the Washington Conference, was that which allowed Marshall Aid dollars to be used to pay Canadian farmers for the wheat they had sold Britain.

Such guidance was not wasted. If Britain had come to believe that the United States was concerned to wreck Britain's socialist experiment, socialists and non-socialists would have united in a deep resentment. Because the men with power in Washington did not believe that they should interfere with that, they allowed the experiment to be worked out where it should have been worked out—in Britain. Their words matched their deeds. And how many politicians honestly expect to find those words as an epitaph on their tombstones?

Something made America learn quickly in 1949. To an observer, between 1948 and 1949 there is something of the difference between early 1941 and early 1942. But it was of vital importance that the right instructors should be at hand, as they were.

CHAPTER XIX

Western Europe and Soviet Russia

European union can come in one of three ways; by catastrophe, by political decision or by economic evolution.

Those who hold that the first is the most likely method by which union will come argue that the states of Europe have failed to see in time the obvious lesson of two wars, that their statesmen have failed to make the most of their opportunities as they arose. Division of Europe will lead to another war, and at some stage in the war what is left of Europe will, almost overnight, find that some minority has taken charge of all its affairs and that unity is a fact. Thereafter, the consequences of the war will be so disastrous that the decision neither will nor can be reversed; the probability is that the unity will be unity in subjection. That might be called the ultra-realistic view and, as with so many ultra-realistic views, it is defeated by its own logic.

Were war to break out now, Europe would be condemned to start again, as it did in the sixth century, and to wait a thousand years for its second Renaissance, if ever one were to come. There would be no point in a second invasion of Europe, of another Omaha Beach. Europe would be ruins in which one savage form of communism struggled with another. It could only be left to find its own way.

For those who believe that the moment has passed when either statesmen or peoples could of their own volition make a difference to the course of events, there is no point in arguing further. They are passengers on what they believe to be a sinking ship. They may make individual plans for their safety. They cannot save the ship itself.

But there are still numbers of people in Britain, and in Europe, who believe that, on this subject, the situation is still one in which free-will and not determination exists. Political decision and economic evolution are closely tied together, but the difference between those two schools of thought lies in something more than emphasis. Those who hold that political decision can and will bring a union of Europe believe that the biggest obstacles are psychological. If a majority of people in Europe want union, they can achieve it, and work out their economic problems afterward.

Those who believe in economic evolution hold, on the contrary, that politicians, to be successful, must follow economic trends, not attempt to move in front of them. If they attempt to do that, their politics will fail. Regarding European Union, this school holds that there are economic urgencies which will produce union in time. Let these do their work. It is for the politician to smooth the way and, at the end, to secure and implement politically what has already happened in economic affairs.

A union for Europe has a long history, but it is not necessary to go back to the Holy Roman Empire. The story can start with Mr. Churchill's offer to M. Reynaud, in 1940, of a political union between Britain and France. If that had come into being then, it would have been potent enough to draw into it, by the end of the war, the whole of the rest of Western Europe. It failed because at that time there existed no unity of thought in France sufficient to carry it through. Between May 10 and June 17, 1940, France was overwhelmed in every way. Thereafter, the people of France and Western Europe fought the war almost as individuals.

Why did not the military unity achieved under General Eisenhower grow into political unity? For two reasons. The governments in exile were only too aware that they did not and could not represent the majority of their peoples at home. Second, the Germans were imposing a form of unity on Europe, but a false and forced unity, which emphasized nationalist feeling among those subject to it, not the reverse. Western Europe finished the war much less in a mood for unity than when the war started.

The main changes of the last five years have been the dying down of the emotions created by the Nazis, a widening general realization of Europe's economic plight, and the growth of this fear of both military and political aggression from the East. Those are the factors now operating in favor of a European federation, and it is on the last two that the chances of European federation really depend.

The vision of European union received its first encouragement in 1948, from a speech by Mr. Ernest Bevin in the House of Commons in January. Mr. Bevin has the reputation for thinking aloud, and in a rather spasmodic way at that; it was pretty obvious, from the surrounding circumstances, that this was an occasion when he had done precisely that. Sir Stafford Cripps was then in the middle of a difficult situation over the French insistence on a devaluation of their own currency. The Foreign Office was not at all happy over the deliberations of the customs union sub-committee of the Paris Conference on ERP. The Admiralty had just announced a scheme which laid up a good part of the British fleet. Obviously, the Foreign Secretary had made no diplomatic preparations for his proposal. Maybe it did not suffer too much from that. It certainly gave encouragement to those who were thinking in terms of a European conference to lead to precisely such a union. They took immediate steps to convene a conference at the Hague, for May.

The Conference at the Hague was the most impressive gathering of personalities yet seen in postwar Europe. Its actual decisions were embodied in three resolutions: political, economic and cultural.

The cultural argument can safely be left out here. The common culture of Western Europe provides a strong reason for union, but it does not provide any serious immediate popular thrust behind any movement towards federation. Politics and economies are too urgent. The most important statement in the political resolution was the declaration that "the time has come when the European nations must transfer and merge some portion of their sovereign rights." It was matched in the economic resolution by a passage which recognized that "no attempt to rebuild the economy of Europe upon the basis of rigidly divided national sovereignty can prove successful." The most ambiguous statement was that in the political resolution which referred to the creation of a "Union or Federation." Those words mask a split on an essential issue. The Hague Congress produced unanimity on a general idea. It did not tackle the specific means of translating the idea into fact.

The real difficulty in the way of European union may seem to be one of form, federation or confederation. The issue is much deeper. The federalists would have all Western European states cede the effective aspects of their sovereignty, the right to decide their own defensive, economic and fiscal plans, into one unity, a government for all Western Europe, popularly elected by universal suffrage. The confederationists would be content to see established a European Council, with power to recommend, possibly with powers of executive action over limited fields, such as transport, patents or standards, but generally without power to do more than advise on the main issues of human activity. What was created at Strasbourg, the Council of Europe, was such a confederation.

The outcome of the Hague Congress was a decision to apply pressure to each of the Western European governments, directed towards securing the calling of a preliminary European assembly to discuss union. There was a certain amount of delay while the International Committee, formed after the Hague Congress, met and drafted its documents. The drafts were not ready until the end of July.

In August, the documents were laid before the French government. It so happened that they reached that government on the day before a cabinet meeting. The French Premier saw the secretary of the French section of the International Committee and told him that if a few minor alterations in the text were made, he would present it to his cabinet colleagues on the following day and recommend a favorable decision. He also added that if the opportunity was missed, it looked as though it would be some time before any French cabinet would again have time and thought enough to spare for such a vote—a very accurate forecast.

The secretary, after telephoning London, agreed to the amendments, the resolution went before the French cabinet, was approved and a statement issued at once. Unfortunately, the amended text, which should have been flown to London immediately after the amendments were verbally agreed, was omitted from the covering letter and so did not reach London until after the release of the French announcement. It therefore arrived at the Foreign Office after the French decision was public, an unfortunate diplomatic lapse, intensely irritating to a man of Mr. Bevin's nature.

In the meantime, Mr. Churchill had tackled the British government. The first response he obtained from Mr. Attlee was purely negative. The second did at least give some answer to the Hague Resolution calling for the convening of a European Assembly. Mr. Attlee wrote that he did not propose to commit the British Government one way or the other until the Commonwealth prime ministers had met in October and discussed the whole issue. That, at least, was an argument with which Mr. Churchill could not openly quarrel.

The Commonwealth prime ministers duly met in October, 1948. They accepted, more readily than had been anticipated, the idea of closer relationship between Britain and Western Europe. They were more "confederationalist" than "federalist" in mind—at least, they were not disposed to argue too strongly against the confederationalist views held by Mr. Bevin and the British Foreign Office. But after that conference, there was no longer any excuse for the United Kingdom Government to hang back. The way was open for the setting up of the organization that finally met at Strasbourg in September, 1949.

The year 1949 saw the creation of a number of instruments designed to further unity in Europe. The European Co-operation Administration had been set up earlier, to make decisions over and organize the distribution of American aid to Europe. In the process of carrying out that task, it had built up an intelligent and well-informed international secretariat capable of assembling the facts upon which decisions could be made, and of implementing those decisions when they were made. But save when its executive body met, it had no power to insist. And its executive body was made of the foreign ministers of Western Europe.

The Brussels Treaty and the North Atlantic Treaty were both military treaties and the councils they called into being were confined to military defense. Under them, the technical experts went to work and produced rather more concrete results than were apparent in the political or economic fields. The final defense plans for Western Europe were completed in December, 1949, to coincide with the arrival of the first installments of military aid from the United States. But again, defense plans do not of themselves produce unity. The forces of Western Europe had had some experience of fighting together under a single command. Soldiers are soldiers whatever their nationality, and defense ministers can make comprehensive and unified plans because those plans are no more than plans—they do not require to be immediately tested in action—and in any case such plans are bound to be secret. By the end of 1949, the stage had been reached when the military staffs likewise needed something more than plans if their drive and enthusiasm were to be maintained.

They were in a state of mind in which failure on the political and economic side could easily jeopardise the co-operation they had already built up in their own sphere of responsibility.

The situation, then, before the opening of the Strasbourg meeting was this. The Hague Conference of 1948, the political and emotional drive behind it and the impetus which the success of the conference had given to that drive, had carried Western Europe to the threshold of a conference capable of laying quite a number of foundation stones. What obstacles were left?

The Strasbourg Conference did set up a Council of Europe. The body created consists of two chambers, the Council of Ministers and the Consultative Assembly. The Council of Ministers is made up of the foreign ministers of each of the member states. It alone can take action, and that action can only take the form of a recommendation to the governments of the member states. The Consultative Assembly is exactly what it is called. It consists of delegates from the parliaments of each member country, nominated by the governments. The numbers in each national delegate bear a relationship with the population of each country. The Assembly meets no more than once a year, and its agenda for that meeting is subject to the approval of the Council of Ministers. On paper, the Assembly looked like nothing more than a talking shop. In itself, it contains no power to initiate action, and carries no responsibility for what is done and what is not done in Europe. Such a Council of Europe, as a congress, could be considered a bad joke.

In fact, the proceedings at Strasbourg showed that the Assembly did possess a potential as a European parliament. The majority of the delegates were men who carried the cares of Europe in the forefront of their minds. They did not cease to be themselves, nationals of a particular state and men of a particular political cast of mind. Yet the Assembly left on observers the impression that, given opportunity, here was a parliament of Europe, and that, given time, the delegates would make the opportunity.

The national delegations varied. The most solid and earnest came from Norway and Denmark. The Swedish delegation was slightly ambiguous. Belgium supplied the chairman, M. Spaak, who exemplifies all that a good European can be. The Italian delegation was intelligent and co-operative. The Greeks were an unpleasant experience, the Turks rather confused by it all, the French notably poor, the British—what was wrong with the British delegation? It was not that it thought in terms of party. That is British parliamentary life and at least such an approach did help to make certain that the Assembly as a whole would think in terms of European parties, not of European states. Perhaps the Labour members of the British delegation were inclined to assume that Europe's salvation must lie in the adoption of British Labour party policy; certainly, they were uneasily aware that there was not the slightest chance that Europe would do anything of the kind. (And to a socialist delegate, it must be a little galling to see so plainly that Europe still rates Mr. Churchill much above Mr. Herbert Morrison.)

But the question remains unanswered: why did Strasbourg fail to become a Philadelphia Constitutional Convention for Europe? One thing should be said at once. Americans assume too easily that the parallel between the creation of the American Republic and of the creation of a Union of Europe must be close. They attribute too much vision and foresight to their ancestors. If the founders of the American federation, the men of the thirteen states, could have even glimpsed the federal machinery that grew out of their decision, they would have shrunk back appalled. Politicians in Europe today can see that to make an effective political union among themselves, they would be compelled to surrender to a European federal government all the powers over the constituent states possessed by the United States federal government, probably more. They, too, are apt to shrink back, dismayed by such a demand on their imaginations.

The political influences at work in Britain towards Western union were assembled in the United Europe Movement, of which Mr. Churchill was the spearhead. Under Mr. Churchill, that organization tended to attach more importance to political and military defense against the East than to the economic aspects of union. There was fear of Russian aggression but also a deep and positive belief in the importance to the world of European culture. It was, and is, nonpartisan because no one party can be said to be unanimously in support of its objectives.

Here, very briefly, are the party reactions to union.

The bulk of the Conservative party is confederationist. They think that the defense pacts and the O.E.E.C. organization, together, do all that is required for the moment. They are dismayed at the political consequences of handing real power (and nothing less would suffice) to a composite body of even more composite Europeans. Mr. Churchill remained more clear-sighted. He would go further than the bulk of his party, partly because he has always had the conviction that he could dominate any European Assembly, and so control its external policy, partly because he had never felt deeply—or thought deeply—on economic issues. He had never willingly been a spokesman of big business; far more is he a spokesman for his ancestor Marlborough.

There was the official point of view, that of the Foreign Office, and voiced by Mr. Bevin. Mr. Bevin as Foreign Secretary was not a man to accept traditional views, save when they filled a gap in his own thinking and experience. The traditional Foreign Office view always has been that Britain should have a minimum of continental entanglements, and effective union would mean the end of a separate British foreign policy. Mr. Bevin does not hold traditional views. He is an individualist, shrewd and instinctive, arrogant and proud. He has little use for theory; his one aim has always been to win for the ordinary man a little more security and comfort than he had before. His motto could be "here and now." But there was nothing about an immediate union of Europe which, so far as he could see, would improve the security or comfort of the ordinary man in Britain here and now. On the contrary. So both the Foreign Office and Mr. Bevin, for different reasons, could see no cause for enthusiasm in the whole project.

The Labour party itself was divided, almost by instinct. Some thought that a united Europe would be a good thing, provided that it were socialist. It would be intolerable, they thought, if Britain were compelled, for instance, to serve the same economic gods as Belgium. For the greater part of 1949, this section of the party still unconsciously assumed that the merits and successes of British socialism were self-evident. The German elections disillusioned them considerably, and in consequence their interest in European union waned. But there were many others who accepted the grimmer theory that Europe is too diverse to be safe without a strong federal government. The leader of that section is Mr. R. W. G. Mackay, a Labour M.P., an immigrant from Australia and a federalist by upbringing

and conviction. The party most solidly behind European union was
the Liberal party, exemplified in Lord Layton, but on this issue the
Liberal party could not hope to count for more than its small total
of individual voices.

"European union can come only by political decision or economic
evolution." That is to oversimplify the situation.

Politics and economics do not work in vacuums but in inter-action.
There are forces capable of driving Europe towards unity, and the
machinery through which they work is more economic than political.
Their first effects were to be seen in Benelux, Fritilux and the Anglo-
Scandinavian union (pray that this escapes a similar name), but
they are more the result of an accumulation of forces stretching back
into history, not of present emergencies and present decisions. And
they move with the speed of a glacier.

Two things stand out. Continental Europe will not unite itself
without Britain; both meanings of that sentence are true. The continental nations of Europe can neither exclude Britain from their
union nor make Europe one without some assistance from Britain.
If they could, they would have done so before now, for the rest of
Europe does not relish the need to carry Britain with it in any such
plans, particularly a Britain reluctant with the reluctance of Mr.
Bevin.

The actions of the United States are equally important, but no
more important, for not even the United States could create a united
Europe without Britain. The task the American people face is to decide which acts will help and which will hinder. Good intentions
are almost irrelevant.

The reluctance that all parties in Britain have shown towards the
reality of a complete merger with the rest of Europe is not just a result of obstinacy. It springs from two positive roots. One is remem-
brance of the past. Britain has not been wholly within Europe for
400 years. There are countless pieces of evidence of that. The other is
that Britain still plans its policy in terms of the whole world. To
Britain, the world is not a background against which national life
is played. It is the stage on which national life is lived. The most
concrete evidence of that is the continued existence of the British
Commonwealth. Why has no other European nation ever created
such a political organization? Other European countries have had the

chances to do so. Some still have the colonial possessions. The Commonwealth did not come into existence simply because at one time a quarter of the globe was nominally under the British flag. Size has little to do with it. The difference in the relationship between the states of this Empire and those existing between any other country and its overseas possessions is one of kind. Whatever the explanation of this organization may be, the Commonwealth remains as much a reality in world affairs as the Gulf Stream.

There are plenty of other differences between Britain and continental Europe. Britain is carrying the burden of maintaining the dollar reserves of the whole sterling area. It is a voluntary act, and presumably Britain intends it to be profitable in the long run. But certainly over these five years she has paid, by the exports of her goods, a large annual sum in reduction of her war debts to such countries as India, Pakistan and Egypt as a price for maintaining the sterling area in working order. Britain is paying for a higher proportion of her imports from the dollar area with exports to that area than any other country in Europe. Britain does make her citizens pay their taxes and obey the currency regulations designed to support the whole national economy, and, complex though the system may be, it has worked to the general advantage, in the shape of stability for world trade. To British eyes—not just to socialist eyes, nor to the eyes of the austere economists of the Treasury—there are in Europe too many bankers and merchants who will betray any currency for temporary gain, who sell any measure of international economic justice for a profit in American dollars or Swiss francs. Britain has poured out capital equipment for the benefit of the colonies throughout this period, and any plan for European union must take into account this British attitude towards, and relationship with, her colonies. Otherwise it will have no appeal to Britain, and, if it does not appeal to these deep instincts in Britain, Britain will not co-operate.

Faced with a reaction of that kind, it is always open to the United States to say that she washes her hands of the whole project, that aid to Europe must stop, and that Europe must take care of itself. Obviously, a great many individual Americans would like to do just that. If the majority did so decide, then the experiment would have failed. It would mean return to real isolation, but her people might think that the lesser of two evils. And even that decision would be better for Europe than the wrong kind of American action.

But it would be a pity. If the United States wishes to encourage capitalism to grow and to expand and to face the real problems of world trade and world betterment (which it is not doing at the moment), if she believes that capitalism and its freedoms are a creed that can mean more to mankind than communism and its regimentation, then she must plan her campaign so that her economic policy does make sense to the rest of the world.

I should prefer to assume that the people of the United States will not throw this responsibility out of the window. If they do not, they must make two big decisions to guide their future actions. Americans must decide what it is, in and about Europe, that they want to integrate, and on what terms and for what purposes. Britain clings to its colonies, the sterling area, the whole complex of imperial relations, because by instinct her people know that they are the lifeblood of her trade, of international trade, in fact of European society. The Commonwealth might collapse; some Americans might like to see it scrapped anyway. But before allowing the one to happen or encouraging the other to take place, it would be as well to think carefully from where exactly the whole system derives its vitality, and what there is about it that can be improved.

This first decision must involve the conclusion that aid to Europe in dollars is not the full answer. Nor is technical convertibility between pound sterling and dollar, nor a closing of the dollar gap by more imports into the United States of goods from Europe. If the United States wishes to revitalize all the Western area, her plans must take into account the whole of its system, not just a part. It is no use strengthening only those parts of Europe that happen to be in contact with Soviet Russia, nor of stopping short with Europe itself. President Truman's "Point Four" is not an afterthought. It is the keystone to the whole structure.

That does not mean more dollars in the shape of direct aid. It means far more, making plans which will get the equipment and technical skill—lacking in every underdeveloped area of the world —to the places where they are needed, whatever the local currency, without requiring that part of the world first to find the dollars necessary to pay for them. For it is not as though a child can earn enough to pay for its own schooling.

The other problem that faces the American people is adjusting to the time scale involved in all this. Every time the Congress, even a single American senator, says that aid to Europe is conditional upon European union's happening right now, and that in any case aid will end in 1952, if not before, as many disintegrating forces are created in Europe as integrating ones. It is as though the master of a sinking timber ship, that had lost all its lifeboats, were to bellow at the crew, "Get busy carpentering another lifeboat, then we'll all be saved." There is always a risk that men in that crew will reply, "To hell with that. There isn't enough time, anyway. I'm going over the side with a couple of baulks of timber on my own, before the ship goes and takes me with it."

I think this quotation from a leading article in the *Economist* puts this point very clearly:

. . . America has the power, if it will be patient, to impel Europe along the road to real integration; but it must recognise the fact that it may take a generation of planning and adaptation to reach the stage at which it brings real economic benefits to the Continent. It has also the power to persuade Europe to take all the risks involved in quickly creating a free market—if it will underwrite the venture. What is not possible, what might indeed shatter the Marshall Plan and frustrate the whole purpose of American policy, is a spectacular attempt to combine short-term recovery with a long-term reorganisation of Europe, to telescope into one great act of policy a process which took over three generations to complete in the pre-industrial United States.

The United States is a world power and in world politics the time scale must be the generation, not the year.

PART VI

BRITAIN TOMORROW

CHAPTER XX

The Impasse and the Future

> In the British election campaign, the Conservatives
> are saying that they accept most of the Labourites'
> social program but promise to do everything more
> efficiently. It will be interesting to see whether the
> formula works better over there than it did here.
>
> *Harold Brubaker in The New Yorker*

As a summary, true or false?

As a summary, I feel it was very near the mark indeed, but I would alter one word. I would substitute the word "cheaply" for "efficiently." It was the desire to spend less, not the desire to get better value for the same money, that seemed to be emphasized in Conservative propaganda during the election, and a considerable number who heard it were left with the vague feeling that in this dark and deceitful world the less spent meant the less provided. But this is to anticipate. How was it that this elaborate and deeply felt campaign produced in the end two strong parties—and two groups of voters—nearly identical in size, and a Liberal party too small even to hold a balance between them?

The total number of voters eligible for the election of February 23, 1950 (the registers being those prepared in the third quarter of 1949), was 34,212,915. Voting took place in 622 out of the 625 constituencies into which Britain was divided, since in two there was no contest and therefore no vote, while in the third, the Moss Side Division of Manchester, the Conservative candidate had died after nomination but before polling day, which necessitated a later poll, held March 9.

The following analysis of the votes cast and comparison with earlier elections is based on the figures prepared by the *Economist*, and excludes the three seats mentioned above and the university constituencies which had been abolished before the 1950 election.

	1950	1945	1935
Labour and Co-operative........	13,248,935	12,106,964	8,302,970
Conservative and Supporters.....	12,467,212	9,962,436	11,718,396
Liberal......................	2,618,891	2,242,714	1,386,243
Others.......................	389,899	645,630	486,130

(In 1950, the Communist poll was 91,575, roughly three out of every 1,000 votes cast.)

The seats gained and percentages of the vote polled by the parties were:

	1950		1945		1935	
	Seats won	% of total vote	Seats won	% of total vote	Seats won	% of total vote
Labour..............	315	46.1	391	48.5	141	37.9
Conservative..........	294	43.4	210	39.9	397	53.5
Liberal..............	9	9.1	11	9.0	16	6.4
Others..............	4	1.4	12	2.6	11	2.2

(In the 1950 election 84% of the electorate voted, the highest figure recorded. In both 1935 and 1945, the percentage was 74.5%.) To give the final allocation of the 625 seats, it is necessary to add the results in the three constituencies excluded from the 1950 totals given above. As mentioned, there was no contest in two constituencies and in the third, the Moss Side Division, the Conservatives won, giving them the three seats. Further, to give the practical voting strength of the two main parties it is necessary to disregard the Speaker (who was a Conservative) and the two Labourite chairmen of committees who, at times, may not be free to vote. The effective voting strengths of the two parties in the House of Commons were: Labour 314; Conservative 297. Even without the factors of death and illness, this was a precarious position for the Labour party.

Was the result of the election a surprise? I think it must have been to many who allowed themselves to be swayed by the optimistic forecasts of both sides in the final weeks, but I doubt if it was to the responsible men in any party. The total party votes were very accurately forecast by the Gallup poll organization, but that calculation does not attempt to estimate the seats each party will win as a result; yet even those could have been roughly forecast. I claim no powers of political divination, but in June, 1948, in *London Newsletter,* I made the following estimate of the position:

The only safe guide to the result of a possible general election is to attempt to forecast the general trends of opinion in the country as a whole and then to apply the observed tendency to each constituency individually.

The record of the by-elections fought in the English constituencies during 1947 and 1948 shows that the average "swing" in the poll from the Labour to Conservative candidate was 7.2 per cent. The highest changeover took place in the urban districts—in the main, middle-class—such as North Croydon (London) 9 per cent, and Edge Hill (Liverpool) 12 per cent. The lowest was in this year's by-election at Brigg, an industrial-cum-farming area in North Lincolnshire, where it was 3.6 per cent.

Another element of complication introduced is the effect of the changes in constituencies themselves contained in the Representation of the People Bill, [This became the Representation of the People Act, 1948.] which reached its report stage in the House of Commons yesterday and today. In the form in which it is likely to pass, it will reduce the membership of the House of Commons from its present total of 640 members. The exact figure for a new House is not yet certain, but it is likely to be about 625. [This was the final figure.] From the missing fifteen seats the Labour party is likely to lose ten and the Conservatives five.

The 1945 general election gave the Communists two seats, the Liberals twelve seats, the Conservatives and their "National" allies 213 and the Labour party and ILP (likely to be absorbed in the Labour party next time) 397 seats. If the constituency adjustments in the new bill are made to those figures, they give the Government 387 seats and the Conservatives 208.

There is one final factor—the constituencies in which the majority of the sitting candidates was less than 500 votes. The Labour party holds 12 such seats, the Conservatives nine and the Liberals three. Despite any general wave of change, it is always likely that one or two of these seats on either side will go the other way, next time.

If there has been a 9% swing in middle-class areas and a 5% swing in working-class areas, the Labour party, were a general election to be held now, must, in my estimation, reckon with a probable loss of the following seats:

London Boroughs.. 7
English Boroughs... 40
English Counties... 31
Wales... none
Scotland.. 6
                                                                    ———
                                                        Total   84

As against this, I think one should estimate that it may gain six seats, one from the Communists, two from marginal seats, three from the Liberal party. This would give it a net loss of 78 seats and a net gain to the Conservatives of 81. The composition of the new House would therefore be:

Labour party.. 309
Conservative.. 289
Liberals... 9

(Figures excluded minor groups, Irish Independents, Communists, etc.) This would leave the Labour party with a majority of twenty votes over the Conservatives and eleven over both Opposition parties. It would leave the Labour administration insecurely perched, but capable of carrying out a center-of-the-road program. Such a government would probably last twelve to eighteen months—more if times were bad.

What is surprising about this calculation is its indication that the basic political conditions in Britain changed so little in the eighteen months after it was made. The explanation for that is not that politics in Britain are sterile, but that they were, over the whole five-year period, in essence negative. For all its emphasis on planned prosperity for the common man, the Government's policies were still based on fear, not hope. But first, what was the course of the election campaign itself?

The date of the general election was announced on January 11, 1950. The decision to choose February as the election month was made some time in the previous November. The choice was, of course, the responsibility of Mr. Attlee as Prime Minister, but among the senior members of the Cabinet around Mr. Attlee, Mr. Morrison was the man with the greatest influence on that issue. Mr. Morrison, in fact, during the second half of 1949, reasserted a great deal of his former power and prestige as party manager.

February or June were the practical alternatives for an election in 1950, before Parliament automatically dissolved in July at the end of its fifth year of existence. Late March, April and May could be ruled out by reason of the fact that the budget must be presented in April, and its main provisions must be discussed and passed, at the start of the financial year. January is not an electioneering month, by choice. To have allowed Parliament to reassemble in January for a new session of no more than a month or six weeks in length would have been futile, and politically dangerous because of its futility. The alternatives were, in fact, an election before or after the budget and, if before, in February rather than March. Sir Stafford Cripps made it clear that his projected budget for 1950–51 was not likely to be one on which a popular election campaign could be based. He could hope neither to lower taxation nor to increase the subsidies on food. With that prospect, the practical answer was to fix the general election for the end of February, and dissolve the old Parliament. The date chosen was February 23, which would enable the new Parliament to meet before the state visit of the French President, already announced for the opening days in March.

The preliminary skirmishings of the campaign were over the subject of election expenses. The principal target was Tate & Lyle, Ltd., the major company in the sugar refining industry, which, in September, 1949, had authorized its directors to organize a public campaign against the whole notion of sugar nationalization. The directors used the well-known advertising device of personalizing their product, and invented a "Mr. Cube" as a symbol of private enterprise in the coffee cup.

Mr. Cube soon became very present. He appeared on the cover of every package of Tate and Lyle sugar sold to the public (and 10,000,000 were sold every week). He became news. Whether he was of any immediate benefit to the shareholders of Tate & Lyle, Ltd. is more doubtful—their shares on the Stock Exchange fell during January by some thirteen per cent as compared with a general fall of no more than two per cent—but Mr. Cube certainly provoked a considerable public argument between Mr. Morrison and Lord Lyle, head of Tate and Lyle, Ltd. Mr. Morrison suggested that the cost of the Mr. Cube campaign might be treated as an election expense of the Conservative party, and therefore be illegal, as an ex-

pense unauthorized be each Conservative candidate. Lord Lyle re-
torted that it could be nothing of the kind, that it was no more than
an educational campaign designed to give the public the facts about
sugar, and that it certainly was not a campaign designed to procure
the election of a particular candidate. So the election campaign began—and by the design of the Labour party—with an essentially
trivial issue in this problem of election expenses, one that could
only have any meaning at all because a general election in Britain
takes place under a very strict set of rules that serve to protect the
voter from certain irresistible forms of persuasion.

A political party may promise the earth, or more, to the electorate
in general, provided no individual candidate offers any individual
elector even so much as a free drink. The argument over Mr. Cube
was whether he was intended to educate the electorate or influence
the individual voter, and even the law officers were a little reluctant
to give a definite opinion on that.

The echoes aroused by Mr. Cube died away (but not Mr. Cube
himself). The Royal Proclamation, dissolving Parliament and sum-
moning its successor, was signed by the King. The next step in the
campaign would be the publication of the parties' election manifestos, statements of policy for the election.

The Labour party was the first to publish its platform. Like all
the manifestos, it was a condensation of the detailed program
adopted during the course of 1949 at an annual conference of the
party. Because it was a condensation, there was almost as much to
be learned from what had been left out as from what had been included.

A party holding office and seeking re-election can only with difficulty avoid a defensive attitude. It has a recent record and it must
defend that record. But it can, of course, go beyond that. It can attack the record of its opponents, and it can also build up a prospect
for the future. The Labour party did two of these things thoroughly;
it defended itself, and it attacked the record of the Conservatives for
the period when they had last been in office. It was most vague about
the future.

Its concrete proposals were for the nationalizing of beet sugar
manufacture and sugar refining, water supply, the cement industry,
the wholesale distribution of meat, all cold storage plants, all

suitable minerals, and all inadequately used land capable of producing food. The manifesto also mentioned industrial life insurance, but stated that this would be the subject of a separate statement of policy to be published later. In addition, there were vague references to the chemical industry and to the shipbuilding and repairing industries (where the prospect of full employment in 1951 and onward was already beginning to look doubtful), sufficient, perhaps, to provide some justification for legislative action later, if time and the political situation then allowed. But, to quote the *Times* leader on the morning of its publication, "Labour's election banner bears two devices; full employment and 'fair shares'."

Where the manifesto left what might be called the concrete for the aspirational, there was a long list of objects that were promised future help or thought. The party announced that it would establish new and competitive public enterprises where privately owned monopolies did not provide all that the public required, and at a competitive price. Equally, it promised aid—in the form of both buildings and finance—to new privately owned enterprises seeking to establish themselves. It promised freedom to open shops, and consumers' advice centers to test and report on goods. And it promised every family a separate home.

But the list of omissions is significant. There was no reference in the manifesto to the level of taxation or its effects, no direct reference to the defense services or their cost, or to compulsory military training. There was no reference to American aid—Conservatives commented later that the word "dollar" appeared nowhere in it—no reference to the situation envisaged when it ended, and no reference to foreign affairs beyond a condemnation of Munich, and a promise to work "realistically" for peace. Plainly, the party wanted to fight the election on domestic issues only, and on the forties versus the thirties at that.

On the political level the appeal was shrewd enough. Those who believed in planning sufficiently to want to know the full range of plans for the next five years were left somewhat unsatisfied, but did that matter? Most of them were already inside the Labour party camp anyway. The manifesto reflected what was still the prevailing mood of the party, belief that everything was under control. But the shabby backdrop of expediency could be seen more clearly when the party's proposals about industrial life insurance were finally revealed; and it is, I think, worth looking at them in some detail.

Industrial life insurance in Britain sprang from the grim fact that the family of an industrial worker in the early nineteenth century had a horror of a pauper funeral—being buried "by the parish," as it was called. Small collecting societies came into being—locally organized, and usually run on a voluntary basis—into which each family paid a penny or so a week in order to receive ten pounds when the breadwinner died. Side by side with the voluntary society, there grew up the industrial life insurance company, living on a vast network of agents collecting small weekly premiums.

At various times and by various statutes (in 1913 and in 1926, for example) the worst of the abuses of these companies were eliminated. Policy holders became entitled at least to a paid-up policy for their money. Larger proportions of the profits earned by the industrial life branches of the companies went back to the policy holders by way of bonuses. The companies, and their collecting agents, acquired an increasing number of scruples in the conduct of their business. Industrial insurance became honest and respectable. But it could still be said to be wasteful and inefficient. That was the argument of Lord Beveridge, and of an earlier investigator, Sir Arnold Wilson, a Conservative M.P. who was killed in action in 1940.

They pointed out that fourteen insurance companies handled nearly all the business, and that the total premium income was some £100,000,000 a year, of which nearly all was collected by some 65,000 full and part-time agents. Each agent had a "book," or list of customers, and a territory. Each territory might contain fourteen different agents, each of a different company, each covering the same streets, often each calling on the same house. If there was only one agent collecting premiums for all policies in each area, the costs of collection—about 6s. in every pound collected—would fall drastically, with advantage to the policy holder.

To this, the socialists added two further criticisms. They claimed that there was no longer any justification for a shareholder, in any industrial insurance company, receiving any share in the profits of that branch of the business. By now, they argued, virtually all the money used in the business had come from the accumulated funds provided by the policy holders, and the policy holders should receive all the net profits resulting from the employment of their money.

They also pointed out that the industrial life insurance companies had come to be one of the largest national agencies for the accumulation of savings. It was socially dangerous, they said, to allow the investments of these funds—estimated at some £1,300,000,000 and growing every year—to be controlled by private individuals on the boards of the companies, and not responsible to any democratically elected body.

These criticisms were at least based on fact. Life insurance companies have vast sums for daily investment, and they can and do use that money to build up industries and individual concerns which they think will prosper. The two biggest companies in the business are the Prudential Assurance Co., Ltd., and the Pearl Assurance Co., Ltd. Their combined funds exceed £400,000,000. I have given an instance of how the Prudential Company financed a particular concern (Rootes Motors, Ltd.) with considerable advantage to the British automobile industry, to the two brothers Rootes, and to the Prudential itself. But there is, of course, an obvious comment on this state of affairs. If the Prudential had not backed Rootes and similar concerns, at the start, before their success was certain, who would have done it?

At a very early stage, the Labour party had said that industrial life insurance should be nationalized and fitted into the general plan of national insurance. It was a logical proposal, but there were two practical difficulties. One was that if the industry were reorganized, a large proportion of the 65,000 collecting agents would lose their jobs, and most of them would not only become anti-Labour voters but would also become anti-Labour agitators on their rounds, as soon as the proposal became a serious risk. The other inconvenient fact was that one of the fourteen companies in the business was the Co-operative Insurance Society, Ltd., owned by the co-operative societies, and the co-operators had no intention of seeing their child nationalized without making a loud cry of protest. And the co-operative movement was not just a mere trading concern. It was the Labour party's political ally, in Parliament and in the field.

The final result, announced a few days after publication of the main Labour party manifesto, was the advocacy of a policy of "mutualization" for the industrial life insurance companies. Mutualization, as proposed, meant that the ordinary shareholders in each company would be given some form of fixed interest-bearing stock in the company, in exchange for their shares, and likewise would surrender their right to vote at company meetings. The directors of each company would be accountable to the policy holders, not the shareholders, and all the profits of each company—after paying the interest on the fixed-interest stock—would belong to policy holders. Save for that, the companies would be permitted to operate as before as separate entities, but lest the directors of any company conclude that the campaign against them was abandoned, mutualization was coupled with a proposal to set up an industrial assurance board to watch over the conduct and progress of the industry.

To avoid the risk of any loss of votes among the 65,000 collecting agents, the mutualization proposals left each agent carrying on as before with his employment assured—and it left the policy holders paying 6s. in every pound to provide it. To avoid any loss of support among the co-operative societies, they were left in full possession and control of the Co-operative Insurance Society, Ltd. The full blast of the Labour party's disapproval was turned on one group alone, the shareholders whose money had originally started the companies.

The plan bears all the stigma of a smart political trick. There is indeed a case for concentrating the whole business of industrial life insurance, and for cutting out the wastes of overlapping administrations. Politics being what they are, there is also a case for not interfering with a powerful organization in an election year. But there can be no case for manipulating an industry so as both to gather the votes and to perpetuate the waste, still less for calling that another step in the march of progress.

The Conservative party manifesto appeared a few days after that of the Labour party, under the title *This is the Road*. It was better written, had a little more force in its appeals to the emotions, and certainly was more aggressive. "We shall bring Nationalization to a full stop here and now," it said, and a statement so unequivocal in an election manifesto stood out as a chunk of solid beef does in a can of inferior soup.

There were many points about which the two manifestos could be said to be in agreement. The Labour party claimed that it would free small businesses from the coils of the monopolies; the Conservatives that they would give a fair field to any enterprise. Both promised support for a policy of full employment; both agreed that home agricultural production should be encouraged. Both accepted rationing of food as necessary until there was enough, in the Conservative phrase, to bring "the prime necessities of life within the reach of every family and every individual." Both supported the social services, and each claimed to have been the authentic parent of the brood. And it was the Conservative manifesto that promised to abolish the direction of labor, not that of the Labour party. But the common ground between the parties has been made clear already. To suggest that the manifestos even appeared to agree on fundamental policy would be completely misleading.

The main claim of the Conservatives was that the socialists had failed. The socialist deception, the platform said, lay in its claim that it is the Labour Government that has brought prosperity and full employment to Britain. In fact it has brought an inflated currency and less value for money. "Devaluation is not the last crisis, nor have we seen the worst of it yet."

Nationalization was to stop. The industries already nationalized were to be decentralized (but only road transport was to be restored to private ownership); waste was to be cut ruthlessly, the cost of defense reviewed, taxes lowered, controls reduced to a minimum, the policy of bulk–buying ended. On the other hand, the health service was to be maintained and improved, war pensions increased, and increases given in the amounts which pensioners could earn before suffering cuts in their state pensions.

There was a little more in this pamphlet than in the other on the subject of foreign affairs. The emphasis was on the British Empire and Commonwealth, on the expansion of trade within the empire, and the need to build up, with British and American capital, the productive capacities of each colony. For the rest, an inevitable reference to "the ideals set forth in the Charter of the United Nations" and "above all, we seek to work in fraternal association with the United States to help . . . all nations . . . to resist the aggression of Communism. . . ."

Yet the impression left by the manifesto—perhaps the occupational hazard of all election manifestos—was that the Conservative party would like to be all things to the vast majority. Taxes were to be cut, but which taxes—income tax or purchase tax—and by how much, were not specified. The government should spend less; yet, on some things, it should spend more. "We shall . . . give appropriate incentives to farmers of marginal land." What incentives, and how much would they cost? The positive and detailed statements of intention were few; that over nationalization was one. "The Liverpool Cotton Exchange will be reopened" was another. We, the Conservatives, the document seemed to say, can do the same things, only better and more cheaply; an assertion which made sense to a Conservative but which might leave the skeptic unmoved.

There was a third party manifesto (I doubt if it is worth while summarizing that of the Communists) put out by the Liberal party under the most sober title of them all, *No Easy Way*. Read in isolation, it presents a solid picture of the need for economy, to stabilize the present gains in social welfare, and to restore at least some of the rights of the individual already eaten away. The country was living beyond its means, it said. Government expenditure must be cut, and the number of government departments drastically reduced. Alone among the parties, it was specific in what departments should be merged. It advocated, as did the Conservatives, the cutting of food subsidies and a concentration on house building. The first requirement, it said, was to give the people "decent living conditions"; questions of whether houses should be built for sale or rent were subservient to that. Again, like the Conservatives, the Liberals claimed credit for empire development—it was the Liberals, it asserted, who had created a commonwealth out of an empire. In these matters, its proposal to abolish conscription for military service was the real distinction between this statement and the other two; that and its insistence that the time had come when the country must look to the restoration of its ancient civil liberties.

But in the light of what subsequently happened, the most important section in the pamphlet is that dealing with nationalization. It was quite definite that the Iron and Steel Act must be abandoned, and that road transport should be freed. "Monopoly," it said, "when it is not inevitable is objectionable and must be broken up. If it cannot be broken up, it should be controlled in the public interest. Only when neither the restoration of competition nor control is possible should nationalisation be considered." The Liberal party organization might still be struggling back to life, harassed by old men who still thought of old Mr. Gladstone and young Mr. Lloyd George, but at least it provided a reasoned and clear-cut stand on nationalization.

After reading all three one could hardly escape the conviction that the Labour party offered one picture—in substance a continuation of the previous five years—and that the other two parties were offering two variations of another picture; that, between themselves, the Conservatives and the Liberals were differing more in emphasis than in substance. Perhaps the importance of the Liberal party was not that it was ever likely to become an effective alternative either to Labour or the Conservatives, but that it remained the parliamentary conscience, and while conscience can function successfully with a small voice, it cannot do so if that voice is finally stilled.

The last day on which candidates could file their nomination papers was February 13. Each candidate on nomination must produce a nomination paper in which he is proposed and seconded by two local electors, and supported by eight more. In addition, he must deposit £150 in cash, to be forfeited if he fails to poll at least one-eighth of the total votes cast in the constituency he is contesting. The candidates nominated were divided as follows:

Labour and Co-operative	617
Conservative and Allies	614
Liberals	478
Communists	100
Others	55

In two constituencies, both in Northern Ireland, only a single candidate was nominated. Accordingly that candidate was at once returned as a member, unopposed. Both were Conservative supporters (Ulster Unionists).

The election campaign entered its last phase cautiously, economically (to husband the moneys in the election coffers) and not very obtrusively. Most of it consisted of 623 little battles in 623 separate constituencies, each with its own characteristics. For instance, side by side in the same issue of *The Times* were the following two reports on the importance of the issue of nationalization of iron and steel. One came from Middlesborough in the northeast of England, the other from South Wales:

No one on Tees-side appears to doubt that the nationalisation of iron and steel is the main issue here.

Electors in South Wales and Monmouthshire show small interest in the nationalisation of iron and steel as an election issue of major importance, although it affects one of the basic industries of the area.

In those areas, the candidates were at least discussing an issue involving nationalization.

But first, what is an election campaign? It is easy to use the word glibly, without being at all sure that it is conveying anything like a true picture of what is going on. The election campaign itself, which in Britain lasts only three weeks, has three purposes. Each party tries to impress on the mind of the elector a last-minute flash of the issues between the parties and equally to impress on his mind the need to make a personal decision on how to vote and finally to make a personal move to vote. The instruments by which this is being done are those local to each constituency, the candidates, the speakers at their meetings and the party canvassers and those general to the whole country, press, radio and news reels in cinemas.

There is little point in attempting to follow any local campaign, but there is something to be said on the organs with the nation-wide appeal. The news reels were recorders, not propagandists. It is doubtful if they influenced a single vote. One can say the same for the press, for different reasons. The press was propagandist, but as a rule each newspaper reached a reader whose mind was already conditioned to accept that newspaper as propagandist at election time. Most readers chose a daily paper suiting their habits of mind.

I doubt if the newspapers made many converts during the election itself. But the radio is a different case because the listener heard the voices, and so something of the personalities, of the broadcasters of all parties. And the radio is an instrument of party political education only at election times, and so novelty heightens the impression it can make. It is impossible to estimate the effect of that influence—there is no data available. But it existed.

By its charter, the B.B.C. must remain independent of party politics, and at an election it strains every nerve to avoid anything which might be thought political. It drops most of its talks on current affairs and kindred subjects; it even cuts from its comedians' scripts any jokes having reference to party politics or personalties. But it places at the disposal of the parties a series of broadcasting periods, ranging from ten to thirty minutes each. (Any party putting fifty or more candidates into the field can claim its share of the allotted time.) The allocation of the periods is settled by the parties themselves. By agreement, the parties choose their speakers and the B.B.C. does not even see the scripts until the speaker arrives in the studio. At this election the series was seventeen in number and ended on the Saturday before polling day, to give the electors time in which to brood on all they had heard. It was a remarkable demonstration of disinterested public enterprise.

By common consent, the two most effective talks, judged as radio talks, were those given by Mr. J. B. Priestley, the author and dramatist, and by Dr. Charles Hill, a Conservative candidate known to the listening public as the "Radio Doctor" from his weekly five-minute talk on every known form of disease given on Fridays after the 8 A.M. news. Both were experienced and excellent radio speakers. Again by common consent, the worst in the series came from Mr. Ernest Bevin, who was either too tired or too unimaginative even to begin to think in terms of radio technique.

Without a great deal of research it will be impossible to estimate what influence these talks had on votes. Clearly, they had an influence on the election, in that they made certain the electorate knew the party arguments and appeals; it is probable that their listening public each day was about 15,000,000. What is uncertain is their influence in swinging a vote. In so far as votes are swayed during the weeks immediately preceeding an election, I should rate these radio talks as the most potent influence.

What were the specific issues in the campaign? A fortnight before election day, the *Financial Times* listed them in this order:

1. The cost of living.
2. Housing.
3. The future of subsidies.
4. High taxation.
5. Full employment.

At that stage, foreign affairs were hardly being mentioned at all.

Nationalization was an issue, but not a prominent one. Outside the areas immediately affected by iron and steel, outside the areas in which the Labour industrial vote was solid enough to make the Labour candidate's campaign a long round of self-congratulation, nationalization was not a point that the Labour candidates preferred to stress. Public control, yes. Public ownership, no. It was necessary, they said, to make permanent the controls over credit and export, over the movements of capital and the location of industries. If possible, they preferred to leave it at that.

The voters preferred it so. They preferred to discuss concrete issues, the cost of food and the provision of houses, pensions and subsidies, but particular pensions and subsidies, why the local secondary school still had too few free places, and why the local industry was likely to lay off a few men soon.

When the election campaign was well under way, the editor of the *New Statesman* wrote:

. . . I heard a Fleet Street editor complain that, although the Press was doing its best, it had not succeeded in 'hotting-up' the electorate . . . My impression, from a few days of speaking and gossiping, mostly in the Birmingham area, is that the public remains obstinately cool.

Were the voters unmindful of the importance of the election to the future of their country? I don't think so, judging by the heavy poll, but I doubt if it can be said that the issues involved in that future were so presented to them that their vote represents an expression of their decision on them.

The first move from the Conservative side was an abortive one. In one of his earliest campaign speeches, at High Wycombe, Sir Stafford Cripps suggested that it might be desirable to limit or tax capital gain on the sale of a prewar house at an inflated postwar figure.

The Beaverbrook press took that up quickly; a capital levy in a disguised form, it suggested. The public remained uninterested. It looked as though it was not going to be an election in which that kind of riposte would help.

A heavier attack on housing seemed more successful. That was an issue which each candidate was bound to handle differently; it depended upon local conditions. The general line of attack was that the Labour Government had not done enough, that it had failed in its promises to give every family a separate house before the end of the 1945 Parliament. With that came the promise that the Conservatives would free the private builder and that he would build faster and more cheaply. As late as February 21, three days before polling day, the Conservative central office sent out in its *Daily Notes* a reprint of a four-point pledge given by Lord Woolton, the chairman of the party, the previous week: "We will make housing Priority No. 1. We will house the people of this country." Some of the Labour candidates in the prosperous industrial areas were apprehensive. Too many of their electors possessed savings sufficient at least to make an initial payment on a house of their own, once builders were free to build to sell.

But the appeal was two-edged. The bulk of the electorate seemed well aware that the Conservatives, if returned, could neither double the number of trained men in the industry nor induce the same number of men to build twice as many houses in the same time. Either houses would be built for sale, or they would be built for rent; there was no chance that both would happen at once. The stronger the appeal to those with money enough to buy a house, the less the appeal to those without money enough to buy—the people whose one chance of a new home depended on their local council building enough houses to bring their names to the head of the list of waiting applicants. It is very difficult to say if the Conservatives gained or lost the more on housing. Clearly, judging by the final result, it was no trump card.

An issue that did strike an immediate response was that of gasoline rationing, first raised by Mr. Churchill. Mr. Menzies's new government in Australia, in fulfillment of his election promises, abolished gasoline rationing as of February 9, and the repercussions of that election promise were already at work in Britain. On the same day, speaking at Devonport in support of his son's candidacy, Mr. Churchill said:

. . . We are determined to put an end to it at the earliest possible moment. We cannot make any definite promises at this stage because we do not know all the facts . . . We believe . . . Even if it may not be possible to abolish petrol rationing altogether, it may soon be all right . . . to increase greatly the basic ration.

Mr. Aneurin Bevan, speaking in the same town later in the evening, made a counter thrust. Speaking of Mr. Churchill's reference to it, he said:

. . . He should be ashamed of himself in trying to bribe the British people by an increase in the basic petrol ration. That is why he is a short-term merchant, concerned only about election results on the twenty-third of this month, and not with the future of Great Britain.

Mr. Hugh Gaitskell, the Minister of Fuel and Power, produced his answer, in greater detail, the following day. After explaining that he was trying to obtain more gasoline without spending more dollars, he said: "To provide the extra petrol needed without rationing it would probably cost Britain alone 40 million to 50 million dollars and for the sterling area as a whole a much larger figure." They were often advised, he went on, to imitate other countries in Europe and abolish rationing. "We can do this tomorrow if we are prepared to let high prices and lower wages do the job instead of coupons." One would say that Mr. Gaitskell had the better of the argument, but that, of course, is not the whole story. Mr. Churchill at least heartened those who hoped to have more gasoline for pleasure. But did that gain his party any votes?

By far the most important issue raised by Mr. Churchill during the campaign concerned foreign affairs, his advocacy of a fresh appeal to Soviet Russia on atomic control. He first made his proposal during the course of an election speech in Edinburgh on February 14. He said:

. . . I have not, of course, access to the secret information of the Government, nor am I fully informed about the attitude of the United States.

Still, I cannot help coming back to this idea of another talk with Soviet Russia upon the highest level.

The idea appeals to me of a supreme effort to bridge the gulf between the two worlds so that each can live their life, if not in friendship, at least without the hatreds and manoeuvres of the cold war. . . .

It is not easy to see how things could be worsened by a parley at the summit if such a thing were possible. . . .

The following night, Mr. Bevin was due to give his speech in the broadcast series and obviously he could not avoid some reference to the suggestion Mr. Churchill had already thrown out, but his comment bears all the signs of an interpolation—and not a very adroit one at that—in the middle of a speech already prepared. He said:

. . . Until now every effort made by the United States and ourselves has failed. Russia is a closed book and at present her people are being more cut off than ever. But if peace is her objective, as it is ours, inspection and control of atomic energy is not too great a price to pay.

I think it is clear from what I have said that this is not a problem which can be solved by any stunt proposals.

"Stunt proposals" is not the happiest of phrases. It gave Mr. Churchill an admirable opening for a reply when he came to make his broadcast on the night of the 17th:

. . . Mr. Bevin, the Secretary of State for Foreign Affairs, dismissed all this by the scornful word "stunt". By this he only showed how far his mind dwells below the true level of events. Why should it be wrong for the British nation to think about these supreme questions of life and death, perhaps for the whole world, at a time when there is a general election? . . . What a reflection it would be upon our national dignity and moral elevation . . . if at this time of choice, this turning point in world history, we found nothing to talk about but material issues and nice calculations about personal gain or loss! What a humiliation it would be if proud Britain, in this fateful hour, were found completely absorbed in party and domestic strife! I am glad I put a stop to all that. . . .

But already it was clear that Mr. Churchill was shying away from some of the implications in his original suggestion. He had covered himself on the first occasion by disclaiming any close information on

United States policy. On the second occasion, he seemed content to ride away with the thought that, after all, he had intended no more than to inject a little reality into what had been, so far, a very domestic election.

Was Mr. Churchill's Edinburgh reference to the possibility of a direct appeal to Soviet Russia intended simply to embarrass his political opponents? Was it a valid and independent act of statesmanship? I doubt if the real answer is a plain "yes" or "no," even if one could uncover it. I think all the evidence shows that Mr. Churchill's motives were mixed.

There is no doubt that Mr. Churchill had, during 1949, become increasingly impatient with, and contemptuous of, Mr. Bevin's handling of the external policies and relations of the United Kingdom. That much is apparent from his references to Mr. Bevin, more cutting than ever before, in the last foreign affairs debate in 1949. Mr. Churchill disliked Mr. Bevin's apparent reluctance to press actively ahead with Western European Union; he disliked still more the reputation for such a reluctance that Mr. Bevin was building for Britain in Europe, and in the United States. After the election, the diplomatic correspondent of the *Manchester Guardian* wrote of Mr. Bevin's last year in that government:

. . . Politically, however, his policy has had unfortunate results. Britain has been branded as the brake on the movement for European unity. Holding the views he has, Mr. Bevin could only have avoided this by presenting his case in a far more positive manner than he has done. His case has, in fact, been unbelievably ineptly and unimaginatively presented. . . .

Mr. Churchill would have subscribed to every word of that.

Mr. Churchill feared that Mr. Bevin, tired and ill, but unwilling to give up his post, was missing chances to create situations favorable to Britain which Mr. Churchill was convinced that he (Churchill) could both create and exploit. Given a majority at election, and restored to the position in relation to Europe that he once held, Mr. Churchill was satisfied he could deal with the threat of atomic warfare in a very different and far more successful way. He thought there was everything to be said for telling the electorate, and the rest of the world, of that conviction.

There are indications that Mr. Churchill chose his moment and his words with an eye to his own electorate—not the rest of the world. It was all very well for him to say, a little disingenuously, that he was not "fully informed about the attitude of the United States." True, he did not have access to the official reports of the British Ambassador in Washington, but Mr. Churchill has certainly never been ill-informed on the state of both official and unofficial opinion in the United States, and the first sounding he took there would have told him that the State Department did not favor an immediate "highest level" approach to Moscow. Some day, possibly, but not around February 23, 1950.

Another indication is the timing of the speech itself. Considering the importance of the topic, it came very late in the campaign. Was it a coincidence that it was made only after the return to Britain of Lord Beaverbrook, and only after Lord Beaverbrook had talked to Mr. Churchill? Lord Beaverbrook may not be among the leaders of the Conservative party but he remains a man to whose opinions Mr. Churchill has always paid a great deal of attention. Mr. Brendan Bracken and he were Mr. Churchill's closest collaborators in the conduct of the 1945 election campaign. Despite that, Lord Beaverbrook remained a close guide in 1950. A personal appeal to Stalin, a sudden flying visit to Moscow; that was the way newspapers were run. To Lord Beaverbrook, could diplomacy possibly hope to find better methods?

As an election issue, this subject had one main disadvantage. The reactions it provoked cut across existing feelings in the two parties, and it was raised too late in the campaign for either party to clear its mind on it. It might not have been wholly a "stunt"; it certainly did not prove to be a heaven-sent inspiration.

The fair, dry weather held for election day. There could be little excuse for anyone staying at home; besides, the facilities for postal voting had been discovered by increasing numbers of voters and they made good use of them. There was every sign that the vote would be heavy, and so it proved to be. Mr. Churchill recorded his vote in London, and then went out to Woodford. Mr. Attlee was already in Walthamstow, his constituency. He voted in Westminster—for his Downing Street residence—by mail.

The polling places closed at 9 P.M. The only incident was in Coventry South, where two polling places ran out of ballots and so disenfranchised some hundreds of irate citizens. (Despite its thoroughness, this was one contingency for which even the latest Representation of the People Act provided no answer.) The first result declared was from Salford, in Lancashire. Labour held the seat. Some 250 results came in that night, and at the end the Labour Party held a majority of 61. The Conservative clubs and parties were dispirited and went early to bed; gatherings of Labour supporters were jubilant. Mr. Morgan Phillips, secretary of the Labour party, said that he thought the lead was enough to win the election. The Conservative central office seemed to agree with him, for a member went on the air over a Columbia broadcast to Canada at 2:30 A.M. to say that only with a lead of over 50 was the Labour party likely to win. But already the writing was on the wall. The Labour candidates had been doing well, and were polling record votes, but the Conservatives were increasing their 1945 vote by a higher percentage. The first results are invariably those from the towns in which Labour had majorities. The county seats would not be counted until Friday, and if the Conservative poll there mounted in the same way, a number of Labour seats, won in 1945, would go Conservative. There was no such hope for the Liberals. On Thursday night, the Liberal Party had one member.

The change came as soon as the Friday results began. The number of Conservative seats started to mount, far more quickly than those of the Labour party. Both home programs of the B.B.C. were broadcasting light music, broken by election results as they came in, with a statement of the parties' positions every fifteen minutes. At 4 P.M. Labour held 256 seats, Conservatives 244, Liberals 6. By 5 P.M. the figures were: Labour, 268, Conservatives, 262. A batch of Scottish results pushed Labour ahead, 280 to 268; but more Conservative seats reduced the lead again. By 6:30, the results were Labour 309, Conservatives 281, Liberals 7. Labour needed another three seats to win an absolute majority in the Commons. It was nearly 8 P.M. before it reached that point.

So the election ended, with all the excitement of a six-hour horserace. The Labour party had won a technical victory. It was almost certain to form the next government, but for how long would that government last?

When I planned this book, I expected that, after the 1950 election, it would be possible at least to know who would have the responsibility of piloting Britain through the difficult waters of the following two or three years. Despite my prediction of June, 1948, I did not really believe that neither party would fail to win a working majority in that election. For the last hundred years the electoral system in Britain has never failed to give Britain a government with a working majority, based either on a single party or a reasonably cohesive coalition of parties. But the unlikely has happened.

The major figures in Conservative affairs over the five years were Mr. Churchill (head and shoulders above the others), Lord Woolton and the policy-making group centered around Mr. Anthony Eden and Mr. R. A. Butler.

How can one hope to describe Mr. Churchill without falling headlong into one or another of the pitfalls in the course? How can one convey to anyone outside Britain the reasons why, on two occasions, the majority of his fellow-countrymen have declined to accept his leadership of a peacetime government? One difficulty is that in times of crisis, the natural leader of a country—and between 1940 and 1943 Mr. Churchill was certainly that—stands above his people like a great shadow thrown on the gray clouds overhanging them. He becomes far greater than himself; his stature increases, so that every success is his and every failure is passed unnoticed. He is far more than himself, and it is thus that he is seen by the distant observer. The crisis ends, the clouds disappear and, for his fellow-countrymen, the shadow is no longer there. They see this man again for what he must always be, a man—a great man—but no longer the embodiment of all they schooled themselves to be when circumstances demanded. And this man they know, by instinct, must be judged practically. Can he make his transition from war to peace? They are entitled to ask that question and to make that judgment. Nations have suffered grievously from their failures to do so.

But the distant observer is less conscious of the need for this adjustment. Lacking contact with the current scene, he still sees that gigantic figure in the clouds. So he assumes—because Mr. Churchill once typified an heroic Britain—he must forever typify Britain; and those who differ from him become dogs snarling at his heels. And if the distant observer is not careful, he will allow himself to think that those who do differ must therefore represent all that is unheroic in Britain.

The plain fact is that as his years increased, Mr. Churchill declined to learn any new trades. He declined to learn how to lead a Conservative opposition in Parliament to the best advantage. He declined to learn the economics of the mid-twentieth century. He declined to learn the attitudes needed in the government of a country that had ceased to be as strong as any in the world. Mr. Churchill has written and painted. He has fashioned his occasional thunderbolts. He has spoken to Europe, and to America, as the embodiment of all that each would like to think Europe actually is. But he never played his proper part in the day to day task of plotting and planning, in Parliament and out, how to win votes and convert people, how to build up the percentage of Conservative vote from its 39% in 1945, back to its 53% in 1935. Nor, which is more reprehensible, did he resign and leave someone else to do it. He remained, a basking Gulliver in Lilliput—fretful, uncertain and yet always the main feature on the landscape.

Lord Woolton, chairman of the party, did apply his mind relentlessly to this task. He could never hope for open leadership of the party, for he had accepted a peerage, and today no party in Britain can be led from anywhere but the House of Commons. Between 1919 and 1939, Lord Woolton built up a magnificent retail store business by his capacity to organize and to choose and train his staff. Once he accepted office as chairman, he did precisely the same for the Conservative party. Left to himself, Lord Woolton is probably more Liberal than Conservative, but he likes power, real power, and this he has won inside his party. In three years, he gave the party an efficient organization, good enough to outpoint that of the Labour party in February, 1950.

Furthermore, he did it without disrupting the traditional pattern of Conservative organization. The Conservative party organization is built around its county associations, which are constituency bodies possessing considerable autonomy. It is they who select the candidate, not the central office of the party, although candidates are usually scrutinized by central office and recommended to the constituencies. Of all parties, the Conservatives had a reputation for allowing their local organizations to be dominated by wealth or social position, preferably both if they could happily be combined. That state of affairs became less and less true. It was easier for the energetic young Conservative, without money, to break through the protective crust of the old organization; in fact rather more easy than for the aspiring middle-class socialist to be accepted in a safe trade-union seat.

Not only that. The Conservative party possessed and used excellent talent in the creation of a policy for the times. Mr. R. A. Butler headed the team that produced the series of policy statements. Alongside him was Mr. Anthony Eden, the tactician and the mouthpiece. He interpreted rather than originated, but he understood men—particularly men at work in the House of Commons. Together, this headquarters team created both a policy and the philosophic reasons for believing in it. Yet even that cannot produce the force necessary to convince an audience that here is something in which they must believe.

Conservatives may not need a formal and detailed policy to the extent that the Labour party does. To the socialists, a party program is the standard of battle, the colors around which the regiments will be expected to fight and, if need be, to die. To the Conservatives, a detailed policy is an affair hatched up in the back rooms—essential, no doubt, just as the general staff are needed in battle—but not requiring detailed discussion and debate in party conferences, summer schools and similar innovations. The real policy of the Conservative party is an assembly of instincts and loyalties. A large section of the British people like old habits; animals, the countryside, loyalty, snobbery, cricket, the idea of a Royal Family and the reflected glory of the great achievements of the past. Most of these vote Conservative, and they are the core of the Conservative party. They do not need an industrial policy. At home, "Fair play all round" and, for a foreign policy, "Keep friendly with the colonies and be kind to the natives" are two slogans which would serve as perfectly adequate substitutes. The bulk of Conservative party supporters are still drawn from those interested in property, those who live on accumulations of property, who manage or deal in property, or those dependent upon various forms of property; just as the bulk of the Labour party's supporters are to be found among those who live upon wages, for whom property considerations have no personal meaning. But numerous as the natural Conservatives are, they do not exceed 45% of the electorate. The problem (a problem for both parties) was to secure the essential six to ten per cent. Put another way, the task for each party was to obtain the backing of more than one class.

This marginal group of six to ten per cent may be small in numbers, but it is of the greatest importance, and not only tactically. It is the balance consisting of those who, for various reasons, are susceptible to political argument, who are not immovably held by economic considerations, who need something more than a well-written election pamphlet. It is among these people that the theories of politics have some play—the theories of socialism and capitalism, of freedom and discipline, of incentive and exploitation. They are a large section of what is termed the floating vote, and they can be won if they see that policy is also accompanied by that indefinable element, leadership. The floating vote is not uninterested in its own economic position. A large factor of its judgment is its opinion of the effectiveness of a party as a set of administrators, and the test for that is the impact of government on their own lives. And Mr. Churchill failed to find the right appeal to the floating vote; the appeal that rang true for 1950.

Only for his party could he do it. While he retained leadership of his party, no one but he had the right and authority to make the appeal. If he did not speak, all the words of the others were in vain. But Mr. Churchill remained the prisoner of his former greatness, a man who, having once made the sun stand still, forever after thinks it is still high noon.

As a record of events, this book ends with the King's Speech on the opening of the first session of the Parliament elected in February, 1950, but surmise on the future of this Parliament is not out of place. I think all one can do is try to estimate the limits of time within which another election is most likely to take place. It is not difficult to forecast the latest date by which the Opposition will try to force another election. Section 11 of the Iron and Steel Act, 1949, reads: ". . . all securities of the companies specified (to be taken over by the Government) shall, on the first day of January 1951 or such date later, but not more than twelve months later than the date aforesaid, as the Minister may by order substitute for the date aforesaid, vest in . . ." the new Iron and Steel Corporation set up by the act. In short, unless an amending act is passed, the steel industry will be nationalized by January 1, 1952. The Conservatives will make every effort to obtain a parliamentary majority in order to be able to repeal the act before January 1, 1952.

The main factor in the final decision to be made by the party that does take the initiative and force the election will be its confidence of winning more of the Liberal vote. Both parties need time to woo that vote, just as they need some time to overhaul their electoral machinery and build up their party funds.

There, the salient fact is that in February, 1950, 85% of the electorate, after a fully publicized campaign, reached certain conclusions on the facts known to them and the arguments placed before them. Unless circumstances change, it cannot be assumed that a large number of people would change their decisions given a second chance to vote. That was the experience in the two elections of 1910—no change in the issues between elections and a net change of one seat in the second election.

Another fact stands out. After a poll of that size, each party must recognize that it has polled very nearly its maximum vote in the existing circumstances. There are no votes to the left that the Labour party can still hope to win, no votes to the right that the Conservative party can sweep up. Both parties must recruit additional votes from the center, from the Liberal vote of February; and if either can manage it, from those who voted for the other party. Regarding the Liberal vote, each can, with reason, cherish some hope of success. It is possible, but unlikely, that the Liberal party would again put 470 candidates into the field for a second election. It is possible, but unlikely, that were they to do so all those who voted Liberal in February would vote Liberal the second time, and so repeat the electoral pattern. But if there are fewer Liberal candidates and fewer reasons for voting Liberal, which way will those 2,500,000 people vote?

That demands a survey of the individual constituencies. Liberal voters in Britain are not of uniform political thought. In Wales, for instance, the Liberals were successful in five of the county constituencies; no doubt Liberal candidates will stand again in those constituencies and no doubt they will win. So, too, might the Liberals expect to win the two seats they hold in the North of Scotland. Those Liberal voters will probably not be called upon either to change their allegiance or stay at home.

Again, there are considerable differences between the Liberals of the North of England and those of the West. The Liberal of the north is quite as much an anti-socialist as he is anti-Conservative—those whose anti-socialism was the stronger almost certainly voted for the Conservative candidate in February. Without a Liberal candidate for whom to vote, many would abstain altogether. Of those who did vote, the majority, I estimate, would vote for the Conservative. But in the west it is the radical tradition that lingers, not the old free-trade individualism of the north. There, the Labour candidate might well gain the majority of the votes from those Liberals who felt that it was their duty to make some positive choice. In the south particularly, among the Liberal voters, there is an appreciable number of men and women who voted Labour in 1945, but who were disheartened by the antics of some of the Labour leaders in the five years that followed. These would vote for a Conservative candidate with the greatest of reluctance. A gesture of conciliation from the left, one they could take seriously, might draw their votes to the Labour candidate again.

But it will be necessary for the Labour Government to make such a gesture. An effective gesture would be a budget concession in taxation. But I doubt if that alone would be sufficient. A gesture to Liberal principles would be needed as well. If the Labour party is to hope to win a majority of these former Liberal votes it must at least abandon its nationalization plans for the iron and steel industry during the Parliament then to be elected. The Liberal party leaders demanded this in their election campaign in February. Those voters who supported them will expect nothing less if they are to give their support to a Labour Government. Once again, the key to the problem is iron and steel.

Provided the Labour party will abandon the Iron and Steel Act, in the next Parliament, as the price to be paid, I think that it has the greater chance of winning the majority of any transferred Liberal votes, particularly in the west and south. I do not envisage any formal pacts between the parties. They are in no mood for pacts. But I think it is possible that the Labour party might hope to win, in these circumstances, a net gain of some ten seats, which would give it a majority in the Commons sufficient to last from two to three years. But will the Labour party pay the price required for this chance of Liberal gain? The indications are that at least some of the party leaders would. Every speech that Mr. Morrison makes, for instance, is evidence that he is one of them.

So, on the evidence, would Mr. Attlee. His cabinet-making, immediately after the election, showed that. Mr. Jack Jones, a trade-union official in the iron and steel industry, lost his former post in the Ministry of Supply, the Ministry sponsoring the Iron and Steel Act. Mr. Gaitskell, who received considerable advancement by his appointment as principal assistant to Sir Stafford Cripps, is a middle-of-the-road socialist. For the first time no left-wing member of the party was promoted or given office. Those of the party who would like to make a stand for further nationalization—cost what it might in immediate success at the polls—are grouped around Mr. Aneurin Bevan, still at the Ministry of Health, and Mr. R. H. S. Crossman, who has yet to be given any office.

The Cabinet, in the week after the election, was clear enough from the terms of the King's Speech of March, 1950, announcing the government's program for the first session of the new Parliament:

In view of the restricted time available and the heavy volume of financial business to be transacted, my Government proposes only a limited programme of legislation for the present session:

Then came the proviso:

Nevertheless, should other measures prove in their view to be immediately necessary for the maintenance of full employment and the national well-being, my Ministers will not hesitate to submit them to Parliament, even though they may seem likely to prove contentious.

The government was not looking for trouble, but if it came up they would tackle it, as they did in September, 1950.

In these careful phrases one can hear the voice of Mr. Attlee at his most typical, summing up the discussion in the cabinet—and his own quite decisive point of view. "We need not," he seems to say, "make this kind of decision here and now. Let us come back to it later, in the light of events." And Mr. Aneurin Bevan would grunt in a noncommittal way. To some extent, then, the final decision will turn upon Mr. Aneurin Bevan, on his influence in the Labour party, and the importance of Mr. Bevan should be neither ignored nor exaggerated.

Mr. Bevan believes in all that he has so frequently said. His political strength comes from the fact that he does, with complete sincerity, see politics in emotional terms, and with such intensity. It is true that in the twenties and thirties, men in the mining districts of Britain—and Mr. Bevan is part of a mining district, in speech and thought—were permanently seared by the treatment the system gave them. It is still possible for a Northumberland miner to write (as he has) that, whenever he thought of Tories, he saw himself back in an ambulance driving the crushed body of a mate to the mortuary, and finding that the rules of the local council (Tory) refused the dead body admittance because it was still dirty with coal dust; it should first have been washed.

Five years ago, Mr. Aneurin Bevan was well in the running for ultimate leadership of his party. He has determination and ability and—far more than any of his colleagues—the gift of arousing emotion in others. He was the youngest member of the 1945 Cabinet. He had remained in opposition throughout the war, and so had no commitments likely to handicap a leader of the left. He had only to show that he was capable of accepting responsibility in the practice of government to secure a firm place.

He has half succeeded. He had patience enough to work at his housing plans throughout the bad times, when nothing seemed to come from them but information about his mistakes. He inherited from the Coalition Government the national health plan which could, in 1948, have been built up to a tremendous fanfare of triumph, for the program itself and for the name Aneurin Bevan. He carried the plan through, although he created a great deal of resistance to it by his methods.

But his trouble is that he never ceased to play politics, inside the cabinet and out, as when, for example, he attacked Mr. Shinwell be-cause he thought him principal rival for the leadership of the left wing of the party. Too often he has thought the applause of a politi-cal meeting another political triumph. He has frittered away some of his strength and influence. Like a bad cavalry leader, he has chased those in front of him too far and returned to find that the real battle has been decided without him. He is the natural leader of a group in revolt. I doubt if he now has sufficient influence to compel a reluctant party to revolt.

There is one final question affecting the relations among the three parties. Will the Labour party—will either of the main parties, for that matter—seriously advocate some revision in the British electoral system designed to insure minority parties a fairer representation in the House of Commons? I doubt it, whatever the alteration—pro-portional representation, the alternative vote—may be, despite the vague proposal thrown out by Mr. Churchill during the debate on the King's Speech, suggesting a committee of inquiry into the whole problem. I think that each party would regard a serious proposal of this kind too high a price to pay even for the prospect of a greater number of Liberal members in the House and therefore a smaller number of their opponents. Each of the two parties believes that sooner or later it will win the five to ten per cent additional votes needed to give it a working majority. In the past, when there was a minority third party in the Commons, neither party benefitted much from its presence. It would need more than one situation like that resulting from the February election to persuade the major parties to depart from the present system. Nor do I think that even the Lib-erals anticipate that these views will be changed within the twelve-month.

The fourth question is the effect of this close result on Britain's ex-ternal relations, and there I feel I should say at once that some of the confusion outside Britain seems to spring from a mistaken em-phasis on the part that theoretical politics plays in the final result. Pure theory influenced the 90,000 Communists, few others. The vote of February was not a judgment on textbook socialism. It was far more a practical judgment on how a particular set of men—grouped within the party that had governed Britain for nearly five years—

had succeeded or failed in their tasks. And because they had succeeded in some things and failed in others, the result was as it was. Quite as many voted against what they felt to be stupid controls—such as those affecting the keeping and killing of domestic pigs—as they did against the theory of socialism.

It may be said that the British people should have looked ahead, that they should have looked where events were carrying them, that they should have shortened sail to meet the storms of 1951 and 1952. But is that not asking too much in the way of foresight? Neither party had the courage of its worst fears. And would the people of Britain necessarily have chosen more wisely if they had been in a panic about the future?

What have other countries to fear from the situation that resulted in Britain from the February election? It should not be feared that the main lines of Britain's foreign policy, political or economic, will be subject henceforward to erratic and unforeseen changes of course. It is clear from the previous five years that there is no very great difference in external aims between the Conservative party and the Labour party, and it is even doubtful that the methods of either, when in power, would have differed from the methods of the other. Mr. Churchill emphasized the need for closer unity in Western Europe in terms which seemed to promise more positive and favorable action than that contributed by Mr. Bevin. Any opposition leader could have said the same. There is no evidence that, had he been faced with the concrete task of welding together the economies of Western European countries, he would have been any more ruthless (mainly at the expense of his own country's immediate interests) than was Mr. Bevin during 1949. It may be true that Mr. Churchill would have appointed a more vigorous Foreign Secretary than Mr. Bevin seems likely to be. Perhaps, in this respect, the election result does constitute a loss to the world, for had either party won a majority substantial enough to give it a five-year prospect of office, I doubt that Mr. Bevin would have returned to the Foreign Office. But lack of vigor is very much less disastrous than disagreement over what should be attempted.

I feel that the core of the disappointment felt in the United States has a different origin. It is clear that during 1949, the State Department had been preparing its future plans for a free world economy, plans needed when Marshall Aid ended. It is reasonably clear that these plans were intended to cover Britain's external liabilities— within the sterling area and outside it—and that they had as their main intention the freeing of international trade in general, and American export trade in particular, from the restrictions imposed upon free exchanges by the world shortage of dollars. Any such plans would be bound to cut across the present lines and methods of British external trade.

The reactions of the oil interests in the United States to the prospect of market limitation resulting from currency shortages were perhaps the most vigorously expressed, and so the most evident, among American industries concerned about a possible shrinkage of business, but it was no more than typical. The American interests, in the mind of the State Department during the preparation of its plans, were all the American trading interests that were suffering, or likely to suffer from the barrier between the dollar and the sterling areas.

It is also a reasonable supposition that these plans were discussed in outline at the Washington conference in September, 1949, that they were elaborated in detail by official contacts during the winter months. And no doubt the general hope was that after February 23, a Foreign Secretary and a Chancellor of the Exchequer would have time and authority to take them a stage further. It was also well understood in Washington that a British Chancellor of the Exchequer would need all the authority he could muster; for the plans would confront Britain with the prospect that its closed markets within the sterling area would be thrown open by an infusion of dollars. So perhaps a part of American disappointment had its origin in the fact that the election result imposed on all concerned another period of waiting. From all that was said and hinted when the election results were announced, it is obvious that the State Department thought this delay a bad thing, if only because by the fall of 1950 the United States itself would be involved in its own elections.

At the present moment, the United States is faced with the supreme task of the second half of this century, that of discovering how to transform the capitalism of the last century into an effective means of transferring goods and commodities in a free world society, without recourse to a system based on a Politburo. I believe that now is the time to think again, forced on the United States by events in Britain, and that the opportunity could be used to produce at least the beginnings of a better solution.

The February election did not leave Britain with a government lacking power and authority, but it has clearly left those who deal with that government uncertain of the duration of its power and authority. That is a handicap. Yet a great many matters of moment have found the more solid solution because of the handicaps that had to be overcome in the process.

CHAPTER XXI

Some Personal Comments

I want to make it clear from the start that this chapter is a patch-work of personal opinions. As a whole, this book is concerned with events and comments on those events, the comments of a fallible man at least attempting to be objective. This chapter cannot help being subjective, since it is concerned mainly with ideas. The three ideas I wish to discuss are the nature of socialism in Britain; prospects for Anglo-American relations, and nuclear fission.

I have the impression that in the United States the word "socialism" has come to have a black-and-white meaning. It seems to be used, mainly by people who believe in free enterprise, as a description interchangeable with communism, indicating the existence of a slave state or police state; in any case something wholly bad. If such a view exists, it seems to me superficial, misleading and at variance with the facts.

Here let me enter a caveat. I do not believe that there can be any simple yet satisfactory definition of socialism in the abstract, because I do not believe that there can be a satisfactory text-book definition of any political system in the abstract. A political system is an expression of the life of a nation or political group; it is the life that it leads, and it cannot be reduced to a formula. The political system in Britain today, whatever the adjective used to describe it, is a product of British history, British economics, British geology and British climate. Each of these is absolutely unique, and their sum is likewise unique. If the United States, for example, were to "go socialist," the pattern its government would then assume might well be more different from that in Britain than it is at present.

The first point I would like to clear up is whether socialism is identical with communism. The simplest illustration of the difference between the two is, I think, that it would be impossible to think

417

of communism existing in what the West calls a democratic society, in a country in which the political machinery is designed to give the people a chance to express their views. The essence of a communist state is one party which claims both the monopoly of all political wisdom and the right to stay in office forever. Socialism, in distinction, involves a belief that the voters must be left the right to reject socialist policies if they so wish. Socialism may abandon that belief; if it does, I would say that it had become communistic.

It may be argued that socialism must inevitably lead to communism. I can see no evidence of that. It is a possibility, just as it is a possibility that a capitalist democracy may become a fascist dictatorship. Certainly, there has been no demonstration anywhere in Western Europe. Neither of the social democracies that existed in Italy and Germany after World War I led to the communist form of dictatorship. Anything can happen; it depends on the vigilance of the people. Only communists use the word "must" in this connection, and I am not persuaded by the arguments they advance for doing so.

In Britain, the vote in 1950 was as free as it was in 1945, or in 1935. The Conservative party could have won the election if a majority of the electors had voted for its candidates; and had it won, its political powers would not have been impaired by anything the Labour Government had done between 1945 and 1950. Britain has not been subject to a real dictatorship since the death of Oliver Cromwell. The parliaments of Great Britain between 1660 and 1832 were by no means fully representative of the people. At times they were corrupt, at times no more than an instrument of an oligarchy, yet they were never without some independence, and that prevented a real dictatorship.

The next question, I think, is whether socialism is purely economic theory, purely political theory, or a combination of both. Here, too, is a cause of much confusion, because the word "socialism" is used indiscriminately to describe all three, singly or together.

Can the word be limited purely to economic theory? I believe not. To do so limits its application too rigidly to make it of any use in this discussion. For instance, it may be used, in economic matters, to describe a state in which the industries are nationalized. That certainly has happened in Britain. But to use the word "socialism" to describe no more than the single act of nationalization produces a very limited result. In that case, socialism would describe only the transfer of the legal ownership of an undertaking from an individual, or from a corporate body, to another corporation owned by the state. Such a definition gives no indication of the future management or operation of that industry. The individuals who formerly owned the industry may remain, with powers and privileges unabated, as managers for the state. If one is to see the real picture, one is forced on to a consideration of the political system which governs the appointment of the managers.

The word may be used to imply some form of workers' control of industry. Again, I do not think we need pursue this very far. Workers' control has never lasted very long anywhere. It was possible to see it, for example, in Czechoslovakia in 1945 and early 1946. It faded. A manager always reappeared and thereafter what mattered was the system which controlled his appointment.

Again, "socialism" may be used to describe some form of state regulation of industry in general, the industry remaining in private ownership. That too is happening in Britain, but it seems to happen just as freely in a state which calls itself capitalistic. The various federal commissions in the United States have many such powers of regulation over privately owned industry. To use the adjective "socialistic" to describe such a state would produce only more confusion.

Socialism can be used as the equivalent of statism, but one is no further forward. For what is statism? Perhaps an attitude of mind, an urge to give the state more power and the individual less? But that becomes almost metaphysical.

I think we must say that socialism is a word intended to describe a theory embracing both the political and the economic life of a country, and that it has a democratic base, inasmuch as it may be modified or reversed by popular vote operating through a reasonably honest electoral system. Under that definition, a democracy may be either capitalistic or socialistic. To distinguish them, one must look further and examine not only the way of life itself—which is a means—but also its aims. It must be important to decide whether the distinction between a capitalist democracy and a socialist democracy is to be found more in the means or in the ends.

The single-minded capitalist may claim that the capitalist state provides equal opportunity for all. Does it? Take one instance alone. When Britain "discriminated" against the interests of the oil industry, the motion-picture industry and the tobacco-growing industry in the United States, did each win the same measure of attention and support from the State Department? Has the watchmaker in the United States a guaranteed price for his product, as has the farmer? The examples could be multiplied.

I am not arguing whether the capitalist state favors employers and the socialist state favors the working class. If this alone were the case, the gulf between the two types would be far wider than it is. I am suggesting that both kinds of state favor all sorts of interests, in preference to others that would seem—in strict theory—to have equal title to support. I would claim, too, that there will be alterations from time to time in the groups supported, and in the extent to which they are supported. For instance, in Britain, has the Labour Government treated the primary school teachers as well as it has the miners or the dockers? Did the Labour Government subject the "capitalist" farmer, who owned his land, to the same rough treatment as it gave to the "capitalist" who owned stock in a nationalized gas undertaking? It did not.

My first point is that no country can allow itself to become neutral or passive in its attitude towards its constituent elements. If it is to live, if it is alive, it must possess a certain dynamic quality. If it is to move, it must desire to move in a particular direction, and it must favor those elements which will help it progress.

My second point is that a democratic state is not governed by economic interests alone, any more than is an individual.

An individual is capricious, in the sense that it is impossible to predict absolutely his decisions and movements. So is a democratic state, capitalist or socialist. True democracy cannot be otherwise. A democratic state cannot be logical, because to be logical it must employ force. It can use force to impose a minimum standard of behavior on its citizens. It cannot use force to impose uniform behavior. The free world must accept inequality, because inequality is a condition of freedom. Equality, because it is logical, can only be procured by a dictatorship. The basic similarity between Britain and the United States is that they are both democracies, and therefore that both must favor and cajole, not order and compel.

Another similarity may be found in the ends which each attempts to reach. The day has gone when the government of a capitalist democracy could say, in effect, "We are in office to favor the rich at the expense of any interest or consideration which conflicts with the right of the individual to get as rich as he can, as quickly as he can, by any means he can." Any democratic state, once it is based on universal adult suffrage, must seek to establish a minimum standard of living, below which it will not willingly allow its citizens to descend. In that sense, it must be a welfare state. The main difference between capitalist and socialist democracies lies in the methods each adopts to its search for those very simliar ends.

The argument began with an attempt to find a definition for socialism. At its conclusion I would offer a definition—my definition, that is—in these terms, and with the knowledge that the definition will be incomplete. I would say that in a democracy, socialism is the tendency of the government to seek to favor those elements in society which will maintain a minimum and if possible produce a rising standard of living and well-being for the least capable of its citizens.

A separate but related aspect of a definition of socialism as practiced in Britain is whether or not this experiment has any relevance to the life and customs of the people of the United States. I think it has. I think it should be of value for them to see the similarities between their capitalist democracy and the socialist democracy of Britain. I think it should be of equal value for them to study the experiment as one parallel to that which they themselves may have to make later.

I am not suggesting that the United States will turn socialist in the British fashion. The trade union and progressive political leaders in America would not duplicate the policy or the experience of a Labour Government in Britain. They are a part of their political and economic environment and while the basic problems in each country may have many similarities, the remedies will be much further apart. But I am suggesting that, as a world power, the United States will sooner or later be compelled to go through something akin to the experience borne by the British people at the present time.

The changes in economic strength, and so in terms of world trade, demanded changes in Britain. The significance of the Labour Government to Britain was not that its political theories were wholly right or wholly wrong. It was that the men responsible for that Government had theories that were different from those which influenced the governments of the decades between the wars. A most useful part of the work done by the Labour Government can be described as winter ploughing. It had broken up the land used too long for pasture, land that had become sour and barren in the process. It made the opposition parties think again.

The greatest risk facing Britain in 1950 does not come from any political theory. It comes from the deep-seated respect that the British still feel for their civil service. The civil service dealt so admirably with the tasks set fifty years ago that the socialist theoreticians assumed it would be equally able in solving the quite different problems they intended to present. Britain stands in danger of being strangled by the red tape of a million government files.

Against that, one must set the achievements of the Labour Government. It has faced up to many of the problems inherent in any democracy which claims to be a welfare state, and its failures are as illuminating as its successes. Any welfare democracy, whether it calls itself capitalist or socialist, must see to it that its system provides a minimum supply of food for all, at prices which all can afford to pay. It must seek to establish a healthy nation, in which all are able to benefit from the achievements of medical science, whether they can afford a doctor or not. Likewise, it can only flourish if it creates a nation-wide educational system providing a fair chance of full development for each individual. I believe it to be a sign of civilization that a nation is careful not to waste any of the capabilities of every citizen.

But the main achievement I should claim for the Labour Government is that it has been less afraid of money, as such, than any of its predecessors. The reformist Liberal Government of 1906–1910 eliminated most barriers of social privilege in Britain, but it had no urgent need to fight any real battle with money. The financiers—the interests of those whose main concern lay in possessions already existing, not in the creation of fresh wealth—all these interests had things very much their own way in the twenties and thirties. That was a day in which a National Government in Britain could only find the money needed to rearm for defense by enticing it with specially created gilt-edged securities, which is equivalent to paying members of a fire company a special bonus to induce them to turn out for each fire.

Very few economists of today would suggest that a nation can safely leave its economy and its financial pattern solely to chance. The stability of a nation's economy depends on the balance between what is saved out of its national product and what is spent. The most devoted adherent of a free–enterprise economy does not argue that the economy needs no controls at all; his claim is that the free enterprise economy provides its own automatic controls. The argument is always over how the controls shall be operated, by alternations of boom and slump, by overproduction leading—through the inevitable crisis—to the remedy, a stimulus to the production of consumer goods.

The day of belief in these automatic adjustments, and in nothing else, has gone. Today, no country is without its central bank and a positive central banking policy, worked out in conjunction with government. No administration will knowingly risk another crisis of the 1929 type, and every administration will take some positive action to avoid a repetition of that collapse.

The point I wish to make is that the Labour Government has been grappling with this question of controls precisely as every industrial state must grapple with it, and the answers it has found, right or wrong, are part of the common experience of all Western civilization. Any failure, complete or partial, is not a matter for rejoicing. It is a matter for study; it is a part of the preparations for the next experiment.

Further, it is essential that this process of experimentation continue and that the United States should avoid thinking of its economy as rigid, guided by a single economic theory in which every event must be made to fit. What is fluid can be remolded. What is set can only be broken. The proof of that comes from Soviet Russia. It is not to be found in the fact that Soviet communism is less efficient industrially than is the free enterprise of the United States. It is to be found in the death in Russia of all art, literature, of every work of challenge and imagination.

There are a great many pitfalls in the path of Anglo-American relations over the next decade. One obvious difficulty is that the first installments of Britain's postwar debts to the United States will come due. A sum of $90,000,000 was due at the start of 1950, that being the net balance of the Lend-Lease transactions between the two countries as agreed upon in 1948. As international figures go, $90,-000,000 is not a great deal of money, but from the beginning of 1952, the first installments of principal and interest due under the 1945 Loan Agreement are to be paid. The capital debt is $3,750,-000,000, and the interest 2½% per annum. From January 1, 1952, Britain should begin to pay the fifty annual installments of principal and interest on this liability. At the same time, and in the same way, Britain must meet the repayment of the Canadian dollar credit of $1,250,000,000.

From the end of 1952, the installments of principal and interest due under the European aid program will be added. Interest is at 2½% per annum. The installments of principal required under the plan are low at the start, no more than $750,000 in the first year. By 1982, the annual capital repayment will have risen to $20,900,000. Again, during the course of 1950, Britain has to come to terms with Canada for the repayment of the balance of principal (about half is outstanding) of the Canadian interest-free dollar loan of $700,000,-000, made in 1942. By the end of this decade, Britain's annual liability for interest and installments of principal on her postwar borrowings alone will be of the order of £70,000,000 a year.

Since 1945, Britain has been repaying some of the earliest of the wartime loans made to her, the Canadian loan of 1942 and the American Reconstruction Finance loan of 1940. These repayments took £32,000,000 in 1946, £36,000,000 in 1947 and £24,000,000 in 1948, all in dollar currency. But a jump to £70,000,000 is a considerable one. There are waiver clauses in the loan agreements, but not in the E.R.P. agreements. The dollars must be found for these repayments—if they can be found—from the total dollar earnings of the United Kingdom, estimated by 1952 to be running at $830,000,000 per year; and that estimate was made on the basis that all will go well with international trade. Maybe no American president will say again, "They hired the money, didn't they?"; but a lot of Americans may be tempted to if there is any sign of a default.

Another concrete difficulty may be over oil.

"It is the essence of this policy," said the British official statement when the British plan to limit the amount of dollar oil imported into the sterling area was announced, "that we are substituting British oil companies' oil not because it is British but because it saves us dollars. Our aim is not to provide an expanding or protected market inside the sterling area for the production of British-controlled companies as such."

Such a policy is understandable and defensible; possibly more understandable and defensible than the policy of the United States itself in excluding Egyptian cotton from the United States when it competes with domestic cotton. Yet the reasons for that policy have obviously not been sufficient to appease the American oil producers. Suppose—whatever the initial intentions behind the British Government's decision—the actual result of the limitation plan proves to be the creation of both a protected and an expanding market for British-produced oil in the sterling area? It might be that the dollar content of British oil is less than that of dollar oil. That would not seem very relevant to the American oil producers who were losing what they had come to regard as an established market. It would console them still less if they were driven to price-cutting which, starting among individual companies, might well extend throughout the world. Nor would American oil interests be the only ones affected. What, for instance, would the effect in the Caribbean area be if action by the British Government could be shown to have depressed the value of their oil production as well as of their sugar crop?

I doubt that there are any international interests stronger and better organized than those of the oil industry. Will they be content to sit back and watch actions by a British Government which, calculated or not, might lead to a disorganization of their business? And if they do not remain inactive, will any action of theirs improve Anglo-American relations?

But debt repayment and the international oil market are only two aspects of the central problem that the United States faces with respect to relations with the rest of the world. And that problem can, I think, be stated with the utmost simplicity. It is that the rest of the world can only send back to the United States, for every purpose, no more dollars than America has previously sent out. If the United States buys $1,000,000,000 worth of commodities from the sterling area, the sterling area can buy $1,000,000,000 worth of goods from the United States, or it can buy $500,000,000 dollars worth of commodities and reduce its debts to the United States by $500,000,000. The one thing it cannot do is to buy $1,000,000,000 in commodities and pay even $10 in reduction of its debts.

The O.E.E.C. interim report, a mid-term survey of what had been achieved in the first two years of Marshall Aid, gave this estimate of the recovery Europe had made. Its initial task had been to restore European production, country by country, as best it could. It was remarkably successful in that; by the end of 1948, the back of that task had been broken. In 1949, industrial production in Western Europe was between 30% and 40% better than in 1947, and 25% better than in 1938. Agricultural production was 25% better than in 1947 and had nearly reached its pre-war level (but there were more mouths to feed). The second task was to increase European sales to the United States and a good deal was done to achieve that in 1949. The third task was even wider and, at the time of the survey—made late in 1949—that still lay ahead. It was to induce the United States to spend more abroad, in the purchase of both goods and services. In 1920, the United States spent about 1½% of its total national product outside its own territories. In 1938, the percentage was down to one–half of one per cent, and it had not even climbed back to the 1938 percentage by the end of 1949.

Europe is expected to sell more to the United States. The O.E.E.C. report anticipated that, provided everything went well, Europe might increase her 1948 level of exports to North America, some $1,250,000,000 to $2,250,000,000 in 1951–52. But that would still leave a dollar gap of $2,250,000,000. Only the United States can find a solution, and until she does it is useless for the American producer to think in terms of expanding exports. There will be a smaller world market, not a larger one, for American agricultural produce, automobiles and films.

Until a solution is found, Anglo-American relations will never be free from friction, for the American merchants will blame the sterling area for stealing their trade away from them. If Ceylon buys one bulldozer from Britain when she would like to buy five from the United States—but can't for lack of dollars—the American exporter will attribute his loss of that sale to British machinations and nothing else. Yet, lacking dollars, the rest of the world will trade as best it can, and it will use sterling as the medium with which to settle its net balances of payments rather than abandon trade altogether. To become an international medium of exchange, a currency must have three attributes, of which the third is the most important. It must have some value, it must have some stability, and it must be plentiful. The value of the pound sterling may have been a little shaken, but it is not scarce.

There are, it seems to me, two ideas struggling for mastery in the United States. One is international trade, with the emphasis on the word "trade." It is based on the attractive belief that those who want good American products must pay good American dollars for them. That is the philosophy of the Anglo-American loan agreement. It is the philosophy behind any new loan for the benefit of the sterling area. It is based on the belief that everything in this world must be paid for in cash, that you can settle any trouble in the world in terms of cash, in the last resort by gifts of cash. I have not myself found that theory to be true.

The other idea is more nebulous. It looks on the American surplus—what can be called the exportable surplus—as an accumulation of tangible things that the world needs and that have no real value unless used; wheat and corn, tobacco, machinery, chemicals. Somehow, the task is to get this accumulation of things shipped about the world to the places in which they are needed and can best be used. International trade is the obvious channel through which to arrange for this movement, but trade is basically exchange. Supposing that "trade" breaks down, for the simple reason that the United States wants so little back in exchange that trade becomes impossible? What then? Is there no alternative? Must the United

States plough under its tobacco and cotton crops, bury its wheat in caves and aircraft hangars, throw so many of its automobile and chemical workers out of employment? Or does it go on with the search for this alternative way of disposing of its surplus? There are those who believe that this alternative must be found, distasteful as a non-trading solution may seem to a trading nation—at least to the traders of a nation. These people, I feel, are in the tradition of Lend-Lease and UNRRA.

It is not my purpose to suggest a solution. I lack the effrontery to put forward any ready-made solution and in any case it is rather late in this book to attempt even to discuss possible solutions, or possible lines towards a solution. To that extent I stand to be criticized for raising questions for which I have no answer, but I should be content if I saw any critics throwing their own proposals into the ring. For I feel most strongly that an answer must be found if capitalism is to survive. Capitalism has no divine right to continue forever. It is no more than a technique for distributing goods, and the time has come for it to make a new advance in that technique. If it can steal some of the clothes from its opponents' wardrobes, so much the better, for it will be called something far worse than thief if it remains inactive.

Those believing implicitly in the merits of capitalism may regard the expression "full employment" as something little better than a catchword. They are right. Like most catchwords it is, in itself, literally meaningless, but like most catchwords, it is an oblique way of stating a fundamental truth. Mankind not only wants full employment, but he also wants full employment for a longer life, with a fuller stomach while he works, and with a real expectation of a rising standard of living for his children. He believes, rightly or wrongly, that all those things can be provided. If capitalism does not provide them, if it leaves him with only the expectation of insecurity, he will try something else. But capitalism can supply them if individual capitalists will surrender some of the natural individual sovereignty they have hitherto claimed. If they do not, then I am afraid that communism may destroy the whole individual sovereignty of man, capitalists included.

Some may think it unrealistic to leave any reference to atomic fission until the final pages of this book. I do not agree. I feel that the subject of atomic fission, and its consequences, has little place in this book, and for these reasons: it is possible that the world may be destroyed in our lifetime, and the words of the biblical prophets that the heavens will be rent asunder will be literally and completely fulfilled. For myself, I accept this, intellectually, as a possibility. I do not accept it emotionally, in the sense that I have made no attempt to alter the pattern of my life in consequence. I think the reason for it is that as an individual I am conditioned to interpret the whole universe in individual terms. Disaster, triumph, boredom, happiness, and final extinction; these for me are the concerns of each individual, an individual who is a part of a community but who lives and dies— above all who feels—by himself. Mine is an egocentric world inhabited by millions of other individuals equally isolated and equally important. Further, not only the content but also the end of each life is separate from that of all others; and, normally, separate in point of time. It is quite alien for me to believe—and quite impossible for me to act as though I believed—that all human individuals are destined to die simultaneously. Because I have survived so many people, so will many others survive me.

That is more than a personal belief. It is the basis of our human civilization. As a people, we believe in continuity. Some look for that continuity in the family, some in the small community or tribe, others in the nation or race. This sense of continuity, this belief that the unsolved questions of today may someday be seen in another and a simpler perspective, just as the threatening cloud changes and softens as it passes across the sky. This is the vital breath of any civilization. When that goes, a civilization dies. And, as yet, although civilizations have died, there has never been a time when the world did not contain some man who believed passionately and completely that there was still a future for the world.

If, in the 1950's or the 1960's, the envelope that enfolds us is to be split into other elements, and the old familiar surface of this globe is to be scorched and blasted in the process of that transmutation, then this book is meaningless. Every book is meaningless. But I will not accept it. While there is a chance that what I would call human sanity exists, this book shall be written; other books shall be written. They must be written for, with purpose or by chance, anyone may supply an idea sufficiently vital in itself to diminish the chances of final disaster.

This book is not in itself a challenge to disaster. It is a weapon in the armory against disaster. It is not blind to the consequences of atomic destruction. It is written with the human belief that the man who accepts disaster before it comes hastens the day of his destruction. If the human race has any merits at all, one must accept its capacity to fight until the last second of the last hour.

Others may advance what at first sight appears to be a more practical objection. Why, they may say, spend time in discussing the problems of an age that is already superseded? When atomic energy is in the full service of man, today's problems of production and distribution will be meaningless. But is that true? Granted that atomic energy were to become plentiful, granted that every political problem associated with it were to be solved, does that render useless all the experience that man has assembled? Of course not.

Atomic energy in itself solves nothing. The core of the malaise that now infects the world, the causes of the strains and tensions that are everywhere so apparent are to be found in one circumstance, the fact that the rate in the expansion of material production throughout the world is unbalanced. The social pattern of the world is like a metal globe of which various sections are being subjected to differing degrees of heat. The metal is expanding at differing rates, and folds and fissures are appearing along the edges of each section. The difficulties of adjustment within each section are far less serious than the difficulties of adjustment between one section and another.

Today, the people of China cry out against the foreigner because they say that the foreigner has exploited them. They mean that the foreigners they have seen and known, the foreigners who trade with them, have built up a standard of living and life expectancy far better than their own. If the United States has a hundred tractors to China's one, will it change the relations between the two countries if the United States converts its atomic fission plants into the equivalent of a thousand tractors to each Chinese one? The sense of exploitation is a product of contrast, and making the contrast more pronounced will neither diminish its intensity nor change its root cause.

Ever since steam put the first large gift of energy into the hands of Western man, the problem for him has been to spread, with sufficient rough justice, the fruits of that energy among his own people. Now he must go further, because the barriers across the world are down, and every man of every color can see the gains of another continent and can justifiably ask that those benefits be shared. The problems posed by atomic energy are exactly the same in kind as those presented by the discoveries of practical uses for steam and electricity. Each state, in the eyes of its saner members, is no more than an organization intended to divide up among its people the varying products of each man's work. To triple the product over 25 years does not alter the nature of the problem. It only imposes a greater strain on the machinery and the method each state uses to solve it.

Science does not solve our problems for us, nor does it alter the nature of the contest. It shuffles the cards in the deck; it alters the values of some of the cards. It is part of the terms of reference, not of the issues. Nor are relations among states different in kind from the relations among individuals in those states. The fundamental discovery the world has yet to make is how to give things away, and it matters little if the surplus is oil, cotton, tobacco or atomic energy.

We are still children of the twilight, struggling with forces we do not fully comprehend, for goals that we can never see wholly or for long. We are not even fully persuaded that this twilight is the first glimpse of a bright dawn ahead, or the end of a day whose noon we had not wit enough to recognize. All we know, by some deep instinct, is that the central struggle lies within us, within each of us, and that until we have each settled this issue for ourselves, we cannot be sure who is foe and who is friend, for what we must fight and to which we must give our service.

British War Losses and Recovery

The figures on wartime losses are taken from a white paper published by the Government in connection with the Anglo-American Loan Agreement negotiations.

LOSS OF OVERSEAS INVESTMENTS

In all, between 1939 and June 30, 1945, Britain realized £1,118,000,000 of overseas investments, including £203,000,000 in the United States, £225,000,000 in Canada, £564,000,000 in the remaining parts of the Commonwealth and £96,000,000 in South America. They were outright sales. The money raised was spent in buying war equipment and supplies. Some investments, of course, remained; largely investments in countries occupied by the enemy and therefore, during the war, not easily salable, in any case of doubtful value, and certainly non-income-producing. The net income of Britain's overseas investments fell to an estimated figure of £97,000,000 in 1945.

INCREASE IN EXTERNAL DEBT

In the case of an individual, this might be described as the rise in the amount which he owed to others. In 1938, Britain's external liabilities were £760,000,000. In 1945, at the end of the war, they were £3,355,000,000, and that was before the United States loan.

LOSS OF RESERVES

These reserves were holdings of gold and United States dollars. In 1938, they were £864,000,000 (which included private holdings of gold and dollars subsequently requisitioned). By December 31, 1940, they had fallen to an all time low of £74,000,000. By June, 1945, they had crept back to £453,000,000. The importance of these reserves was far greater than their intrinsic worth. They were, and are, the working capital of the whole business.

To summarize this, the six years of war cost Britain, in the form of reduced external assets and increased external liabilities, some £4,198,000,000, a considerable portion of it in other currencies. By VJ day, on current account, Britain was insolvent.

There were other items on the list:

LOSS OF SHIPPING

The cause of this requires no explanation. The balance sheet for shipping was:

Figures in millions of deadweight tons

Total of merchant shipping on British Register on September 3, 1939		22.1.
Add: Gains:		
New Building	8.7.	
Captures	0.7.	
Acquisition		
(returnable)	4.6.	
(non-returnable)	1.3.	15.3.
		37.4.
Less: Losses:		
Pre-war tonnage	13.0.	
Tonnage acquired during the war	5.0.	18.0.
Position as at 30th June, 1945		19.4.
Less returnable tonnage still in hand		3.5.
Net balance of British-owned shipping at end of war		15.9.

Over half the original tonnage had been lost. Only part had been made good during the war. Whenever made good, the process was a burden on the country's resources.

LOSS OF PROPERTY

There were 210,000 dwellings completely destroyed by enemy bombs or rockets, another 250,000 were so badly damaged that they could not be rebuilt, and another 3,500,000 received damage which could be repaired. In all, about one house in every three received some damage. In addition, 25,000 factory buildings were hit. Damage to installations of one kind and another was equally extensive, proportionately more in the case of docks and dock areas, as they were specific targets.

In all, the estimated cost of repairing war damage in Britain, on the 1945 level of costs, was £1,450,000,000. The actual cost increased considerably over the five years.

There is also the general loss suffered by the inability of industry to maintain, repair and replace its equipment during a war, the effects of which are difficult to estimate, but equally difficult to overcome.

In summary, the Government's statement, put forward at Washington, and used as a basis in the loan agreement negotiations, was that the war had cost Britain about £7,500,000,000 out of a total estimated prewar national capital of £30,000,000,000. About 25% of the total of Britain's material wealth had gone; moreover, the 25% that had gone consisted of the most liquid, or easily convertible assets.

LOSS OF LIFE

Killed and missing in the fighting services....................	297,762
Killed in merchant shipping...............................	35,453
	333,215

In addition, some 60,000 civilians were killed by enemy action.
Who would dare estimate the loss of these men and women in terms of cash?

All European countries involved in the war suffered in the same way and from the same causes; Germany most of all. But Britain encountered an additional complication; she shared with Soviet Russia the role of principal European victor. She had to meet the consequences of military victory over a wrecked country, and had to pay some proportion of both the cost of the occupation and some measure of rehabilitation.

In 1948, the United Nations published a survey of the economic situation and prospects of Europe. It covered 1946 and 1947. On page 59, the report says: "Europe emerged from the First World War with some reduction in its overseas investments but with the greater part intact in countries relatively undisturbed by the war, and still capable of producing large returns. The shipping position had deteriorated more seriously but still yielded substantial revenues. These receipts . . . made a large contribution towards financing the deficit on trade account in those years [1919 and 1920].

"Since the Second World War the situation has been completely different. Incomes from investments are only half as large as in the earlier postwar period. Shipping payments have made heavy drafts on dollar resources, and the war has left in its train a burden of military expenditure by European countries in other parts of the world."

Here are figures showing Europe's balance of payments with non-European countries (figures in billions of dollars):

	1919 and 1920	1946 and 1947
Europe's imports f.o.b.	19.7	22.4
Europe's exports f.o.b.	7.7	10.4
Deficit	12.0	12.0
Income from investments (net)	+1.8	+0.9
Other current transactions (net)	+2.2	—2.2
Total deficit in current account	8.0	13.3

To continue from the report: "These changes stand out even more sharply in the estimates for the United Kingdom. . . . Here also the deficit on trade account during the past two years [1946 and 1947] has not been greatly different in amount from that during the first two years after the First World War . . . Still more impressive, however, is the change in investment income and service receipts. Whereas after the First World War these receipts were more than adequate to cover the trade deficit, in 1946 and 1947 they have added some £500,000,000 to the deficit on trade account. This has been partly the result of sharply reduced returns from investments and shipping, but the largest item in the accounts for 1946 and 1947 is the figure of £500,000,000 for Government transactions, which includes military expenditure, relief and rehabilitation expenditures, the cost of supplies and services to the civilian population of Germany and other Government transactions.

"One result of this has been to limit the amount of aid which Europe could afford to buy from the United States, over and above the aid that was given or facilitated by loans. In 1919 and 1920 the United States exported to Europe 4.4% of her gross national product. In 1946 and 1947 she exported (and this figure includes every form of Government and voluntary aid) no more than 2% of her gross national product for those years. The total was greater, the proportion was less.

"The outstanding fact which emerges from this comparison of the two postwar periods, both for Europe as a whole and for the United Kingdom in particular, is that after the First World War Europe was still able to count on very substantial earnings from investments of past years and from shipping and other services currently rendered, whereas at present these invisible receipts have been greatly reduced and are more than outweighed by extraordinary expenditures abroad of one kind or another."

So much for the direct and measurable consequences of the war. Before we leave this summary of statistics, let us include some figures showing what recovery was made between the years 1945 and 1950.

DEBT REPAYMENTS

Britain's external indebtedness in June, 1945, was given at £3,355,000,000 (estimated in the value of the pound sterling at that time). Between that date and 1949, Britain has received aid from outside resources as follows:

(Figures in millions of pounds)

From the United States and Canada

Loans	£1,192
Aid under European Recovery programs	335
From I.E.P.A.	7
From the British Commonwealth (remainder)	
Australia and New Zealand	38
South African Gold Loan (net)	30
	£1,602
Other capital transactions (drawings from International Monetary Fund and the like) resulted in a net loss of	64
leaving the net total of receipts at	£1,538

But during the same period, Britain has herself granted aid, made repayments on account of debts, and transferred to others some of the aid received from the United States. The exact figure is not only open to argument, it is openly the subject of argument. In December, 1949, the *Observer* made an estimate of this which produced the following picture:

(Figures in millions of pounds)

Gifts by Britain	400
Loans by Britain	493
Transfers by drawing rights under I.E.P.A.	44
Reductions in sterling balances held outside Britain	423
Other capital transactions (investments less sales and redemptions)	138
TOTAL	1,498

It is arguable, therefore, that Britain retained for her own immediate use a comparatively small proportion of the aid given her. It is also worth noting that Britain has reduced the over-all debit balance on her overseas trade from £630,000,000 in 1947 to £10,000,000 in the first half of 1949.

REPLACEMENT OF SHIPPING LOSSES

The tonnage of new shipping launched in Britain during the period is as follows:

1946	1,120,000 tons.
1947	1,193,000 tons.
1948	1,176,000 tons.
1949	1,267,000 tons.

These figures represent just over one half of the total of merchant shipping launched throughout the world during the same period, and the new shipping constructed brings Britain's merchant fleet to not far short of what it was in 1939.

REPLACEMENT OF DAMAGED HOUSING, ETC.

During the period from 1945 to the end of 1949, Britain built 623,347 new permanent dwellings and erected 157,146 new dwellings described as temporary, most of which will undoubtedly be occupied for more than their estimated life of ten years. In addition, 39,254 houses totally destroyed by enemy action had been rebuilt. In all, the grand total of dwellings provided, new and temporary, including damaged houses repaired and service camps made usable for civilian families, was 1,104,319.

DISPOSITION OF NATIONAL INCOME

Taking 1948 as a reasonably average year, the total national income was estimated to be £10,700,000,000. Of that, some £2,352,000,000 was invested in various capital projects, of which only £120,000,000 represented gifts and loans from abroad. Of the capital investments made, somewhat more than half were made by trading corporations in additions to reserves etc., one–third represents capital investments by government activities and the balance, some £220,000,000, is private saving.

Three Representative Family Budgets

1. June 1947. Man, wife and two children. Man's earnings £9.15s. (including rent from part of house.) Purchasing house on mortgage repayable by installments.

General expenditure (weekly)	£.	s.	d.
Income tax		11.	6.
Trade-union subscriptions		1.	.
National health payments, etc.		3.	1.
Payments on house mortgage, local taxes and repairs	1.	12.	.
Fares to work		6.	.
Dinners at work		8.	5.
Snacks		5.	.
Children's pocket money		4.	.
Newspapers		1.	.
Cigarettes		10.	.
Electricity		4.	6.
Telephone		3.	6.
	£4.	10.	.

Housekeeping expenses:

General purchases (including groceries and vegetables)	£2.	.	.		
Bread		3.	6.		
Milk		6.	.		
Fish		3.	.		
Sausages and offal		4.	6.		
Coal		3.	.		
Insurance		12.	.		
Clothing and household replacements	1.	9.	.	5.	. .
				£9.	10. .

Weekly balance (surplus) 5s.

2. May 1947. Man, wife, one son, aged 18, in Navy, and one younger son. Man's earnings £6.9s. a week, additional income of £1. a week from lodger. House rented.

General expenditure (weekly)	£.	s.	d.
Income tax		2.	.
Union subscriptions, etc.		9.	6.
National insurance		2.	10.
Rent	1.	10.	.
Food	2.	9.	6.
Gas and electricity		8.	6.
Clothing and household repairs		8.	.
Coal		5.	.
Life and sickness insurance payments		7.	6.
School meals and pocket money (younger son)		2.	6.
Husband's spending money		6.	.
	£6.	11.	4.

Weekly balance (surplus, subject to payments by lodger) .... 18s. 8d.

3. October 1948. Man, wife and one young child. Man's earnings £7.15s. a week. House rented.

General expenditure (weekly)	£.	s.	d.
Income tax		6.	.
National insurances		5.	
Union subscriptions		2.	6.
Rent and rates	1.	16.	8.
Cigarettes		10.	.
Holiday savings		3.	.
Newspapers and entertainments		8.	3.

Household expenses:

Groceries	£1.	.	.
Vegetables		6.	6.
Milk		4.	.
Bread		4.	6.
Meat		4.	.
Fish		2.	.
Laundry		2.	6.
Gas (heating and cooking)		12.	.	2. 15. 6.
		£6.	6.	1.

Weekly balance (to cover fares, shoe repairs and minor domestic purchases) 18s.1d.

British Agricultural Income and Expenditure

The following statistics are taken from the report of the Cambridge School of Agriculture, based on a survey of forty holdings averaging 134 acres apiece. The figures are for the year 1943, and cover a typical farm in Central Norfolk, in the east of England.

Gross Receipts	£
Dairy Produce.	537
Horned Stock.	273
Pigs.	26
Poultry and Eggs.	73
Sheep and Wool.	47
Wheat.	294
Barley.	667
Sugar Beet.	260
Other Crops.	16
Miscellaneous.	46
	£2197.

Expenditure	£
Labour.	615
Food Stuffs.	110
Livestock.	158
Rent.	145
Fertilizers.	84
Seeds.	82
Miscellaneous.	372
	£1466.

Gross Profit £731.

In considering these figures, the following points must be borne in mind:

1. Prices for livestock and fodder crop are adjusted for price changes during the year.
2. Depreciation of stock and equipment is allowed for on the expenditure side at normal rates of write-off.
3. Included in labor costs is an estimated amount to cover the work of the occupant's family even though no cash wage is paid.
4. Nothing is charged on the expenditure side for the personal expenses of the occupant or his family or for their personal use of farm equipment (e.g., for their living quarters on the farm, for the use for pleasure of their automobile).
5. No allowance on the expenditure side is made for the work of the occupant himself, or for his skill, or for interest on the capital employed by him in the undertaking.

Figures were obtained in 1943 for 160 sample farms in Norfolk, Essex and Cambridge. The average acreage of the individual holdings was 174, and the average profit per farm was £889. The highest level of profit was from Cambridgeshire, where it was £1019 per farm, due to a slightly higher average acreage and, possibly, to the fact that there is slightly more horticulture in that area.

There has been some change since 1943 and the balance of that change has gone against the farmer. Based on the figure 100 as equaling the 1936/1938 average, the price of all farm products advanced from 185 in 1943 to 208 in 1946. And while the cost of fertilizers advanced only from 138 to 141 in the same period, wages have risen considerably. The latest figures available are those prepared by the National Farmers Union, based upon information collected from over 4,000 farms in Britain. These show the present-day profit and loss account for the average farm:

Acreage Group	Average Acreage		Average Revenue		Average Expenditure		Average profit per acre		Average profit per farm	
	1947	1948	1947	1948	1947	1948	1947	1948	1947	1948
Mainly Arable										
50 and under	39	37	£1524	1641	£1190	1274	£8.0	8.6	£309	£314
51–150.....	104	102	2690	3008	2189	2496	5.0	4.5	522	457
151–300.....	214	214	4666	4902	4018	4389	3.2	2.4	689	510
Over 300....	483	501	11277	12289	9876	11172	3.2	2.2	1527	1108
Arable and Mixed										
50 and under	37	40	1270	1276	968	1135	8.6	3.6	316	143
51–150.....	109	112	2389	2547	2086	2275	3.3	2.5	356	282
151–300.....	213	213	4267	4483	3639	3948	2.8	2.5	598	539
Over 300....	584	521	10811	11236	9965	9943	1.0	2.1	1069	1092
Mainly Dairying										
50 and under	41	41	1411	1374	1188	1188	5.4	5.5	224	226
51–150.....	100	99	2245	2323	1876	2033	3.6	3.6	362	353
151–300.....	201	203	3692	3991	3192	3486	2.2	2.8	448	572
Over 300....	511	513	8068	8928	7102	8232	1.8	1.3	916	656
Mainly Livestock										
50 and under	31	31	1033	1208	942	1153	1.6	2.3	50	71
51–150.....	106	109	3013	3254	2666	3055	2.1	2.7	220	295
151–300.....	219	222	3642	3912	3213	3615	1.6	2.1	350	468
Over 300....	669	620	6923	6790	6094	6432	0.9	1.1	567	697
Livestock and Mixed										
50 and under	38	35	752	1172	584	1065	3.0	3.1	111	109
51–150.....	109	109	1934	2221	1618	1947	2.2	3.1	244	341
151–300.....	213	211	3238	3475	2794	3074	1.8	2.6	378	543
Over 300....	459	471	6923	7971	6069	7061	1.6	1.6	711	747

In these figures the cost of the farmer's own time is not included as an expense, and the result is plainly shown in the fall of the profit earned per acre as the cost of hired labor per acre increases.

Basic Weekly Rations and the Availability of Food in Britain

Table of Basic Weekly Rations

	1945	1948	1949
Bacon and ham	3 oz.	2 oz.	4 oz.
Cheese	3 oz.	1½ oz.	2 oz.
Butter	3 oz.	3 oz.	4 oz.
Margarine	3 oz.	4 oz.	4 oz.
Cooking fat	2 oz.	2 oz.	2 oz.
Meat	1s. 2d.	1s.	1s. 6d.
Sugar	8 oz.	10 oz.	8 oz.
Tea	2½ oz.	2 oz.	2½ oz.
Liquid milk (pints)	2	2½	3.

Average weekly consumption of foodstuffs

(based on corresponding 10 months in each year)
Figures in thousands of tons

	1934–38 (average)	1948	1949
Flour	82.6.	100.8.	98.8.
Sugar	40.6.	34.8.	38.8.
Fresh and frozen meat	40.5.	29.8.	28.5.
Bacon and ham	10.4.	3.9.	4.5.
Fish	16.9.	21.0.	19.0.
Butter	9.7.	5.3.	5.7.
Margarine	3.6.	7.7.	7.9.
Cooking fat	3.9.	3.5.	4.7.
Cheese	3.6.	3.6.	4.2.
Tea	4.4.	3.5.	3.5.
Potatoes	62.8.	102.2.	108.9.
Shell eggs (million dozens)	12.6.	10.1.	12.9.
Milk (million gallons)	108.3.	134.8.	145.6.

In detail, the increases and decreases in food consumption are as follows:

Increases

POTATOES: Over two-thirds as many are eaten as before the war. Almost all are home-produced; imported potatoes make up about one week's consumption in the year. Potatoes are not rationed. There was temporary rationing in the first half of 1948, due to heavy loss of stocks in the spring floods.

MILK: Almost 50% more milk is drunk than in 1938. Over half the present consumption forms part of the special allocations to expectant and nursing mothers, children and invalids, and is generally made available at below cost. Milk rationing ended in January, 1950.

FISH: The increase in consumption is about 20%. Fresh fish is not specifically imported, but foreign trawlers do land and sell their catches at British ports. Fish is not rationed and the price control over fish was removed early in 1950. A feature of the recent period has been the rapid growth in the number of quick-freezing plants.

FLOUR: Increase in consumption about 25%, and this was maintained even during the period of rationing. The rationing system was introduced to prevent consumption from rising, not to cut it down.

Three-quarters of all wheat supplies are imported.

Rationing is no longer in force, but each wholesaler is limited—in the amount of flour he can draw from the mills—to approximately his former consumption.

CHEESE: Increase in consumption 11%, almost entirely accounted for by the extra rations given to certain classes of heavy workers.

Most home-produced cheese is rationed. About 95% of supplies are imported, but the "free" cheeses include most of the French cheeses. New Zealand is the largest single supplier of cheese.

JAM, MARMALADE AND HONEY: Increase in consumption about 50%. The rationing of jams ceased by stages as supplies became more plentiful. The last jams were de-rationed in December, 1948, honey in May, 1949.

MARGARINE: Increase in consumption 100%, mainly caused by the decrease in butter ration. The total consumption of edible fats and oils is about 25% below that of 1938.

Margarine is rationed. (Four ounces per head per week from July 1948).

Decreases

(All these are rationed foods)

MEAT: The most noticeable decrease. The actual decrease is 25%, so far as carcass meat is concerned. But demand is more widespread. So, too, is the distribution of the inferior cuts and grades. Result: More people are conscious of the limitations imposed by the ration.

The bulk of meat eaten in Britain is imported; home production accounts for about one–third of the supply. In 1948, farmers were allowed to hold back 20% of their grain crop for feeding livestock, which produced a considerable improvement in supplies available in 1949. Rationing is on a cash basis and all retail prices are fixed.

BUTTER: Consumption about 50% of pre-war, but increasing (see margarine above). The present weekly ration is 4 ounces.

BACON: Consumption now about 50% of the pre-war figure. This is a noticeable deficiency for those who were accustomed to the pre-war English breakfast.

Sixty-six per cent of requirements are imported and European supplies are improving. Home production showed a poor increase up to 1948 because of shortage of animal feed, but it is now improving steadily. However, even if everything goes as planned, Britain will not return to her pre-war level of home-produced bacon before 1952.

SUGAR: Consumption is not quite up to the pre-war level. Home production provides about one-third of requirements, and the 1949 harvest was light owing to drought. No sugar for consumption in Britain is now imported from the dollar area. The inability to free sugar from rationing is due mainly to the fact that Cuban sugar is from the dollar area and other sources of supply have not yet filled the gap.

SHELL EGGS: Consumption is now about equal to the pre-war figure. Home production increased very rapidly in 1949, and the general shortage is nearing an end.

TEA: Consumption about 75% of pre-war. The main reason for the present shortage is the reduction in supplies from Indonesia, over the last five years.

Government Estimate of the Cost of National Insurance

Classification of the Population of Britain in 1948
(numbers in thousands)

	Men	Married women	Other women	TOTAL
Insured Persons: Employed.........	13,300	1,400	4,600	19,300
Self-employed......	2,200	100	500	2,800
Non-employed.....	700	8,100	1,200	10,000
Persons above pension age who have retired from work..............	1,700	1,700	2,300	5,700
Children under 15, or 15–16 at school	5,300	—	5,100	10,400
TOTALS.....................	23,200	11,300	13,700	48,200

Estimated cost of Program: 1948–1978
(figures in millions of pounds)

Estimated Expenditure on Benefits	1948	1958	1968	1978
Retirement pensions..............	238	301	421	501
Widows' benefits and guardians' allowances........................	22	35	42	40
Unemployment benefit.............	94	94	94	89
Sickness benefit..................	70	83	86	81
Maternity benefits................	9	8	8	8
Death grant*.....................	1	6	9	12
Cost of Administration............	18	18	18	18
TOTALS.....................	452	545	678	749

* Not fully in operation.

Estimated income of the National
Insurance Funds

Interest on existing capital assets (reserve fund) taken over from earlier plans............................	21	21	21	21
Receipts from contributions:				
Insured Persons.................	175	189	189	176
Employers......................	138	145	146	136
TOTALS.....................	334	355	356	333
Estimated cost to National Exchequer (excess of cost of benefits over contributions)........................	118	190	322	416

(NOTE: These figures were calculated before Parliament altered the bill to
provide for the payment of sickness benefits to self-employed persons
after the third day of illness, instead of after the twenty-fourth day.
The estimated cost of sickness benefit should, therefore, be greater.
The contributions were not changed.)

The administrative machine within the Ministry of National Insurance will cost about £25,000,000 a year, and the present total of its staff is 39,000 men and women, which includes about 2,000 temporarily taken on to cope with the initial rush and 1,450 who are employed on the separate family allowance program. It is estimated that the "Approved Societies" employed about 10,000 people full time on national health work. About 7,300 of these have been absorbed into the ministry. During the first year of operation, to July 5, 1949, these people dealt with 10,000,000 claims, involving 40,000,000 separate payments.

The ministry is now organized into twelve regional offices, and 960 local offices. It is intended to increase the number of local offices to about 1,100. In the first year, 28,000,000 people visited local insurance offices. The number of approved societies taken over was about 6,000, but these included about 5,000 small branches, locally administered, but centrally controlled.

Before the plan came into operation, the last records showed that about 15,550,000 men and women were covered by unemployment insurance plans, and some 15,203,000 were covered by the former National Health Insurance program (these figures are not cumulative). The ministry's estimate of the total of men and women on their books on July 5, 1949 was 24,000,000.